# SECRETS *of* THE NATIONAL ARCHIVES

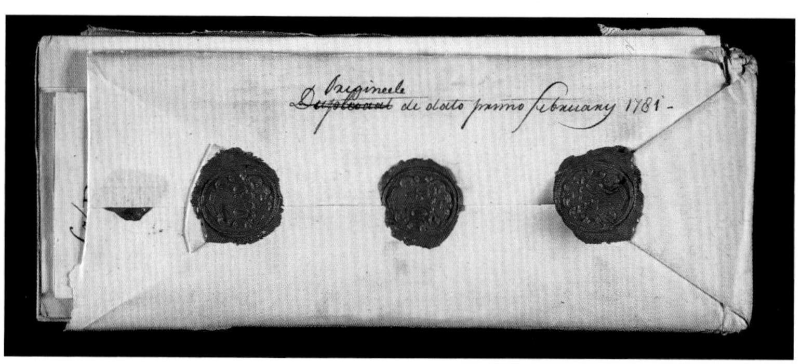

# British Justice

King's Proctor showed a paper for rescission of decree but publicly say the went.

Mr Simpson dined at York House with the King who coveted his wife & broke the Commandment of God.

Photo: Hugh Cecil, London

~~HIS MAJESTY KING~~ Mr EDWARD ~~VIII~~ I address unknown gone abroad.

otherwise "Mr X" 2 the Co-respondent in the arranged Divorce for Mrs. Simpson at Ipswich Oct 1936.
Mr Simpson was not guilty he was paid and squared.

43

# SECRETS *of* THE NATIONAL ARCHIVES

Richard Taylor

EBURY PRESS

*TO ISOBEL AND MARY*


## Acknowledgements

THIS BOOK COULD not have been written without the generosity of a great many people: generous with their time, patience, organisation, hospitality, sharing of expertise and/or just plain hard work. I would like to thank in particular Edward Field, Caroline Kimbell, Laura Simpson and Hester Vaizey of The National Archives' publications department; Nicola Crossley and Carey Smith of Ebury Press; David Fordham our designer; my secretaries Jane Hurst and Michelle McIlduff; Charlie, Christa, Sidney and Frank Panton and my mother Gillian Taylor for their endless hospitality; and the National Archivists: Adrian Ailes, Nick Barratt, Catt Baum, Amanda Bevan, Paul Carter, Audrey Collins, James Cronan, Sean Cunningham, Bruno Derrick, Mark Dunton, Ed Hampshire, Chris Heather, Sarah Hutton, Roger Kershaw, Katy Mair, Jackie Marfleet, Rose Mitchell, Jacqueline Moon, Jess Nelson, Jenni Orme, Briony Paxman, James Ross, William Spencer, Stephen Twigge and James Travers. Thank you all so very much.

# CONTENTS



## 11th–14th CENTURY

## 15th–16th CENTURY

## 17th CENTURY

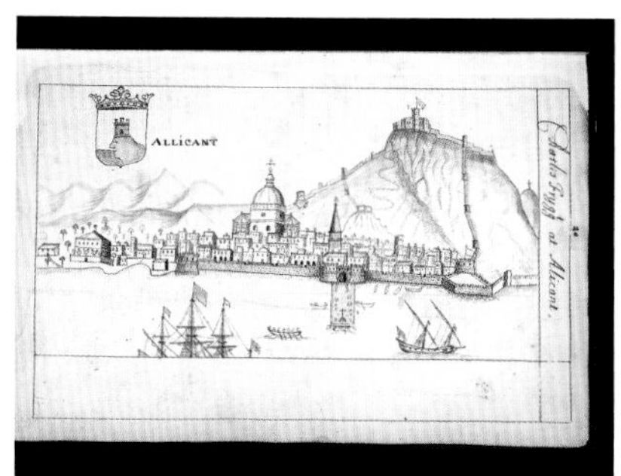

## 18th CENTURY

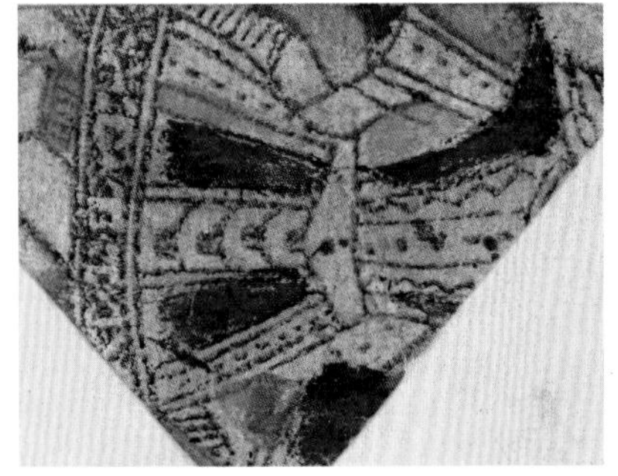



## 19th CENTURY

## 20th CENTURY

# FOREWORD

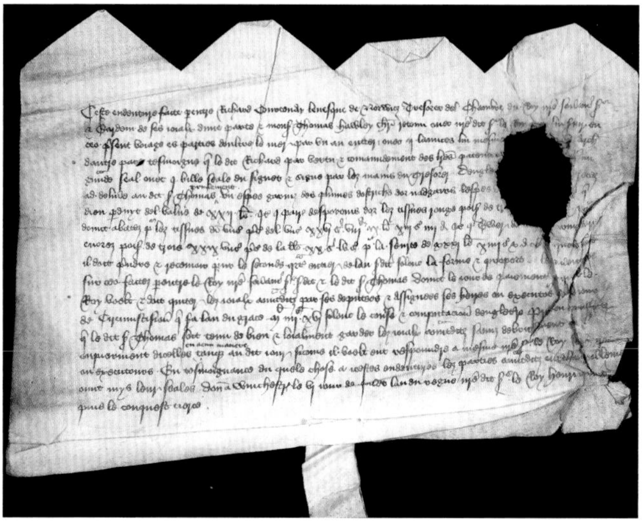

RIGHT: *Indenture for men to fight for Henry V in France at the Battle of Agincourt.*

THE REPOSITORIES OF The National Archives are brimming with material that relates to the past thousand years of our nation's history, and with over 120 miles of documents, there are always new discoveries to be made from such rich and varied holdings. This book covers every era from the start of the historical record to the modern day, pulling together an exciting collection of extraordinary, surprising and world-changing documents – in its own way, each document discussed, be it large or small, has helped to shape the world we know today.

Several the documents included here have been chosen by the people who know the records best. Staff of The National Archives were asked to name their favourite document, and the result was an overwhelming range of suggestions. People from all sections took part in the poll, from curators and conservators to the authors of books based on the material they deal with on a daily basis, and those who give children the opportunity to hold historical documents in their hands for the first time. Richard Taylor talked to staff who had nominated records to discuss the significance and rationale behind their choices. The poll highlighted the wealth of knowledge that exists across the organisation.

**Jeff James**
Chief Executive of The National Archives and Keeper of the Public Records

TERRA REGIS. · SCARVEDELE WAPENTAC ·

IN Neuuebold cum . vi . bereW. Witintune . Brimintune . Tapetune .
Cestrefeld . Bintorp . Echintune . ibi sunt . vi . car . 7 . i . bouat . ad geld . Soca
huj . ☩ . In Wingreurde . ii . car . ad geld . In Stechersst . 7 padine . iiii . bouat . ad
geld . Wast . e . In Normantune . V [ta] . pars uni car . ad geld . In Honestune . tcia
pars uni car . ad geld . In Dranefeld . i . car . ad geld . In Rauenesholm 7 Upetu-
ne . i . car . ad geld . In Toptune 7 Hortune . ii . bou ad geld . Ad has tras soch adiacent
. vi . ac pti . Silua . v . leuu long . 7 . iii . leuu lat . De plana tra . lx . acr . · ii . ☩ . 7 . B .
In Onestune . 7 Normetune . hab leuuine 7 Edunne . vii . bou . 7 . iiii . acr . ad geld . ☩ . In
Waletune . hab hundulf . ii . car . ad geld . Wast . e . HAMENSTAN WAPENTAC . In Derelei
hab Rex . E . ii . car . ad geld . In Ferlei . 7 Cotes . 7 Berlei . i . car . 7 . ii . bou ad geld . In Mes-
tesforde . hab Rex . E . ii . car sine geld . Wast . e . Ad hoc . ☩ . adiacent hee Berenuich . Mes-
lach . Suuttretone . Woonesleie . Bunteshale . Ibeholon . Teneslege . In hus . vii . car ad geld .
In Werchesworde . sunt . iii . car . ad geld . In Crunforde [. ii . car .] . In Middeltune [. ii . car .] 7 Opetune [. iiii . car .] . 7
Welledene [. ii . car .] . 7 Gersintune [. ii . car .] . 7 Caldelaue [. ii . car .] . 7 Hiretune [. iiii . car .] . ad geld . x viii . car . In Esseburne .
sunt . iii . car ad geld . Wast . e . BereW huj . ☩ . In Mapletune [. ii . car .] . 7 Bradelaue [. ii . car .] . 7 Torp [. ii . car .] . 7
Benedlege [. ii . car .] . 7 Ophidecotes [. ii . car .] . 7 Ochenauestun [. iiii . car .] . ad geld . x iiii . car . Wast sunt . In Perewic
sunt . ii . car . ad geld . Wast . e . Colne de Rege ten . Ad hoc . ☩ . adiacent . iii . Berenuite . Elles-
hope . hanzedone . Eitune . ibi sunt . ii . car ad geld . Wast . e . In Waletune 7 Redlaues-
ton . hab Algar comes . vi . car ad geld . In Westone . ii . part . ii . car . 7 in Smalei 7 Chites-
lei . iiii . bou . In Neuueton . 7 Bretebi hab Algar . vii . car ad geld . In Mileburne hab
Rex . E . vi . car ad geld . hec soca ptin ad Mileburne . In SCARVESDELE WAPENTAC . In Ba-
reuue . x ii . bou 7 dim . In Suerchestune . i . car . In Celerdestune . i . car 7 dim . In Osmun-
destune [. ii . bou .] 7 Codetune [. iiii . bou .] [. ii . car 7] . In Normanestune . i . car . Ad geld . viii . car . 7 . ii . bouat . In Rapen-
dune 7 Middeltune hab Algar comes . vi . car ad geld . In Wuuleslei . ii . car . ad geld . In
Tichenhalle . ii . car . 7 . ii . bou . 7 . ii . part . i . bou ad geld . In Trangesbi dim car ad geld .
In Messeham . ii . car ad geld . In Caldecote . iii . car ad geld . Hae ad Cliftune ptin in Stadford .

# INTRODUCTION
## On Documents . . .

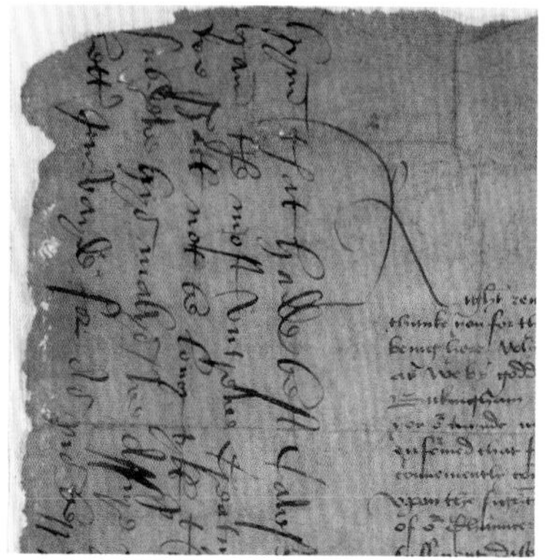

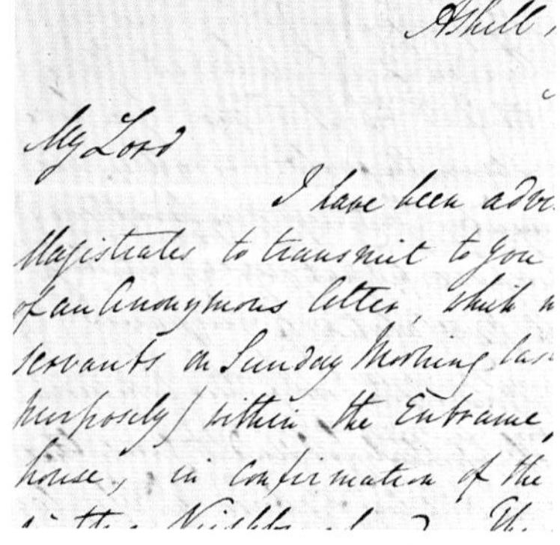

My Lord

I have been adv

Magistrates to transmit to you

of an Anonymous letter, which

servants on Sunday Morning las

purposely) within the Entrance

house, in Confirmation of the

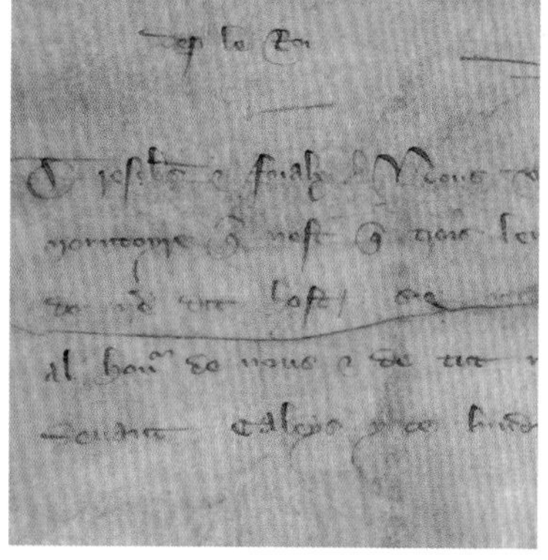

M16307

Russian East Asiatic S.S. Co. Radio-Telegram. 526

S.S. "Birma".

| Origin.Station. | Time handed in. | Via. | Remarks. |
| --- | --- | --- | --- |
| Titanic | 11 H.45M.April 14/15 1912. | | Distress cal Ligs Loud. |

Cgd - Sos. from M. G. Y.

We have struck iceberg sinking fast come to our assistance.

Position Lat. 41.46 n. Lon. 50.14. w.

M.G.Y.

OPPOSITE: *A page from the Domesday Abbreviato, which may be the first image of a black person in Britain.*

TOP TO BOTTOM: *Extracts from Richard III's letter; the covering note to the 'Anonymous Letter'; letter from Edward III; telegram from the* Titanic.

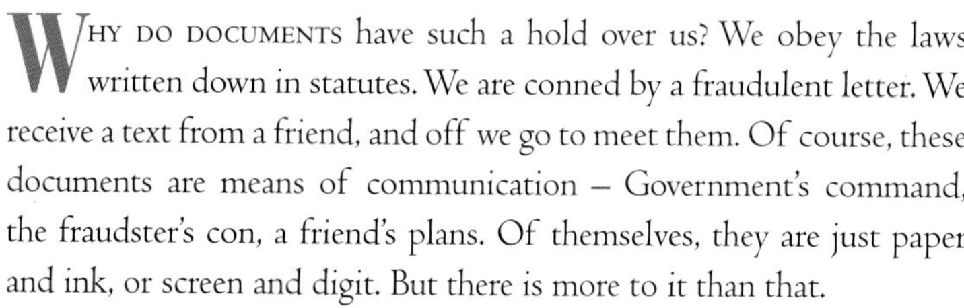

WHY DO DOCUMENTS have such a hold over us? We obey the laws written down in statutes. We are conned by a fraudulent letter. We receive a text from a friend, and off we go to meet them. Of course, these documents are means of communication – Government's command, the fraudster's con, a friend's plans. Of themselves, they are just paper and ink, or screen and digit. But there is more to it than that.

Tell someone you love them, and it is a beautiful moment. Set the words down on paper, and you raise the stakes. You show the person you love that you have had time to think about these words, to choose and order them. You are saying, 'Look, here are my feelings, considered, recorded. I love you. I really mean it.' 'I really mean it' holds true for those statute-book laws, too. By capturing the commands in a document, Government is saying, 'Pay attention. You have to do this. It is written down.'

Emotion recorded in a document is distilled, intensified from the day-to-day. When Richard III grabs the quill from his scribe's hand, and scrawls out his fury at an old friend's treachery (see page 49) boy, does he mean it. When Norfolk labourers wrote a sinister, anonymous threat to local gentry, the menace is still palpable (page 158). Documents distil emotions and they capture moments. The letter from Edward III (page 34), written as the enemy army approaches; the heart-rending telegrams from the *Titanic* (page 237) – you see these documents today exactly as they were at the moment when they left the king's hand or were received from the sinking ship.

This is why the term 'historical document' is misleading. We give this label to documents that have played a part in events we think of as history.

ANTI-CLOCKWISE: *Extracts from a suffragettes' spoiled census form; the Tide Letter; Captain Cook's Journals; Manorial Rolls during the Black Death; section of a satirical cartoon; a Ripper letter.*

But, like the email or text that you wrote last week, any document is past-tense from the moment it is written. Time passes, but the document stays the same. They are not historical – they are evergreen. The forms that suffragettes spoiled during the 1911 census (see page 235) capture the women's protest as freshly now as they did then. The letter from the terrified young woman who would go on to become Elizabeth I (page 58), is still pleading for her life, more than 450 years after it was written. In his ship's log (page 120), Captain Cook is still at anchor in Botany Bay, just after his first encounter with Australian Aborigines. You may have read or learnt about the events in these documents. Here, you are looking at the events as they happened.

Documents are witnesses. The Manorial Rolls from Great Waltham and High Easter (see page 36) were written in the midst of the greatest horror that Europe has ever seen, the first strike of the Black Death. They were actually there. And, as witnesses, they tell us what they saw: death, after death, after death. But often what is most telling is not what a document says, but how it says it, or what it doesn't say. The Manorial Rolls show that, in the midst of death, life was going on – courts were convened, land was farmed, taxes gathered. The outrageous cartoons that satirise the Prince Regent (page 162) don't just poke fun; they also show that, in England at the time, you could portray a future king as a fat-bottomed fool without losing your head. Indeed, documents can tell you things that the writer doesn't mean you to know. The Ripper letters (page 224) positively betray their writers. They pretend to be from Jack the Ripper, but not one of them is likely to be real. Rather, these horrible mimics are celebrating Jack's mad butchery.

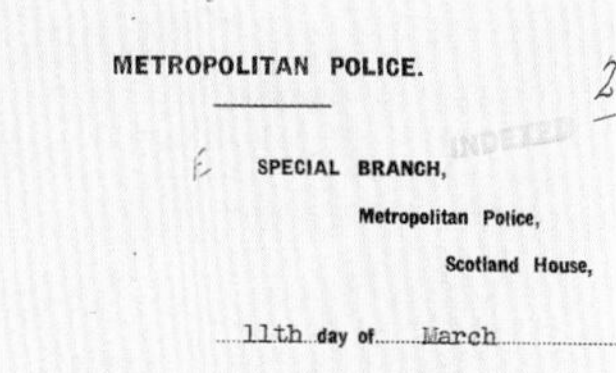

METROPOLITAN POLICE.

SPECIAL BRANCH,
Metropolitan Police,
Scotland House,

11th day of March

With reference to the attached correspo
m the Chief Constable, Wigan, respecting Eric A.
as George ORWELL :-
Enquiry shews that this man's correct n
c Arthur Blair. He is by occupation a journalis
hor, and writes under the name of George Orwell.

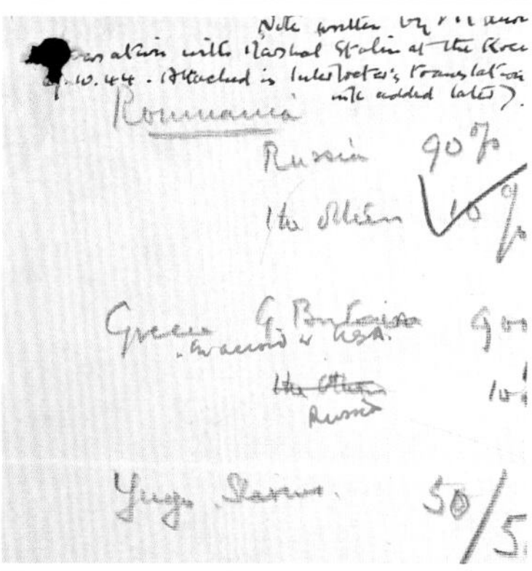

Roumania
Russia 90%
The others 10%
Greece
Yugo-Slavia 50/5

Some of these documents were secret. They may have been personal secrets, like the registers of clandestine marriages (page 113), or the 'scarlet pimpernel' cards that could get you past crooked customs officials during the French Revolution (page 154). Others contain government secrets, such as the surveillance files on George Orwell (page 258), or Churchill's 'Naughty Document', which records a covert, late-night pact with Stalin (page 274). You might expect people not to record their secrets, but they do. Indeed, sometimes they have to. If they were not recorded in a document, then the clandestine marriage could be denied, the diplomatic deal reneged upon. These secrets don't want to disappear.

Other documents are not just public; they are really, really public. They mean to shout as loudly as possible, in as many places as possible. The American Declaration of Independence was a rallying cry to a country that was fighting for its life. The signed original is displayed today at the US National Archives in its own marble rotunda, a sacred space for a nation's founding document. But at the time, the declarations that really mattered were the copies (page 126), rolled out through the night at a nearby printing press and then rushed across America to be nailed at public crossroads or declaimed in town centres.

A fine example of the power of the copy is Caxton's first printed document (page 46). This modest document is the first little breeze of an impending hurricane. You can see what was going to happen, right there on that page – the process of printing made it easy to manufacture Indulgences (documents sold by the Church, which claimed to offer relief from torment after death) and they swamped the market, with

Clockwise from top left: *A register of clandestine weddings; the symbol of the 'scarlet pimpernel'; extract from Special Branch's file on George Orwell; Churchill's 'Naughty Document'; the United States Declaration of Independence; an Indulgence.*

PART VII.

PENALTIES.

ARTICLE 227.

The Allied and Associated Powers publicly arraign Willi
formerly German Emperor, for a supreme offence against
and the sanctity of treaties.

A special tribunal will be constituted to try the accused
the guarantees essential to the right of defence. It will
judges, one appointed by each of the following Powers
States of America, Great Britain, France, Italy and Japan.

In its decision the tribunal will be guided by the highest n
policy, with a view to vindicating the solemn obligations
takings and the validity of international morality. It will
punishment which it considers should be imposed.

The Allied and Associated Powers will address

the result that the Catholic Church looked tawdry. Simultaneously, printing made it easy to mass-produce Bibles, giving people direct access to the word of God without the mediation of priests. And so printed Indulgences and printed Bibles ushered in the Protestant revolution, and Europe split between a Protestant North and Catholic South. You can hardly overestimate the impact, on alliances and wars, on buildings and art, even on our national personalities. And it all starts here.

Whether public or private, documents are about permanence, even immortality. In a letter, my love is captured forever; so is Richard III's hatred of his treacherous former ally. That permanence is important at a personal level; at a public level, it can be indispensible. William the Conqueror's great survey of England became known as the Domesday Book, which means the 'Book of the Day of Judgement' (page 16). The book seemed to stand for eternity. It gave permanence to the landholdings it records and, above all, permanence to William as king. In a quieter way, the same holds true for a little eighteenth-century congregation of a non-conformist chapel in Nottingham, who recorded their baptisms in the margins of a genteel ladies' magazine (page 109). The document legitimised their poor but proud community, and gave it a sense of permanence, stability, history.

That quality of permanence means that documents take on their own lives, independent of their creators. A stunning example of this is the Magna Carta (page 20). It is astonishing, really, that a document sealed in a damp field in Surrey, between a little mafia of English barons and a king who would be dead the following year, should resonate down the centuries. Not just resonate as a record of a moment in history, but resonate day by day, in a practical way, as a document deferred to by governments and courts around the world. Or take the Treaty of Versailles (page 250). How can it be that this paper and ink had the power to end a war that had killed millions, and to lay the ground for another war that would kill millions more?

So, why do documents have such a hold over us? Because they mean something. Because they are independent and permanent. Because they are time capsules. Because they are witnesses and betrayers. Because they can be secret, or personal, or public. Because, without them, we would be very different people. Documents may just be objects. But if the documents themselves aren't shaping our lives, they are giving a pretty good impression of it.

FROM TOP: *Extract from the Domesday Book; a non-conformist register of baptisms; the Magna Carta; the Treaty of Versailles.*

Left: *The UK National Archives' building at Kew houses one of the most extraordinary collections of documents in the world. Centuries of British government records are stored there, as well as key papers relating to many other countries.*

# . . . *and* On Archives

Tens of thousands of document archives exist in the UK. An online register, the UK Archives Hub, lists more than 27,000, a number that is still nowhere near the total. Counties, cities, towns and parishes hold archives filled with local records, of births and deaths, ancient maps, the papers of local grandees. There are specialist archives that hold, say, ecclesiastical or military documents, and corporate and community archives.

Archives preserve a community's memory. More than that, they give a community a sense of itself. When Edward I of England defeated the Scots in 1296, he wanted to obliterate Scotland's sense of its own nationhood. What did he do? He stole their records, carting them off to England like defeated captives. The tactic did not work, but when some of the records that Edward took were accidentally lost, it left a permanent hole in Scotland's history.

The archives of living communities are never closed. They are organic, added to, growing. After all, an archive is a bid for immortality by the powers of the day, a means of preserving their acts and deeds for posterity. Like the phrase 'historical documents', it is misleading to describe an archive as historical. Archives reflect pride in the present, a sense of the past and hope for the future.

The UK National Archives is one of the most extraordinary collections of documents in the world. There are 126 shelf-miles of them, at the last count. The National Archives contains documentary records of centuries of British government, courts, administration, records and information about its people and their deeds; and through British exploration, its colonies and Empire, The National Archives also contains foundation records for a large part of the rest of the world.

But The National Archives is not a museum. Records are preserved and retained but they are not kept behind bars or in glass cases. You can, if you wish, visit, sign in, call up the documents you want to see and inspect them for yourself. The documents on these pages represent a sliver of its extraordinary collection. They belong to us all.

# 11th–14th Century

## The Domesday Book *to the* Manorial Rolls

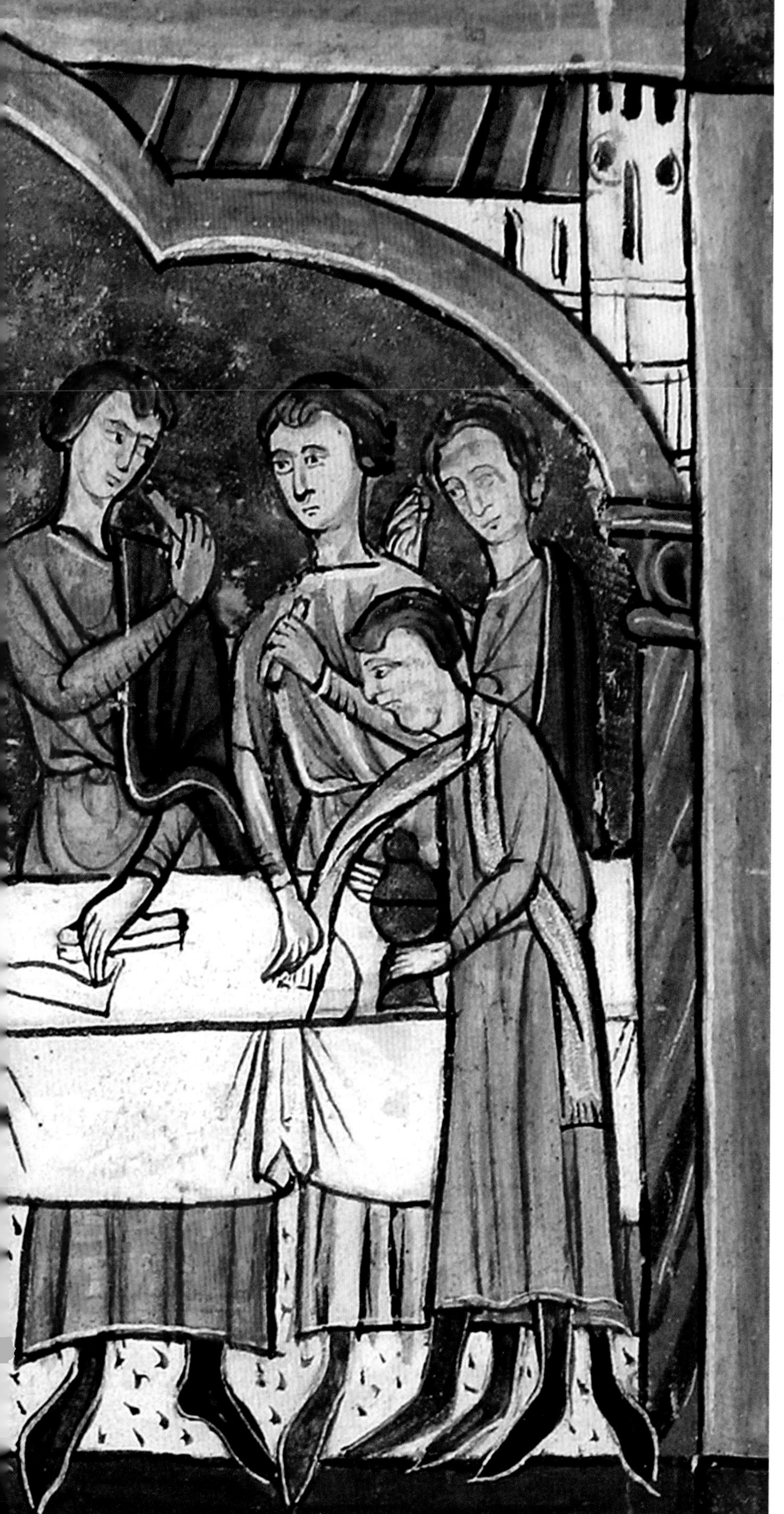

LEFT: *Illumination from the Domesday Abbreviato of Edward the Confessor, the Anglo-Saxon king from whom the Normans claimed royal authority, at a banquet.*

In Burgo Malmesberie habet rex .xxvi. masuras hospitatas. 7 xxv. masuras in quib' sunt dom' que non reddunt geld' plusquam uasta tra. Vna quaeq; harum masurarum redd' .x. den' de gablo. hoc est simul .xl.iii. sol' 7 vi. den'. / seruitiu' reddit.
De feudo epi baiocsis. e ibi dimidia masura uasta. que nullu'
Abb malmesbie ht .iiij. mas 7 dimid. 7 foris burg' .ix. coscez q' geldant cu burgsib'. Abb Glastingbiens' ht .ii. masur'. Eduuard' uicecom .iii. masur. Radulf' de mortem' .i. 7 dimid. Durand' de Glouuec' .i. 7 dim. Witts de ow .i. Hunfrid' de insula .i. Osbn' Gifard .i. Alured' de Merlebge. dimid mas uasta. Goisfrid' marescal similit' [illegible] .i. 7 tcia parte uni' mas. Drogo f. ponz. dimid. Uxor Edric .i. Rog' de berchelai .i. mas de firma regis. 7 Ernulf' de hesding .i. similit' de firma regis. qua in cautte accep. he due nullu seruitiu reddunt.
Rex ht una uasta masuram de tra qua Azor tenuit.

Hic Annotantur Tenentes Tras In Wiltescire.

.i. Rex Willelmus.
.ii. Eps Wintoniensis.
.iii. Eps Sarisberiensis.
.iiii. Eps Baiocensis.
.v. Eps Constantiensis.
.vi. Eps Lisiacensis.
.vii. Abbatia Glastingberiens.
.viii. Abbatia Malmesberiens.
.ix. Abbatia Westmonasterii.
.x. Abbatia Wintoniensis.
.xi. Abbatia Creneburnens.
.xii. Abbatissa Scefesberiens.
.xiii. Abbatissa Wiltuniensis.
.xiiii. Abbatissa Wintoniensis.
.xv. Abbatissa Romesiensis.
.xvi. Abbatissa Ambresberiens.
.xvii. Aeccla Beccensis.
.xviii. Giraldus pbr de Wiltune.
.xix. Canonici Lisiacenses.
.xx. Comes Mortoniensis.
.xxi. Comes Rogerius.
.xxii. Comes Hugo.
.xxiii. Comes Albericus.
.xxiiii. Eduuard de Sarisberie.
.xxv. Ernulf de hesding.
.xxvi. Aluredus de Merlebergh.
.xxvii. Hunfridus de Insula.
.xxviii. Milo crispin.
.xxix. Gislebertus de Breteuile.
.xxx. Durand de Glouuecestre.
.xxxi. Walterius Gifard.
.xxxii. Witts de ow.
.xxxiii. Witts de Braiose.
.xxxiiii. Witts de Moiun.
.xxxv. Witts de faleise.
.xxxvi. Walscinus de Dowai.
.xxxvii. Waleran uenator.
.xxxviii. Willelm filius Widonis.
.xxxix. Henricus de fereres.
.xl. Ricard filius Gisleberti comitis.
.xli. Radulf de Mortemer.
.xlii. Robertus fili Giroldi.
.xliii. Robertus fili Rolf.
.xliiii. Rogerius de Curcelle.
.xlv. Rogerius de Berchelai.
.xlvi. Bernard panceuolt.
.xlvii. Berenger Gifard.
.xlviii. Osbernus Gifard.
.xlix. Drogo filius ponz.
.l. Hugo Lasne.
.li. Hugo filius baldrici.
.lii. Hunfrid camerarius.
.liii. Gunfrid malduith.
.liiii. Alured de Ispania.
.lv. Aulfus uicecomes.
.lvi. Nigellus medicus.
.lvii. Osbernus pbr.
.lviii. Ricard puingiant.
.lix. Robtus marescal.
.lx. Robertus flauus.
.lxi. Ricardus Sturmid.
.lxii. Rainalds canud.
.lxiii. Maci de Moretania.
.lxiiii. Gozelin Riuere.
.lxv. Godescal.
.lxvi. Herman 7 alii seruientes regis.
.lxvii. Odo 7 alii taini regis.
.lxviii. Herueus 7 alii ministri regis.

Rex habet de Burgo Wiltvnie .L. lib. Xdo Herueus recepit ad custodiend' reddeb' .xxii. libras.
De Wiltescire ht rex .x. lib p accipitre 7 .xx. solid p sumario. p feno .c. solid' 7 v. oras.
De dimid molino ap Sarisberie ht rex .xx. solid' ad pensum.
De tcio denario Sarisberie ht rex .vi. lib. De tcio denario Merleberge .iiij. lib. De tcio denar' Crichelade .v. lib. De tcio denario Bade .xi. lib. De tcio denario Malmesberie .vi. lib.
De Cremtone .lx. lib ad pondus. h reddit Eduuardus uicecom.
Walterius hosed de .ii. parab burgi Malmesberie redd' .viii. lib regi.

Quantu' reddeb ipsu burgu T.R.E. 7 in hac firma erant placita hundret de Cicemtone 7 Sutelesberg q regi ptineb. De moneta redd' ipsu burg' .c. solid.
In eod burgo habuit heraldus .un. agr' tre in q sunt .iiij. masure 7 vi. alie uaste 7 un molin redd .x. solid. hoc tot reddeb .c. sol. T.R.E.
Qdo rex ibat in expedition' t tra t mari: habeb de hoc burgo aut .xx. solid ad pascendos suos buzecarl. aut unu homine ducebat secu p honore .v. hidaru.

## Terra Regis.

Rex tenet Cauna. Rex. E. tenuit. 7 nunq geldauit. Ideo nescit quot hide sint ibi. Tra e .xxx. car. In dnio sunt .vij. car. 7 vij. serui. Ibi .xxx. uitti 7 lxxviij. bord. 7 x. colibti. hntes .xxi. car. Ibi .xl.v. burgenses. 7 vij. molini reddtes .iiij. lib 7 xii. sol. 7 vi. den. 7 L. ac pti. 7 pastura .ii. leu lg. 7 una leu lat. H uilla redd firma uni' noctis cu omib' csuetud'.
Hui' m ecclam ten Nigell' de rege cu .vi. hid tre. [illegible] Tra e .v. car. In dnio st .ii. 7 vi. serui. Ibi .vij. uitti .ii. bord. 7 xi. cozet. cu .iii. car. Ibi .ii. molini de .xx. sol. 7 xxv. burgses redd .xx. solid. Silua .ii. qz lg. 7 una qz .xxiij. ac lat. Pastura .iii. qrent lg. 7 ii. qz lat. Tot ual .viij. lib.
Alured' de hispania ten .v. hid tre. qs Nigell' calumniat. H tra testimonio scire ptinuit ad ecctam T.R.E.
Rex ten Beduinde. Rex. E. tenuit. Nunq geldauit nec hidata fuit. Tra e qt .xx. car una min. In dnio sunt .xii. car. 7 xviii. serui. Ibi qt .xx. uitti 7 Lx. cozets 7 xxiiij. colibti. Ibi .viii. molini redd .c. sol. Due silue hntes .iii. leu lg. 7 una leu lat. Ibi .cc. ac pti. 7 xii. qz pasture lg. 7 vi. qz lat. Huic m ptin .xxv. burgenses. H uilla redd firma uni' noctis cu omib' csuetudinib'. In hoc m fuit T.R.E. lucus hns dimid leu lg. 7 .iii. qz lat. 7 erat in dnio regis. Modo tenet eu henric de fereres.
Rex ten Amblesberie. Rex. E. tenuit. Nunq geldauit nec hidata fuit. Tra e .xl. car. In dnio sunt .xvi. car. 7 L.v. serui. 7 ii. colibti. Ibi qt .xx. 7 v. uitti 7 L.vi. bord. hntes .xxiij. car. Ibi .viii. molini redd .iiij. lib 7 x. sol. 7 lxx. ac pti. Pastura .iiii. leu lg. 7 .iii. leu lat. Silua .vi. leu lg 7 iiij. leu lat. Hoc [illegible] cu appendic suis redd firma uni' noctis [illegible]
In hoc m numerant tre .iii. tainoz quas [illegible] T.R.E. has ded Witts com in Amblesbie p mutatione Bovecome. De hui m tra .ii. hid ded rex. E. in sua infirmitate abbatisse Wiltuniensi. qs nunq antea habuerat. postea u eas tenuit. Has Witts com ded Quintone 7 Suindone 7 Cheuerel que erant tainlande. p tra de insula de Wit que ptineb ad firma de Amblesberie.
Rex ten Guerminstre. Rex. E. tenuit. Non geldauit nec hidata fuit. Tra e .xl. car. In dnio st .vi. car 7 xxiiij. serui. 7 xiii. porcarii. Ibi .xv. uitti 7 viii. cosc 7 xiiii. colibti. cu .xxx.vi. car. Ibi .vi. molini de [illegible] lib. 7 qt .xx. ac pti. Pastura .i. leu lg. 7 dim leu lat. Silua .ii. leu lg 7 .ii. lat. Ibi .xxx. burgses. Hoc m redd firma uni' noctis cu omib' csuetudinib'.
Rex ten Chepeha. Rex. E. tenuit. Non geldauit nec hidata fuit. Tra e .c. car. In dnio sunt .xvi. car 7 xxv. serui. Ibi .xl.viij. uitti 7 xl.v. bord 7 xx. cot 7 [illegible] porcarii. Int' oms hnt .lxvi. car. Ibi .xii. molini de .vi. lib [illegible] ac pti. Silua .iiii. leu lg 7 lat. pastura .ii. leu lg 7 [illegible] lat. Hoc m cu append suis redd firma uni' noctis cu omib' csuetudinib' 7 ual .c.x. lib ad numeru.
Hui' m ecclam cu .ii. hid ten Osbn eps ex T.R.E. Vna ex his hid e tainlande. altera ptin ecclie. Tot ual .l.v. solid.
Huic m ptin una tra qua rex. E. dederat Vluiet uenatori suo. 7 erat de dnio suo. H in firma regis e m. 7 p una hida [illegible]. Tra e .ii. car. 7 ipse ibi st. 7 ii. serui 7 iii. uitti 7 iiij. coscez cu .i. car. Pastura .iiij. qz lg. 7 una qz lat. Val .iij. lib.
In firma hui' m e dimid v tre que fuit tainlande. Edricus tenuit T.R.E.

# THE DAY *of* JUDGEMENT

## The Domesday Book

## 1086

ABOVE: *The cover of the Domesday Book, added by the Tudors. The Book was relied upon to determine land rights for hundreds of years.*

THE DOMESDAY BOOK is a grinding, relentless, powerhouse of a document. The world at this point might have seen great armies, great buildings, great kingdoms. But no document had yet compared to the Domesday Book as an expression of brute, naked power.

Twenty years after William the Conqueror defeated the Anglo-Saxons and proclaimed himself king of England, he ordered a detailed survey of his new land. Commissioners were sent on circuits to inspect and record local manors. The Book is organised into counties – the page opposite is from Wiltshire – and landowners. Land listed opposite under 'Terra Regis' is land held directly from the king. The amount of land that each person held is identified with the word *tracar* and a number. *Tracar* is short for *Terra Carracutas,* 'plough land', this being the measure of land that ten oxen could plough in a day; and the number shows how many measures of such land each man held. The land entries are followed by an enumeration of the landowners' possessions – cows, pigs, fish ponds, ploughs and so on. The Domesday Book contains the odd flash of colour – the vineyards that the Normans optimistically planted in London, for example – but mostly it is page after page of who-owns-what.

The Domesday Book is an expression of remorseless control. Its immediate, practical purpose was to tell William what resources were available to him, and at that level the Domesday Book is nothing more than a gigantic tax return. But there is a sense that by reducing the wealth of England to writing and holding it in a book, the King was conquering it all over again, ploughshare by ploughshare. The process of compiling the Book meant that every landowner in the country, however high their standing, had to have their possessions inspected by the King's appointed commissioners, checked by the King's appointed committees, and listed in the King's book. It would have left people in no doubt about who was in charge. By far the most common and important words in the Book are *ten de,* from *tenuit de,* meaning 'held of'. A landowner might hold land of a

OPPOSITE: *A page for Wiltshire. Top left is a description of the town of Malmesbury; below that is a summary of the county's landowners, headed by 'Rex Williamus' – King William.*

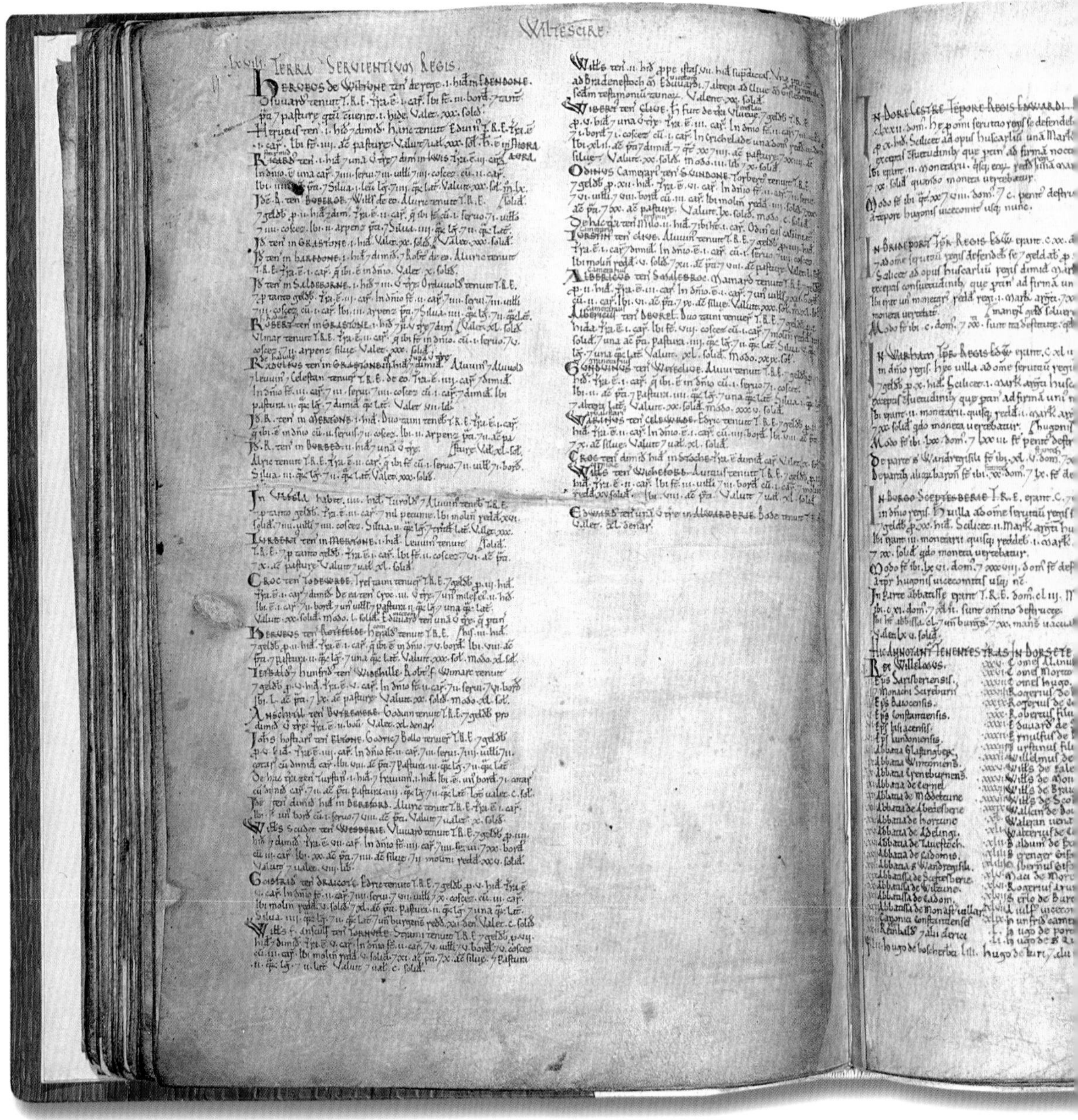

knight, who might hold it of a bishop, but each and every chain starts with *Tenuit de rege* – 'held of the King'. Ultimately, the King owned every inch of land, every fish pond and every pig in England.

The Book includes some fine propaganda. At various points it refers to land holdings as 'TRE', *Tempus Rex Edwardi*, meaning that particular lands were held from the time of Edward the Confessor, the revered Anglo-Saxon king who had died in 1066. William wanted to be seen as following Edward in an unbroken chain of royal authority in England. He wanted to obliterate the memory of the intervening Anglo-Saxon king, Harold, whom he had killed in battle. Where the Book needs to refer to Harold, he is described merely as

*Left: The description of Wiltshire finishes to the left, and Dorset starts to the right, following the same pattern – principal towns, key landowners and land held from the King. The red lines through words were intended to highlight them.*

'Lord'. At a couple of points, though, the mask slips, and the scribes refer to Harold as *Rex*, 'King', perhaps showing that many unofficially used his proper title. Airbrushing history is harder than you might think.

The Domesday Book shows how the Conqueror had almost completely filled the landowning classes with his fellow Normans. The names recorded for the bishops, abbots and tenants-in-chief are virtually all Norman (and male, of course – the Domesday Book contains more cows than women). But the Book itself is a product of both cultures. The Anglo-Saxons had developed an organised infrastructure that was far more advanced than anything the Normans had to show; while only an all-powerful top-down force such as the Normans could have commanded such an enterprise. It was this combination of dictatorship and organisation that led to the unprecedented triumph of the Book.

Almost the entire Book was written by one man, known to us simply as 'Scribe A'. He had a small amount of help from a second scribe, 'B', who seems to have covered for A for short spells (perhaps when Scribe A stepped outside to scream at the tedium of it all). Although anonymous, Scribe A has achieved his own kind of immortality. 'Domesday Book' means 'Book of the Day of Judgement', a name that it acquired around one hundred years after it was written. It had become a book of absolute authority, as if written by a divine hand. If land was designated in the Domesday Book as belonging to a particular person, then that was the end of it, and the Book was cited in legal disputes about land title for several hundred years after it was compiled. In the Tudor and Stuart periods, the Book was held in such reverence that when parts needed to be copied, they were reproduced exactly, down to the appearance of the handwriting itself. Recently a special font was created to emulate the handwriting of Scribe A. This extraordinary document retains its power, even in the digital age.

# GREATER THAN *the* KING

## The Magna Carta

1215

RIGHT: *A coin minted during the reign of King John, showing the King's head. John imposed taxes at unprecedented levels.*

THE MAGNA CARTA is the document that rules the ruler – the very first British document that sought to set out laws to bind a king. It is a legal cornerstone, its words still echoing today in the US Constitution and the Universal Declaration of Human Rights. And yet this document, sealed in a windswept field in Surrey, was nothing more than a bargain struck by a few self-serving barons and a mendacious monarch. It is concerned with property rights, not human rights, and arguably had no legal force at all. How did a document with such an unpromising beginning become so important?

The background to this constitutional eruption was, as is so often the case, bad government. When John was crowned King of England in May 1199, he inherited vast territories. In addition to the English throne, his father, Henry II, had accumulated much of western France, from Normandy in the north to the Pyrenees in the south. But within a few years, John 'Soft-Sword' had lost great tracts of it to Phillip II of France, including – for the first time since the Norman Conquest – the land mass of Normandy. In the eyes of medieval Europe, John was humiliated. He was also considerably poorer. Not only had the expense of a war not been compensated for by conquest, but the loss of land meant that future revenues for the Crown fell on a smaller band of subjects. The process of taxing a population has been compared to plucking a live goose. The trick is to extract the maximum number of feathers with the minimum amount of hissing. John would now pluck very hard.

John increased the sums payable by sheriffs for holding their lucrative offices, and they in turn squeezed the people from whom they extracted funds. The King demanded hefty payments from his tenants-in-chief on inheritance, marriage or wardship. John also exploited the system of 'scutage', payments by tenants in lieu of military service, at a frequency and at rates never seen before. To enforce his rights, John seized land, took hostages and imprisoned debtors. One baron debtor died in exile, his wife and son allegedly starving to death in the King's castle at Windsor.

A lesson from all this is just how much you can get away with. The goose endured this vigorous plucking until, ten years after he was driven out of Normandy, John tried invading France again. This adventure was even more catastrophic than the last. John lost Anjou,

OPPOSITE: *The 1225 reissue of the Magna Carta. When Henry III reissued the 'Great Charter', it reassured the barons and brought peace and stability to England.*

*'No free man shall be taken or imprisoned or dispossessed, or outlawed or exiled, or in any way destroyed, nor will we go upon him, nor will we send against him except by the lawful judgment of his peers or by the law of the land.'*

Maine and Touraine, the heart of the empire he had inherited. To John's English barons, it seemed as if the years of squeezing would now stretch indefinitely into the future. Enough was enough. At Christmas 1214, disaffected barons demanded that John should restrain his abuses. The King refused the demands, and a group of rebel barons renounced their allegiance to him. By June they had taken London, and John risked losing everything. But behind the scenes, negotiations had been taking place. A party of rebel barons met the King's representatives at Runnymede, a field by the Thames, which lay halfway between the King's castle at Windsor and the barons' camp at Staines. The principles of a peace deal were captured in a document known as the Articles of the Barons. On 15 June, full agreement was reached: the Magna Carta.

You have to look very hard at Magna Carta to see it as an embryonic statement of human rights. The overarching intent was to put a stop to arbitrary government, especially financial caprice. It fixed the level of fines payable by heirs, limited the King's powers of wardship, defined the rights of widows, and set out the circumstances in which scutage could be levied. These provisions of course all related to the King's tenants-in-chief – there was no overarching principle at stake. But buried at clauses 39 and 40 are two of the Magna Carta's most celebrated clauses:

*39: No free man shall be taken or imprisoned or dispossessed, or outlawed or exiled, or in any way destroyed, nor will we go upon him, nor will we send against him except by the lawful judgment of his peers or by the law of the land.*

*40: To no man will we sell, to no one will we refuse or delay, right or justice.*

These are two of the three paragraphs to remain in force today (the third concerns the independence of the Church, with which John had also had running battles). The Magna Carta provided for its own policing: clause 61 established a commission of twenty-five barons to ensure the King's compliance with the agreement. They were empowered to seize the King's possessions if he breached its terms.

Strictly speaking, the Magna Carta had legal force for just ten weeks – or, possibly, no legal force at all. Two years previously, to resolve a long-running dispute with the Church, John had surrendered his kingdoms of England and Ireland to the Pope, who leased them back to him for an annual fee. It was questionable whether John could agree to the terms of the Magna Carta at all without the Pope's consent, but in any event the Pope denounced the document as 'unlawful ... unjust ... base and shameful'. John's battles with his barons continued, with companies raising arms across England and even an unsuccessful French invasion. But before these battles could be resolved John died, of dysentery, in October 1216.

If John had lived, the Magna Carta might have become an historical footnote. But after his death, the document proved itself to be a remarkably effective tool for establishing stability. John's son and heir, who would become Henry III, was then only nine. The Magna Carta was quickly reissued in a slightly amended form. The barons were reassured, and peace followed. After he had come of age and ascended to the throne, Henry III made his own reissue in 1225 (which is the document shown here) and the peace continued. And that is the reason that this document enjoys its remarkable status – because ruler and ruled discovered its power to bring stability and peace.

# JEWS *in* ENGLAND: *Dependence and Loathing*
## Jewish Tax Roll

## 1233

Above: *(detail) Medieval English Jews were forced to wear spiked hats.*
Below: *Jews and demons mingle in the clerk's doodle.*

THIS DOCUMENT CAPTURES medieval England's dependence on its Jews, and its hatred of them.

In 1070, William the Conqueror invited Jewish financiers to settle in his new land. The Bible prohibits usury, the charging of interest on loans. It was believed that this prohibition applied to Christians but not to Jews, and so Jews took up the role of moneylenders and financiers. By the mid-twelfth century there were Jewish communities in the south of England, the Midlands and East Anglia.

Jews were valuable. In 1189, England's Jewish community paid as much as the entire Christian population towards the 'Saladin Tithe' for the conquest of Jerusalem. Aaron of York, the greatest financier of the reign of Henry III, funded the building of Westminster Abbey, the creation of the windows at York Minster and the expansion of the Tower of London.

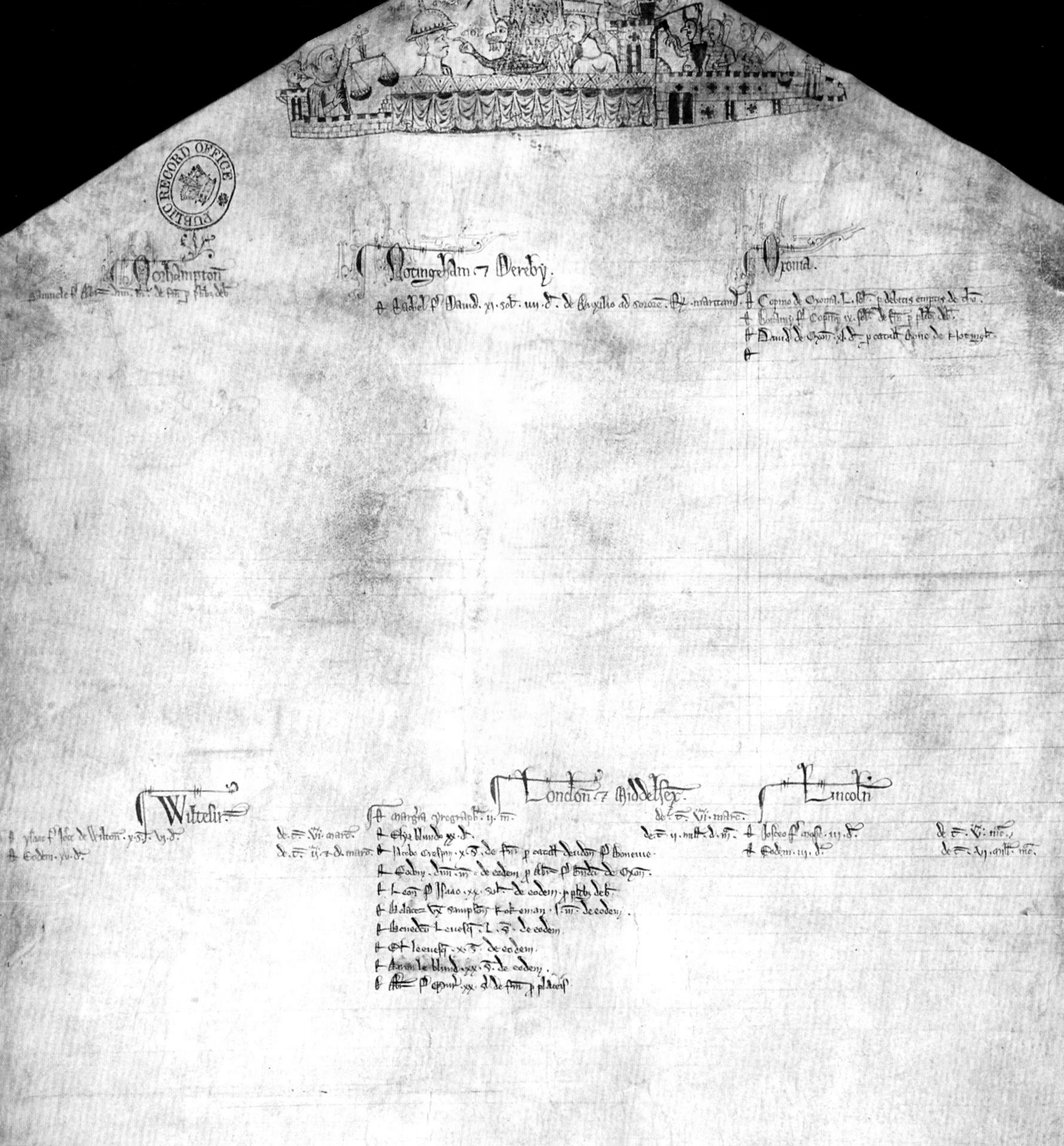
PUBLIC RECORD OFFICE
Norhampton
Notingeham 7 Dereby
Oxonia
Wiltesir
London 7 Middelsex
Lincoln
Glouc

OPPOSITE: *The roll succinctly captures medieval England's reliance on, and hatred of, the Jews – above the description of taxes payable is a demonic cartoon.*

And England loathed them for it. Jews were despised for their perceived wealth, and for the royal protection that they enjoyed. Not only were Jews not part of the Christian majority, they were part of a group that was thought to have actively participated in the death of Christ. Jews were regularly accused of the ritual killing of children. In Norwich, for example, a Jewish moneylender, Odartson Benedict, and three fellow Jews were tried and hanged for the kidnap and murder of a Christian child.

The fate of Odartson Benedict would have been known to the subject of the document opposite, a fellow member of the Jewish community of Norwich, Isaac fil Jurnet. The body of the document is a receipt roll for the taxation of Isaac, the richest man in Norwich, in 1233. He had property interests that included the Norwich docks, and was chief moneylender to the Abbot and monks of Westminster. The taxes levied on Isaac in the body of the roll are enormous and, of course, were an excellent source of income for the State.

But at the top of the roll is a cartoon, doodled by an anonymous clerk. In the cartoon, Isaac fil Jurnet is portrayed as a devil, with three faces and a triple beard. The triple image may allude to Isaac's different business interests, and suggests a demonic hypocrisy. Isaac is accompanied by named demons, 'Colbif' in the centre and 'Dagon' to the right. Colbif touches the hooked noses of the people on either side, as if they are devil's marks. The figure to the left is Mosse Mokke, Isaac's debt collector, wearing the spiked hat that Jews were forced to wear. Seven years after this was drawn, Mosse was dead, executed on the accusation that he had clipped precious metal from coins. To the right is Mosse's wife, Avegaye, who was accused of charging excessive interest on loans. The clerk was clearly local, familiar with Isaac and his circle, and with local attitudes towards them. The theatrical setting for the drawing suggests that the clerk was also familiar with the Mystery Plays of the time, in which biblical stories were dramatised, and in which Jews were portrayed as Judases and Christ-killers. With its images of devils, scales and balances, the cartoon attacks Isaac's business of moneylending – a business that was, of course, the very reason for the existence of the tax roll on which it was drawn.

*The figure to the left is Mosse Mokke, Isaac's debt collector, wearing the spiked hat that Jews were forced to wear. Seven years after this was drawn, Mosse was dead, executed on the accusation that he had clipped precious metal from coins.*

Things would get even worse for Jews in England in the following years. The State continued to gouge as much money as it could out of them, while at the same time passing laws that made it harder for them to charge interest and enforce security. Tax receipts from Jews fell from around £4,000 a year in the 1240s to around £900 in 1278. Jews were becoming a lot less valuable. They also no longer held their monopoly on lending, with the rise of the great Italian banking families (the Christian bankers got around the biblical prohibition on usury by not charging interest as such, instead requiring periodic payments for insurance on their loan).

In 1290, Edward I ordered the expulsion of England's Jews. Most fled to France, until their further expulsion from France in February the following year. A few went to Egypt, some to Scotland, others across the Mediterranean to the Levant. It would be 350 years before Jews returned to England.

# A BLACK MAN *in* BRITAIN
## The Domesday Abbreviato

# 1241

LEFT: *Perhaps the earliest image of a black man in Britain, gripping the letter 'I'.*
RIGHT: *The book is filled with doodles; some may be imaginary, some drawn from life.*

THE DOMESDAY ABBREVIATO is a mystery. On the face of it, it seems to be a summary of the Domesday book, a kind of working copy. But whereas the great Domesday Book is a grim, almost featureless record of ownership rights, the Abbreviato is rather pretty, with illuminated images in its early pages and artistic little doodles in its margins. Our best guess is that it was compiled at Westminster during the reign of Henry III. But we cannot be sure when, where or why it was made.

The most famous image in the book is this one (left), which may be the earliest surviving portrayal in Britain of a black person. His appearance here is as mysterious as the rest of the book. The page on which he is doodled concerns land rights in Derbyshire, which we can be fairly confident he has little to do with. At a first glance, the image can seem shocking, a grotesque caricature. The man hangs from the letter that opens the page. His grimacing face is locked in a snarl, showing rows of animal teeth.

But look again. The man's arm is bent. He isn't hanging from the letter, he is reaching up and grasping it. He is beautifully dressed, in a banded orange tunic and blue stockings with orange cross-garters. The artist carries the orange of his clothes through to the depiction of his skin, a detailed study of iridescent beauty. And, as for those teeth, doesn't he simply have an overbite?

Was this drawn by someone who had seen a black person, perhaps a visitor to court or a nobleman's servant? We cannot say, not least since the same skilled artist also draws convincing mythical creatures in the Abbreviato. But, to me, everything about this drawing says that it was drawn from life or memory. The artist is not denigrating this man – he is simply fascinated by him.

OPPOSITE: *Unlike the Domesday Book, the Domesday Abbreviato contains illuminations. Here are legends from the life of Edward the Confessor.*

n Rs E: Conf
dlkedge Johem
) in Sacramento
comite
udus abbas
nter decem

Rs E: conf.
um Abbatem
o pag: 397
dem Sanctus
i Evangelista
odo eundem

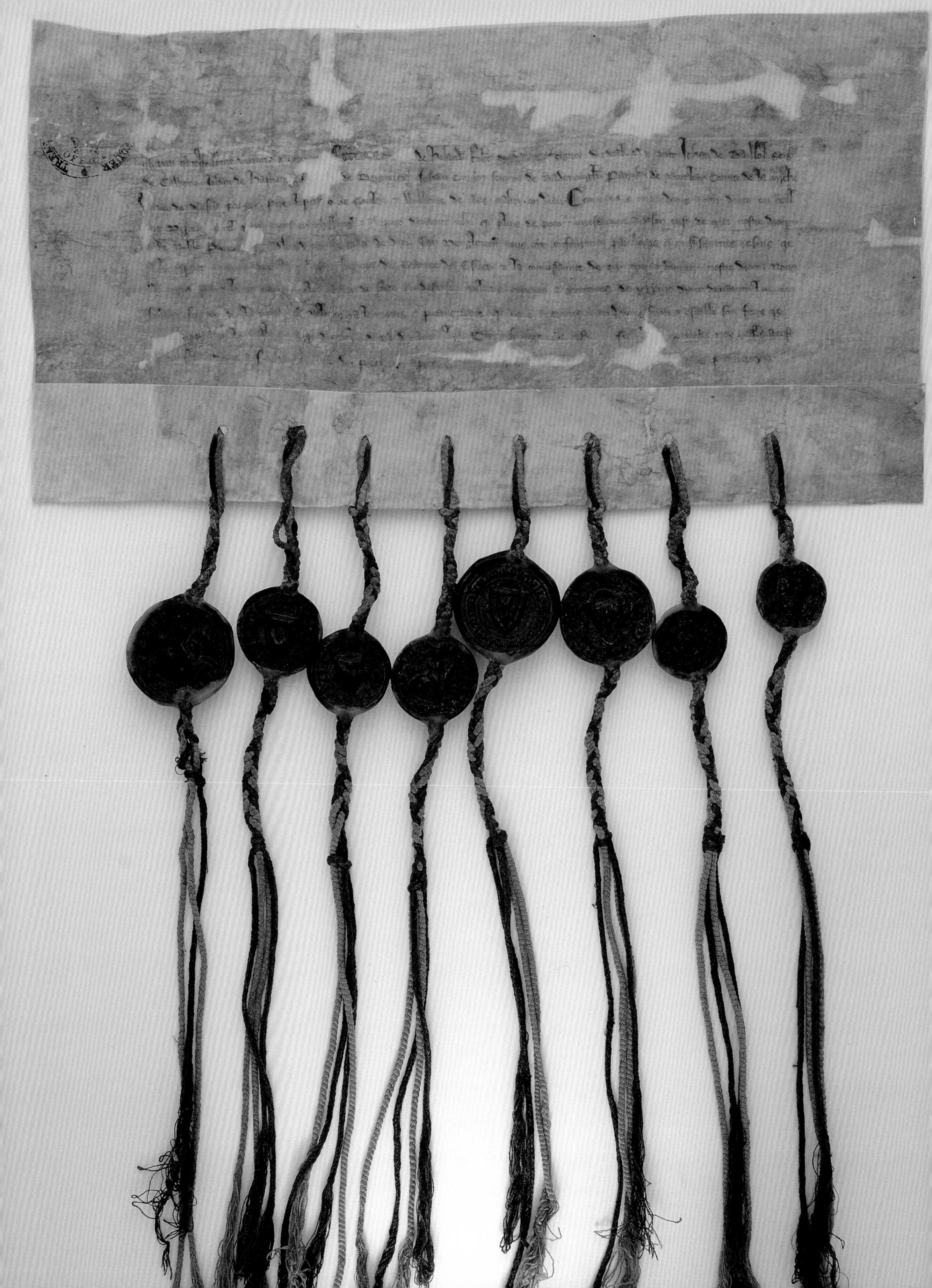

# *The* GREAT CAUSE
## Claimants to the Scottish Throne

LEFT: *One side of the seal of John Balliol, a lead contender to be king of Scotland.*

## 1291

THIS ELEGANT PARCHMENT still raises hackles over 700 years after it was written. Each of the men who set their seals to it was submitting their claim to be king of Scotland to a special tribunal – presided over by the king of England. The English would later enjoy claiming that the Scottish king was merely an appointee of the English; while the Scots would angrily respond that the document shows no subservience or submission. Either way, the document set the tone for hundreds of years of stormy relations between the two nations.

It could all have been so different. In the early thirteenth century, Alexander II (a descendant of Malcolm, the man who killed Macbeth) used violence and diplomacy to organise the northern kingdom into much the shape that we recognise today. His son, Alexander III, married a daughter of the English king, Henry III, creating a real prospect of the union of the Crowns. But in the space of a few years, through a series of mishaps, Alexander and his direct heirs all died. Scotland was left without a clear line of succession.

Civil war was a real possibility, most likely between the two strongest claimants to the Crown, John Balliol, Lord of Galloway, and Robert Bruce, Lord of Annandale. To avoid this catastrophe, a process was needed to decide who would be king. That process became known as Scotland's 'Great Cause'.

It would have stuck in Scottish throats, but Edward I of England was the natural choice of arbiter in the Cause. Edward had ruled Scotland's nearest neighbour for almost twenty years. It was in his interest to ensure stability and peace in Scotland. Moreover, Edward was not someone you wanted to provoke. A hard-bitten veteran of the crusades, he had ruthlessly crushed rebellions in Wales and elsewhere. Wise counsel said that he should be kept onside.

It was also sensible – and this was a key purpose of this document – to ask that all the claimants should agree in advance to abide by the decision of his tribunal. No one wanted to go through the process, only for a failed candidate to rise up against the chosen king.

OPPOSITE: *Claimants to the Scottish throne each fixed their seals to agree to abide by the decision of Edward I's tribunal. Bruce's and Balliol's seals are first and second from the left.*

Edward required the claimants to come to Norham Castle in Northumberland, where each attached his seal to the document, on emerald-green wax attached at the end of red and green silk cords. Bruce's seal is a sword-wielding knight on horseback; Balliol's is a shield.

Edward assembled 104 men to decide the competing claims, but Balliol and Bruce were the only compelling candidates. After some seventeen months, in November 1292 Balliol was named as Alexander's successor. He travelled to Scone where, seated on the famous Stone of Destiny, he was proclaimed king of Scotland.

It was a miserable monarchy. The English missed no opportunity to embarrass the hapless Balliol. Edward was a royal back-seat driver, interfering in Scottish affairs and demanding Scottish troops for his French wars. When Scotland signed a treaty with France, Edward massacred the people of Berwick and Dunbar, had Balliol paraded in front of him and stripped him of his royal insignia. Edward carried off key symbols of Scottish independence, including the Stone of Destiny, and archives of documents. Scotland was without a king for ten years, but then reasserted itself with great victories against the English, first under its most famous hero William Wallace, and later under Bruce's grandson Robert the Bruce, crowned king of Scotland in 1306.

This document, cornerstone of the Great Cause, is solidly pragmatic and almost certainly saved Scotland from tearing itself apart. But pragmatism rarely stirs the soul and, besides, it was a grubby kind of agreement. England was pleased to rule the Scottish nobles by belittling and dividing them, while the Scottish nobles were quick to press their personal interests over national feeling. Echoes of suspicion, recrimination and mistrust would reverberate from this document for hundreds of years.

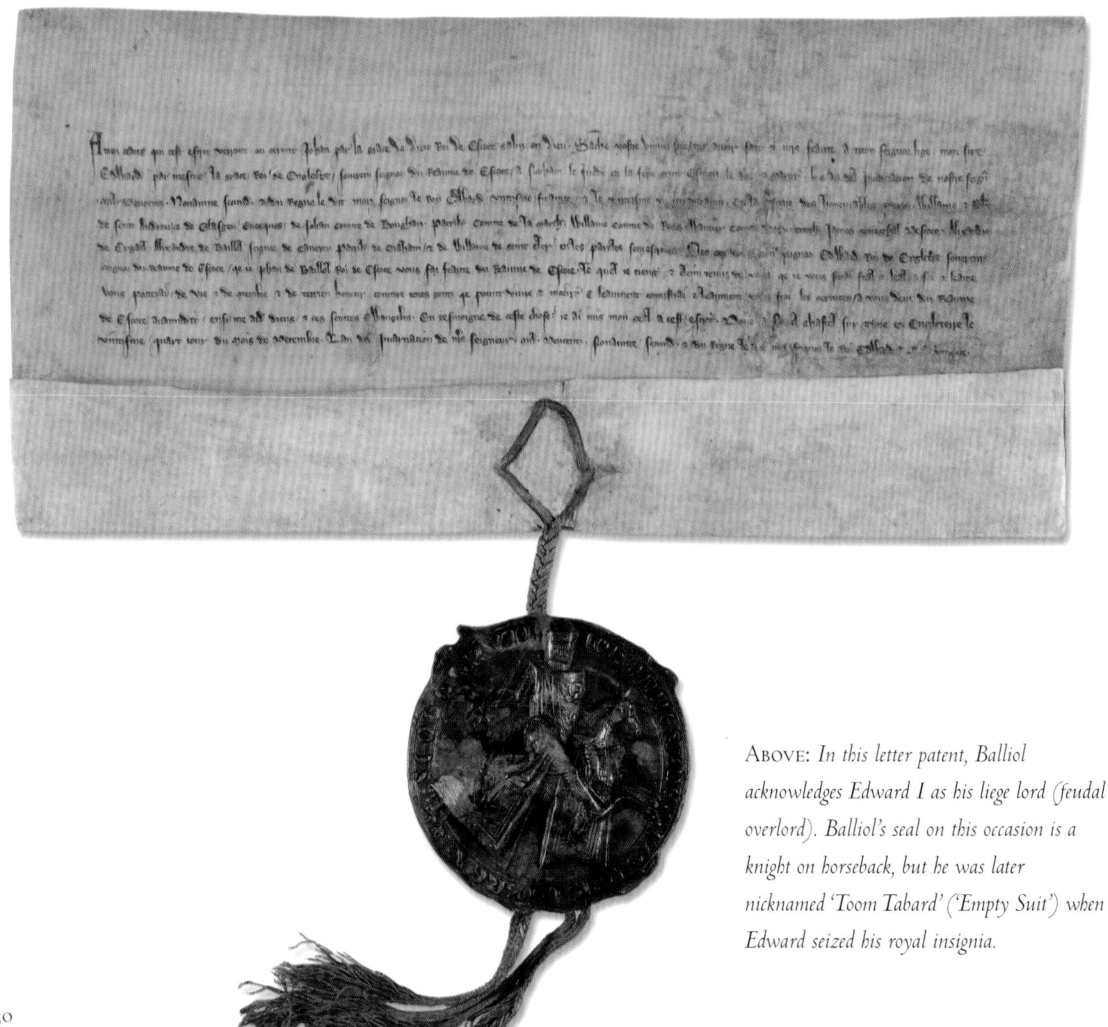

ABOVE: *In this letter patent, Balliol acknowledges Edward I as his liege lord (feudal overlord). Balliol's seal on this occasion is a knight on horseback, but he was later nicknamed 'Toom Tabard' ('Empty Suit') when Edward seized his royal insignia.*

# *A* CLERK'S MUSIC
## Early Music in Multiple Parts

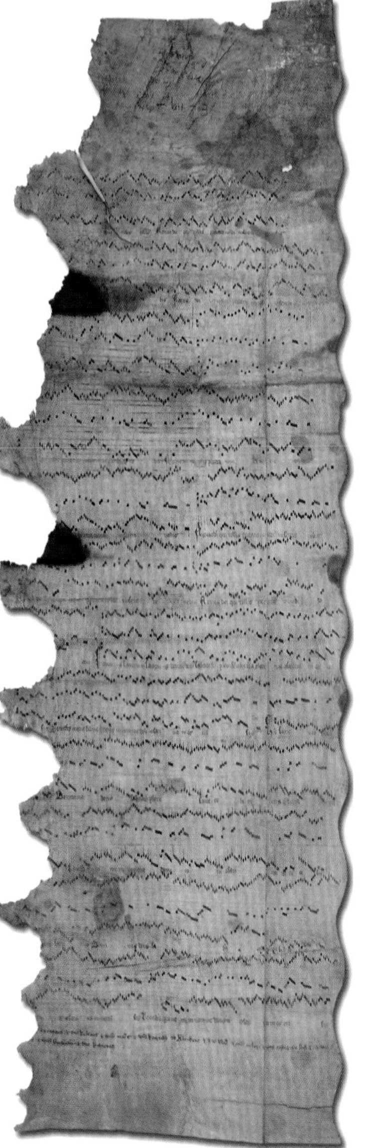

**1325**

RIGHT: *Torn sheepskin parchment – on one side, death duties; on the other, an amazing musical survival.*

ONE SIDE OF this sheepskin parchment contains a commonplace record, the assessment of death duties for lands in Tamworth, but on the reverse is something remarkable – one of the very earliest settings of music in multiple parts in England, written out by an anonymous government clerk.

The music is in three parts, with the lines set one above the other, and, below, the words of the *Agnus Dei*, an ancient Christian prayer to Jesus. The music was written later than the record on its reverse. The assessment was written out twice, once for Crown records and once for the heir, and the two versions divided by an irregular cut, so that they could be matched and verified if the terms were ever in dispute. Since the music was written entirely within the borders of the half shown here, it must have come later. The musical clerk who wanted to record this setting had simply come across an old scrap of parchment that seemed good for the purpose. Government records were frequently recycled in this way.

The setting is complex, the writing elegant. The clerk who wrote this was a highly skilled, musical man and almost certainly a priest. Churchmen were closely involved with government, and the line between religious and administrative life was blurred. Given such intermingling, the piece may well have been sung at one of the churches near the heart of government, such as St Stephen's Chapel, Westminster.

The document gives tantalising hints about the lives of such priest-clerks at a time when the machinery of government was still settling down. The government was itinerant, and there was no professional civil service as such. The distinction between public and private, as well as between State and Church, was hazy. Government jobs were for life, and clerks regarded official documents as being in some sense their personal property. Government papers are scattered around the country, as clerks would take them back to their abbeys and estates. They would undertake official work as and when they needed to, in taverns, at breakfast, over dinner. Many records in the National Archives are streaked with the grease of meals centuries old. It is unclear why the musical priest-clerk wrote out this gorgeous music. Had he composed it, or sung it, or heard it and wanted to capture it? This document gives you space to imagine.

LEFT: *The irregular cut (to the left) of the record of death duties enabled it to be verified against the heir's copy.*

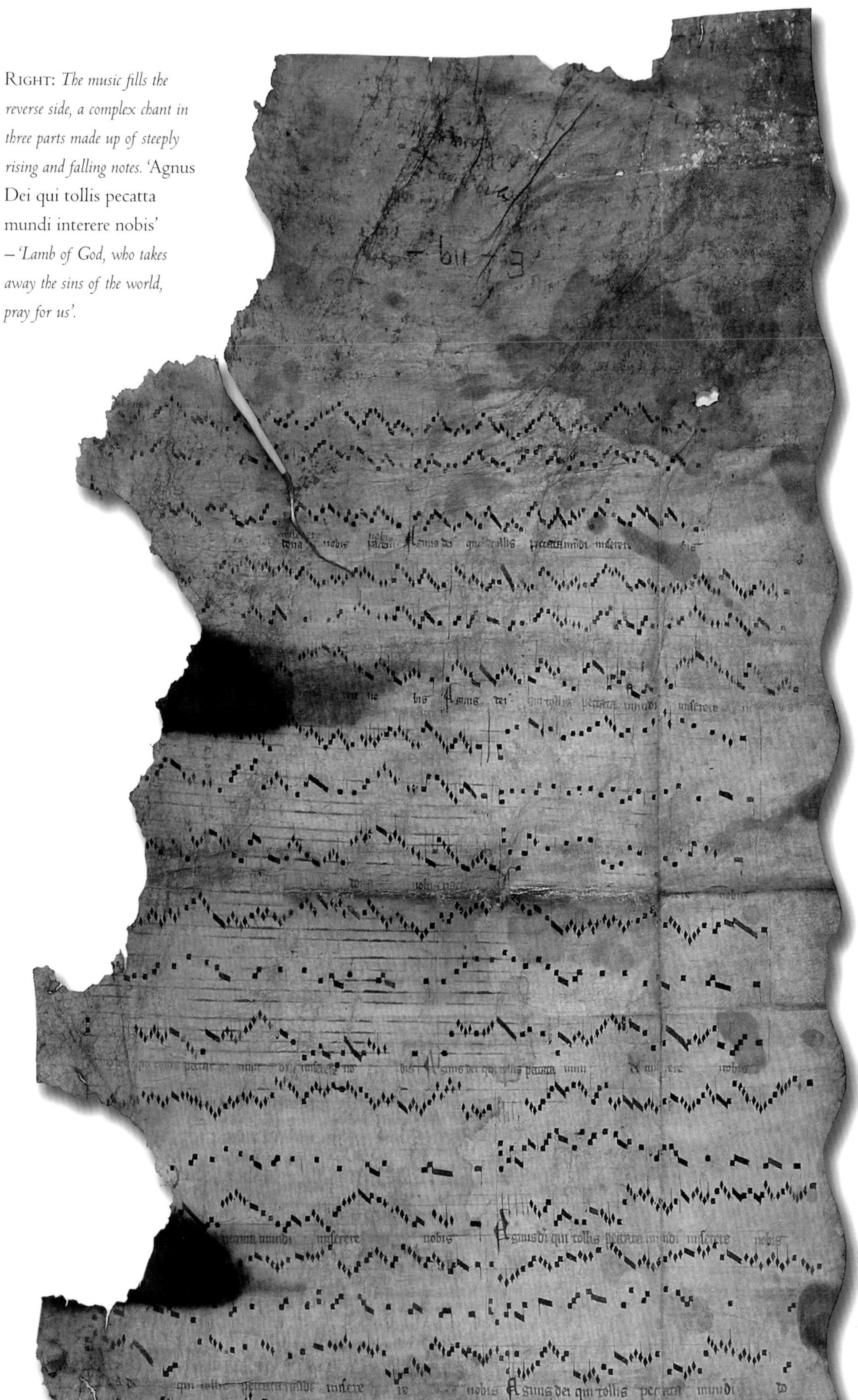

RIGHT: *The music fills the reverse side, a complex chant in three parts made up of steeply rising and falling notes.* 'Agnus Dei qui tollis pecatta mundi interere nobis' *– 'Lamb of God, who takes away the sins of the world, pray for us'.*

# PRAYERS *from the* BATTLEFIELD

## Letter from Edward III

RIGHT: *Edward III. His military ventures included the Crusades, brutal campaigns in Britain and war in France.*

## 1347

On the evening of 23 July 1347, an English king wrote home from his army camp in France:

*Most dear and faithful. We signify you for certain that our adversary of France with all his power encamps beside Mount Owry which is only three French leagues from our host and if we are able to see their tents and encampment outside of our said host then we hope with the aid of our Lord Jesus Christ on them speedily to have a good journe* [day] *with regard to our right quarrel to the honour of us and our realm whereby we pray you devoutly make prayer for us. Given under our secret seal at Calais the Monday after vespers.*

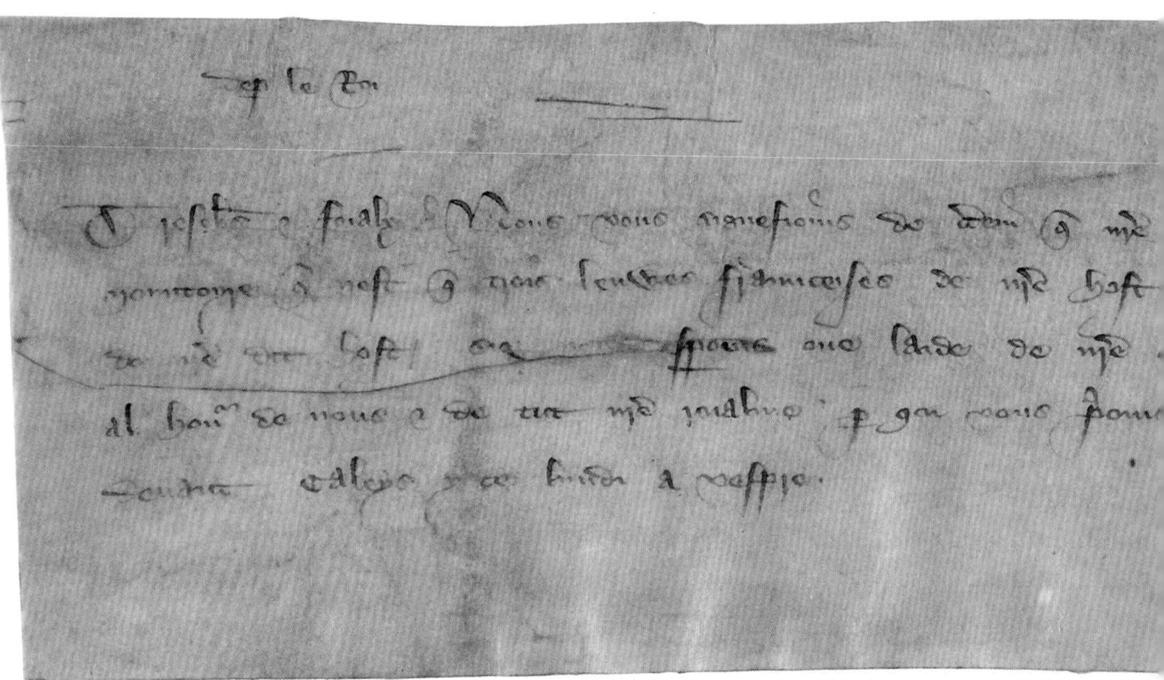

The Hundred Years' War between England and France began in 1337 when Edward III, who had then been king of England for around ten years, asserted a claim to the French throne through his grandfather, Philip IV of France. In the summer of 1346, Edward invaded. At the time, France was the European superpower and Edward's claim was bold, to say the least. But that August, his army of around 35,000 won a spectacular victory at Crécy over the 100,000-strong army of Philip VI of France. Crécy was an extraordinary upset for the French. The victory owed much to the new technology of the English longbow, but nevertheless Edward must have felt that Christ was with him.

Edward's victory gave him glory but no material gains, and so he decided to offset his expenditure by taking the seaside town of Calais. But the town's defences were too strong for Edward to take it by storm, and it was keeping itself provisioned from the sea. The French king meanwhile had regrouped, and was advancing on the English lines. This is the moment the letter captures.

Edward's letter was probably going across the Channel to the English Chancellor. The slits at the top are designed to carry the king's seal – a secret seal in this case, for personal communications.

It is difficult to say whether Edward's prayers were answered. Edward was occupied with a siege, and was expecting to have to fight only if he saw the enemy's 'tents and encampment outside of our said host' – in other words, if the French brought the fight to him, not the other way around. The French king did not advance, and so Edward did not get his 'good journe'. But he did get Calais. Edward summoned ships to block the port, threatening it with starvation, but saying that he would spare the city if six of its leaders would surrender themselves to him. They were to come to him nearly naked, with nooses around their necks and carrying the keys to the city and castle. In the event, the men were spared execution, but Calais was to remain in English hands for the next two hundred years.

Below: *Edward III dictated this letter from his army's camp outside Calais; the French army was three leagues (about nine miles) away.*

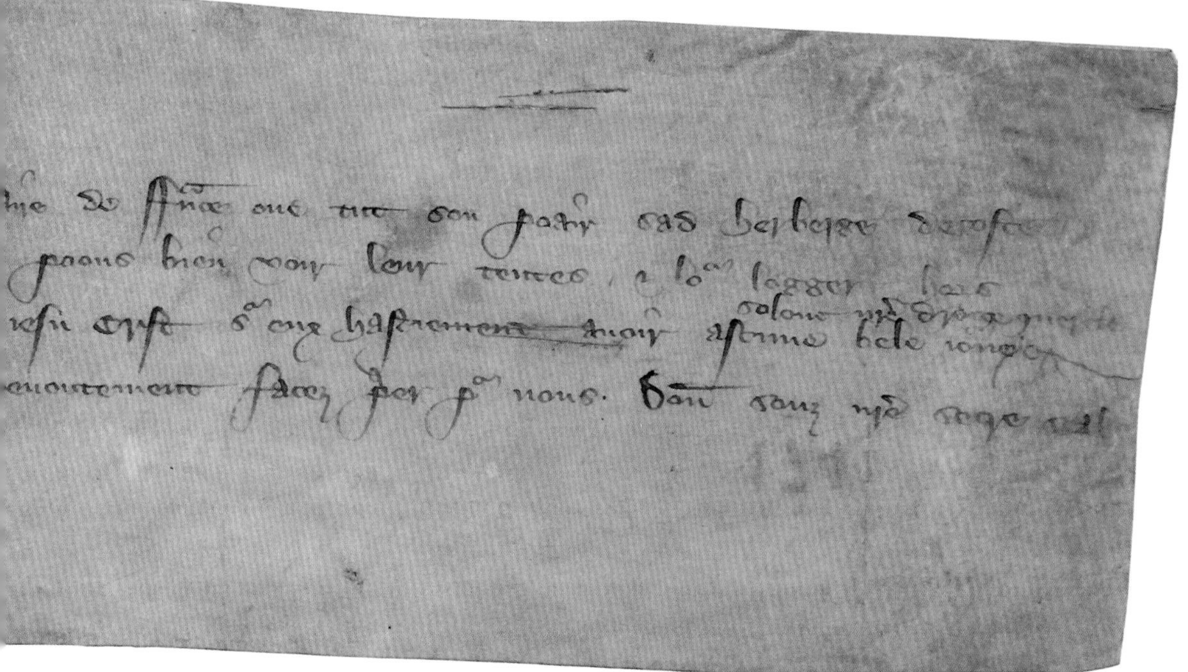

# *The* BLACK DEATH
## Manorial Rolls

# 1349

RIGHT: *Woodcut showing plague victims.*
OPPOSITE: *The manorial roll of Great Waltham indicates a death-rate of around 60 per cent.*

THESE DOCUMENTS WERE written in small English villages where the people were living through the most devastating event of the Middle Ages, or of any age. The world of the Black Death was one in which more or less every other person was killed, seemingly at random, in the space of a few months; in which the dead in their homes were discovered only by the stink of their rot; in which care for the dying and dead was forgotten; in which parents abandoned children, and children their parents; in which families fled from each other. These documents contain just a glimpse of the horror.

The Black Death – thought to have been caused by the bacterium *Yersinia pestis* – originated in southwest China. It was carried to the Mediterranean on merchant ships, first to Sicily, and onwards to ports in Italy and France, from where it began to race its way inland. The Italian poet Boccaccio described the plague as he encountered it in Florence:

*It began in men and women with a kind of swelling in the groin or under the armpit. Commonly called 'tumours', they grew to the size of a small apple or egg. Soon these tumours spread all over the body. After this the symptoms changed and black or purple spots appeared on the arms, thighs or elsewhere, sometimes large, sometimes small. These spots were a certain sign of death ...*

The pestilence reached England in the summer of 1348, probably through the port at Bristol, and by November had reached London. The manors of Great Waltham and High Easter in Essex, where these documents originated, knew then that the plague was at their door.

The documents were written the following summer, at Pentecost 1349. They are the rolls of the local manorial courts. The ordinary business of the courts was to regulate local issues and determine payments owed to the lord of the manor. Today, they are invaluable in helping us understand the impact of the plague. Manors imposed a 'frankpledge' on their adult males, in effect a quarterly tax of one penny per man. By calculating the fall in frankpledge between 1346, when the plague was just a rumour, and 1349, when it had fully hit, you can count the scale of the devastation. The rolls show that in High Easter in 1346, 16 shillings and 7 pence was the sum paid, so 197 adult males lived there. At Pentecost 1349, the frankpledge had collapsed to 6 shillings and 5 pence. Only 71 adult males were still alive in the manor, a loss of more than 60 per cent.

[illegible] ... [illegible] iiij d.

Dna Gatton — misericordia iij d. — Capitalis plegius de Gatton presentat quod Ricardus Godman [illegible] ... [illegible]

misericordia iij d. — Et quod Johannes Colmere [illegible] ... [illegible]

Et quod Ricardus Godman, Johannes Hebbere, Ricardus Hebbere [illegible] ... Johannes [illegible]

[illegible] — et [illegible] de [illegible] ... [illegible]

[illegible] — Et quod quilibet [illegible] ... [illegible]

[illegible] — Johannes [illegible] et Johannes [illegible] de [illegible] ... [illegible]

misericordia iij d. — Et quod [illegible] ... [illegible]

misericordia iij d. — Et quod Johannes [illegible] ... [illegible]

[illegible] — [illegible] quilibet [illegible] ... [illegible]

misericordia iij d. — Et quod Johannes [illegible] ... Chapman [illegible] ... [illegible]

Et quod [illegible] ... [illegible]

Et quod [illegible] ... [illegible]

[illegible] — [illegible] ... [illegible]

misericordia iij d. — Et quod [illegible] ... [illegible]

Et quod Johannes [illegible] ... [illegible]

[illegible] — [illegible] ... Johannes [illegible] ... [illegible]

[illegible] ... [illegible]

Et quod [illegible] ... [illegible]

[illegible] — [illegible] ... [illegible]

[illegible] — Et [illegible] ... [illegible]

Et quod Johannes [illegible] ... [illegible]

[illegible] — Johannes [illegible] ... [illegible]

[illegible] — Et [illegible] Johannes [illegible] ... [illegible]

[illegible] — Et quod [illegible] ... [illegible]

misericordia iij d. — Et quod Johannes [illegible] ... [illegible]

condonatur — Et quod Thomas de [illegible] ... [illegible]

misericordia iij d. — Et quod [illegible] ... [illegible]

Et quod [illegible] Johannes [illegible] ... [illegible]

[illegible] — Et quod [illegible] ... [illegible]

[illegible] — Et quod [illegible] ... [illegible]

misericordia iij d. — Et quod Johannes [illegible] ... [illegible]

[illegible]

condonatur — Johannes [illegible] ... [illegible]

[illegible] — Et quod [illegible] ... [illegible]

Et quod [illegible] Johannes [illegible] ... Gilbertus [illegible] ... [illegible]

[illegible] et [illegible] capitalis [illegible]

Et est [illegible] in manu domini j. gardinum terre custumarie in quo Willelmus Ulgar obiit seisitus. Et [illegible] in manu domini j. mes' & iiij acr' terre custumarie post mortem Johannis Wrongy. Et [illegible] gardinum de Mallond post mortem Alicie Wrongy. Et [illegible] in manu domini j. mes' & iiij acr' terre in quibus Johannes [illegible] obiit seisitus. Et de [illegible]

Ad hanc curiam venit Petrus Fabyngton & sursumreddidit in manu domini [illegible] j. mes' & [illegible] acr' terre [illegible] Alicie [illegible]. Et dominus de gratia sua speciali concessit [illegible] Petro filio [illegible] & Alicie de [illegible] habendum & tenendum de domino eisdem Petro & Alicie & eorum heredibus [illegible] et fecit fidelitatem. Et dant domino de ingressu [illegible] Johannis Cornewaille

ff. iii. iiij d.

Releu' iiij d. Johannes filius Johannis [illegible] fecit fidelitatem domino pro [illegible] acr' terre in quibus Johannes [illegible] pater eius obiit seisitus. Et dat de releuio [illegible]

ff. [illegible] Walterus Shach fecit fidelitatem domino pro uno mes' & [illegible] acr' terre de Mallond in quibus Johannes Shach pater eius obiit seisitus. Et dat domino de fine pro ingressu [illegible] Johannis Cornewaille

Johannes filius Johannis Parker fecit fidelitatem domino pro j. mes' & [illegible] acr' terre de Mallond [illegible] in quibus Johannes Parker pater eius obiit seisitus. Et [illegible] acr' terre in quibus [illegible] Parker filius [illegible] Johannis Parker [illegible] obiit seisitus. Et dat domino de fine pro ingressu [illegible] Johannis [illegible]

ff. [illegible]

Johannes filius [illegible] fecit fidelitatem domino pro uno mes' [illegible] acr' terre de Mallond in quibus [illegible] pater eius obiit seisitus. Et eadem [illegible] Johannes fecit fidelitatem domino pro [illegible] acr' terre in quibus [illegible] obiit seisitus. Et eadem [illegible] Johannes fecit fidelitatem domino pro [illegible] acr' terre in quibus Willelmus [illegible] obiit seisitus. Et eadem [illegible] Johannes fecit fidelitatem domino pro [illegible] in quibus [illegible] obiit seisitus. Et dat domino pro ingressu [illegible] Johannis Parker

ff. [illegible]

[illegible] Johannes [illegible] qui tenuit de domino [illegible] terre custumarie [illegible] morte [illegible] et nullus [illegible]

Et est [illegible] in manu domini j. cotlond post mortem Gilberti Russel. Et [illegible] in manu domini [illegible] acr' terre post mortem Johannis Russel & [illegible] Russel. Et [illegible] in manu domini [illegible] acr' terre de Mallond post mortem [illegible]. Et [illegible] in manu domini j. cotlond post mortem Johannis [illegible]. Et [illegible] in manu domini j. gardinum terre custumarie post mortem [illegible]. Et [illegible] post mortem Alicie [illegible]. Et [illegible] j. cotlond post mortem Johannis [illegible]. Et [illegible] terre post mortem [illegible]. Et de [illegible]

Johannes [illegible] qui tenuit de domino [illegible] terre de [illegible] post [illegible] mortem [illegible] Et ad hanc curiam venit [illegible] & [illegible] terre [illegible] concessa. Et faciunt [illegible] Et fecit fidelitatem

[illegible] fid.

Johannes [illegible] qui tenuit de domino [illegible] terre custumarie j. gardinum de Mallond & [illegible] acr'

Opposite and left: *These rolls were completed a year after the Black Death struck. They list the dead, but also show that, for all the horror, life went on.*

Of the 126 men missing from the rolls, a few may have died of other causes, some will have run away, but the overwhelming majority will have died from the Black Death. The roll is peppered with the words 'post mortem' against the villagers' names, with their date of death.

Fourteen miles down the road at Great Waltham, the story was a little different. There, the frankpledge fell from 15 shillings and 6 pence in 1346, to 9 shillings exactly in 1349 – or from 186 men to 108, a fall of 44 per cent. Significant differences in the death rate occurred from place to place, both in England and across the Continent. The Black Death was carried by lice and fleas and so villages with clean running water fared better, because the cleaner you were, the better your chances of survival. Some villages were better organised than others and were quicker to quarantine their sick.

The rolls give you a sense of the personal impact as well. When landowners died, the land would pass to their next of kin on payment of a fee and oath of 'fealty' (feudal loyalty) to the lord of the manor. Here, you can see one John Purt going through the process:

*John, son of Osbert Purt, makes fealty to the Lord for one messuage, and twenty acres of 'molland'* [land on which rent is paid] *in which Osbert Purt his father died seised. And also the said John makes fealty to the Lord for three acres of land in which Michael Purt, his uncle, died seised. And also the said John makes fealty to the Lord for three acres of land in which William Purt, his uncle, died seised. And also the said John makes homage to the Lord for two and a half acres and one rod of land in which Walter Purt, his uncle, died seised.*

In other words, in the space of those few months, John had lost his father, Osbert, and his uncles William, Michael and Walter. He may well have lost cousins, too, since he is the male inheritor of all the estates.

The rolls also tell a more positive story. In spite of the devastation, the manorial courts of High Easter and Great Waltham were convened and attended, business was transacted and records were kept. In fact, life for many survivors improved. With a shortage of workers, wages went up and rents went down. We can revisit these villages thirty years later, in the rolls for the collection of the 1381 poll tax. John Purt's son Richard and his wife, Agnes, were now thriving on this land. They have named their son after his grandfather.

*The roll is peppered with the words 'post mortem' against villagers' names, with their date of death.*

# 15th–16th Century

## Agincourt Indentures *to* The Ealing Census

Left: *An image from* Valor Ecclesiasticus; *Henry VIII sits in state, his courtiers avert their eyes.*

Lincoln'

Particule compoti Thome Chaworth militis defuncti tam de donis ipsius Thome quam de vadiis suis ac [illegible] hominum ad arma et [illegible] sagittariorum [illegible] retentis [illegible] consilio [illegible] hominum ad arma [illegible] [illegible] in comitiva sua [illegible] Regis Anglie [illegible] Regis [illegible] [illegible] regni sui [illegible] infra [illegible] indenturas inter [illegible] prefatum [illegible] factam [illegible] die Aprilis [illegible] anno [illegible] de [illegible] sigillo [illegible] die [illegible] regni sui [illegible] Thesaurario et Camerariis [illegible] in memorandis [illegible] inter [illegible] de termino [illegible] [illegible] Regis [illegible] articulorum [illegible] inclusa [illegible] quarum quidem indenturarum [illegible] et articulorum tenores conditiones et [illegible] in titulo compoti Roberti Babthorp [illegible] in viagio predicto [illegible] predictas [illegible] compotorum de huiusmodi viagiis [illegible] [illegible] Regis Henrici [illegible] de magno sigillo suo dato primo die Octobris anno regni sui primo Thesaurario et Baronibus huiusmodi [illegible] directis [illegible] in memorandis de eodem anno primo inter [illegible] directis Baronibus de termino [illegible] primo [illegible] Regis [illegible] de [illegible] super [illegible] Thome [illegible] militis [illegible] in [illegible] Regis Henrici [illegible] de [illegible] suo [illegible] anno [illegible] eiusdem Regis [illegible] in [illegible] per [illegible] in Lincoln' [illegible] eodem defuncto [illegible] tam de donis et [illegible] per ipsum [illegible] de [illegible] ipsius Thome et retinencie sue predicte [illegible]

[illegible]

Idem reddit compotum de [illegible] de Thesaurario et Camerariis [illegible] termino Pasche [illegible] anno [illegible] hominibus ad arma [illegible] et sagittariis [illegible] ad [illegible] Regi in viagio predicto [illegible] predictos [illegible] die [illegible] in pelle memorandis ad eandem [illegible] de termino et anno predictis [illegible]

Et [illegible] redempcionibus [illegible] aliis [illegible] prisonariis [illegible] moneta auro argento [illegible] valorem [illegible] in viagio predicto capto non [illegible] redempcionibus [illegible] prisonariis predicta moneta auro argento vel iocalia in viagio predicto per ipsum Thomam vel aliquem de retinencia sua capta fuerunt ut dicit super sacramentum suum [illegible]

Nec [illegible] de [illegible] Regis Francie filiis [illegible] consanguineis suis aut de aliquo Rege de quocumque regno fuit vel de locumtenente aut alio capitaneo [illegible] de [illegible] de Francia in viagio predicto per dictum Thomam vel aliquem de retinencia sua capto [illegible] formam indenturarum predictarum [illegible] capti in viagio predicto faciendo [illegible] prefato Thome [illegible] per ipsum Thomam vel aliquem alium de retinencia sua capti fuerunt in viagio predicto iuxta formam indenturarum predictarum ut dicit super sacramentum suum

Summa [illegible] [illegible]

[illegible]

Idem computat [illegible] hominibus ad arma [illegible] sagittariis [illegible]

# OFF *to* AGINCOURT

## Agincourt Indentures

LEFT: *This indenture for service was started in Southampton, as Henry V amassed an army and fleet to invade France.*
RIGHT: *Back in England, authorisation was needed to pay the men. The red mark shows where the chamberlain's seal was attached.*

# 1415

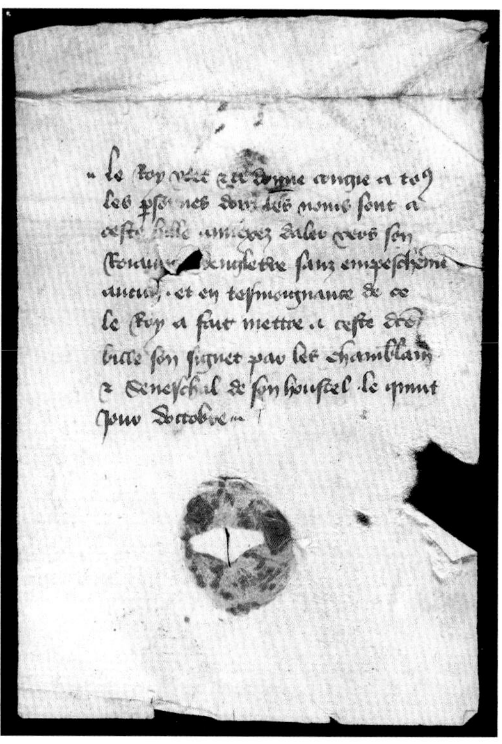

THESE DOCUMENTS WERE written by a government clerk near the quayside at Southampton, in the summer of 1415. They are indentures for the men who were about to join Henry V's invasion of France and who, a few months later, would fight alongside him at the legendary battle of Agincourt.

Henry V had succeeded his father to the throne two years previously. He quickly consolidated his position, and the remarkable stability he achieved in domestic affairs allowed him to turn his attention abroad, in particular to France. France was in a mess. Its king, Charles VI, was prone to bouts of mental illness and his dukes fought one another for power. Henry's great grandfather, Edward III of England, had had a claim to the French throne and adopted what remains the motto of the British monarchy: *Dieu Et Mon Droit* – 'God And My Right', 'My Right' being the English king's right to the Crown of France. With France so unstable, it was a good moment for Henry to reassert that right.

Henry's first act was to get his finances in order, cutting unnecessary costs and insisting on full payment where due. He borrowed extensively and was granted double taxation by Parliament. The royal coffers were soon overflowing with cash.

And here you see a little of what he spent it on. The old feudal system of military service in return for land had broken down (not least under the impact of the Black Death – see page 36), but the King still expected his tenants-in-chief to accompany him to war. However, instead of being bound by traditional loyalty, they entered into legally enforceable indentures. In the rolls shown here, a nobleman called Sir Thomas Hawley is agreeing to bring certain men and horses to battle. The rolls set out the terms of employment for the men, their pay and levels of compensation for any lost horses. Standardised rates of pay are shown: 12 pence per day for men-at-arms, 6 pence per day for mounted archers and 4 pence per day for foot archers.

The rolls also list the jewels that the Crown is pledging against the sums to be paid. The men were well aware of how often the Crown ran out of money, and were not about to risk their lives and possessions on trust. The records in the National Archives are the Exchequer copies. The leaders named on each roll would retain their own copy. It was crucial both for the men and for the Government that the document should be

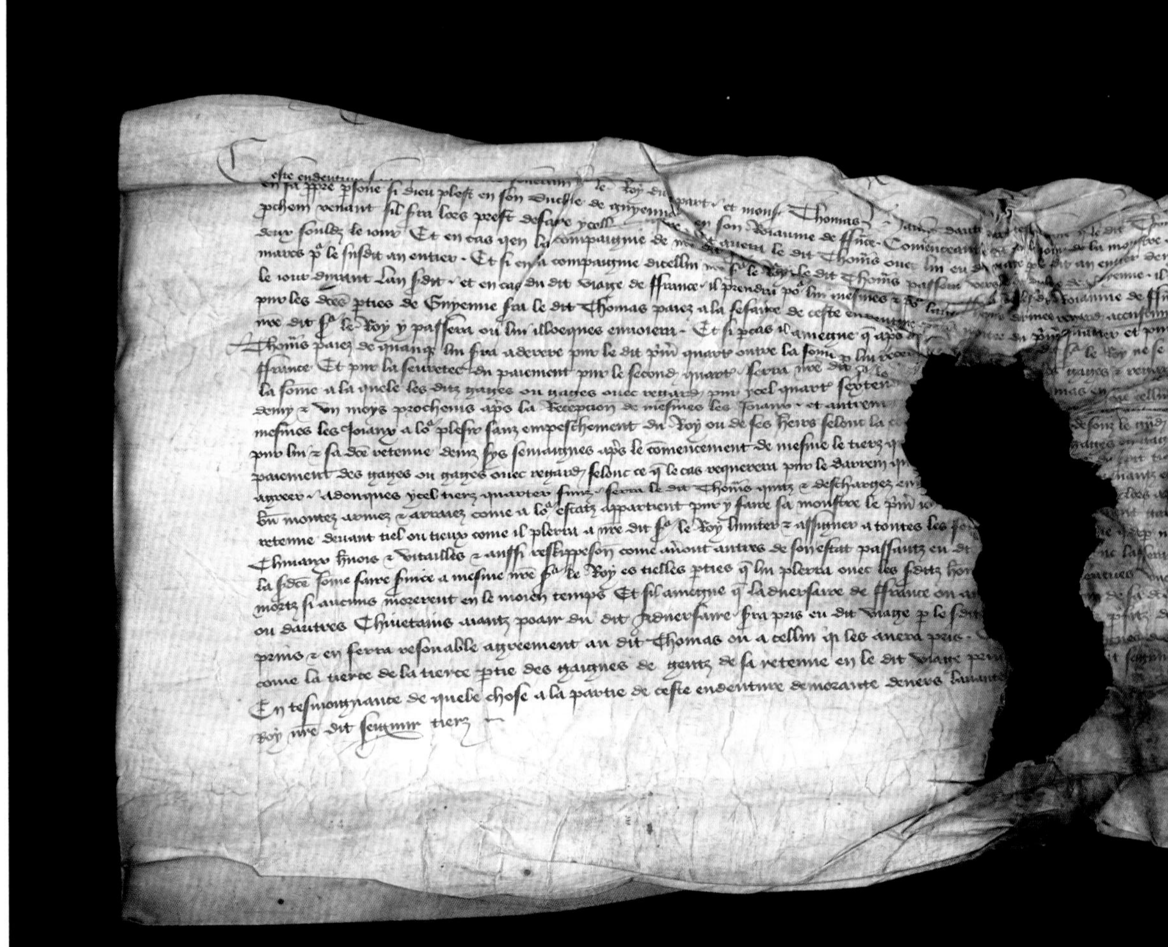

accurate – for the fighting men because they didn't trust the Crown, and for the Crown because it wanted to redeem its security once the men were paid. On completion, the rolls were kept in individual white leather bags. Any further documents about the company would be added to the bag, but otherwise each one would remain unopened until the men did – or did not – return.

These rolls give human faces to the famous campaign, as they list the names of those who would fight. Thomas Hawley's man-at-arms was Roger Kynder, and they were accompanied by six named archers. A small company like this would have stayed together for the whole campaign.

We can imagine Hawley, Kynder and the archers setting off together from Southampton, dazzled by the sight of the 1,500 ships that carried the army of 6,000 men across the Channel. After joining a division and beseiging the port of Harfleur, they would have carried on overland, increasingly tired, dirty and riddled with the dysentery endemic in the ragged English army. Two-and-half months after landing, they would have found themselves near the small village of Agincourt in northern France, facing the massed ranks of the French army, pennants fluttering, armour gleaming, as many as ten times their number. They would have known that, whereas Hawley might be taken alive for the ransom, for the others it was kill or be killed. Luckily for them, the French had made a terrible choice of battlefield – a muddy field, narrowly hemmed between woods,

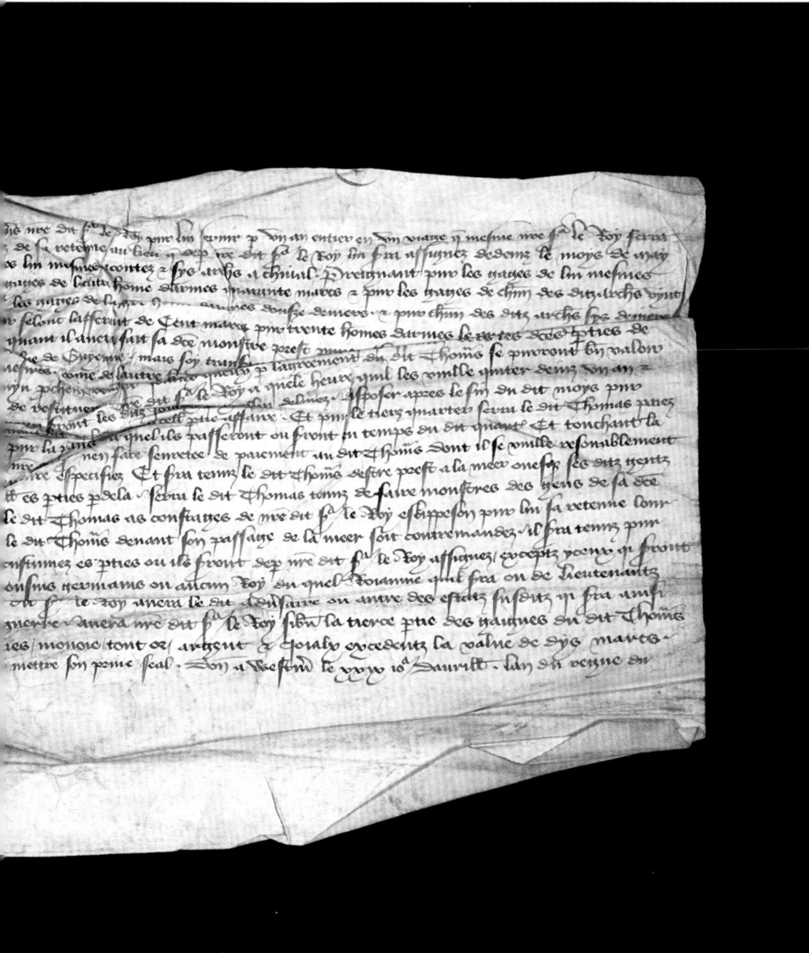

LEFT: *Although this document has suffered later damage, the indentures were stored very carefully. It was vital to know who owed what to whom. This one was between Richard Curtenay, Bishop of Norwich and Treasurer of the King's Chamber, and Thomas Hawley, Knight, who was to die at Agincourt.*

which gave the superior French numbers no space for maneouvre. The archers' arrows would have been among the thousands that took flight in the first English volley; so many that they darkened the sun. As the French vanguard advanced, its knights struggled in the heavy October mud and the archers could have fired point-blank through the enemy's armour, eventually abandoning their bows to attack the bogged-down French with swords and mallets.

After three hours of fighting the battle was over. Several thousand Frenchmen lay dead, including the flower of French nobility. Only a few hundred English had been killed. As the roll relates, Hawley was counted among the English dead. The survivors of the group will have prayed for the soul of their lost leader, but they themselves were now safe.

The army re-embarked at Calais, and when the group arrived back in England, their bag was pulled out again, and a reckoning made. The rolls were living documents, and the marking '*Apud Bellum de Agincourt*' shows what was written after the battle. Still the accounting continued: what was owed, what was paid, what was pledged and what redeemed. The price of Hawley, his man-at-arms and archers over the whole campaign was £31 14 shillings and 10 pence. The men were paid and they disappear from our view. But the victory of Agincourt was so stupendous, so glorious, you can be sure that they were fêted as heroes wherever they went.

# *The* SPARK *of a* REVOLUTION
## England's First Printed Document

The fourth tractate and the last of the progressyon and draughtes of the forsayd playe of the chesse

The first chappitre of the fourth tractate of the chesse borde in genere how it is maad capitulo primo

We haue deuysed aboue the thynges that apperteyne Unto the formes of the chesse men and of their offices, that is to wete as wel of noble men as of the comyn peple / Than hit apperteyneth that we shold deuyse shortly how they yssue and goon out of the places where they be sette, And first we ought to speke of the forme and of the facion of the chequer after that hit representeth and

ABOVE: The Game of Chess, *a book printed by Caxton on the Continent before he moved his press to Westminster in 1476.*

# 1476

THIS DOCUMENT IS momentous, the very first surviving document produced in England by the new technology of the printing press. It is also profoundly ironic – a Catholic document that illustrates perfectly why, within a few decades, Europe was to experience a Protestant revolution.

The document is an 'Indulgence', issued on 13 December 1476 by John, Abbot of Abingdon, to Henry Lanley and his wife. The purpose of Indulgences was to reduce the time that their subject would spend in Purgatory. In medieval Catholic belief, sins committed on Earth would condemn the sinner to hell or, more usually, to Purgatory, where for a period of time the sinner would undergo torments designed to purge them of their sins and make them ready for entry to heaven: gluttons would be fed on worms, the proud raised and lowered on crushing wheels, the avaricious dipped in molten gold. The living could take steps to minimise their time in Purgatory whilst alive through the sincere repentance of their sins. The sincerity of the repentance might be demonstrated by some sacrifice commensurate with the sin, such as prayers, pilgrimage or a payment of money. Over time, a system evolved whereby sacrificial payments could be made to the Church in return for the promise of reduced time in Purgatory. A payment of a few shillings might reduce your torment in the afterlife by a few days. The greater the payment, the more time you got off.

This Indulgence was a big one. After a preamble setting the Lanleys' Indulgence in the context of their contrite hearts ('*nobis confessoribus peccata vestra humiliter confessi fuistis* …' – 'having humbly confessed your sins to our confessor …'), it gets down to the payment ('*Ac pro armata ac manutencione classis contra turcos perfidos*' – 'you have contributed a sum to a naval expedition and its maintenance against the

OPPOSITE: *The large wax seal was meant to give England's first printed document a look of grandeur, but the red ink betrays where the abbot simply filled in the blanks.*

Johannes Abbas Abendon Sanctissimi in xp̄o p̄ris et dn̄i nostri dn̄i Sixti diuina puidencia pape quarti Ac sedi
aplice ī Regnū Anglie Wallia et hibernia vna cū collectore fructuū et puentuū Camere aplice in regno p̄dicto debitoris
Nūcius ꝛ Cōmissari⁹ specialit̄ deputat⁹ dilectis nobis ī xp̄o [illegible]
Salutē in dn̄o sempiternā Qm̄ autē iugi cōsideracōnis oculo fragilitatis huāne infirmitates cōsiderātes sepius corde
estis compuncti timētes hui⁹ seculi delectacōibus velud magni maris fluctibus inuolui absorberi antiqui serpētis iaculis
indies vulnerari Sciētes [illegible]ō nisi p penitencie tabulam vulnera mortes et picula huiusmodi euitari posse Ad nos ple-
nissimaꝝ indulgenciaꝝ dispensatores huilib⁹ cordib⁹ aīsq3 deuotis p salutari remedio confugistis Nos igitur aīaꝝ vraꝝ sa-
luti consulere [illegible] vos ad locū p nos p Jubilei gr̄a consequēda deputatū cōtulisse ꝛ cordib⁹ contritis deputatis ad ho[illegible]
a nobis confes[illegible] [illegible]ccata vrā humilit̄ confessi fuistis Ac p armata ac manutencōe classis contra turchos perfidos
cristiane religio[illegible] [illegible]micos de facultatibz vobis a deo cōcessis terrena in celestia caduca in stabilia felici cōmertio com-
mutando competentē quātitatem cōtulistis plenissimā remissionē oīm pccōꝝ vroꝝ Etiā quantūcunq3 enormiū et grauium
ac ppt̄ q̄ merito sedes aplica esset cōsulenda Necnō absolucionē quarūcūq3 Censuraꝝ ꝛ sniaꝝ tam ab hoīe quā a iure
lataꝝ ac Jubile[illegible] [illegible]ā p inde Ac si basilicas aplōꝝ Petri ꝛ Pauli ac alias Vrbis ecclesias ꝛ loca visitassetis Ac qui[illegible]
vestrū visitass[illegible] [illegible]ionēq3 solēpnē Sanctissimi dn̄i nr̄i pape cōsecuti fuissetis relaxacionēq3 quorūcūq3 votoꝝ si que
emisistis ꝛ rela[illegible] [illegible]bis voluistis Vltra marino sancti Jacobi ī Compostella religionis ac continēcie exceptis vos esse con-
secutos vnitati[illegible] [illegible] et sacramentis restitutos auctoritate aplica qua ī hac pte fungimur declaram⁹ Insup quod ydoneū
Confessorem qui de qui[illegible] [illegible]nq3 criminibz quātūcunq3 grauibz ꝛ ppt̄ que sedes aplica esset merito cōsulenda in mortis
articulo in nō vero Reseruatis confesso[illegible] [illegible]doneus quē duxeritis eligendū tociēs quociēs vobis seu cuilibet vestrū placuerit
de absolucionis beneficio puidere et penitenciā salutarem Iniungere Ac in mortis articulo plenariā remissionē et Jubilei
graciā impertire possit et valeat tenore presencium cōcedim⁹ facultatem. Dat̄ apud [illegible]
Anno dn̄i Millesimoq3 quadringentesimoseptuagesimo [illegible] Pōtificatus p̄fati Scīssimi dn̄i nostri dn̄i Sixti diui-
[illegible] Anno

wicked Turks') and what they are getting for it. The Indulgence is not only absolute (*'remissionem omnium peccatorum'* – 'remission of all your sins'), it is ongoing. Whatever the Lanleys now do, even crimes that only the Pope was normally empowered to forgive (such as wilful murder), they can achieve absolute remission by a deathbed confession (*'ac in mortis articulo plenariam remissionem'* – 'and in death may pronounce a full remission').

The Indulgence was printed at Westminster by William Caxton. Caxton was born in Kent in 1421. He worked outside England as a diplomat and merchant, and in Europe came across a new technology – printing – which had first been developed by Johannes Gutenberg in the early 1450s. Caxton set up a printing press in Bruges, where he printed an English translation of the *History of Troy* and a book on chess. In 1476, he moved to England, and in the autumn rented a house at Westminster Abbey. He must have brought type, punches and matrices with him (the type here is the same as some of his work in Bruges), and possibly the press itself. He wasted no time in selling his services. Strikingly, his print here is similar to the style of handwriting used in government at the time. One of the best ways to market a radical innovation is to make it look familiar.

Rather than have teams of monks laboriously transcribing manuscripts by hand, you could now set each page with prepared letter blocks and reproduce it dozens of times in a single day, greatly reducing the time and cost of producing written works. Information could be disseminated at an unheard-of speed and scale. In time, one impact on traditional religion would be the translation and dissemination of the Bible in English. The ease with which the Bible could now be reproduced meant that the study of scripture was removed from the monopoly of the priests, and put into the hands of the people. Some readers would soon be interpreting scripture in new and radical ways.

*Rather than have teams of monks laboriously transcribing manuscripts by hand, you could now set each page with prepared letter blocks and reproduce it dozens of times in a single day, greatly reducing the time and cost of producing written works.*

Caxton was a jobbing printer, and at Westminster produced everything from *The Canterbury Tales* (the first book printed in England) to chivalric romances to religious texts and translations of classical literature. But it is the way in which his new technology would be applied to the grant of Indulgences that is striking here. The Abbot has tried to emphasise the gravity and importance of the Indulgence by attaching a beautiful wax seal. But he has spotted that, for the content itself, all you would now need to do is to fill in the blanks. This Indulgence could be re-used again and again – just change the names of the recipients, the amount they pay and the amount of time off from Purgatory, and off you go. (Abbot John was a sharp operator. Two years later, he would be investigated by the Pope for unrelated financial irregularities and abuse of his position. He managed to get off scot-free.)

The arrival of the printing press made it easy to crank out Indulgences, debasing the currency of the Church and generating profound resentment. Forty years after this document was printed, in Germany, a former monk, Martin Luther, issued a protest against the Church, including against its practice of issuing Indulgences, and the Protestant revolution began. You can see clearly from this document, the very first of its kind in England, what was happening, and what was about to happen.

# '*The* MOST UNTRUE CREATURE LIVING'

## Letter from Richard III

## 1483

ABOVE: *Richard III, who came to power through an act of treachery. In the letter shown here, Richard is hysterical with rage at the treachery of a former ally.*

SOMETIMES A DOCUMENT captures the whole of a man.

Richard III was crowned king on 6 July 1483. He had won the throne by means of a gross betrayal. When Richard's elder brother, Edward IV, died, he left an unpopular wife, Elizabeth Woodville, and two young heirs. On his deathbed, Edward named his brother as Protector, charging him with care both of his kingdom and his sons until they came of age. But Richard had other plans. After Edward's death, Richard declared that the dead king had contracted another, secret, marriage before his marriage to Elizabeth. That meant that Edward's sons were illegitimate, and lost their rights to the throne. The two boys would later die in the Tower of London, a crime for which Richard has long been the prime suspect.

Richard's coup was conducted in close concert with his friend the Duke of Buckingham. Buckingham had been married as a child to Catherine Woodville, Elizabeth's sister. He had long resented his wife's family, and was an eager accomplice in Richard's betrayal. On taking the throne, Richard showered Buckingham with riches, naming him Constable and Great Chamberlain of England. Buckingham now ranked as the most powerful man in the kingdom, after the King.

All this made Buckingham's subsequent treachery the more extraordinary. Just four months after his coronation, Richard received the astonishing news that Buckingham had rebelled against him. Buckingham was joining forces with the Woodvilles, the very family that he had helped Richard to displace.

The document shown here was written shortly after Richard heard the news. The letter is from Richard to his Chancellor, Bishop John Russell. The neat handwriting in the central part is that of a scribe, who was taking down Richard's request that the royal seal be sent to him at Lincoln (Richard needed the seal so that he could continue to conduct government business during his campaign against Buckingham). Richard has then snatched the letter out of the hand of the scribe and writes in his own hand:

*His band crashed into the men guarding Henry, but before Richard could reach the usurper, he was unhorsed and beaten to the ground. As the blows rained down, Richard's dying words were 'Treason! Treason! Treason!'*

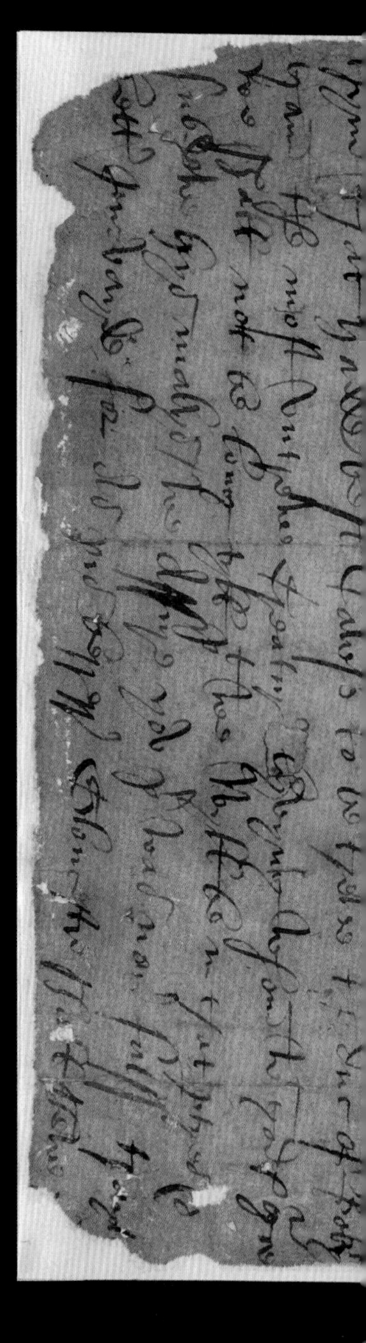

*We would most gladly that you came yourselves if you may, and if you may not, we pray you not to fail, but to accomplish in all diligence our said commandment, to send our seal incontinent upon the site hereof, as we trust you, with such as you trust and the officers pertaining to attend it, praying you to ascertain us of your news.*

This is not the most coherent of messages. Richard was in a state of extreme agitation. The ink starts to fly, and the handwriting becomes even less legible as Richard works up a head of steam. Having reached the end of the page, he turns the parchment on its side, and continues in the margin.

*Here, loved be God, is all well and truly determined, and for to resist the malice of him that had best cause to be true, the Duke of Buckingham, the most untrue creature living; whom with God's grace we shall not be long till that we will be in those parts, and subdue his malice. We assure you that there was never false traitor better purveyed for, as this bearer, Gloucester, will show you.*

As it turned out, Richard did not need to fight Buckingham face to face. Exceptionally heavy rain bogged down the rebel Duke's troops. Harassed by guerrillas loyal to the King, his forces melted away. Buckingham took refuge in the cottage of one of his servants, who promptly turned him in for a thousand-pound reward. Buckingham was beheaded in Salisbury marketplace less than three weeks after Richard wrote his letter.

The impulsiveness and sensitivity to betrayal that Richard shows in this letter continued through his life, and to the very end of his life. Richard reigned for just two years and two months. In August 1485, another challenger for the throne, Henry Tudor, faced Richard III at the Battle of Bosworth. When Richard's scouts spotted the banner of Henry Tudor less than a mile off, he made a sudden decision. Leading a small body

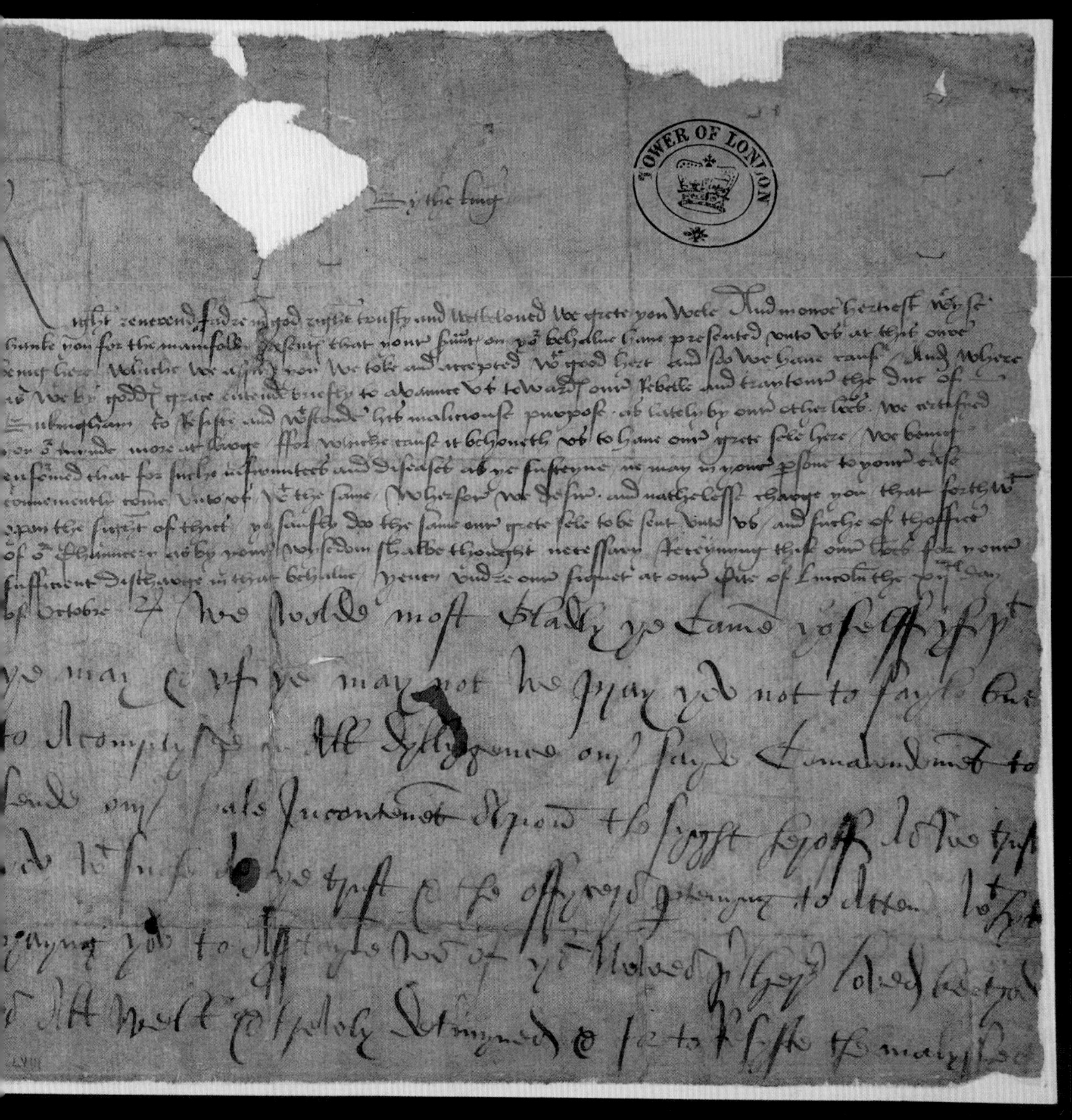

of knights and squires, Richard skirted the battle and thundered towards Henry Tudor. His band crashed into the men guarding Henry, but before Richard could reach the usurper, he was unhorsed and beaten to the ground. As the blows rained down, Richard's dying words were 'Treason! Treason! Treason!'

ABOVE: *Richard III snatched the letter from his scribe and wrote in a state of great agitation.*

# SEALS, STARS *and* STRIPES
## Elizabeth I, Henry VIII and The Wassington Seal

LEFT: *The Great Seal of Elizabeth I – on one side she is a crowned monarch, on the other she is a courtly rider.*

THE LEGAL FUNCTION of a seal is to certify the authenticity and authority of a document. By pressing the seal's image into warm wax attached to the document, the owner guarantees that the document originates from him- or herself and no one else. Since each seal is unique to its owner, it also offers a chance to send a message about how the owner would like to be seen by the world.

The great seal of Elizabeth I is a fine example. One side shows her mounted and in full armour, a determined warrior, albeit that she is trotting against a fashionable floral backcloth. The extent of Elizabeth's dominion is signalled by the Tudor rose representing England, the fleur-de-lys of France and the harp of Ireland; and in case anyone missed the symbols, the words around the edge of the seal translate as 'Elizabeth by the Grace of God, Queen of England, France, Ireland, Defender of the Faith'. On the other side of the seal, Elizabeth is portrayed as the lawgiver, dressed in her coronation robes, crowned and anointed. Her rule is sanctioned by God. On one seal the hand of God emerges from the clouds to bless Elizabeth; on another the Queen is bathed in heavenly rays.

In 1527, Henry VIII of England and Francis I of France tried to outdo each other with the solid gold seals that each attached to their 'Treaty of Perpetual Peace' (perpetual, that is, until 1543, when Henry ordered the invasion of France). Francis's seal is a model of regal elegance. Angels draw back curtains to reveal his throne, while the King sits in a relaxed pose, one knee raised and his head turned to the side. The portrait on Henry's seal is altogether more thuggish. He looks the viewer squarely in the eye, a sceptre clutched in one hand, a crown planted firmly on his head, his family symbol of the Tudor rose placed directly beneath the throne. He seems to be daring you to question his authority. Henry hadn't forgotten that his family had held the throne for just forty years.

But the seal that may have had a more enduring impact than any other is the small, inconspicuous mark of the Wassington family, shown here. The document to which the seal is fixed is an indenture, 1401, by 'Edmond son

OPPOSITE: *In the centre of the small Wassington family seal, 1401, is a shield with three stars above two stripes.*

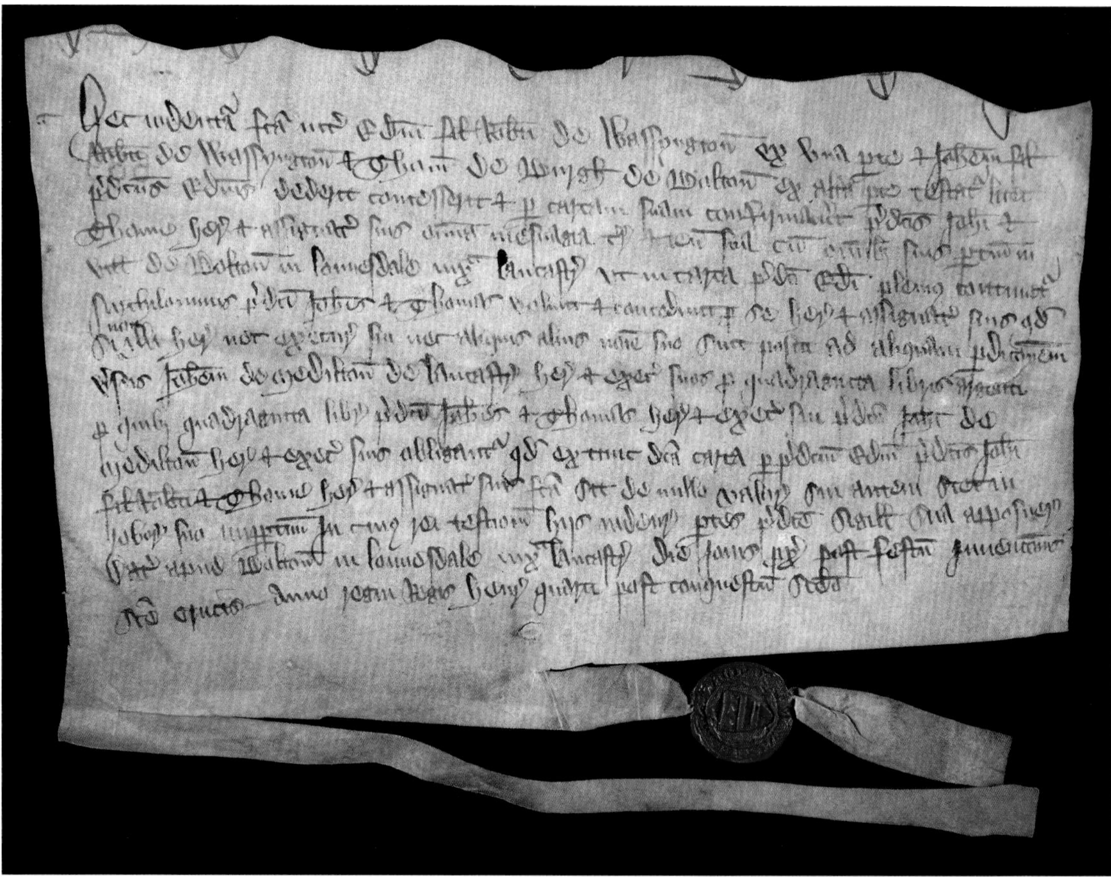

Above: *The little Wassington seal attached to this indenture would become the American Stars and Stripes. Robert De Wassington was an ancestor of George Washington, first US president.*

of Robert De Wassington' concerning lands in Bolton-Le-Sands, Lancashire. The promises given in the indenture would have been written out twice on a single sheet of parchment. Each party's seal would have been fixed at one end, and the two sets of promises divided by an irregular cut. Each party took the half with the other party's seal, and the irregular cut meant that, should the need arise, the two halves of the parchment could be reliably reunited to prove their authenticity. You can make out Robert De Wassington's thumb print on the back of his seal, where he has worked the wax to soften it. The arms on the seal are simple – stars above stripes.

Robert De Wassington was an ancestor of George Washington, first President of the United States. The American War of Independence was fought under the 'Grand Union' flag, which comprised red and white stripes, with a British Union flag in the top left-hand corner. In 1777, a year after the Declaration of Independence, the US Second Continental Congress resolved that the flag of the United States would comprise thirteen stripes and thirteen stars, to represent the then thirteen members of the union. No one knows for sure why the United States adopted stars and stripes on its shield and flag, but the similarity to the family seal of its first president seems an unlikely coincidence. On 14 June each year the US is covered with fluttering stars and stripes to celebrate Flag Day. This little wax seal was to have a lot of descendants.

# PRICING UP *the* CHURCH

## *Valor Ecclesiasticus*

## 1535

ABOVE: Valor Ecclesiasticus *opens with this imposing illumination of Henry himself. The posture of the dominant king and his subservient courtiers emphasises his power as he sits with legs splayed and sporting a scarlet codpiece.*

THE PICTURE ON THE RIGHT is a heck of a way to open a set of accounts. Henry VIII sits on his throne, sceptre in hand. The King's legs are spread, a scarlet codpiece jutting from his pantaloons. His courtiers stand about with eyes averted, fearing to gaze upon his glory. The King looks you, the reader, straight in the eye, as if daring you to defy him. It is a fitting start to a book that was to play a key role in a terrifying exercise of royal power – the greatest land-grab that Britain has ever seen.

This is Henry's personal copy of the *Valor Ecclesiasticus* ('Church Valuation'), the first survey of the value of property held by the Church in Britain, undertaken in 1535. The previous year, after the Pope had refused to grant Henry a divorce from his first wife, Catherine of Aragon, Henry had made himself Supreme Head of the Church in England. Henry's new position gave him the power to divorce Catherine, and had another major advantage: money. Church institutions owned around a quarter of the farming land in England, as well as a treasure trove of jewels and precious metals, all donated down the centuries by benefactors and pilgrims seeking divine favour. The Church in England had paid a portion of its clergy's annual income to the Pope, a kind of tribute known as the 'First Fruits and Tenths'. Now that Henry was Head of the Church, he reasoned that the First Fruits and Tenths ought to be coming to him.

The problem was that no one knew how much money was involved. No one was even quite sure how many churches, monasteries and other religious houses there were. And so the King sent commissioners to every county, to visit every church and religious house in England, Wales and English-controlled parts of Ireland, to find out just what they were worth.

Staff

Hic Inferius continentur valores annuales omnium et singulorum dominiorum Maneriorum terrarum et tenementorum ac aliarum possession[um] quarumcumque temporalium Necnon decimarum Oblacionum pensionum porcionum et aliorum profic[uorum] quarumcumque spiritualium in Comitatu Staff et aliis seperalibus Com[itatibus] inferius specificatis tam Ep[iscop]o Coven[trensi] et Lich[feldensi] quam quibuscumque Abbatiis Monasteriis Prioratibus Decanat[ibus] Archidiaconat[ibus] Collegiis Ecclesiis collegiatis Hospitalibus Rectoriis vicariis Cantariis Liberis Capellis et aliis promocionibus spiritualibus in dicto Comitatu Staff situatis pertinen[tibus] et spectan[tibus] vnacum deduccionibus et Allocacionibus eorundem pro decimis inde Domino Regi Annuatim soluend[is]

videlicet

Decanatus Ruralis de Lapley

et Tresulle in Comitatu Staff Coven et Lich Dioc et infra Archinat Staff Johanne Talbot Johanne Gyfford Militibus Waltero Wrotesley Armigero et Johanne [illegible] generoso Commissionar ibidem

Collegium de Gnosall — Rolandus Epus Covent Decanus ibidem [illegible]

Mordhall — Prebenda Johannes Halle Clerici Prebendarius ibidem — Valet [illegible]

ABOVE: *As this was Henry's personal copy, it is richly illustrated, in particular with images that reinforce the King's authority and power.*

Take, for example, the Priory at Walsingham in Norfolk. Dedicated to the Virgin Mary, this was a major centre for pilgrimage. In the *Valor Ecclesiasticus* the Priory's annual income is recorded as £391 11s 7¼d, plus offerings of £260 12s 4½d. It is impossible to do a direct comparison of the value of money across the centuries, but whereas straightforward price indexation might make that an annual income of half-a-million pounds today, as a proportion of the total economy it would have been worth more than £100 million. The King's eyes must have been widening as he leafed through this book, and it dawned on him just how much he had within his grasp.

So it perhaps isn't surprising that, armed with this book, Henry decided that he wanted rather more than just the First Fruits and Tenths. There were several precedents for winding-up monasteries and sequestrating their assets, and by the 1530s many religious establishments were vulnerable to attack. Monasteries that had flourished in previous centuries were by now severely depleted, many of them too small even to make up the twelve monks or nuns needed to say the Divine Office (a daily cycle of prayers). Writers such as Luther and Erasmus had criticised monastic life, and bawdy satires did the rounds, describing the supposedly luxurious and sexually charged lifestyles of monks and nuns. At the same time that the *Valor Ecclesiasticus* was being compiled, another royal commission was surveying the practices of religious houses and it reported back the failings, particularly sexual failings, of monks and nuns with lip-smacking relish. Henry therefore had an excuse to suppress first the smaller religious houses, and then the larger ones.

OPPOSITE: *This is the opening page of the assessment of religious establishments in Staffordshire. The accounting starts with the two sites at the bottom of the page.*

Within five years of this book being compiled, the religious houses that it lists had gone. Monks and nuns were mostly pensioned off, or monks might become parish priests. Around one hundred sites of monastic worship became (and many still are) parish churches. The rest were stripped of their assets and pulled down or left to the elements. By providing a snapshot of the extent of their riches, this book arguably caused the dissolution of the monasteries. Whether or not it caused the dissolution, it undoubtedly enabled it.

that without cause prouid ...
to go vnto the tower, a place more wonted for a false traitor, tha a
subiect wiche thogth I knowe I deserue it not, yet in the face of
al this realme aperes that it is prouid wiche I pray god I may die the
shamefullist dethe that euer any died afore I may mene any suche
thinge and to this present hower I protest afor God (who shal iudge
my trueth) whatsoeuer malice shal deuis) that I neuer pra[cticed]
conciled nor cosented to any thinge that migth be preiudi[cial]
to your parson any way or dangerous to the state by [any]
mene and therfor I humbly beseche your maiestie to le[t]
me answer afore your selfe and not suffer me to trust [to your]
counselors yea and that afore I go to the tower (if it
be possible) if not afor I be further codemned, howbeit
I trust assuredly your highnes wyl giue me leue to do it [afor]
I ~~be~~ go for that thus shafully I may not be cried out on as now I [shal]
be yea and without cause, let cosciens moue your highnes to
take some better way with me tha to make me be condemned
in al mes sigth afor my desert knowen. Also I most hu[mbly]
beseche your highnes to pardon this my boldnes wiche in-
nocecy procures me to do togither with hope of your natu[ral]
kindnis wiche I trust wyl not se me cast away without d[esert]
wiche what it is I wold desier no more of God but that you
truly knewe. Wiche thinge I ~~thinge~~ thinke and beleue you sh[al]
neuer by report knowe vnles by your selfe you hire. I ha[ue]
harde in my time of many cast away for want of comminge
to the presence of ther prince ~~as~~ and in late days I harde my
lorde of Somerset say that if his brother had bine suffe[red]
to speke with him he had neuer sufferd but the
perswasions wer made to him so gret that he was brogt
in belefe that he coulde not liue safely if the admiral liue[d]
and that made him giue his consent to his dethe thogth
thes parsons ar not to be copared to your maiestie yet I
pray god as euel perswations perswade not one sister again[st]
... that the haue harde false report and

# PLEADING *for* HER LIFE

## The Tide Letter

## 1554

OPPOSITE: *Accused of treason, threatened with execution, Elizabeth begs Queen Mary to meet with her.* RIGHT: *Elizabeth five years later, the young Queen in her coronation robes.*

SHE WOULD RULE England for forty-four years. She would become an icon, 'Good Queen Bess', 'the Virgin Queen', 'Gloriana'. But when she wrote this letter on 17 March 1554, Elizabeth Tudor was just twenty-one years old, and fighting for her life.

Elizabeth's sister, Mary, had been crowned queen of England the previous summer. Both women were children of Henry VIII: Mary by his first wife, Catherine of Aragon; Elizabeth by his second, Anne Boleyn. Frustrated by the lack of a male heir and dazzled by the younger Anne, Henry had his marriage with Catherine declared void. Mary found herself suddenly declared illegitimate, a bastard, and stripped of her royal status. Henry married Anne, and when Elizabeth was born, Henry demanded that Mary, seventeen years her senior, should act as maid-in-waiting to the baby princess. But by the time Elizabeth was two-and-a-half years old, her mother had fallen out of Henry's favour and was executed, and she too was declared illegitimate. Now both girls were legally bastards.

The relationship between Mary and Elizabeth was never comfortable. They were separated by a generation in years. Mary was a granddaughter of the great Spanish Catholic monarchs Ferdinand and Isabella, married a Spaniard, and was devotedly Catholic; whereas Elizabeth was pure English and refused to go to Catholic Mass. Mary would never forget that Elizabeth was the child of the woman for whom their father had deserted her own mother. But you should keep your enemies close. In August 1553, when, in the tumble of Tudor politics, Mary rode to London to be crowned queen, she had Elizabeth at her side.

Popular support for Mary evaporated shortly after her coronation when she married Philip II of Spain. Philip ruled vast territories and, in spite of his attempts to ingratiate himself with his new subjects (even publicly drinking that most English of delicacies, warm beer), it was feared that England would become just another scalp on his belt. In January 1554, courtier Sir Thomas Wyatt raised a rebel force against Mary in Kent. The rebels marched on London, and although they were a force threatening enough for Mary to send messengers to ask for terms, the city held firm and the rebellion fizzled out.

Elizabeth was next in line to the throne, and so naturally was suspected of involvement in the rebellion. For four weeks she was kept in close custody at Whitehall Palace, while the authorities searched for evidence against her. Under torture, Wyatt implicated Elizabeth, and Mary ordered that she be taken to the Tower of London – a terrifying prospect for anyone, but even more so for Elizabeth. This was where her mother had been imprisoned and executed. Before Elizabeth was taken to the Tower, one of Mary's counsellors, the Duke of Sussex, agreed that she should be left undisturbed to write to Mary. Elizabeth gathered her thoughts, and began:

*If any ever did try this olde saynge that a kinges worde was more tha[n] another ma[n]s othe I most humbly beseche your M[aiesty] to verefie it in me and to reme[m]ber your last promis and my last demau[n]de that I be not co[n]demned without answer and due profe wiche it semes that now I am for that without cause provid I am by your counsel frome you co[m]manded to go unto the tower a place more wonted for a false traitor, tha[n] a tru subiect wiche thogth I knowe I deserve it not, yet in the face of al[l] this realme aperes that it is provid wiche I pray god I may dy the shamefullist dethe that ever any died afore I may mene any suche thinge, and to this present hower I protest afor God (who shal juge my trueth) whatsoever malice shal devis that I never practyced conciled nor co[n]sentid to any thinge that migth be preiudicial to your parson any way or daungerous to the state by any mene, and therfor I hu[m]bly beseche your maiestie to let me answer afore your selfe and not suffer me to trust your counselors yea and that afore I go to the tower (if it be possible) if not afor I be further co[n]demned howbeit I trust assuredly your highnes wyl give me leve to do it afor I go for that thus sha[m]fully I may not be cried out on as now I shal be yea and without cause let co[n]sciens move your hithnes to take some bettar way with me tha[n] to make me be co[n]de[m]ned in al me[n]s sigth afor my desert knowen. Also I most hu[m]bly beseche your highnes to pardon this my boldnes wiche innoce[n]cy procures me to do togither with hope of your natural kindnis wiche I trust wyl not se me cast away without desert wiche what it is I wold desier no more of God but that you truly knewe. Wiche thinge I thinke and beleve you shal never by report knowe vnles by your selfe you hire. I have harde in my time of many cast away for want of comminge to the presence of ther prince and in late days I harde my lorde of So[m]merset say that if his brother had bine sufferd to speke with him he had never sufferd but the perswasions wer made to him so gret that he was brogth in belefe that he coulde not live safely if the admiral lived and that made him give his consent to his dethe thogth thes parsons ar not to be co[m]pared to your maiestie yet I pray god al perswatio[n]s perswade not one sistar again[st] the other and al for that the have harde false report and not harkene to the trueth knowen therfor ons again with hu[m]blenes of my hart, bicause I am not sufferd to bow the knees of my body I hu[m]bly crave to speke with your higthnis wiche I wolde not be so bold to desier if I knewe not my selfe most clere as I knowe my selfe most tru, and as for the traitor Wiat he migth paraventur writ me a lettar but on my faithe I never receved any from him and as for the copie of my lettar sent to the fre[n]che kinge I pray God co[n]fou[n]d me eternally if ever I sent him word, message toke[n] or lettar by any menes, and to this my truith I will stande into my dethe.*

The letter finally concludes with two moving postscripts: 'I humbly crave but only one word of answer from yourself … Your Highness most faithful servant that hath, since from the beginning and will be to my end, Elizabeth.' The young princess could not resist a fashionable final flourish on her signature.

The letter is brilliantly judged. It appeals to Mary's sense of the monarch's exemplary role, to their private history together and to Mary's religious sensibilities; and it alludes to the horror of the Tower and to Elizabeth's own royal blood. The letter even has a touch of regal defiance ('yea, and that without cause').

The second page of the letter contains eleven diagonal lines, scratched out by Elizabeth so that no forger could add anything to her plea. These may be the most eloquent lines ever drawn. Not only would they act as a practical bar to forgers, they would vividly demonstrate to Mary that someone might add forged words. The message of these lines is that Elizabeth is true, but that many false people stand between her and her sister.

The letter was brilliantly judged in another way, too. By the time Elizabeth had finished it, the tide on the Thames had risen too high for boats to ride through London Bridge. Hence the name that history has given this document: the 'Tide Letter'. Elizabeth had gained another day in Whitehall, and out of the Tower.

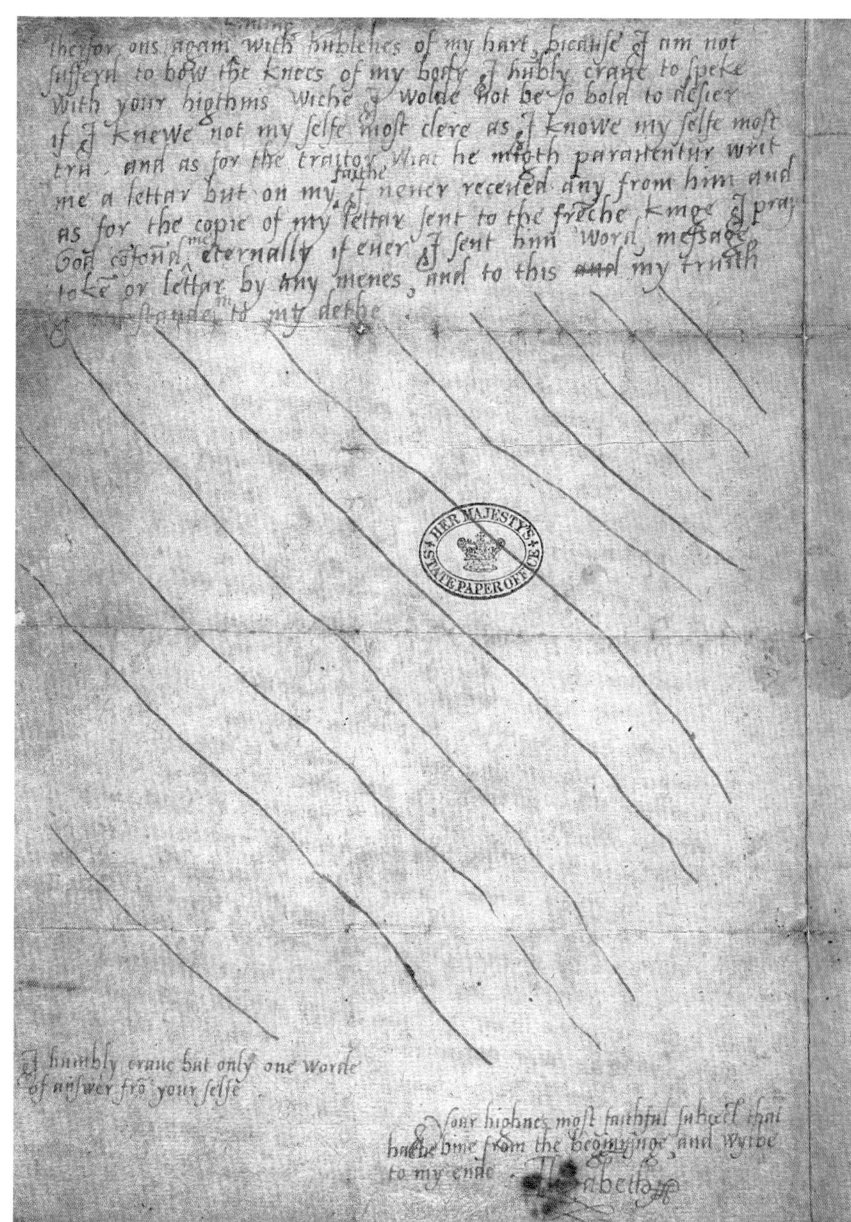

therfor ons again kneling with humblenes of my hart, bicause I am not
suffred to bow the knees of my body I humbly crave to speke
with your highnis wiche I wolde not be so bold to desier
if I knewe not my selfe most clere as I knowe my selfe most
tru. and as for the traitor Wiat he might paraventur writ
me a lettar but on my faithe I never receved any from him and
as for the copie of my lettar sent to the freche kinge I pray
God confound me eternally if ever I sent him word, message
toke or lettar by any menes, and to this ~~and~~ my truith
I will stande in to my dethe.

HER MAJESTY'S STATE PAPER OFFICE

I humbly crave but only one worde
of answer fro your selfe.

Your highnes most faithful subiect that
hathe bine from the beginninge and wylbe
to my ende. Elizabeth

LEFT: *The last page of the Tide Letter contains eleven eloquent diagonal lines. These were to guard against additions by forgers, and so convey the message from Elizabeth to Mary that enemies wanted to divide them.*

When Mary received this letter, she was furious that Elizabeth had been allowed to write to her. She was also, apparently, unmoved. The next day, while Mary took part in a Palm Sunday Procession, Elizabeth was taken in the pouring rain by barge to the Tower, entering by what is now known as the Traitor's Gate. For the next two months there she remained, unaware of what was going on in the world outside, unable to influence the plots against her, not knowing if she might be executed or murdered at any moment.

But Elizabeth was popular, and Philip knew that if she were executed, he would be blamed and Spanish influence in England would be all the more despised. He persuaded Mary to spare Elizabeth and so Tudor politics continued its chaotic tumble. Five years after writing this letter, Elizabeth was queen of England.

# *Who* KILLED AMY ROBSART?

## Coroner's Report

## 1560

LEFT: *Robert Dudley, Earl of Leicester, was rumoured to be the Queen's lover.*

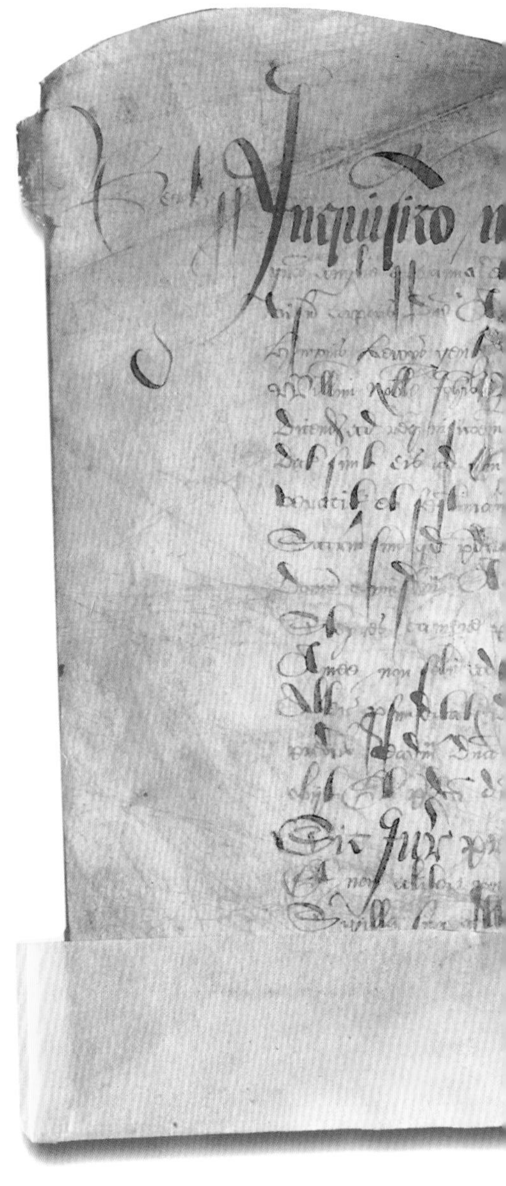

ON 8 SEPTEMBER 1560, Amy Robsart was found with her neck snapped, at the foot of a flight of eight stairs. Her death caused a wave of gossip and speculation to sweep across England and the Continent. For Amy Robsart was the wife of Robert Dudley, favourite and rumoured lover of Her Most Glorious Majesty, Queen Elizabeth I. Was her death an accident? Suicide? Or was it murder?

This report is the coroner's investigation into Amy's death. It lay hidden in the National Archives for four-and-a-half centuries. Its discovery in 2008 was all the more remarkable, because it contains a damning clue.

Robert Dudley was a dashing nobleman – tall, athletic, with red-brown hair and black-brown eyes. Amy was the pretty daughter of a wealthy Norfolk landowner. The couple married when both were just seventeen, and it seems to have been a true love-match.

But Dudley also maintained a friendship with the young Princess Elizabeth, whom he had first met when they were both children. When Elizabeth became queen, she appointed Dudley to the prestigious position of Master of the Horse, and he was constantly at her side. Rumours abounded that the two were more than just friends, and that Dudley paid regular visits to the Queen's bedchamber. Elizabeth was the most eligible woman in Europe, yet while kings, princes and dukes queued to woo her, she declared that if she were to take any husband, it would be Dudley.

But there was a problem – poor, neglected Amy. As her husband attended to the Queen, Amy was left for months on end with only her small retinue for company. In the summer of 1560, she was living at

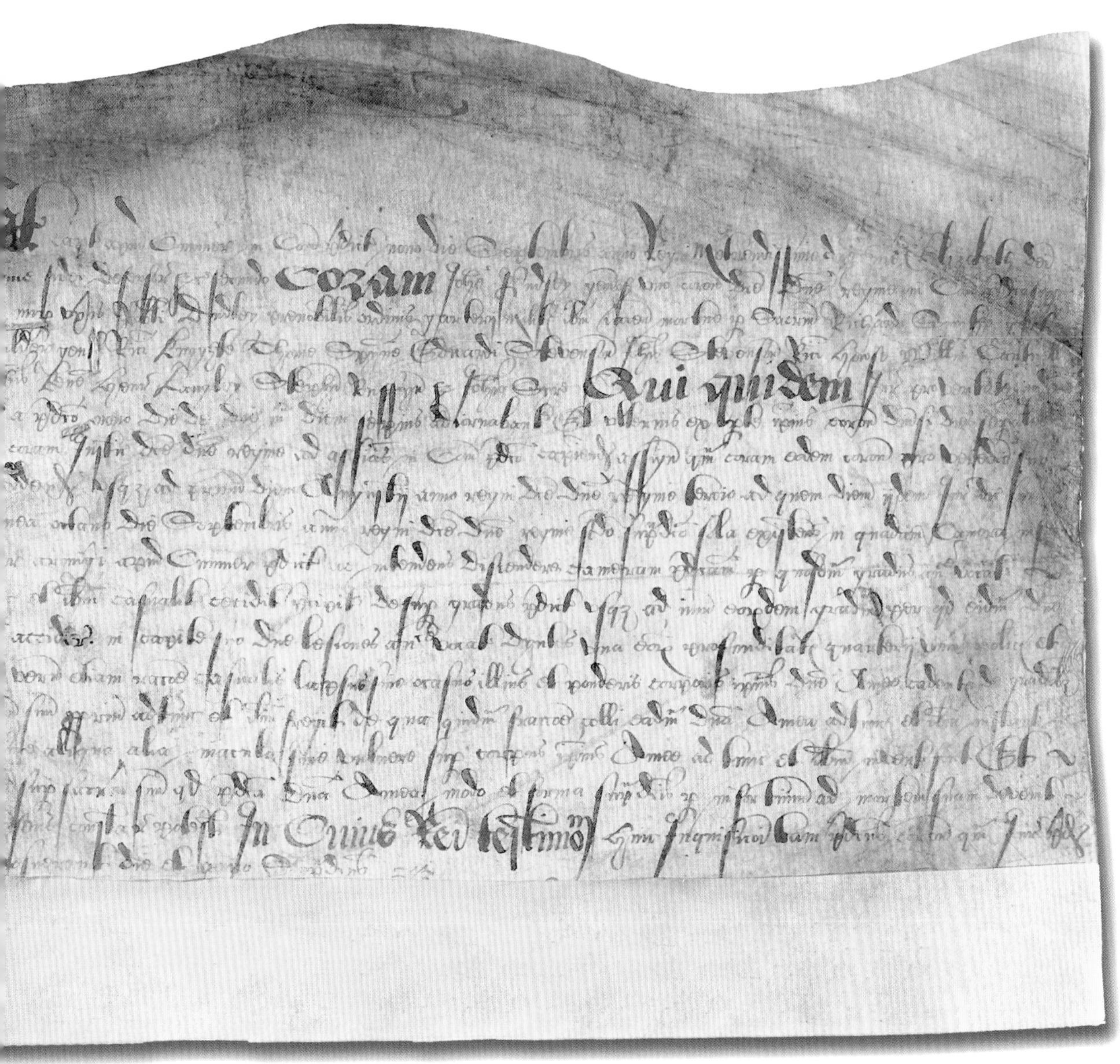

the residence of one of her husband's associates, near the village of Cumnor, Berkshire. On the morning of 8 September, she insisted – against their protests – that her servants should visit a local fair and leave her on her own. Later that day she was found dead.

To investigate the death, a jury of local men was quickly assembled. They found that Amy had broken her neck by accident. For centuries, historians believed that that was all the jury had found. But in fact their report, shown above, contains more. It reads:

Above: *The coroner's report into the death of Amy Robsart lay hidden in the National Archives for almost 450 years. The evidence suggests murder, the conclusion is that it was an accident. Was the jury rigged?*

*Two 'dyntes' in the head? One of them two inches deep? It is hard to believe that such severe head injuries could have been sustained, along with a broken neck, by an accidental fall down a short flight of steps.*

*The aforesaid Lady Amy on 8 September in the aforesaid second year of the reign of the said Lady Queen, being alone in a certain chamber within the home of a certain Anthony Forster, Esq., in the aforesaid Cumnor, and intended to descend the aforesaid chamber by way of certain steps (in English, called 'steyres') of the aforesaid chamber there and then accidently fell precipitously down the aforesaid steps to the very bottom of the same steps, through which the same Lady Amy there and then sustained not only two injuries to her head (in English, called 'dyntes') – one of which was a quarter of an inch deep and the other two inches deep, but truly also, by reason of the accidental injury or of that fall and of Lady Amy's own body weight falling down the aforesaid steyres, the same Lady Amy there and then broke her own neck, on account of which certain fracture of the neck the same Lady Amy there and then died instantly and the aforesaid Lady Amy was found there and then without any other mark or wound on her body; and thus the jurors say on their oath that the aforesaid Lady Amy in the manner and form aforesaid by misfortune came to her death and not otherwise, insofar as it is possible at present for them to agree in testimony of which that for this inquest both the aforesaid coroner and also the aforesaid jurors have in turn affixed their seals on the day.*

Two 'dyntes' in the head? One of them two inches deep? It is hard to believe that such severe head injuries could have been sustained, along with a broken neck, by an accidental fall down a short flight of steps. The jurors at the inquest seemed to have been troubled, reaching their verdict only 'insofar as it is possible for them to agree'. Why were they so sanguine about those 'dyntes'?

The finger points to Dudley. When it came to using his power to influence a jury, Dudley had form. Six months earlier, one of his men had been acquitted at the assizes in Stafford, apparently by a rigged jury. Connections have been made between Dudley and several of the jurors who looked into Amy's death.

The possibility that Dudley rigged the jury does not mean that he was responsible for the murder. He knew full well that suspicion could destroy his reputation and ruin any hope he had of marrying the Queen and so, guilty or innocent, he was desperate for a report that would clear his name. It seems more likely that one of Dudley's associates, impatient to free his friend to marry the Queen, decided to take matters into their own hands. They will have ensured that Amy would be on her own, asking that she send away her servants, perhaps on the pretext of a private meeting. Alone with Amy, the associate (or one of his men) smashed her skull, broke her neck, arranged the body on the stairs and fled. Certainly, that was the gossip at the time. Even among Dudley's enemies, few thought him directly guilty; but persistent rumours accused Sir Richard Verney, one of Dudley's most loyal supporters, of involvement in the 'accident'.

Once Dudley's name had been officially cleared by the coroner's report, Elizabeth welcomed her favourite back to court with enthusiasm. Elizabeth had been the victim of false accusations herself (see page 58), and she was disposed to accept that Dudley was innocent. But she also knew that, for all their flirtation, marriage to Dudley was now impossible. For eighteen more years, Dudley fruitlessly courted Elizabeth, before giving up and marrying again. Elizabeth, of course, would never marry.

# ADVERTISING AMERICA
## The Roanoke Map

## 1585

RIGHT: *A drawing of one of the wives of Wingina, the Native American chief on Roanoke Island, by settler John White.*

THIS IS THE EARLIEST English map of North America, dating from the reign of Elizabeth I. The location, an island named Roanoke on what are now known as the Carolina Banks, shows the first attempts by the English to form a permanent colony in the New World. The map was drawn by people full of hope, but the story was to end in tragedy.

The Roanoke expedition was prompted less by the promise of the New World and more by events in Europe. Hostile Spanish ships in the English Channel made trading with Holland difficult, and other avenues for trade were needed. Walter Raleigh received a licence from the Queen to establish a colony in North America, and in April 1584 he sent his friend Captain Philip Amadas to reconnoitre the North American coast. Amadas reached Florida and headed north, until he and his party found a natural harbour and landed at Roanoke, an island named after the native people, the Roanoke Carolina Algonquian. They made contact with the chief of the local tribe, King Wingina, who received them kindly. In September, the little expedition returned to England, armed with specimens of the local wealth and accompanied by two tribesmen. Raleigh started drumming up support at court for a full expedition.

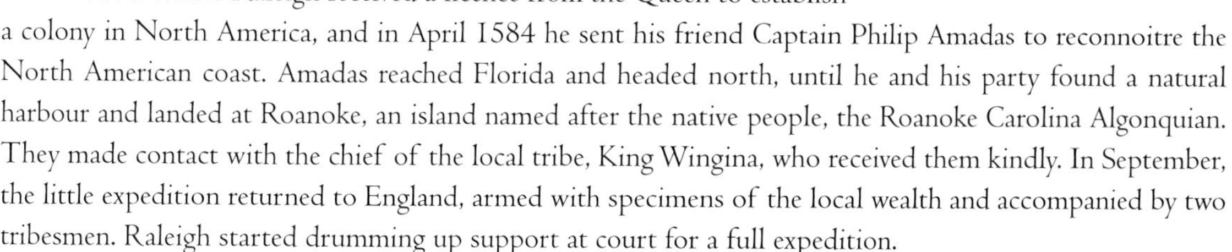

*Appropriately enough, this first map of America is an advertisement. The writer wants to demonstrate to Elizabeth's court just how splendid this new found land is, and to encourage more investment.*

The following year, a fleet of six English vessels arrived at Roanoke under the command of Captain Grenville, together with Captain Amadas, future governor of the colony Ralph Lane, and artist and mapmaker John White. The settlers built a fort and started to explore the mainland, coast and local rivers. This map shows what they found.

Appropriately enough, this first map of America is an advertisement. The writer wants to demonstrate to Elizabeth's court just how splendid this new found land is, and to encourage more investment. The coastline

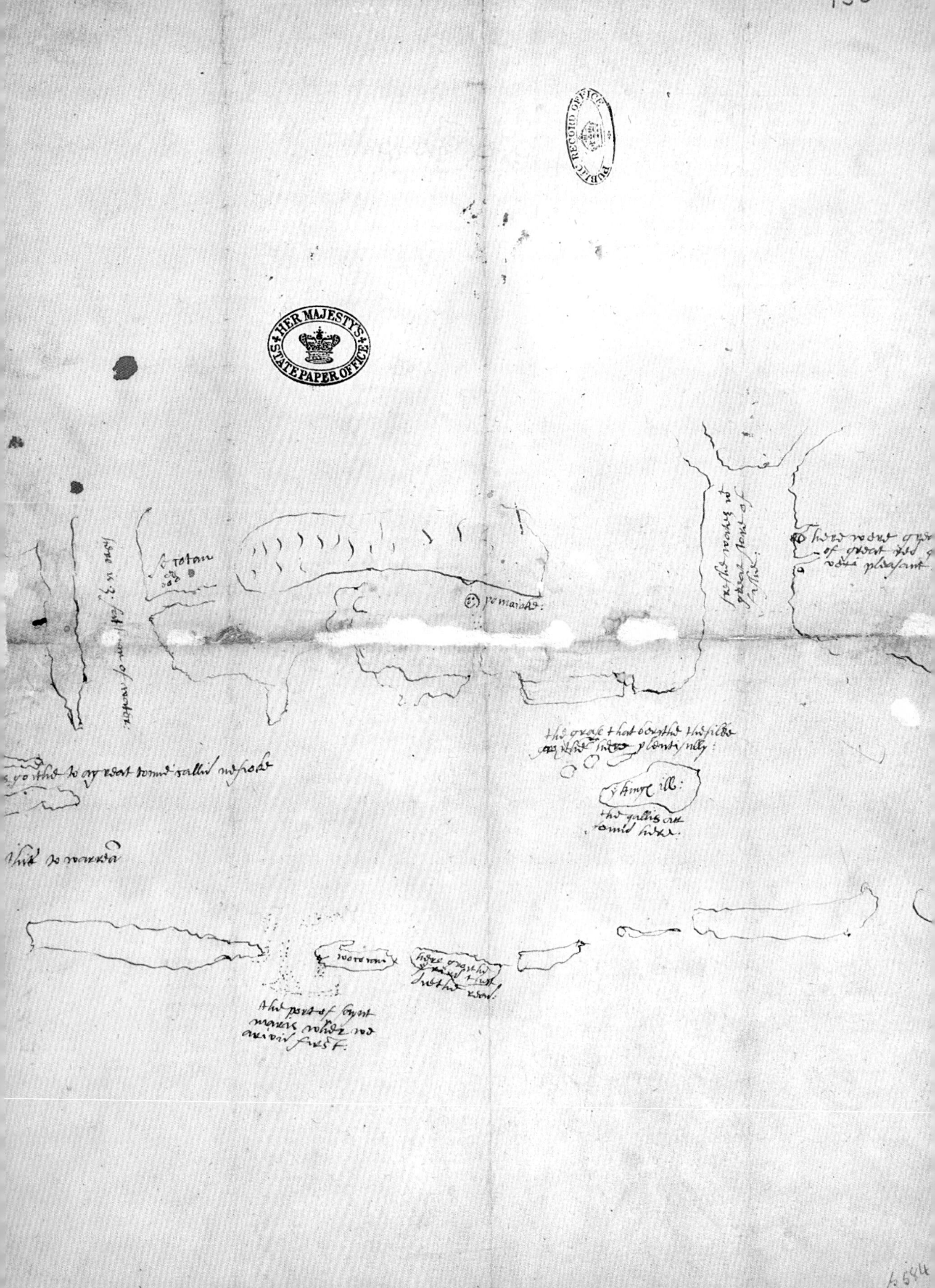
HER MAJESTY'S STATE PAPER OFFICE
PUBLIC RECORD OFFICE
pomaioke

Opposite: *The first map of America shows land, broken up by river mouths, in the top half; and the sea, dotted with islands, in the bottom half. The area is now known as the Carolina Banks.*

*More advertising surrounds the island: 'the grase that berithe [bears] the silke groith here plentifully', and below the island, 'the gallis are found here' (oak gall, which can be used to make ink and is used as a dye).*

shown is about seventy miles long. The landmass and coastal inlets form the upper half of the map, the lower half being sea and islands. A large inlet at the upper left of the map is marked 'here is three fatham of water', to show it as a useful harbour for English ships (particularly ones that might want to ambush passing Spaniards). On the right-hand side there is another inlet, formed from the convergence of two rivers, which is marked 'fresh water with great store of fish'. The praise for the bounty continues on the land to the right of the bay: 'here were great store of great red grapis veri pleasant'. Below the bay, in the lower half of the map, is Roanoke itself, marked: 'Ye kinges ill [Island]'. To give a sense of scale, Roanoke is about eight miles long. More advertising surrounds the island: 'the grase that berithe [bears] the silke groith here plentifully', and below the island, 'the gallis are found here' (oak gall, which can be used to make ink and is used as a dye).

Along the chain of islands at the bottom of the map is written 'here groith the root that diethe read' (here grows the root that makes red dye) and 'the port of saynt maris where we arivid first'. The map is also scattered with the names of Indian towns – Pomaioke in the centre of the coast, Secotan by the left-hand inlet, at the far left directions to towns off the map, 'this goithe to a great toune collid Nesioke', and below that, 'this to Warrea'. The English had come to an area that was already well populated.

This map and much other information – including gorgeous drawings by John White of the local people, fauna and flora, now in the British Museum – was sent home to reassure investors and tease out yet more funds. By September, Grenville decided to return to England, while Lane agreed to stay and await new supplies and colonists in the spring. But Lane fell out with King Wingina, killed him and scattered his tribe. Lane survived the winter but found the environment too much to bear, and returned to England with all the colonists.

The following year another attempt was made to establish the colony at Roanoke, on this occasion led by the colony's artist, John White. At the end of 1587, White returned to England for fresh supplies, leaving behind a substantial number of English. But when he finally returned, some three years later, the colony had vanished. There were no signs of fighting. Items that White had left behind were found buried in the sand, suggesting a quick but not urgent departure. White had left instructions that if the colonists left the island, they were to carve the name of their destination on a post at the fort, and sure enough there was the name 'Croatoan', an island to the south where a friendly native tribe lived. But there was no sign of them there. Expeditions to find the lost colony in 1599 and 1602 failed to establish its fate – although for years rumours persisted that native children had been seen with fair skin and light eyes.

In 1607, a new settlement was established further up the coast at James Town, which became the first English settlement to endure in the Americas. Within thirty years, the English were moving steadily into New England, with thousands emigrating to the new land.

# BRITAIN'S FIRST CENSUS

## The Ealing Census

## 1599

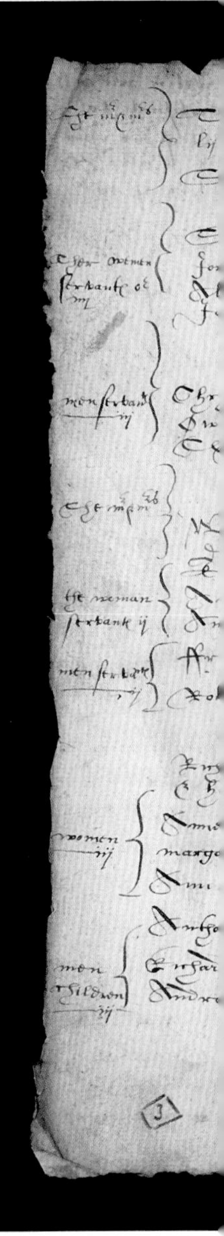

This is Britain's earliest surviving census. When it was compiled, Elizabeth I was still on the throne, and Shakespeare was partway through his career. The Ealing Census, as it is known, was undertaken in 1599 in what is now a smart suburb of London, but was then a country village of eighty-five households.

No census had been undertaken in England before, because they were feared. The Bible records that King David was tempted by Satan to count the number of fighting men in Israel and Judah (2 Samuel 24; 1 Chronicles 21). His officers did so, but when they had finished, God sent three days of plague as a punishment. The Bible isn't clear why God took such a dislike to David's census, but Christian authorities took the warning seriously. If the risk of Divine wrath wasn't enough to put people off, the counting of the monasteries (see *Valor Ecclesiasticus*, page 55), and the traumatic destruction that followed, was a relatively close memory. The next systematic population listing would not happen until the 1660s; the first government census not until 1801.

Why, then, was the Ealing Census made? It simply tells us that: '*The Constable of Ealing is responsible and is collecting the information in response to an inquiry*.' We don't know what that 'inquiry' was, but someone in Government clearly wanted information – financial information, most likely, since the census is on Exchequer paper.

So the census was commissioned, whether the people of Ealing liked it or not. It would have been hard to escape in a place of this size, where the constable would have known everyone. Indeed, the constable may have been able to list the people off the top of his head. If not, he may have gone door-to-door, or required everyone to report to him at a particular time and place.

The census is organised into household groupings, with householders listed under 'name – age – occupation'. The most common occupation is 'husbandman' (farmer), as you would expect in a rural community. The left-hand side of the page shown here records a doctor and his servants: 'Thomas Landthorn, doctor of physic, aged 54 years, or thereabouts'. Below is the doctor's wife, 'Cibbolle Landthorn, his wife aged 51 years'. Underneath are listed the names of their 'men servants' and 'women servants'.

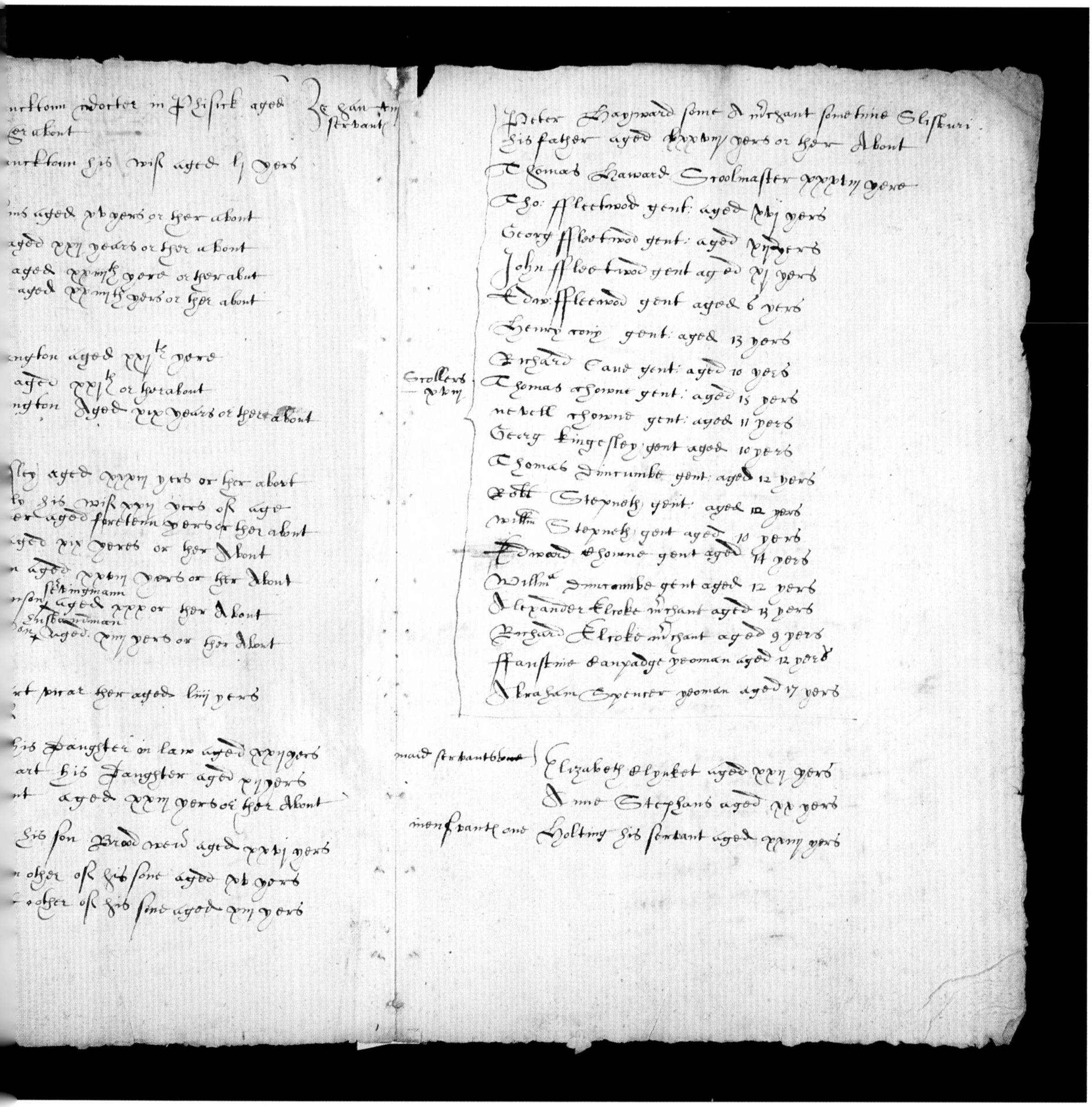

On the right-hand side is 'Peter Heyward, Schoolmaster'. Below is a list of his pupils, their ages all jumbled together, starting off with the 'gentlemen scholars'.

When you get this far back in history, the records that have survived tend to tell the stories of the great and famous. Most of the everyday, ordinary people, simply getting on with their lives, have disappeared. Except as they might appear in parish records of baptisms and deaths, we don't even known their names. The pleasure of the Ealing Census is its unique, evocative snapshot of the people living side by side, in this one little community, at this one moment in time, so long ago.

ABOVE: *The left-hand page lists the local doctor, Thomas Landthorn, and his household servants; the right-hand page lists the local teacher and his pupils.*

ALLICANT

# 17TH CENTURY

## The Revels Accounts *to the* Wills of Nell Gwyn and Catherine of Braganza

LEFT: *How to storm Alicante: Captain Grenville Collins's innocuous seaview of the port was a guide to future invasion.*

# The Accompte of the Office of the Reuelles of this whole yeres Charge in An$^{o}$ 1604: Untell the last of: Octobar: 1605::

## The Chardges

of thos tymes viz betwene the last of October 1604: An$^{o}$ RR$^{s}$ Jacobi 2$^{do}$: untell the last of October: 1605: As well by meanes of Attendinge makinge choise perusinge and reforminge of Playes Showes & Inventions as weare prepared & sett forthe and presented before the kinge Ma$^{tie}$ att tymes Afforsayde: As allso for workmens wages the Officers botewages forninge Bardges wares workmenshipp & Carridges w$^{th}$ other expences thervnto belonginge, Besides the full of sundrey ware for the m$^{rs}$ lodginge for the Rehersales And Ayringes w$^{th}$ suche like Ordinary Allowaunces. The perticulars wherof togeather w$^{th}$ the parties names to whom & wherfor the same is due heare after ensueth viz:

Verra: pstit extra recept a Sety prorausis infra script: viz:

Edmundo Tylney Ar$^{r}$ magistro Revellorum per ipsum exponend versus exoneracionem omnium [illegible] in eo Officio pro hoc anno presenti 1605 per breve sub privato sigillo dormiente dat xxi$^{mo}$ die Decembris 1604 Anno regni sui Anglie Francie et Hibernie secundo et Scotie xxxviij$^{no}$ — 6li

But ther was payed in the sayd terme of S$^{t}$ Michaell unto y$^{e}$ sayd M$^{r}$ of the Revelles y$^{e}$ some of [illegible] six pounds nyne shillings & tenpence being the Surplusage of his Accompt for the year ended the last of October: 1604:

# TRUTH, LIES *and* SHAKESPEARE
## The Revels Accounts

## 1604

OPPOSITE: *The opening page of 'The Account of the Office of Revelles'. Edmund Tylney, named in the second paragraph, was the Master of Revels.*

THESE MAY BE the most romantic set of accounts ever written. They are the accounts of the Office of Revelles from 1604 until October 1605. They list plays performed at the court of James I, the dates of the performances and their cost. The accounts are particularly exciting because of the appearance of a name: 'Shaxberd' – William Shakespeare.

The accounts set out the dates when some of Shakespeare's plays were performed at court:

*Hallamas Day being the first of November ... The Moor of Venis* [All Hallow's Day, 1 November 1604, *Othello*]

*The Sunday following display of the Merry Wives of Winsor*

ABOVE: *Very little is known about Shakespeare's life; the dates of his plays are based on a few scraps of evidence. Even the image above, which was once passed off as being of Shakespeare, is highly dubious.*

*St Stivens night 'A play called Mesur for Mesur'* [St Stephen's night, 26 December, *Measure for Measure*]

*On Inosents night A Plaie of Errors* [Holy Innocents night, 28 December, *The Comedy of Errors*]

*Betwin Newyere Day and Twelfe Day A play of Loves Labours Lost* [1–12 January 1605]

Any contemporary record of Shakespeare takes on the glow of a holy relic, so few records are there of the world's greatest playwright. These accounts make you ache to shuttle back to 1 November 1604 and stand in James's court to watch *Othello* as Shakespeare himself directed it, and most likely see the man himself looking on. The Revels Accounts are doubly important because, for all that any modern edition of Shakespeare's plays will list the plays by date, we actually have very little evidence to indicate when each one was written. The accounts show that the plays listed were written by the end of 1604, which is the earliest record for *Othello* and

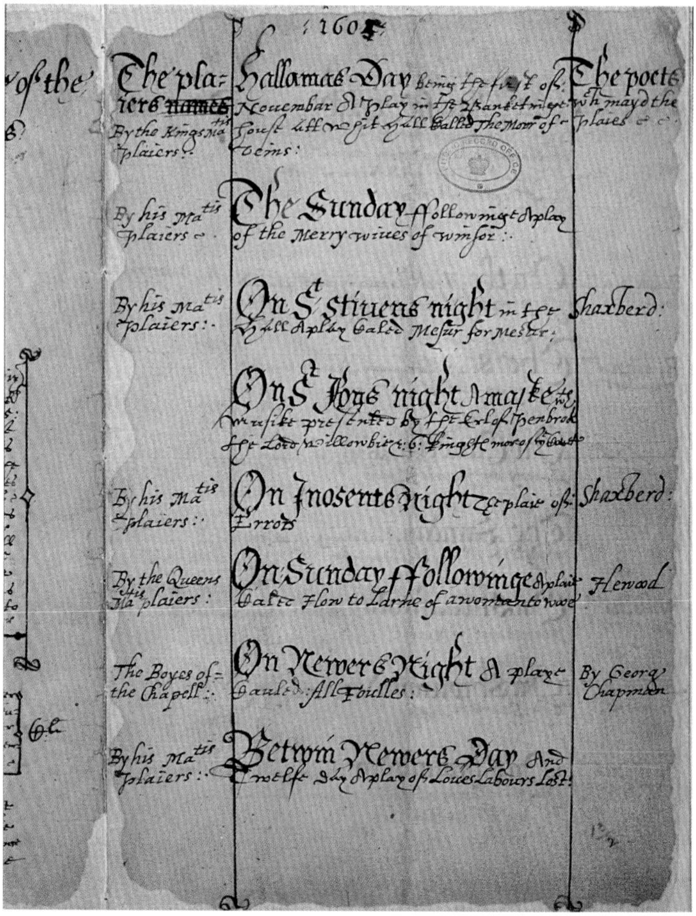

1604

| The plaiers names | | The poets wh mayd the plaies |
|---|---|---|
| By the Kings Ma^tis plaiers: | Hallamas Day being the first of Nouembar A play in the Banketinge house att Whithall Called The Moor of Venis: | |
| By his Ma^tis plaiers | The Sunday ffollowinge A play of the Merry wives of Winsor: | |
| By his Ma^tis plaiers: | On S^t Stiuens night in the Hall A play Caled Mesur for Mesur: | Shaxberd: |
| | On S^t Jhons night A maske | |
| By his Ma^tis plaiers: | On Jnosents night the plaie of Errors | Shaxberd: |
| By the Queens Ma^tis plaiers: | On Sunday ffollowinge A plaie Called How to Larne of a woman to wooe | Hewood |
| The Boyes of the Chapell: | On Newers Night A playe Called All Foolles: | By George Chapman |
| By his Ma^tis plaiers: | Betwin Newers Day And Twelfe day A play of Loues Labours Lost: | |

Right: *This page includes the earliest known records of* Othello *(top of page) and* Measure for Measure *(third from top). The right-hand column lists 'the poets', including 'Shaxberd'.*

*Measure for Measure.* Shakespeare had another twelve years to live – when the accounts were written, he had yet to write, for example, *The Tempest, The Winter's Tale* or *Antony and Cleopatra.*

The documents have been the subject of intense controversy. They were discovered in 1842 by a clerk in the Government's Audit Office, Peter Cunningham, who claimed to have come across them in the basement of his office at Somerset House. Cunningham was an active member of the London Shakespeare Society, but if anyone found it odd that a Shakespeare enthusiast should have found an important piece of Shakespearean evidence in his basement at work, they don't seem to have mentioned it. The find by the young clerk caused great excitement, and no serious attempt was made to authenticate the accounts. In the years that followed, Cunningham became both a noted antiquary and a chronic alcoholic. In 1868, he was caught trying to sell some of the accounts (which were Government property) to the British Museum, claiming a moral right to them. As Cunningham's modest fame turned to infamy, attention turned to the remarkable circumstances of his find. The documents were denounced as forgeries, and chronologies for Shakespeare's plays based on the accounts were held to be flawed. This consensus lasted for around forty years, until fresh salvos of academic papers were exchanged, for and against the authenticity of the accounts. Examinations were undertaken of the ink, the paper, the markings and the extent to which they tallied with other known accounts. Even the holes nibbled through the documents were pressed into service. Were they made by Elizabethan worms or Victorian worms? The latest conclusions are that the accounts are genuine, but the damage was done, and they still tend to be marginalised.

The accounts are a useful reminder not to believe everything you read. The facts and dates of history can sometimes be based on a few scraps, just one scrap, or even a single disputed scrap, of evidence.

# FOILING *the* GUNPOWDER PLOT
## The Monteagle Letter

## 1605

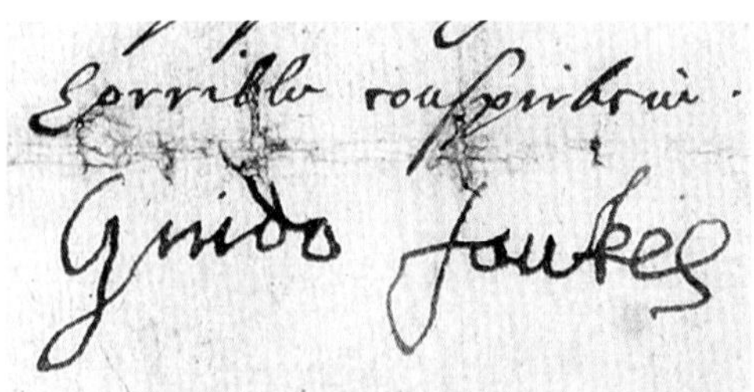

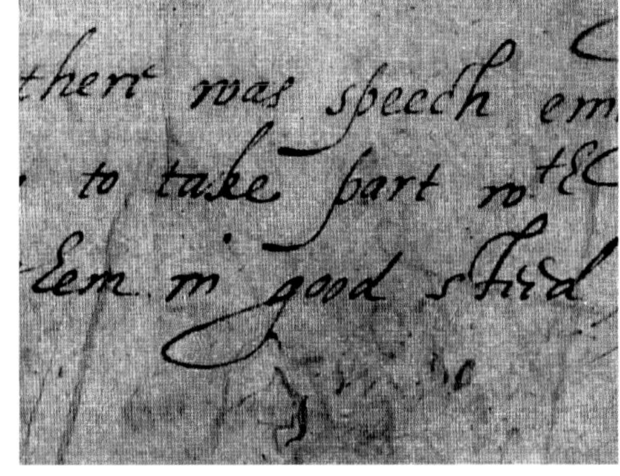

ABOVE: *A horrible contrast: above, the normal signature of Guy ('Guido') Fawkes; below, barely legible, is his signature immediately after torture.*

IF A DOCUMENT could be said to have changed history – or, perhaps, to have stopped history changing – it is this one, the Monteagle Letter. This is the letter that revealed the Gunpowder Plot to the authorities, led to the capture of Guy Fawkes, and saved the British King and Parliament from destruction.

James VI of Scotland became James I of England in 1603, and Catholics hoped that the new king would be more tolerant towards them than his predecessor, Elizabeth I, had been. But English Catholics were to be disappointed. At first, James said that he would not 'persecute any that will be quiet and give outward obedience to the law', but in February 1604, furious to find that his wife had received a rosary from the Pope, James denounced the Catholic Church and reimposed penalties on Catholics.

In sixteenth-century Europe, several attempts had been made by Catholics to assassinate Protestant rulers, and a charismatic Catholic from Warwickshire, Robert Catesby, now began to plot the death of the King. Catesby drew several like-minded men to him, mostly Catholic converts. The plan was to blow up Parliament on its State Opening, killing King, ministers, judges and bishops in one massive blow. With King and Parliament destroyed, the plotters would raise a rebellion in the Midlands, and install the King's nine-year-old daughter, Elizabeth, as a Catholic monarch.

When this letter was written, the Gunpowder Plot was on the brink of success. The conspirators had leased a ground-floor undercroft, directly below the House of Lords. They had ferried thirty-six barrels of gunpowder across the Thames and hidden them there beneath piles of firewood and coal. Guarding the stash was Guy Fawkes, a soldier from York, who had spent years fighting on the Continent and whose face was little known in England. Fawkes could plausibly pass as another serving man around Westminster. When Parliament opened on 5 November, Fawkes was to light a slow fuse on the gunpowder and escape across the Thames.

But on Saturday, 22 October, William Parker, 4th Baron Monteagle, a prominent Catholic lord, was visiting his house in Hoxton. A hooded figure approached the house and handed this letter to one of his servants, who handed it to another servant, who was ordered to read it out to Monteagle as he ate:

11A

my lord out of the love i beare to some of youere frends i have a caer of youer preservacion therfor i would advyse yowe as yowe tender youer lyf to devyse some exscuse to shift of youer attendance at this parleament for god and man hath concurred to punishe the wickednes of this tyme and think not slightlye of this advertisment but retyere youre self into youre contri wheare yowe maye expect the event in safti for thowghe theare be no apparance of anni stir yet i saye they shall receyve a terrible blowe this parleament and yet they shall not seie who hurts them this cowncel is not to be contemned because it maye do yowe good and can do yowe no harme for the dangere is passed as soon as yowe have burnt the letter and i hope god will give yowe the grace to mak good use of it to whose holy proteccion i commend yowe

*My lord, out of the love I bear to some of your friends, I have care of your preservation. Therefore I would advise you, as you tender your life, to devise some excuse to shift your attendance at this parliament; for God and man hath concurred to punish the wickedness of this time. And think not slightly of this advertisement, but retire yourself into your country where you may expect the event in safety. For though there be no appearance of any stir, yet I say they shall receive a terrible blow this parliament; and yet they shall not see who hurts them. This counsel is not to be condemned because it may do you good and can do you no harm; for the danger is passed as soon as you have burnt the letter. And I hope God will give you the grace to make good use of it, to whose holy protection I commend you.*

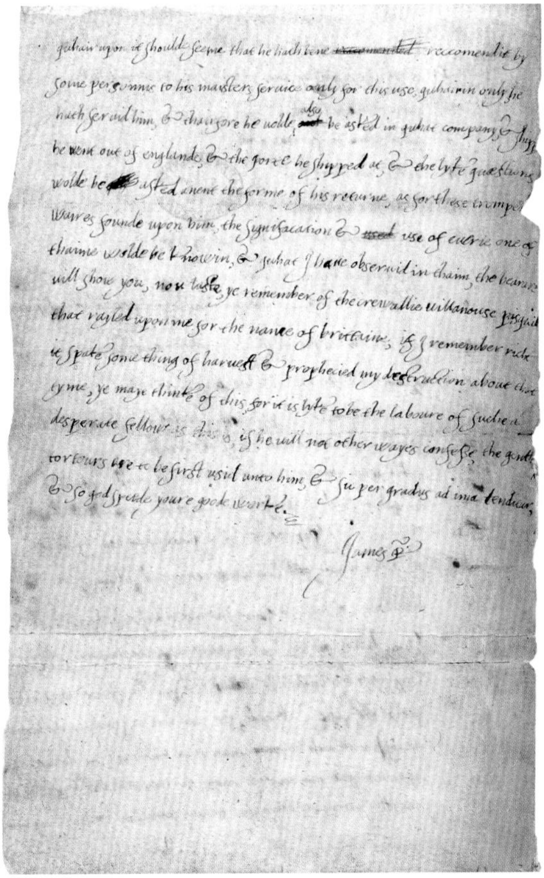
quhairupon it should seeme that he hath bene recommendit by some personnes to his maisters service onlie for this use, quhairin onlie he hath servid him, & thairfore he wolde be asked in quhat companie & shippe he went out of englande, & the porte he shipped at, & the lyke questions wolde be asked anent the forme of his returne, as for these trumperies founde upon him, the signification & use of everie one of thaime wolde be knowin, & quhat I have observid in thaim the bearer will shew you, now lette ye remember of the crewallie villanouse pasquil that raylid upon me for the name of britaine, if I remember richt it spake some thing of harvest & prophecied my destruction about that tyme, ye maye thinke of this for it is lyke to be the labour of suche a desperate fellow as this is, if he will not other wayes confesse the gentler tortours are to be first usid unto him, & sic per gradus ad ima tenditur, & so god speede youre goode worke.

James R.

Opposite: *The Monteagle Letter.*

Above: *The chilling direction from James I that the 'gentler' tortures were to be used on Fawkes at first, 'and so by degrees proceeding to the worst'.*

Who had written the letter? We will never know for sure, not least because the authorities later showed a remarkable lack of curiosity about it. But the prime suspect is Francis Tresham, Monteagle's brother-in-law. Tresham was a childhood friend of Robert Catesby's, and had been introduced to the plotters' circle only a week before. Tresham had at first tried to persuade the conspirators not to go ahead with their plan, anxious that the murders would damn their souls. But if Tresham was the author, why the skulduggery? Why did he not simply approach his brother-in-law in person? Quite possibly, he did. This was the first time that Monteagle had visited his house in Hoxton in several months. That, and his showy insistence that the letter be read out loud to him, suggests that he was expecting it.

Monteagle promptly rode to Whitehall and gave the letter to Lord Salisbury, the head of James's secret service. Parties were sent to search around Parliament on Monday, 4 November, the day before the State Opening. The first search party found Guy Fawkes, who claimed that the pile of firewood belonged to his master. The search party went on its way. The King insisted on a more thorough search, and just after midnight Fawkes was found again, this time dressed in a cloak, hat and spurs for his getaway. The gunpowder was discovered and Fawkes arrested.

You can trace what happened next from further documents in the National Archives. For a week or so the Government had no real idea of what was going on, but the possibility that a substantial uprising was afoot was very real. Fawkes was the Government's only source of information, and they had to break him. The contrast between Fawkes's normal, strong signature on his later confession of 17 November and his feeble, barely legible signature immediately after torture on 9 November is horrible. The conspirators were rounded up, some being killed in the course of their capture, others later executed.

Monteagle, on the other hand, was richly rewarded for his efforts, and protected from his obvious implication in the plot. Without his little letter, British history might be very different indeed.

# *The* ROUND ROBIN
## Petition from Emigrants

# 1621

ABOVE: *The Pilgrim Fathers depart for the New World – from a nineteenth-century coloured engraving.*

OPPOSITE: *This petition to emigrate was risky. The signatories signed it in a circle so that their leaders could not be identified. They included labourers, artisans and professional men.*

THIS DOCUMENT IS an original 'round robin', one of the earliest in the world. Some of its signatories were to found one of the greatest cities on earth.

The words at the centre are a request for permission to emigrate by a group of Walloon Huguenots – Protestants from modern-day Belgium – to Sir Dudley Carleton, English Ambassador to the Hague:

*We promise my Lord Ambassador of the Most Serene King of Great Britain to go and inhabit in Virginia, land under her Majesty's obedience, as soon as conveniently may be, and this under the conditions to be carried out in the articles we have communicated to the said Ambassador and not otherwise, on the faith of which we have unanimously signed this present with our sign manual.*

The Huguenots wanted to escape Catholic Belgium to found a Protestant colony in America. They dreamt of a New Jerusalem.

But the petition was risky. If the authorities did not like it – or it found its way into the hands of hostile agents – then the signatories, and in particular their leaders, risked imprisonment and even death. So they adopted a 'round robin' – originally, a 'round ribbon' – in which each signatory made their mark in a circle around the petition. This way, it was impossible to identify the leader of the group. The round robin was a security device, but it was also an expression of their faith. These Christians stood, or fell, together.

In the petition, 55 men, 31 women and 129 children are named. They were a mixed group. Many were labourers; there were semiskilled workers, including a brewer, weaver and hatter; there were men of learning, a surgeon, a student of theology. Their leader, as it happened, was Jessé de Forest, who signed as a dyer, with

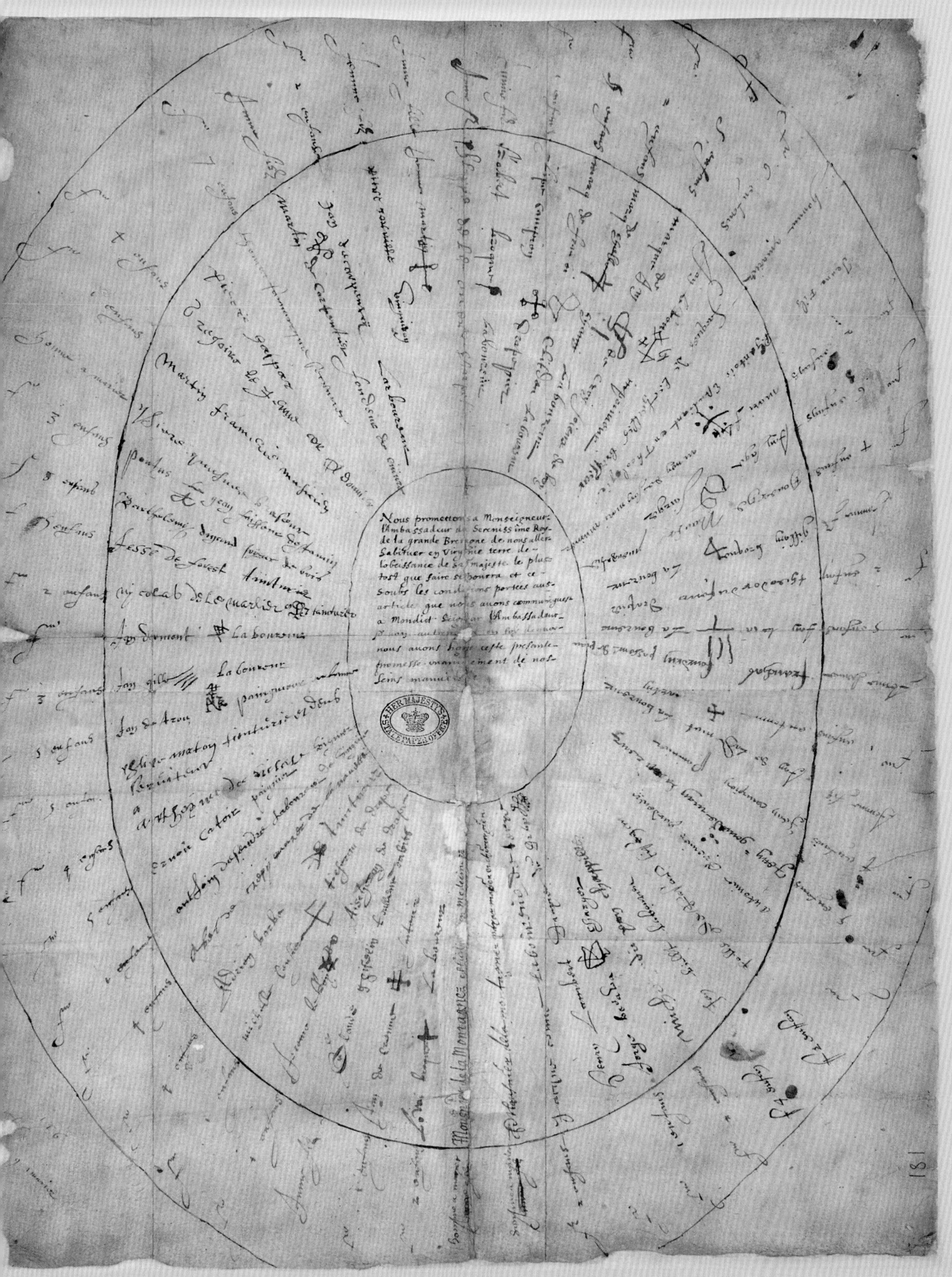

Nous promettons a Monseigneur l'Ambassadeur du Serenissime Roy de la grande Bretagne de nous aller habituer en Virginie terre de l'obeissance de sa Majeste le plustost que faire se pourra et ce soubs les conditions portees aux article que nous avons communiques a Mondict Seigneur l'Ambassadeur [illegible] nous avons signe ceste presente promesse unanimement de nos seins manuels.



181

*'We promise my Lord Ambassador of the Most Serene King of Great Britain to go and inhabit in Virginia, land under her Majesty's obedience, as soon as conveniently may be . . . on the faith of which we have unanimously signed this present with our sign manual.'*

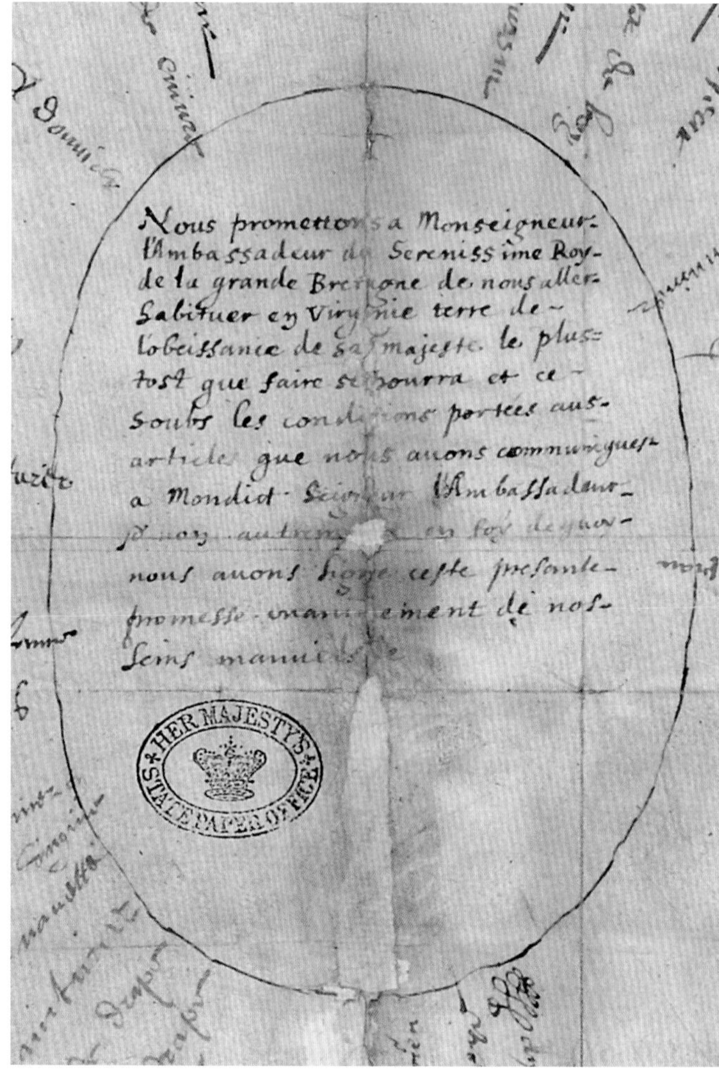

Nous promettons a Monseigneur
l'Ambassadeur de Serenissime Roy
de la grande Bretagne de nous aller
habituer en Virginie terre de
l'obeissance de sa majeste le plus
tost que faire se pourra et ce
soubs les conditions portees aux
article que nous avons communiques
a Mondict Seigneur l'Ambassadeur
par nos autres [illegible] en foy de quoy
nous avons signe ceste presente
promesse unanimement de nos
seins manuels



RIGHT: *In the centre of the Round Robin is the petition to the Ambassador of Great Britain for permission to found a colony in Virginia.*

his wife and five children. He was an associate of the Pilgrim Fathers, Puritans who followed the same dream of a new world, and who had sailed for America in 1620. The petition was submitted a few months after the Fathers had set sail; de Forest was determined to follow.

The petition was granted, but subject to a condition. The settlers were expected to disperse when they arrived in America, and could not live together. For a group prepared to share the risk of the round robin, this was insupportable. They refused to accept the condition.

De Forest would get his chance the following year. His group was eventually given permission to set up a colony in the West Indies as agents for the Dutch West India Company. De Forest crossed the Atlantic but died exploring the Oyapock River between Brazil and French Guiana, and never saw his colony founded. His children, though, survived, and joined a fledging colony of Walloons around the mouth of a vast river that had been found by the English explorer Henry Hudson only a couple of decades before. These democratic Walloons had found their New Jerusalem. It would become New York City.

# KILLING *the* KING

## Transcript of the Trial of Charles I

## 1649

A Journall of the Proceedings of the High Court of Justice erected by Act of the Comons of England Intituled, An Act of the Comins of England assembled in Parliamt for Erecting of a high Court of Justice for the Trying & Judging of Charles Steward King of England

The Act

An Act of the Comons of England assembled in Parliamt for Erecting of a High Court of Justice for the Trying & Judging of Charles Steward King of England

ABOVE: *The opening page of 'A Journal of the Proceedings of a High Court of Justice ... for the Trying and Judging of Charles Stewart King of England'. The Journal also sets out the Act that authorised the trial.*

THIS IS THE ORIGINAL transcript of the trial of Charles I, which captures word for word the momentous events taking place around it. The King of England and Scotland was on trial for his life and this document still crackles with the drama of those proceedings.

How had the King and Parliament reached this point? In the first half of the seventeenth century, Parliament was a body that the ruling monarch could consult, but which could be summoned or dissolved at his or her pleasure. Charles believed that kings were appointed by God, and therefore found the idea that he should consult Parliament impertinent, even blasphemous. And so in 1629, when Parliament had become particularly troublesome, Charles dissolved it. He did not summon Parliament again for another eleven years, finally doing so only after he had provoked a rebellion in Scotland that he couldn't afford to fight. In practice, it was impossible for the King to raise very large sums of money without Parliament's consent and co-operation. But a lot of resentment had built up during those eleven years of absence. On being recalled, Parliament's first act was to present Charles with a long list of grievances, and to force reforms on him. Over the following two years relations between King and Parliament grew more chaotic until, in January 1642, Charles led a band of soldiers to arrest his fiercest Parliamentary critics. The King failed to find them, but left Parliament in an uproar about his use of force against its members. Six days later, Charles left London with his family. By the summer, towns and cities were taking sides, declaring their allegiance either to the King or to Parliament.

Over the next seven years, brother was set against brother, father against son. War and disease claimed almost 200,000 lives in England alone, from a population of around 5 million (as a proportion of population, refused so to doe, upon which his severall defaults this Court might justly have proceeded to Judgment against him, both for his Contumacy & for the matters of the Charge, taking the same for Confessed as aforesaid: Yet neverthelesse this Court for their owne cleare information & further satisfaccon have thought fitt to Examine Witnesses upon Oath, & take notice of other Evidences, touching the Matters conteyned in the said Charge, which accordingly they have done: Now therefore upon serious & mature deliberacon of the premisses & consideracon had of the Notoriety of the Matters of Fact, Charged upon him as aforesaid, this Court is in Judgment & Conscience satisfied that hee the said Charles Stuart is Guilty of Levying warr against the said Parliament & People & of maintaining & continuing the same, for which in the said Charge hee stands accused, and by the Generall Course of his Governmt, Councells & Practices, before & since this Parliament began (which have bin and are Notorious & Publique and the effects whereof remaine abundantly upon Record) this Court is fully satisfied in their Judgmt & Consciences that hee hath bin & is Guilty of the wicked designes and Endeavours, in the said Charge sett forth, and that the said warr hath bin levied maintained & continued by him as aforesaid, in prosecucon & for the Accomplishmt of the said designes: And that hee hath bin & is the Occasioner, Author, & Continuer of the said unnaturall, Cruell, & bloudy warrs, & therein Guilty of High Treason & of the Murthers, rapines, Burnings, Spoyles, Desolacons, Damage, & Mischeife to this Nation, Acted & Committed in the said warr & occasioned thereby: For all which Treasons and Crimes this Court doth adjudge, that hee the said Charles Stuart, as a Tyrant, Traytor, Murtherer and publique Enimy to the good People of this Nation shall be put to death by the severing of his head from his body./

After the Sentence reade the Lo: President said

This Sentence now reade & published is the Act Sentence, Judgement & Resolucon of the whole Court: Whereupon the Court stoode upp & owned it

King — Will you heare mee a word Sir./

Lo: Presidt — Sir you are not to be heard after the Sentence

King — Noe Sir?

Lo: Presidt — Noe Sir by yor favour, Guard withdrawe yor Prisoner./

King

Opposite: *The transcript of the sentencing of the King to death and, at the bottom, his panicked response (continued on the next page).*
Right: *A list of commissioners at the trial; half of those appointed stayed away.*

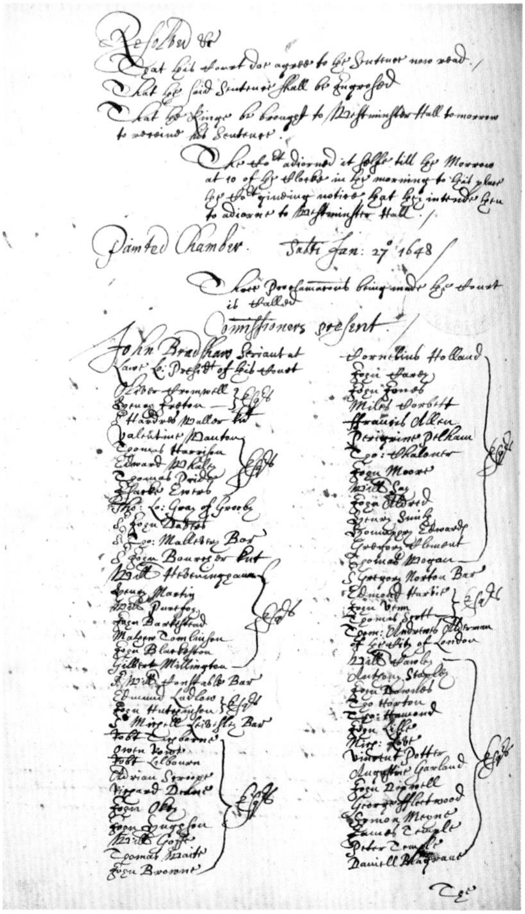
Resolved &c
That this Court doe agree to the Sentence now read.
That the said Sentence shall be Engrossed
That the Kinge be brought to Westminster Hall tomorrow to receive his Sentence.
Painted Chamber. Satr Jan: 27 1648
Commissioners present.
John Bradshaw Serjeant at Lawe Lo: President of this Court

this represents twice the loss of life that occurred during the American Civil War). There were, in fact, two consecutive wars before the trial of the King. The first concluded in 1645 when the King's armies were destroyed at the battles of Naseby and Langport, and the King was captured the following year. The second was provoked in 1647–8 by a secret alliance between the captive King and Scotland, and concluded with Parliament's victory against the Scots at the battle of Preston. The King's secret alliance against Parliament focused minds. Something had to be done about him.

The majority in Parliament did not want to try the King, still less to execute him. Most wanted him to rule with more limited powers, under a new constitution. But in the eyes of many in the Army, he was the tyrant behind the bloodshed, against whom justice must be done. Army regiments 'purged' Parliament, arresting forty-five Members of Parliament and refusing entry to more than three times that number. The remaining 'Rump Parliament' of seventy-five MPs passed a bill authorising the trial of the King for high treason.

Parliament convened what was, in effect, a kangaroo court. Charles was afforded no defence lawyer. The trial took place in the intimidating surroundings of Westminster Hall, crowded with soldiers and spectators. Parliament appointed three judges and 135 commissioners, although more than half of the commissioners had the good sense to stay away. Several prominent jurists refused to act as President and so the job was given to the relatively unknown John Bradshaw, Chief Justice of Chester. Bradshaw sat on one side of the court in a scarlet robe, protected from assassination attempts by steel plates in his hat and clothes. The King sat on the other side, old beyond his forty-eight years, wearing a black cloak and the silver Order of the Garter.

In the middle of it all sat a clerk, furiously writing down the exchanges. You have to admire him. Amid the high drama and heated exchanges, the proceedings are captured word for word, with barely a pause to refill the quill. The frantic speed of his scribbling conveys the urgency and immediacy of what was going on.

The transcript records that Charles was accused of high treason and high misdemeanours; of being a tyrant, traitor and murderer; and of having the blood of Englishmen on his hands. When asked to plead, he

*The President condemns Charles Stuart to be put to death as a 'public enemy' 'by the severing of his head from his body'.*

Opposite: *The King continues to protest against his sentence as he is dragged away. When Charles II came to the throne in 1660, he persecuted the commissioners present that day, who are listed in the bottom half of the page.*

was obstinate. He declared that he was England's lawful King, and refused to acknowledge the authority of the court to try him: 'I would know by what power I am called hither. I would know by what authority, I mean lawful.' Since the King had refused to plead, the court entered a guilty plea. Nevertheless, the judges heard the evidence of witnesses over a few days. The King sat throughout the proceedings seemingly indifferent, occasionally allowing himself a sardonic laugh or wry comment.

The trial lasted one week. What you see on these pages is the awful denouement, which took place on Saturday, 27 January 1649. The President condemns Charles Stuart to be put to death as a 'public enemy' 'by the severing of his head from his body'.

The King seems to have been caught completely off-guard, his composure shattered:

*King:* *'Will you hear me a word, Sir?'*
*President:* *'You are not to be heard after the sentence.'*
*King:* *'No, Sir?'*
*President:* *'No Sir, by your favour, Sir. Guard, withdraw your prisoner.'*
*King:* *'I may speak after the sentence, by your favour, Sir, I may speak after the sentence. By your favour, hold! The sentence, Sir – I say, Sir, I do –'*

Charles was dragged away without finishing. Was he panicking as he realised that Parliament really was going to kill him? Did he finally mean to speak in his defence? Or did he intend to make a last, defiant speech to rally his sympathisers? Whichever it was, he had lost the chance.

The King was executed three days after this transcript was made, on a black-draped scaffold built outside the Banqueting House in Whitehall. A great crowd gathered. The King conducted himself with dignity, and when his head was struck off by a single blow, an enormous groan arose from the people, appalled by the enormity of what they had just seen.

A little over a decade later, Charles's son was returned to the throne. Charles II was generally conciliatory, but he wreaked revenge on many of the people who were involved in his father's trial and who appear on these pages. Bradshaw had died in 1659, but on Charles II's orders his body was exhumed and hanged on a gallows alongside the corpses of Oliver Cromwell and the parliamentary general Henry Ireton; their heads were then displayed on twenty-foot pikes over Westminster Hall. The clerk who transcribed the trial would have been too lowly to attract vengeance, but you can imagine that he would have kept his own head down. Meanwhile, this transcript lay buried in the government records, retaining the electricity of that extraordinary day.

King — I may speake after the Sentence — By yor favour Sr I may speake after the Sentence ever — By yor favour (Hould) the Sentence Sr — I say Sr I doe.

Lo: Presdt — Guard withdrawe yor Prisoner

King — I am not suffered to speake Expect what Justice other people will have

These last words hee spake as hee was going forth of the Cort

The King being withdrawne the Court adiourned it selfe forthwth to the Painted Chamber

The Cort being sate in the Painted Chamber according to adiornmt from Westminster Hall

Paynted Chamber

Commissioners present

John Bradshaw Seriant at Lawe
Lo: President

John Lisle
Will Say
Oliver Cromwell
Henry Ireton
Thomas Harrison
Edward Whalley
Thomas Pride
Isaack Ewer
Sr Hardres Waller knt
Thomas Lo: Gray of Groby
Sr John Danvers knt
Sr Tho Maleverer Bart
Sr John Bourcher knt
Isaack Pennington Alderman of the Citty of London
Thomas Waite Esqr
Will Heveningham
John Downes
Henry Martin
John Berkstead
Mathew Tomlinson
Gilbert Millington
John Blackston
Sr Will Constable Bart
Sr Michell Livesley Bart
John Hutchinson
Robt Tichborne
Nicholas Love
Owen Rowe
Robt Lilborne
Edmund Ludlowe

Esqrs

Adrian Scroope
Richard Deane
John Okey
Symon Mayne
John Huson
Will Goff
Cornelius Holland
John Carew
John Jones
Miles Corbett
Francis Allen
Peregrine Pelham
Thomas Chaloner
John Moore
John Alured
Henry Smith
Humfr: Edwards
Gregory Clement
Thomas Wogan
Sr Gregory Norton Bart
John Venn
Tho: Scott
Edmund Harvie
Esqrs
Tho: Andrewes Aldr of London
Will Cawley
Anthony Stapley
Tho: Horton
Thomas Hamond
Augustine Garland
John Dixwell
James Temple
Peter Temple
Daniell Blagrave
Esqrs

Sr Hardress

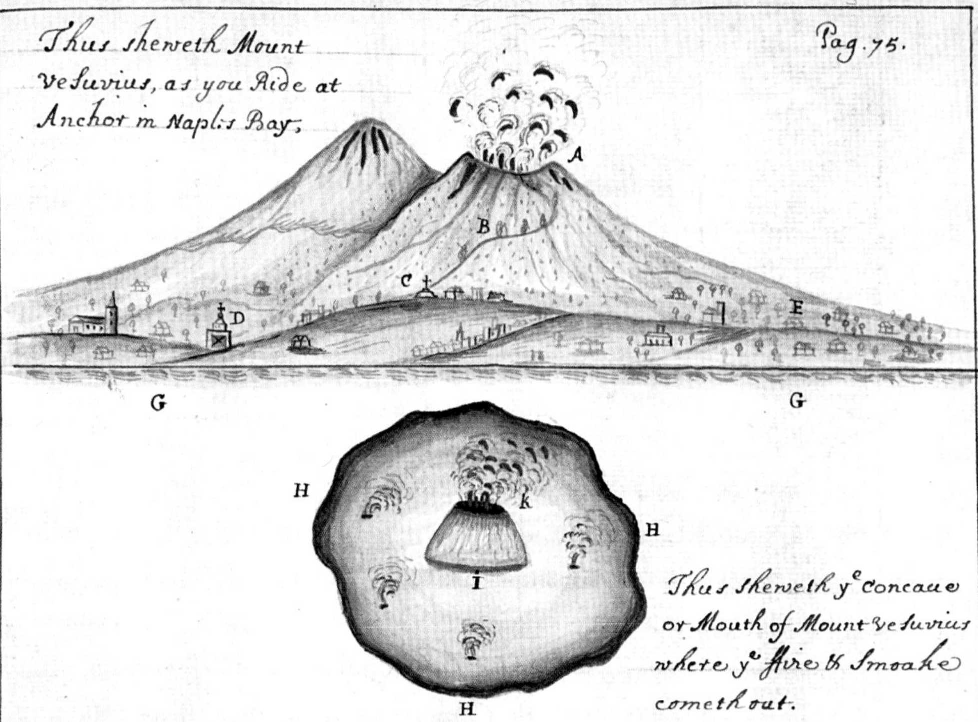


A the top of ye Mountaine

B C the way up to ye top

D a Monument erected about 30 yeares agoe, for soe far the ffire came tumbling downe the Mountaine about 32 yeares since, and Belcht out ffire & Brimstone for three days time, Ejecting Millions of Tunns of Great and Smale Stones, throwing some of them as far as the monument, wch is three English miles from the top, consuming many Brave Villidges, and pleasant vineards and Gardens, for 3 miles round, soe that now there is nothing to be seene, but Stones Sinders and Ashes, of which the ground is covered, which maketh the way very difficult to get up; We Rid up on mules as far as C, and there left the mules, and with much trouble & paines Ascended to the top, where we lookt downe into the Concave, which Shewed as in the ffigure H.I.K. the Circumference I Judg'd to be 5 miles round at ye brimes a H, and the depth from H to I I Judged to be 200 yards, in the midle of wch Pitt there was a Small hill as I K. out of the top of wch comith out the fire and Smoake, in the day time you can see nothing but the Smoake, the decent is perpendicular, and in many Small places

Smoaketh

# SPYING *and* SIGHTSEEING

## Ship's Log of Capt. Grenville Collins

# 1677

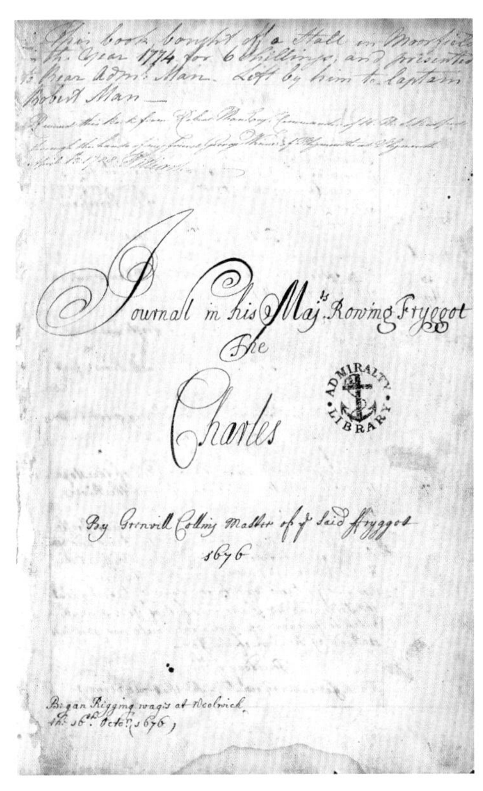

This book bought of a Stall in Moorfields the year 1774 for 6 Shillings, and presented to Rear Adml. Man. Left by him to Captain Robert Man —

Journall in his Majts Rowing Fryggot The Charles

By Grenvill Collins Master of ye said fryggot 1676

Began Rigging wages at Woolwich the 16th Octor 1676

OPPOSITE: *Captain Grenville Collins's panorama of Vesuvius, seen from the sea; below is the inside of the crater, seen from its rim.* RIGHT: *The title page of Grenville Collins's Journal, in effect a reconnaissance report.*

YOU CAN ALMOST smell the brine and hear the creaking of the ship's planks as you read the ship's log of Captain Grenville Collins. Grenville Collins is best known for being the first Englishman to chart systematically the British coastline (if you have ever seen a framed antique map of the British coastline, there is a fair chance that it was drawn by Grenville Collins). But at this point, in the late 1670s, he was in the western Mediterranean, on a mission from the British Admiralty to chart Spanish waters and ports during a period of relative peace. He was spying.

Grenville Collins was an experienced sailor and surveyor, who had taken tours along the South American coast and in the South Seas, and had led an expedition to the Arctic in search of the fabled Northwest Passage to the Pacific. His appointment to chart the western Mediterranean – by one Samuel Pepys, then Secretary to the Admiralty – came in 1676, when Grenville Collins was in his early thirties.

The log shows him working from the moment his ship left Falmouth, sounding the depths of the waters out of port before reaching the open seas. He sailed along the coast of Portugal (at peace with England, of course, since Charles II was married to the Portuguese Catherine of Braganza, page 90), before cutting across to Tangiers and chasing a couple of Algerian ships on the way. Then it was back across to Gibraltar, Alicante, Cadiz and onwards. The journal is filled with charts, plans and drawings, little reconnaissance images of Spanish ports, showing how they looked from the sea and how to navigate into them. Very handy, if you might want to storm them at some point in the future.

By 1677, Grenville Collins had reached the Bay of Naples (Naples was controlled by the Spanish), where he undertook the intriguing little side-trip shown here. He climbed Mount Vesuvius.

Vesuvius had been dormant, presumed dead, since the end of the thirteenth century, and its slopes had recovered their greenery and been laid with vines. Then, in 1631, just a generation before Grenville Collins's

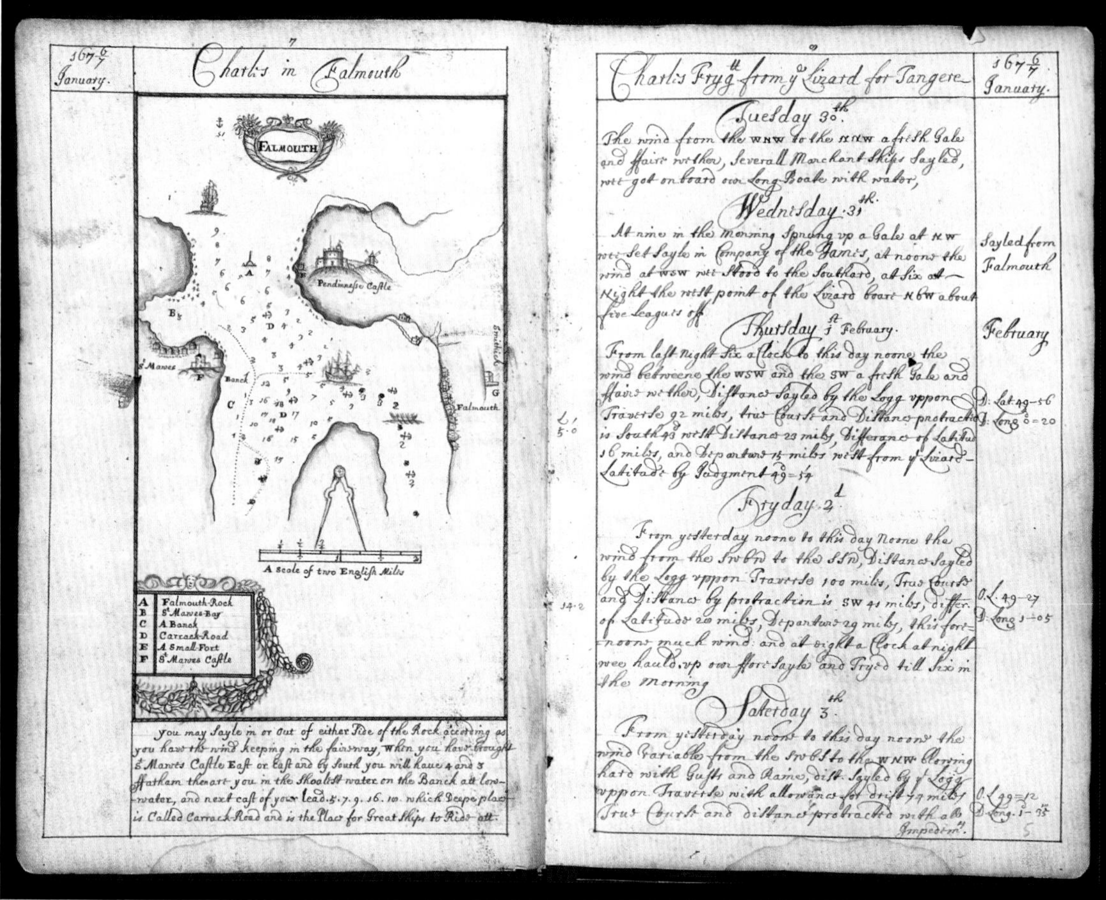

1677/6 January.

Charls in Falmouth



| | |
|---|---|
| A | Falmouth-Rock |
| B | St Mawes-Bay |
| C | A Banck |
| D | Carrack-Road |
| E | A Small-Fort |
| F | St Mawes Castle |

You may Sayle in or Out of either Side of the Rock according as you have the wind keeping in the fairway, when you have brought St Mawes Castle East or East and by South you will have 4 and 3 ffatham then art you in the Shoalest water on the Banck att low-water, and next cast of your lead. 5. 7. 9. 16. 10. which Deepe place is Called Carrack-Road and is the Place for Great Ships to Ride att.

Charls Frygt from ye Lizard for Tangere — 1677/6 January.

Tuesday 30th.

The wind from the WNW to the NNW a fresh Gale and ffaire wether, Severall Marchant Ships Sayled, wee got on board our Long-Boate with water,

Wednesday 31th.

At nine in the Morning Sprung up a Gale at NW wee Set Sayle in Company of the James, at noone the wind at WSW wee Stood to the Southard, at Six at Night the west point of the Lizard beare NbW about five Leagues off — Sayled from Falmouth

Thursday 1st February.

From last Night Six a Clock to this day noone the wind betweene the WSW and the SW a fresh Gale and ffaire wether, Distance Sayled by the Logg uppon Traverse 92 miles, true Course and Distance protracted is South 43d west Distance 23 miles, Differance of Latitude 16 miles, and Departure 15 miles west from ye Lizard— Latitude by Judgment 49=54 — February — D: Lat. 49–56 — D: Long 0=20

Fryday 2d.

From yesterday noone to this day Noone the wind from the SWbW to the SSW, Distance Sayled by the Logg uppon Traverse 100 miles, True Course and Distance by protraction is SW 41 miles, differ. of Latitude 20 miles, Departure 29 miles, this fore-noone much wind: and at eight a Clock at night wee hauld up our ffore Sayle and Tryed till Six in the morning — O. L. 49–27 — D. Long 1–05

Saterday 3th.

From yesterday noone to this day noone the wind variable from the SWbS to the WNW blowing hard with Gusts and Raine, dist. Sayled by ye Logg uppon Traverse with allowance for drift 77 miles True Course and distance protracted with all Impedimts. — O. L. 49=12 — D. Long. 1–35

visit, the volcano sensationally erupted again, claiming some 3,000 lives. It erupted again in 1660. So by the time of his visit, it was once again a blackened, desolate mountain, an object of fascination and fear.

Grenville Collins ascended the lower slopes by donkey, before climbing to the rim of the volcano. He recorded what he saw with his surveyor's discipline:

Above: *The mouth of the river at Falmouth. Grenville Collins began to take soundings as soon as he left port.*

*Thus showeth Mount Vesuvius, as you ride at anchor in Naples Bay.*

*Thus showeth the concave or mouth of Mount Vesuvius where fire and smoke cometh out.*

A *The top of the mountain*

B, C *The way up to the top*

D *A monument erected about 30 years ago, for so far the fires came tumbling down the mountain about 32 years since, and belch out fire and brimstone for three days time, ejecting millions of tons of great and small stones, throwing some of them as far as the monument, which is three English miles from the top, consuming many brave villages and pleasant vineyards and gardens, for three miles around, so that now there is nothing to be seen, but stones, cinders and ashes, of which the ground is covered, which maketh the way very difficult to get up; we rid up on mules as far as C and there left the mules and with much trouble & pains ascended to the top, where we looked down into the concave, which showed as in the figure H.I.K. the circumference I judge to be three miles round and*

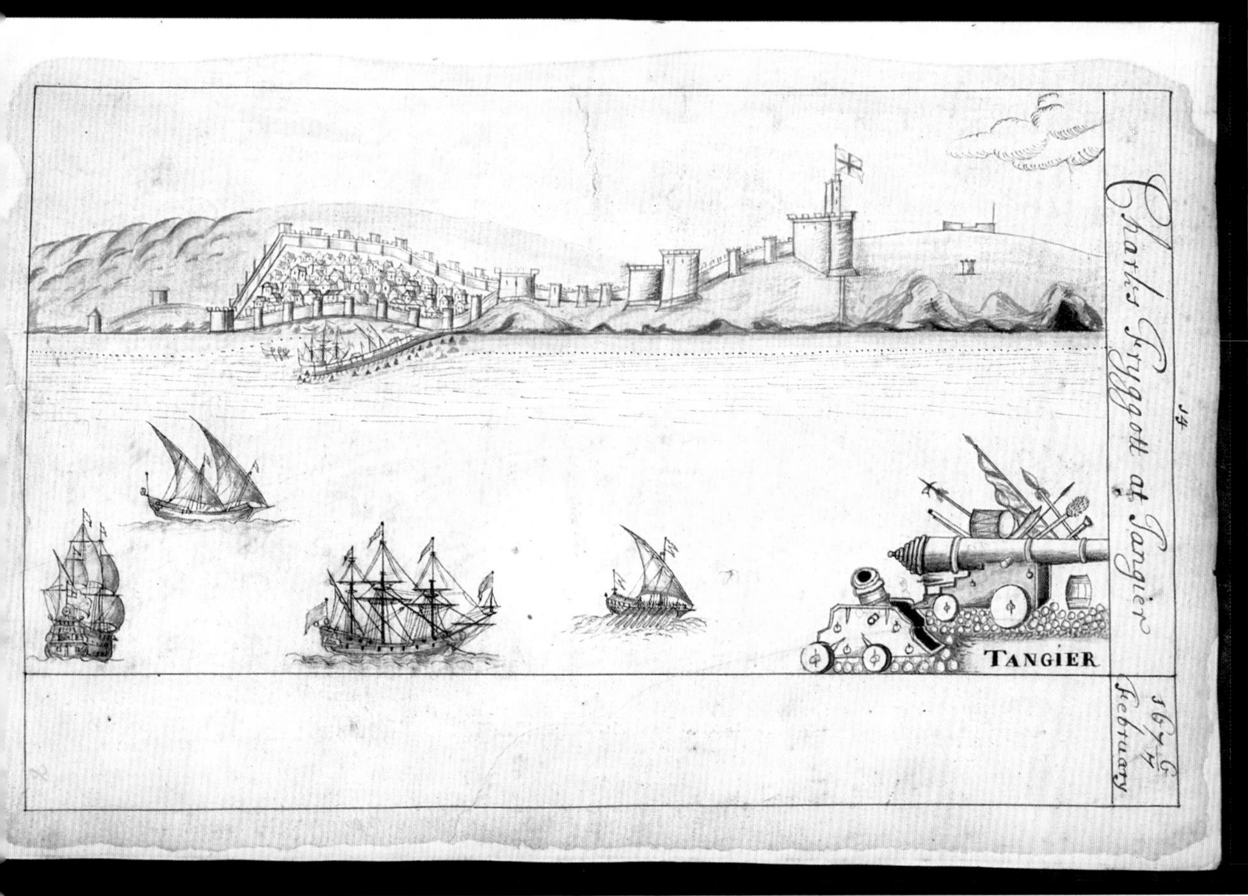


Above: *A seaview of the port at Tangiers. The image told the Admiralty what their ships would see, if they ever wanted to storm the port.*

*at the brims at H, and the depth from H to I I judge to be 200 yards, in the middle of the pit there was a small hill as IK out of the top of which cometh out the fire and smoke, in the daytime you can see nothing but the smoke, the descent is perpendicular and in many small places smoaksth.*

Grenville Collins returned to England in 1679 and handed his log to the Admiralty. England and Spain would be at war again in 1701 and Grenville Collins's charts may have been used in British attacks on Cadiz and, most significantly, in capturing Gibraltar, the first step towards British rule over the rock that continues to this day. Vesuvius would erupt again five years later.

> *'Thus showeth Mount Vesuvius, as you ride at anchor in Naples Bay. Thus showeth the concave or mouth of Mount Vesuvius where fire and smoke cometh out.'*

# *The* MISTRESS *and the* QUEEN
## Wills of Nell Gwyn and Catherine of Braganza

## 1687/1705

FAR LEFT AND LEFT: *Eleanor 'Nell' Gwyn; Catherine of Braganza.* OPPOSITE: *Nell Gwyn's will. Her signed initials 'E.G.' (bottom right) were the only letters she learned to write. She was brought up in a brothel, but her executors include two earls and the Attorney General.*

WILLS ARE LIFE after death; documents that give the dead power over the living. They appoint executors who are authorised to administer the estate of the deceased and to fulfil the dead person's instructions as to how their belongings should be divided. They are, in their way, a person's last expression of themselves. But for a will to be effective in law it must follow strict rules, and their cold legal formulae allow little room for the spirit of their makers. To find a person in their will, you have to read between the lines.

The two wills shown here make a fascinating comparison, each conveying some of the spirit of Restoration England. They are those of Charles II's mistress, Eleanor 'Nell' Gwyn, and his wife, the Portuguese princess Catherine of Braganza.

Nell Gwyn's life was meteoric. Born in 1650, as a child she worked in a brothel run by her mother in London's Covent Garden. An early lover found Nell a job in the theatre. Another lover, the actor Charles Hart, taught her the actor's trade, and Nell achieved fame as a comic actress. She became the mistress of an aristocratic rake called Charles Sackville, with whom she kept house at Epsom before, at the age of eighteen, starting an affair with the King, who was twenty years her senior (she referred to the King as her 'Charles the Third', after Hart and Sackville). It all started when they found themselves seated in adjoining boxes at the theatre. The King invited Nell to dine with him afterwards, an occasion for Nell to display her legendary wit. It turned out that neither the King nor his companions had come out with any money, and Nell had to pay the dinner bill. 'Od's Fish!' she exclaimed, imitating the King. 'This is the poorest company I have ever been in!'

Nell would be the King's mistress, one of several but the most enduring, for sixteen years. She bore him two sons, Charles and James, Charles being the 'Duke of St Albans' who is named as her sole beneficiary in her will (Nell had bullied the King into granting titles to their children; she was no pushover). The position that she had achieved in society is shown by the executors she names, including the Earl of Rochester, the Earl of Pembroke and, for heaven's sake, the Attorney General Robert Sawyer. But for all the bequests of jewels and plate, she was not rich. On his deathbed in 1685, Charles had begged, 'Let not poor Nelly starve.' His brother and successor James II paid Nell's debts and granted her a pension.

CIN

# In the Name of God Amen.

I Ellen Gwynne of the parish of St Martin in the ffeilds and County of Midd<sup></sup> Spinster this Ninth day of July Anno Dni One Thousand six hundred eighty and seaven doe make this my last Will and Testament and doe revoke all former Wills ffirst in hopes of a joyfull resurrection I doe recommend my selfe whence I came my soule into the hands of Allmighty God and my body unto the earth to be decently buryed at the discretion of my Executors herein after named And as for all such Houses Lands Tenements Offices places pensions Annuityes and Hereditamts whatsoever in England Ireland or elsewhere wherein I or my Heires or any to the use of or in trust for me or my Heires hath have or may or ought to have any estate right claime or demand whatsoever of ffee simple or ffreehold I give and devise the same all and wholly to my deare naturall sonne his Grace the Duke of St Albans and to the Heires of his body And as for all and all manner of my Jewells plate Householdstuffe Goods Chattells Credits and other Estate whatsoever I give and bequeath the same and every parte and parcell thereof to my Executors hereafter named in upon and by way of trust for my said deare Sonne his Executors Administrators and Assignes and to and for his and their owne sole and peculier benefitt and advantage in such manner as is hereafter exprest And I doe hereby constitute the Right Honoble Lawrence Earle of Rochester the Right Honoble Thomas Earle of Pembroke the Honoble Sr Robert Sawyer Knight his Maties Attorney Generall and the Honoble Henry Sidney Esqr to be my Executors of this my last Will and Testament desiring them to please to accept and undertake the execution hereof in trust as afore mentioned And I doe give and bequeath to the severall persons in the Schedule hereunto annexed the severall Legacies and summes of money therein expressed or mentioned And my further will and mind (any thing above notwithstan[ding]) is that if my said deare Sonne happen to departe this naturall life without Issue then living or such Issue dye without Issue Then and in such case all and all manner of my estate above devised to him and in case my said naturall Sonne dye before the age of one and twenty yeares Then alsoe all and all my personall estate devised to my said Executors (not before then by my said deare Sonne and his Issue and my said Executors and the Executors and Administrators of the Survivor of them or by some of them otherwise lawfully and firmly devised or disposed of shall remaine goe or be to my said Executors their Heires Executors and Administrators respectively in trust of and for answering paying and satisfying all and every and all manner of my guifts legacies and directions that at any time here after during my life shall be by me any wise mentioned or given in or by any Codicills or Schedules to be hereto annexed And lastly that my said Executors shall have all and every of them One hundred pounds apeice of lawfull money in consideracon of their care and trouble herein And furthermore all their severall and respective expences and charges in and about the execucon of this my will In witnesse of all which I hereunto sett my hand and seale the day and yeare first above written.

E. G.

Signed sealed published and declared in presence of us who at the same time subscribe our names alsoe in her presence

Lucy Hamilton Sandys
Edward Wyborne
John Warner
Wm Scarborough
Ja: Booth.

Translated out of Portuguese

Catherina R.

In the Name of God Amen

Catherine by the Grace of God Queen of Great Brittain, do declare that this is the Paper Signed with my hand to which I refere my Self in my Will and which I desire may take place as part thereof, and that due and full Execution may be Given as to the Bequests and Pious Legacies and other dispositions which I order to be performed after my decease in the order and manner following./

First I leave to be applyed for the Charges of my funerall Twenty thousand Cruzados and in Case the Expences thereof shall not amount to that Sume, I desire that all the Overplus thereof, may be divided Equally amongst the Convents of Fryars and Nuns of Villa Vicosa, besides what I particularly leave to some of them./

I order that on the three days imediately following after my decease there shall be caused to be said for my Soul, as many Masses as can be Celebrated in the Convents and Parishes of this Court and shall Continue the following dayes untill they make up the Number of Ten thousand Masses, for the Almes whereof I give the Sume Ten thousand Cruzados/

I order that there shall be once Given for almes to the Convent of the Sacrament of the Dominican Nuns three

Catherina R.

Donna Catherina por graça de Deos Rainha da Gram Breta nha, declaro, que este he o papel assignado por minha mão q' me remeto no meu testamento, e que quero valha como parte delle, dandose pronta e inteira execução aos suffragios, e legados pios, e outras dispoziçoens q' ordeno, se cumprão depois da minha morte pella ordem, e maneira seg.te

Primeiramente deixo aplicados vinte mil Cruzados p.a os gastos dos meus funeraes, e no cazo q' o dispendio, não chegue a igoalar esta soma quero q' tudo o q' restar della, se reparta igoalmente pellos Conventos de Religiosos, e Religiosas, que ha em Villa Viçoza alem do que particularmente deixo a alguns delles. ——

Mando q' nos tres dias, q' immediatamente se seguirem ao meu falecimento, se fação dizer pella minha alma todas aquelas missas que poderem celebrarse nos Conventos, e Parrochias desta Corte, e que se vão continuando nos outros dias seg.tes até se preffazer o numero de dez mil missas p.a cuja esmolla determino a quantia de dez mil Cruzados. ——

Mando q' se dem de esmolla por hua vez ao Convento do Sacramento das Religiosas Dominicas tres mil Cruzados: a Caza professa de S. Roque da Companhia de Jesus tres mil Cruzados: ao Convento da M.e de Deos de Religiosas Franciscanas da S.ta Regra dois mil Cruzados: ao Convento do Crucifixo das Religiosas Francezas da ordem de S. Francisco mil Cruzados: ao Convento de S. Antonio dos Capuchos desta Cidade mil Cruzados: aos Religiosos da provincia da Arrab.da p.a ajuda da sua vestiaria tres mil Cruzados - ao Convento das Chagas das Religiosas Franciscanas de Villa Viçosa mil Cruzados. a Caza professa da Comp.a de Jesus da mesma V.a mil Cruzados - ao Convento de S. Fr.co de Capuchos da Piedade da mesma V.a

PREVIOUS PAGES: *On the right, the original Portuguese, and on the left, the English translation of the will of 'Catherine R[egina]', 'Queen' Catherine of Braganza. The will is deeply Catholic, providing for gifts to the convent and for masses to be said for her soul.*

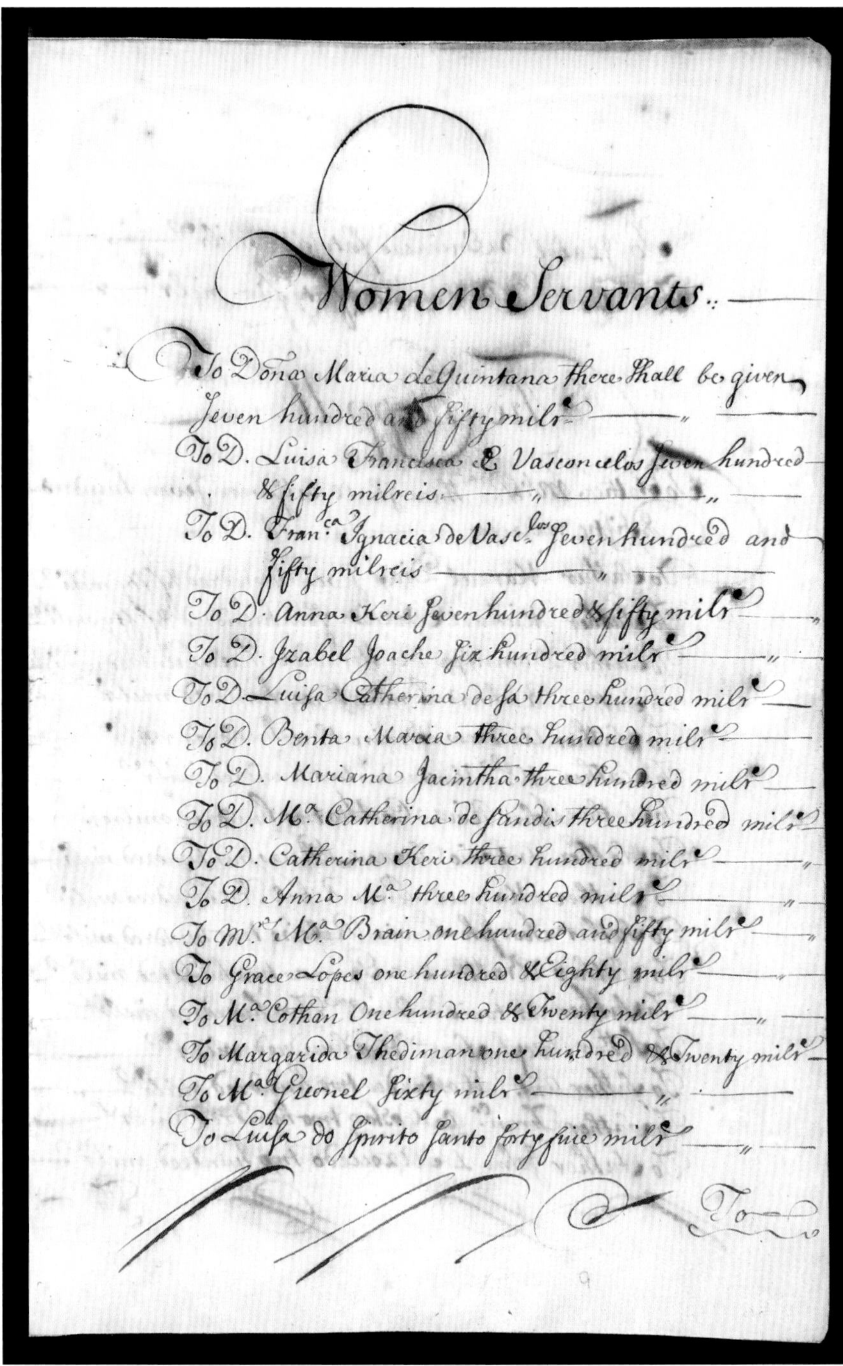

Women Servants.

To Dona Maria de Quintana there shall be given seven hundred and fifty milrs ——"
To D. Luisa Francisca & Vasconcelos seven hundred & fifty milreis ——" ——"
To D. Fran.ca Ignacia de Vasc.los seven hundred and fifty milreis ——"
To D. Anna Keri seven hundred & fifty milrs ——"
To D. Izabel Joache six hundred milrs ——"
To D. Luisa Catherina de Sa three hundred milrs ——
To D. Benta Maria three hundred milrs ——
To D. Mariana Jacintha three hundred milrs ——
To D. Ma Catherina de Sandis three hundred milrs ——
To D. Catherina Keri three hundred milrs ——"
To D. Anna Ma three hundred milrs ——"
To Mrs Ma Brain one hundred and fifty milrs ——"
To Grace Lopes one hundred & Eighty milrs ——
To Ma Cothan One hundred & Twenty milrs ——"
To Margarida Thediman one hundred & Twenty milrs ——
To Ma Gueonel sixty milrs ——"
To Luisa do Spirito Santo forty five milrs ——"

To

*Darkly pretty, Princess Catherine was brought up in the cloistered environment of the Portuguese court.*

ABOVE: *The list of gifts to Catherine's women servants. Note the preponderance of Portuguese names – Catherine kept a Portuguese retinue around her.*

*Catherine was permitted to practise her Roman Catholicism in England, but as a result was never crowned Queen (a fact that her will ignores, since it refers to her as 'Queen of Great Britain'). Catherine was a lightning rod for English anti-Catholicism.*

Nell never learned to read or write: the letters 'E.G.' at the foot of her will (for 'Eleanor Gwyn') were the only two she ever learned. When she executed this will, at the age of thirty-seven at her home in Pall Mall, Nell would have known that she was dying. She had suffered strokes earlier in the year, leaving her paralysed and bedridden. Pretty, witty Nell died four months after signing this document.

The contrast with Catherine of Braganza could not be greater. Darkly pretty, Princess Catherine was brought up in the cloistered environment of the Portuguese court. It was international politics that prompted her match with Charles. The marriage sealed an alliance in which the Portuguese got English help against the Spanish, and the English got Bombay.

Catherine's devout Catholicism rings through her will, with a lengthy hymn of praise to the Holy Trinity, Mary and the Saints, and her long list of gifts to religious institutions. Catherine was permitted to practise her Roman Catholicism in England, but as a result was never crowned Queen (a fact that her will ignores, since it refers to her as 'Queen of Great Britain'). Catherine was a lightning rod for English anti-Catholicism. Her retinue was accused of the murder of a Protestant nobleman and Catherine of high treason; it was only Charles's intervention that saved her.

Catherine's will shows how robustly the little Portuguese princess withstood these anti-Catholic attacks. Her and Nell's stories also show that Protestant–Catholic relations at the time were much more nuanced than is often portrayed. Charles and Catherine, and their respective courts, saw no difficulty in their getting married twice, once in a public Anglican rite and once in a secret Catholic one. Nell's will, with its gift to the Catholic poor of London, shows the same nuance.

Catherine had had to learn early on to accommodate Charles's mistresses and over time her loyalty and affection for the King earned her respect, although through the misfortune of miscarriages she never bore him a child. Charles remembered Catherine on his deathbed, just as he had remembered Nell. She sent him a message: 'To beg his pardon if she had offended him all his life'. Charles responded, 'Alas poor woman! She asks for my pardon? I beg hers with all my heart. Take her back that answer.'

After Charles's death, Catherine lived quietly in Somerset House on the Strand in London (as it happened, only a short carriage-ride away from Nell's home in Pall Mall). Catherine's will was written in Portuguese and translated into English. She always maintained a Portuguese retinue and remained loyal to her Portuguese roots (a connection that benefited England more than it could know; it was Catherine who, in England, popularised the Portuguese practice of drinking tea.) Catherine lived in England through the reign of James II but during the reign of William and Mary her Catholicism caused increasing isolation. She was welcomed back to the Portuguese court in 1892 and died in Lisbon on the last day of 1705.

# 18th Century

## Records from Fort Commenda *to* Secret Border Passes

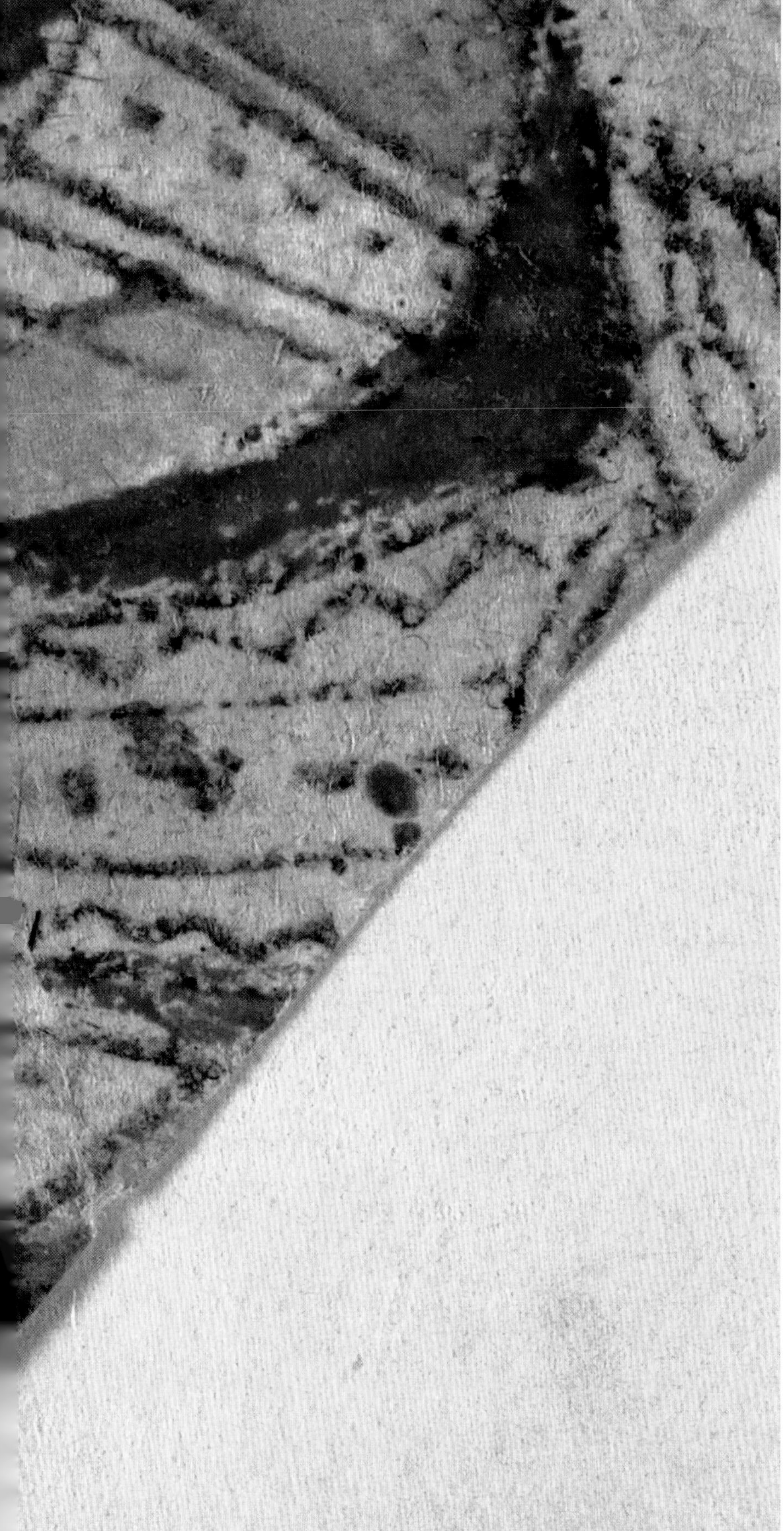

Left: *Card sharp: detail of one of the tokens used by French royalists to slip through English customs without detection.*

# Comenda Fort ye 23d Octob 1714

Arrived here at Commenda with Instructions
to Receive into my Charge from Mr Antho
Francia This Fort with all The Effects what=
soever belonging to the Royall African
Compa & here To Continue as Chief to manage
the Said Compa affaires To the Best of my
knowlege for ye Sole Acctt Intrest & benefite
of ye aforementiond Compa Whereof I Took Posses=
=sion ye 27th & Inventorys of all ye Said Compa
Effects Sign'd by ye above Said Antho Francia
my Self & Edward Richardson & Rich Whaley
Second & Writer here

## Copy of ye Inventory

to be Seen in ye book of
Acctts & of ye Instructions
in ye book of Letters

27th Pursuant to Orders from Cape Coast I Enquired into
ye Truth of Jno Cabess's owing Mr Francia a Mark
of gold for goods delivered him in Octobr 1713 whereof
Mr Francia had wrote To ye Agents upon Jno Cabess's
Refuseing To pay him ~ & find it plain that
he owes ye money Mr Francia haveing a note
attested by Mr Charles Sydenham & Jno Powers
declareing his delivery of a pawn of aggree beeds
(ye he had for that Debt) To Jno only upon his
promise to pay him ~ But Jno notwithstanding
ye note positively Denyes his owing him any thing
at present ~ whereof have this day Wrote ye Genn
ye present day answerd me Wishing they Could agree
but Mr Francia has dropt it Till a further Oppor
tunity ~ Sent To Cape Coast 20 Chests Corn „ 1 „ 14 „ —

29 A Seven hand Canoe Touching at This place from
Dixcove have according To Instructions this day
Recd from Cape Coast Taken out of her 4 Bales Blew pps
at 25 Each and Sent word thereof To Cape Coast ~ 2 „ 15 „ —
and haveing plaid them Recd from Succondee
according To Order have Advised Mr Rob Mason ye of
Recd from Succondee 100 Blew ppss at 4 Ea ~ 3 „ 1 „ — „ —
At the Same Time acquainted ye Genn with

# DIARY *of a* SLAVE MARKET
## Records from Fort Commenda

Opposite: *The opening page of William Brainie's diary, the day of his arrival to take charge of 'Cominda Fort'. Brainie was to buy African captives, store them and sell them as slaves to passing ships.*

## 1714

Above: *Eighteenth-century Ashanti gold. The British Royal Africa Company traded gold, ivory and slaves with passing ships.*

At the turn of the eighteenth century, a 300-mile stretch of West African coast was Europe's shopping strip. The Gold Coast, in modern-day Ghana, offered long beaches interspersed with sheltering headlands that were convenient for visiting ships, and more than sixty European forts had been constructed at points that gave easy access to the African interior. These were not colonies – most were built with the consent of local chieftains; they were, first and foremost, trading posts, selling African gold and, of course, African slaves.

This is the diary of one of those forts, Fort Commenda, which was run by the British Royal Africa Company. It was kept by William Brainie, an Englishman who arrived to take charge in November 1714. Fort Commenda was square-built, with high walls and bastions at each corner that held large and small cannon. It stood beside a crossroads that connected the coast with a number of tribes. Inside there were comfortable apartments for the commander, barracks for around ten soldiers, and a 'Negro House' that could take 150 slaves.

Slave traders from the interior would arrive at the fort with men, women and children captured on raids, or supplied by rival tribes. Europeans exacerbated local disputes by supplying chiefs with money and arms to fight their wars, generating captives and a steady supply of slaves. At the fort, the prisoners would be bartered for, and then 'stored' in the Negro House until the next ship arrived on its way to the Caribbean. They would then be sold at a mark-up.

What is shocking about Brainie's diary is how mundane it all is. We are used to stories of slavery being told in tones of horror and outrage, but that wasn't how Brainie saw it at all. To him, slaves were simply commodities to be bought and sold, fundamentally no different from nuggets of gold or ivory. Mention might be made of a slave's age, sex or health, but only because those were the factors that determined price:

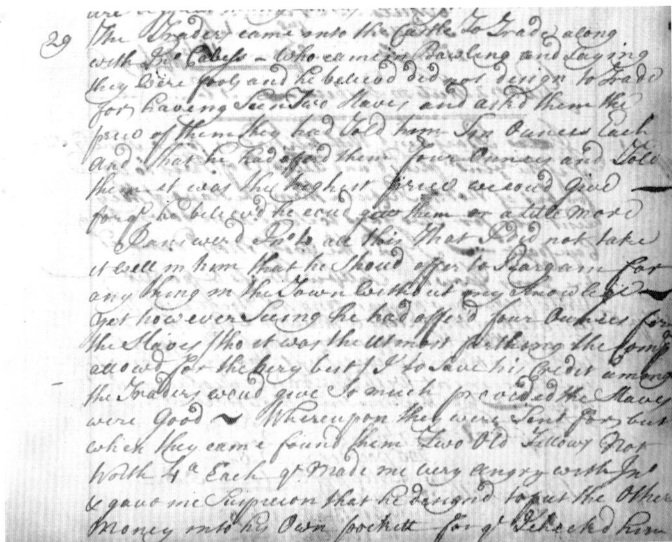
29 The Traders came into the Castle to Trade along
with Jno Cabess – Who came in Bawling and Saying
they Were fools and he believed did not design to Trade
for having Seen Two Slaves and askd them the
price of them they had Told him Six Ounces Each
And That he had offerd them four Ounces and Told
them it was the highest price we could give
for wch he believed he could get them or a little more
I answerd Jno to all this That I did not take
it well in him that he Should offer to bargain for
any thing in the Town Without my knowledge
But however Seeing he had offerd four Ounces for
the Slaves tho it was the utmost Pittance the Compy
allowd for the buying but I to Save his Credit among
the Traders woud give So much provided the Slaves
were Good ~ Whereupon they were Sent for but
when they came found them Two Old fellows Not
Worth 4a Each wch made me very angry with Jno
& gave me Suspicion that he designd to put the Other
money into his Own pockett for wch I checkd him

Left: *A particular irritant to Brainie was a slaver called John Cabess, an 'Ingrain'd Rogue'.*
Opposite: *The diary records the trade in slaves, ivory ('Elephant's Teeth') and other objects. The middle section here records a runaway woman slave.*

*Sent to Cape Coast, three men, two women and one boy.*
*Received one of the men slaves I sent to Cape Coast returned as not good for which I have paid £14 being 10pptts* [a perpet is a bolt of woollen fabric] *& 16 sheets which was paid for him.*
*Received from Cape Coast 1 man slave sold for gold being entered at 10 pptss 16 sheets.*

Brainie's diary records the occasional slave death or runaway in the tone that a cattleman might use to describe wastage among his herd:

*By the negligence of the guard one of the women slaves made her escape three days ago but being captured by some of John Cabess's people had her returned when I made the guard pay 4a.* [i.e. 'Angels', each weighing a 1/16 ounce of gold] *for their pains and to encourage the townspeople, if such occasion should again happen upon this fearing they might do so again, sent them down to Cape Coast.*

The human touches on these pages come not from the slaves – they weren't really seen as human, after all – but from Brainie himself, bored and irritated at this fly-blown posting. A particular irritant to him was John Cabess, one of the slavers who did business with the fort and, in Brainie's words, an 'Ingrain'd Rogue':

*1715, March 29. Traders came into the castle to trade along with John Cabess, who came in bawling and saying that they were fools and he believed did not design to trade for having seen two slaves and on asking the price of them they had told him six ounces each and that he had offered them four ounces and told them that it was the highest price we could give for which he believed he could get them or a little more … I did say his credit among the traders would give so much provided the slaves were good, whereupon they were sent for, but when they came, found two old fellows not worth 4a. each which made me very angry with John and gave me suspicion that he designed to put the other money into his own pocket for which I checked him and told the traders the slaves were not worth buying.*

It has been estimated that, over time, 1.6 million slaves arrived in the British Caribbean from Africa. That does not count the many who died following their capture, or in the forts, or on the sea voyage. The diary is an example of how dreadful acts can, by culture, habit or thoughtlessness, become normal and everyday.

6

Commenda Fort ye 14th Decembr 1714

to this fort

Sold for Gold

10 Small Blew pp^ts -------- 2" 8"-
12 " Sheets ---------- 12"-
21 Gunns ------------ 6" 4"- | 1" 1" 4" —

Barter'd for Slaves 2 Men & 1 Boy

27 Blew ppetts ------ 6" 12"-
52 Sheets ---------- 3" 4"- | 1" 2" — " —

Barter'd for Elephants Teeth

30 Sheets for 120^d Large ------ 1" 14" —

15 By the negligence of ye Guard one of ye Women Slaves made her escape 3 days ago but being catch'd by some of Jnº Cabess's people had her Return'd wch I made ye Guard pay 4^o for their pains & to Encourage ye Towns people if such Occasion shou'd again happen — Upon this fearing they might do so again Sent them down to Cape Coast

Sent To Cape Coast 3 Men 2 Women & one Boy — 2" 2 8" —

Ditto The Traders Leaving the place gave them in Dashes --- 5 Sheets ---- " — " 5" —

18 Rec'd one of ye Men Slaves I Sent to Cape Coast Returnd as not good for wch I have paid 14^o being 10 pp^ts & 16 Sheets wch was paid for him

Rec'd from Cape Coast 1 Man Slave 3 8" —

Sold for Gold being Enter'd ------ "

10 pp^tts ------------ 2" 8
16 Sheets ------------ 1" — | 3" 8" —

at the Same Time Rec'd Permission to Come to Cape Coast at Christmass — wch I desired in my Last Letter having Some Business there Also Orders to Enter Two Young Women into pay who formerly were Reco'd Girles —

19 Wrote To Cape Coast Castle of my Design of being there at Xmass & Sent down ye Teeth wch I purchas'd these Two Months Viz

Sent To Cape Coast 378 in 7 Teeth
112 Small in 13 d^o ---- " — " 6.12" 6

# *How to* CATCH *a* PIRATE
## Reports of the Hunt and Killing of Blackbeard

# 1718

ABOVE: *Captain Edward Teach, 'Blackbeard', depicted with the smoking fuses that he jammed under his hat.*

THE 'GOLDEN AGE' of piracy in the Atlantic ran from the mid seventeenth century to the first quarter of the eighteenth. There were rich pickings to be had in the trade around the Atlantic, and the British Royal Navy was tied up in wars with foreign powers, principally the French. Pirates ran riot along the coasts of the Americas, West Africa and the Caribbean.

Many pirate captains are infamous: Captain Kidd, John 'Calico Jack' Rackham, the vicious Henry Avery. But the most infamous of them all is Edward Teach, or 'Thack' – the pirate better known as Blackbeard. Teach was a terrifying figure, his vast beard twisted with black ribbons and reaching up to his eyes. When Teach attacked he would light smoking fuses on either side of his hat, to make himself appear even more demonic, a true figure from hell. In *Peter Pan*, J.M. Barrie invoked his legend. Captain Hook, he wrote, had been Blackbeard's bosun.

Blackbeard commanded a fleet of four or five ships, one of them a forty-gun warship. In the winter, he would plunder around the West Indies before making his way up the American coast as the weather warmed. His most outrageous act took place in 1718 when, for five days, he blockaded the harbour at Charleston, holding the town to ransom and plundering any ships heading towards the port.

OPPOSITE: *Lieutenant Robert Maynard's report of the final battle with Blackbeard ('Thatch') and his crew. Maynard hid his men below deck and ambushed Blackbeard when the pirates boarded.*

Enough was enough. The Governor of Virginia, Alexander Spotswood, issued a proclamation that put £100 on the head of Blackbeard. He approached Captain Gordon of HMS *Pearl* to persuade him to chase down the pirate. Blackbeard was thought to be lurking in the Ocracoke Inlet (around fifty miles south of Roanoake – see page 65), and so Spotswood

Honord: Sr:

Having aquainted you yesterday for their Lordsps: information that I had reason to finde fault wth the account Lieut: Maynard [illegible] of his Maties: Pearle under my command made to his Matie in his petition lately layed before him in Counsell.

In order to this I shall, very briefly lay before their Lordsps: all ye steps of that action with Thatch called Blackbeard

After they were so near, that the compliment past betwixt them of not giving each other quarters; Thatch observing all his men upon deck gave them a broade side; his guns being sufficiently charged with swan shot, partridge shot, and others; with this broad side he killed and wounded (most by the swan shot) one & twenty of his men, Mr: Maynard finding his men thus exposed, and no shelter order his men down into the hold, going himself into the cabin abaft; ordering the midshipman that was at the helm, or Mr: Butler his pilate to aquaint him with any thing that should happen. Thatch observing his decks clear of men presently concluded the vessel his own, and then steers on board Lieut: Maynards sloop, enters himself the first man, with a rope in his hand to lash or make fast the two sloops: Mr: Butler aquainting Lieut Maynard with this, turned his men upon deck, and was himself presently among them: where in less then six minuets tyme Thatch and five or six of his men were killed; the rest of these rogues jumped in the water where they were demolished, one of them being dyscovered some dayes after in the reeds by the fouls hovering over him: the sloop in wch the Lymes people were in, had the misfortune to have the thre officers that commanded them killed a head of his sloop: & another shot through the body in Thatchs sloop by one of our men, takeing him by mistake for one of the pirates

This Sr: is the true, and real steps of that action, given in upon oath at his Maties: Court of Admirty: in Virginia, by himself & people the truth of which if need be Lieut: Governor Spotswood can justifie & also Capt: Brand: there being no such thing given out there [illegible] boarding Thatch sword in hand; as he is pleased to tell his mand of Captn Ge: Gordon, at Kiquotan in Virginia

# Remarkable Occurrences &c

Moderate gales & fair weather.

The former part moderate & fair, the latter fresh gales & cloudy weather; yesterday in the afternoon came aboard 29 bushells of Callavances & 25 firkins of Butter.

hard gales & squally rainy weather most part of this 24 hours; yesterday PM came aboard the Pork that was sent ashore to be cut into mess pieces; at 4 AM lower'd yards & Topmasts.

The former part fresh gales & rainy weather the latter fair. yesterday in the afternoon the longboat brought aboard of 4 inch One coile new, of 3 inch twice layd one, of 3 & one of 2½ —

Moderate gales & fair weather; yesterday in the afternoon the longboat brought abd. 12 hundred weight of bread from hampton, & four Barr:les of Tarr from the sd place

The former part moderate & fair, the latter hard gales & much rain; at 2 AM lowerd yards & Topmasts; gott up the spare cable & an old cast cable, got about 4 Tunns of ballast into the longboat for a sloop taken up to go against the Pyrats in No. Carolina.

The former part fresh gales & cloudy weather, the latter moderate & fair, about noon gave an Order to My 1st Lt. Mr. Robt. Maynard to go comander in chief by sea of two Sloops the Jane & Ranger, hird by Governour Spotswood, & mann'd & Arm'd out of his Matie's Ships Pearl, & Lyme to proceed to North Carolina to attack one Edward Thack, commonly call'd Blackbeard; this day he sail'd from hence, with one months provisions at whole Allowance for 35 men, in the Jane which I mann'd out of the Pearl, & 25 in the Ranger mann'd Arm'd & Victual'd &c, by Capta: Brand out of the Lyme

Moderate gales & fair weather, dry'd all the sails; unbent M.sail F.sail, stay-sails & put them down

Winds & Weather Do: yesterday in the afternoon the longboat came aboard with her load of water; this morn sent ashore 20 Sick persons to Sick Quarters in hampton

Moderate gales & fair weather; the longboat came aboard with water.

Weather for the most part the same; the longboat came aboard with water.

Weather Do, hoisted yards & Topmasts.

Weather Do; the longboat came aboard with water 556 lb fresh beef

Weather Do the longboat came aboard with water Do put her ashore to return

OPPOSITE: *Captain Gordon's journal. In the largest middle section, Gordon records sending his First Lieutenant Robert Maynard to attack Blackbeard.*

provided funds for Gordon to hire small sloops that could navigate the shallow channels around Ocracoke.

As Gordon recorded in his journal, on 17 November he sent his First Lieutenant, Robert Maynard, to hunt down the pirate:

*The former part fresh gales & cloudy weather, the latter moderate fair, about noon gave an Order to my first lieutenant, Mr Robert Maynard, to go commander in chief by sea of two sloops The Jane & Ranger, hired by Govenor Spotswood, & mann'd & armed out of his majesty's ships Pearl & Lyme to proceed to North Carolina, to attack one Edward Thack, commonly called Blackbeard ...*

Maynard heard from passing ships that Blackbeard was anchored on the inner side of Ocracoke Island. Arriving in the evening, Maynard waited overnight before launching his attack. Maynard's report takes up the story:

*'Mr Butler acquainting Lieutenant Maynard with this, turned his men upon deck, and was himself presently among them, wherein in less than six minutes tyme Thatch and five or six of his men were killed; the rest of these rogues jumped in the water where they were demolished, one of them being discovered some days after in the reeds by the fowls hovering over him . . .'*

*In order to this I shall, very briefly lay before their lordship's all the steps of that action with Thatch, alias Blackbeard. After they were so near, that the compliment passed betwixted them of not giving each other quarters . . .*

(Blackbeard's actual words were more colourful: 'Damnation seize my soul,' he roared, downing a glass of liquor, 'if I give you any quarter or take any from you!').

*Thatch observing all his men upon deck, gave them a broadside; his guns being sufficiently charged with Swan shot, Partridge shot and others; with this broadside he killed and wounded (most by the Swan Shot) at one and twenty of his men, Mr Maynard, finding his men thus exposed, and no shelter ordered his men down into the hold, giving himself unto the cabins avast; ordering the mid shipman that was at the helm, or Mr Butler, his pilot to acquaint him with anything that should happen. Thatch observing his decks clear of men presently concluded the vessel his own, and then sheers on board Lieutenant Maynard's sloop, enters himself the first man, with a rope in his hand to lash, or make fast the two sloops; Mr Butler acquainting Lieutenant Maynard with this, turned his men upon deck, and was himself presently among them, wherein in less than six minutes tyme Thatch and five or six of his men were killed; the rest of these rogues jumped in the water where they were demolished one of them being discovered some days after in the reeds by the fowls hovering over him . . .*

*Blackbeard fought on, until cut by a broadsword wielded by one of Maynard's crew. 'Well done!' he shouted to the man on the first blow, before the second struck his head from his shoulders. Some of Blackbeard's crew escaped; one of them, as Gordon reports, being discovered in reeds because of the birds hovering above him. But Blackbeard's legend, at least, would not die.*

In other words, Maynard hid his men below deck until Blackbeard leapt on board, whereupon they rushed out to overwhelm the pirates. Maynard and Blackbeard fought sword to sword, and when Maynard's sword broke he pulled out his pistol and shot Blackbeard. Blackbeard fought on, until cut by a broadsword wielded by one of Maynard's crew. 'Well done!' he shouted to the man on the first blow, before the second struck his head from his shoulders. Some of Blackbeard's crew escaped; one of them, as Gordon reports, being discovered in reeds because of the birds hovering above him. But Blackbeard's legend, at least, would not die. It was later said that when his headless body was pitched overboard, it swam several times around the boat.

Gordon's journal gives a gruesome final touch:

*3 January 1719: Little wind & fair weather; this day the Sloop Adventure Edward Thack formerly Master (a Pirate) anchored here from North Carolina commanded by my first lieutenant Mr Robert Maynard who had taken the Athelsted Sloop & destroyed the said Edward Thack and most of his men; he also brought Thack's head, hanging under his bowsprit in order to present it to the Colony of Virginia …*

The assault on Blackbeard was part of a wider effort to suppress piracy in the Atlantic. Peace between England and France freed up the Royal Navy to pursue pirates, just as Gordon and Maynard had done. Idle privateers, no longer allowed to attack the French, were licensed to go after pirate ships instead, and substantial rewards were offered for capturing them. The law was changed so that pirates were no longer taken to England for trial, but were tried and executed in the larger ports, their bodies hung to rot in gibbets as a warning to others. The authorities used carrots as well as sticks. In 1717, George I proclaimed that pirates who gave themselves up to the authorities would be pardoned.

Piracy quickly collapsed in the face of these efforts. It has been estimated that in 1720 there were some 1,500 to 2,000 pirates operating in the Caribbean and along the coast of North America (to give an idea of the scale of this, the entire population of New York at the time was just 18,000), who were responsible for forty to fifty attacks a year. By 1726, there were no more than 200 pirates, and barely half a dozen attacks. The days of the Atlantic pirate were over.

# DICK TURPIN'S INDICTMENT

## Indictment Papers

RIGHT: Dick Turpin *magazine, from the 1900s. The romantic legends that surround Turpin are at odds with the violent reality of his life.*

## 1739

THIS INDICTMENT FOR horse-theft tethers us to reality – and a pretty sorry reality at that. If ever there were a distance between a person's real life and the myth about him, it is in the story of Richard 'Dick' Turpin. Galloping by moonlight on his charger Black Bess, the dashing highwayman was in reality an habitual thief, housebreaker and murderer. This document is his final indictment for horse-theft, for which he was hanged. It also shows how rough justice was in the eighteenth century.

Richard Turpin was born in Essex in 1705, the son of a butcher. He probably followed his father's trade, which also gained him some criminal connections when he began reselling stolen deer. He was tall (well, 5' 9", which was tall for the time), but badly scarred with smallpox. In his twenties, Turpin moved from the outskirts of criminal activity into its heart as a member of the 'Essex Gang'. The gang's method was to break into remote homesand then terrorise and torture their victims into handing over their savings. One housebreak involved the rape of a maidservant and torture of the owner, who was forced to sit bare-buttocked on his own fire. The sum of £50 was offered for the capture of the notorious gang.

The Essex Gang was eventually betrayed and hanged, their bodies left to rot in gibbets on the Edgware Road. But Turpin escaped capture, and now turned to the business for which he is best known, that of a highwayman. With accomplice Thomas Rowden, he robbed coaches in areas that now form part of Greater London: Epping Forest, Putney, Barnes and Hounslow in the west, Blackheath in the southeast. Rowden was captured and transported, and two years later Turpin reappeared with another accomplice, Matthew King. When the pair was ambushed, King was shot but, slippery as ever, Turpin made good his escape and went into hiding in Epping Forest. In the forest, Turpin shot and killed a man who tried to apprehend him. He was now a murderer, with a reward of £200 on his head.

Turpin headed north and for several months lived under an assumed name in Lincolnshire. When he was arrested for affray in 1738 – he shot his landlord's cockerel, then threatened to shoot his landlord – suspicious Justices of the Peace uncovered a series of accusations of horse-theft against his new persona. His true identity was discovered by chance, when his handwriting on a letter to London was recognised. He was indicted and tried at York Assizes.

Below: *This indictment of Dick Turpin lay on the desk of the judge who sentenced him to hang.*

The indictment is for the theft of three horses belonging to a Thomas Creasy: a mare worth £3, a foal worth 20 shillings and a gelding worth £3. The indictment shows that even though the authorities knew that they had captured a notorious murderer, they did not trouble themselves with that particular crime. The charges of theft would be enough to hang Turpin. The eighteenth century is notorious for the number of crimes – more than 200 – that were punishable by death, most of them crimes against property. It did not matter that Creasy had recovered his horses by now. Nor did it matter that the indictment is wrong, about both the date and place of the alleged crimes. Turpin had no defence counsel. The judge, on whose desk this indictment would have laid, was meant to protect the interests of the accused. Reports from the trial are pathetic. Turpin asked for more time for his defence, the judge refused to give it, and Turpin was at a loss as to what to say. Turpin was sentenced to death and was hanged at Knavesmire in York.

Turpin enjoyed some notoriety in his own lifetime, principally because he remained at large while so many accomplices were captured. The story of his life was rushed out on his execution to cash in on public interest, but he was still portrayed as a violent crook. It was his relocation from London to Yorkshire that provided the yeast for a more romantic story to arise, that he had ridden the entire 200 miles in a day. The myth was adopted in one of the nineteenth century's most successful novels, *Rookwood* (1834) by Harrison Ainsworth, a gothic tale set in a gloomy manor, involving a supernatural curse and doomed romantic love. It followed the current fashion of introducing a real historical criminal. Turpin pops up in the novel without much purpose apart from being charming and suitably gothic, riding his black horse by moonlight. The novel was a sensation. Less than one hundred years after this indictment was written, a waxwork of Turpin stood in Madame Tussauds. Documents like this bring legends back down to earth.

# FAITH *and* REASON, RICH *and* POOR

## Non-conformist Baptism Book

## 1740

RIGHT: *The blank pages of a ladies' magazine served as a baptism book for Presbyterians in Nottingham.*

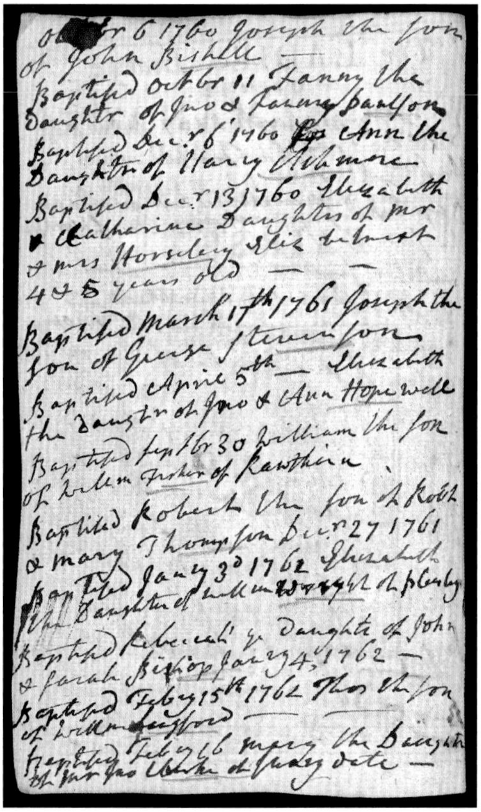
[illegible] 6 1760 Joseph the son
of John Bishell —
Baptised Octbr 11 Fanny the
Daughter of Jno & Fanny Paulson
Baptised Decr 6 1760 [illegible] Ann the
Daughter of Mary [illegible]
Baptised Decr 13 1760 Elizabeth
& Catharine Daughters of mr
& mrs Horsley Eliz [illegible]
4 & 5 years old — —
Baptised March 17th 1761 Joseph the
son of George Stevenson
Baptised April 5th — Elizabeth
the daughter of Jno & Ann Hopewell
Baptised Septbr 30 William the son
of William Fisher of Rawthern
Baptised Robert the son of Robt
& mary Thompson Decr 27 1761
Baptised Janry 3d 1762 Elizabeth
the Daughter of William [illegible]
Baptised Rebeccah y Daughter of John
& Sarah Bishop Janry 24, 1762 —
Baptised Feby 15th 1762 Thos the son
of William [illegible] —
Baptised Feby 16 mary the Daughter
of mr Jno Clarke of [illegible] date —

THIS SWEET LITTLE book captures the eighteenth century's opposites: science and religion, wealth and poverty, establishment and non-establishment, all jostled together in this accidental meeting place.

The book is a record of the baptisms of children born into a congregation of poor Presbyterians in Nottingham in the mid-eighteenth century. Presbyterianism was the established religion of Scotland, and Presbyterian congregations in England usually had Scottish links. But non-conformists remained outside the establishment, prohibited, for example, from holding public office or attending university. Members of non-conformist groups tended to come from the artisan and lower classes, and many of the people listed here will have been involved in textiles (Nottingham was known for its lacemaking), trade or service. Presbyterian theology and organisation was a source of tremendous strength and pride. The congregation was led by democratically elected elders, not Anglican bishops appointed by the established elite. They were confident that God's chosen ones were saved, regardless of wealth or status. A source of pride, too, would have been their plain meeting house – no ornaments or stained glass, just a prominent pulpit from which to preach the word of God, and benches or chairs from which to hear it. Baptisms were important for welcoming newborns into the community, and were performed in front of the congregation, with a sprinkling of water.

Non-conformist congregations were not obliged to keep registers of baptisms but many did so anyway. Making a formal record of such an important event was the proper thing to do, and if a register was good enough for the Anglicans, it was good enough for them. But there was no need for highfalutin register books. The blank pages of a women's magazine – here, the 1740 edition of the *Ladies Diary* – would do them just as well.

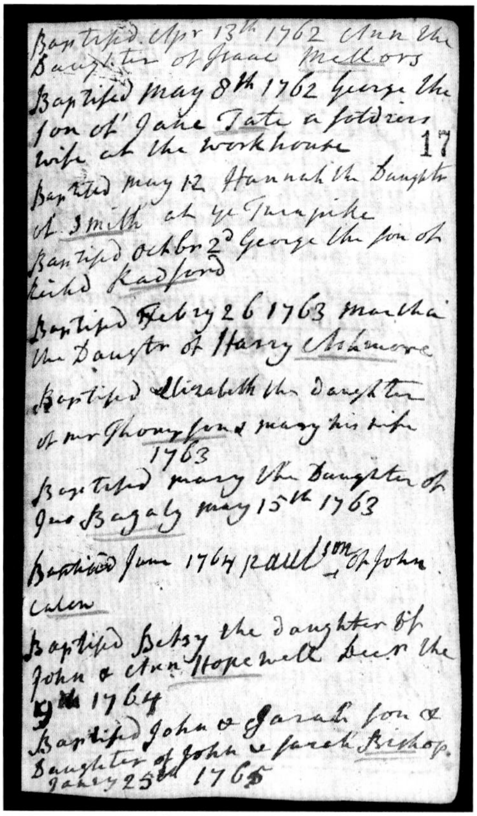
Baptised Apr 13th 1762 Ann the
Daughter of Isaac Mellors
Baptised May 8th 1762 George the
son of Jane Tate a soldiers
wife at the workhouse 17
Baptised May 12 Hannah the Daughter
of Smith at ye Turnpike
Baptised Octbr 2d George the son of
Richd Radford
Baptised Febry 26 1763 Martha
the Daughter of Harry Ashmore
Baptised Elizabeth the daughter
of mr Thompsons mary his wife
1763
Baptised mary the Daughter of
Jno Bagaly may 15th 1763
Baptised June 1764 Paul son of John
Calen
Baptised Betsy the daughter of
John & Ann Hopewell Decr the
9th 1764
Baptised John & Sarah son &
Daughter of John & Sarah Bishop
Janry 25th 1765

LEFT: *On the blank pages of the magazines, the local congregation recorded their baptisms.*

OPPOSITE: *The front page of the 1740 edition of the* Ladies Diary. *The publication was famous for its puzzles, and became the world's first printed forum for mathematical exchange.*

On one page appears the record of children baptised:

*October 6, 1760, Joseph the son of John Bishill*
*Baptised October 11, 1760, Fanny the daughter of good Fanny Baullon*
*Baptised December 6, 1760, Anne the daughter of Harry Robmore*
*Baptised December 13, 1760, Elizabeth Katherine the daughter of Mr & Mrs Horsley Eliz B almost four and five years old*

(The book records more female than male baptisms; boys were more likely to be baptised in the Church of England, to give them a better chance of education and work.)

On the opposite page are the printed pages of the *Ladies Diary*. Towards the end of the seventeeth century, publishers began to realise that women could form a distinct readership group, and the *Ladies Diary* was the very first annual almanac targeted at women. Its tone was courtly, as evidenced by the rhyme around the picture. The earliest editions contained recipes and romantic fiction, but it became apparent that its most popular features were its mathematical puzzles and verbal riddles. This was an age of popular science. Public lectures were attended by men and women alike. Mathematics came to dominate the magazine, and made it popular with men, too. Puzzles were sent in by readers (to my shame, I couldn't solve any of them), with answers provided the following year. And the *Ladies Diary* thus became, believe it or not, the world's first printed forum of mathematical exchange.

By the time of this edition, the print run was a huge 30,000 copies, and the almanac had become – ironically, given its use by our poor congregation – a favourite of the leisured and establishment classes. To please its smarter readership, each edition contained a list of feasts and festivals of the Church of England. The Presbyterians carried on filling the blank pages without batting an eyelid: 'Baptised April 13, 1762, Anne the daughter of Isaac Mellors'; 'Baptised May 8, 1762, George the son of Jane Tate, a soldier's wife at the workhouse'; 'Baptised May 12, Hannah the daughter of Smith at the Turnpike'.

Who knows how a book like this came to be the one used – through a mathematically-minded member of the congregation perhaps? Its journey to the National Archives started in 1837 when civil registration was introduced. The Registrar General called for all registers to be sent to Somerset House in London, which would be a central point for holding the records of baptisms. But this little book is more than a record of births: it captures the Spirit of the Age.

# *The* LADIES *Diary*:

## OR, THE

# Woman's ALMANACK,

## For the YEAR of our LORD, 1740.

Being the *BISSEXTILE*, or LEAP-YEAR:
Containing many Delightful and Entertaining *Particulars*, Peculiarly Adapted for the *Use* and *Diversion* of the

# FAIR-SEX.

Being the *Thirty-Seventh* ALMANACK ever Publish'd of this Kind.

1. HAIL! happy LADIES of the *BRITISH* Isle,
On whom the GRACES and the MUSES smile.

2. LONG had your lovely *Shape*, and matchless *Mein*,
The Wonder of the Neighb'ring Nations been;

3. NATURE to make your *Triumph* more compleat,
To peerless CHARMS has added piercing WIT.

4. NO more let *SCYTHIA* vaunt her FEMALE-HOST,
Nor their SEMIRAMIS th' *Assyrians* boast:
WIT join'd to BEAUTY, *Fame* shall now record;
Which lead more Captive than the Conqu'ring Sword.

Printed by *A. Wilde*, for the Company of STATIONERS, 1740.

May 2 1744

Joseph Sealy of Woodford in Essex Husbandman a Batchr. and Eliz Cayford of Ditto Spinster.

2

Henry Lowton of St Pauls Covent garden Gents Sert a Batchr. and Jean Waller of Ditto Spinster.

2

William Thomas St George's Hanr Square Corkcutter a Batchr and Mary Chilcott of St Giles in ye Fields Spinster.

2

Richard Floyd of St Georges Middx Sailsman a Widower and Eliz Leake of Do Spr

2

Richard Crakenthorp of St Andrews Holborn (Gent) a Batchr and Ann Otway of St Georges Hanr Square Spinster

3

The Honble Henry Fox Esqr a Batchr and Lady Caroline Lenox (Daughter to his Grace the Duke of Richmond) Spinster

3

William Giller of St Peter le Poor Gent Sert a Batchr and Mary Johnson of Ditto Spinster.

3

Patrick Brady of St Giles in ye Fields Labr a Batchr and Margt Fanning of Ditto Widow.

LEFT: *The register of 'clandestine' weddings conducted by the Reverend William Dare on 2 May 1744. The registers were valuable for proving the marriages' validity. Sixth from the top is a particularly valuable one – the clandestine marriage of a daughter of the Duke of Richmond.*

*One Fleet parson said that he married 1,000 sailors a week when the ships were in: sailors intoxicated by their first woman in months, women intoxicated by the sailor's shore-leave wages, or both parties just plain intoxicated.*

# *The* CLANDESTINE WEDDINGS

## Records of Fleet Marriages

RIGHT: *Print of 'A Fleet Wedding', beside St Paul's Church, Covent Garden. A sailor is about to marry his landlady's daughter, in front of a 'Fleet Parson'.*

**1744**

THESE ARE RECORDS of 'irregular' or 'clandestine' weddings: shotgun weddings for pregnant girls, drunken weddings for sailors on shore-leave and that staple of romantic fiction, secret weddings for eloping lovers.

In the eighteenth century, the conduct of clandestine weddings had become something of an industry, built up around the debtors' prison in London, the Fleet. The Fleet had a regular churn of impecunious clergymen, who found that they could earn cash-in-hand by conducting quick marriages in the prison chapel. The prison authorities eventually prohibited weddings in the chapel, and the practice spread to the area around the prison. The area became known as the 'Rules of the Fleet', or the 'Fleet Rules', and was bounded by Fleet market (now Farringdon Street), Ludgate Hill, the Old Bailey and Fleet Lane. 'Marriage Houses' sprang up within the Fleet Rules, often in rooms over coffee houses and taverns. It was good business. Money could be made from conducting the wedding itself, from issuing a certificate of the marriage, for food and drink, and for room hire.

The Fleet registers in the National Archives alone record over 200,000 weddings. Why did people opt for a Fleet wedding? Many were simply inexpensive weddings for the less well-off, since Fleet weddings were much cheaper than those provided by the Church of England. Others were more spontaneous. One Fleet parson said that he married 1,000 sailors a week when the ships were in: sailors intoxicated by their first woman in months, women intoxicated by the sailor's shore-leave wages, or both parties just plain intoxicated. For some, there were sound commercial reasons. Paupers seeking relief from a parish might need to marry a resident of the parish. Marriage was also a good way for a woman to shift her debts, because a married woman's debts fell to her husband. A number of newlywed men would find themselves 'having and holding' rather more than they expected.

There were other advantages. Fleet weddings were quick, and they were private. Then as now, some couples wanted to avoid the stress of a large wedding and a quick trip to the Fleet Rules provided a solution. There was also the thrill of doing something a bit naughty. A clandestine marriage might seem rather racy to your friends, and annoying your parents never goes out of fashion.

The marriage registers – often tall, thin notebooks – were more than records of interest. They were valuable, carefully kept and often bequeathed to descendants of the owners. They were proof that the wedding had

Right: *The Reverend Dare's scruffy original notebook. Notes of the weddings, including that between Henry Fox and Lady Caroline Lenox (left and second from the top), were scribbled down immediately after the ceremonies had been performed.*

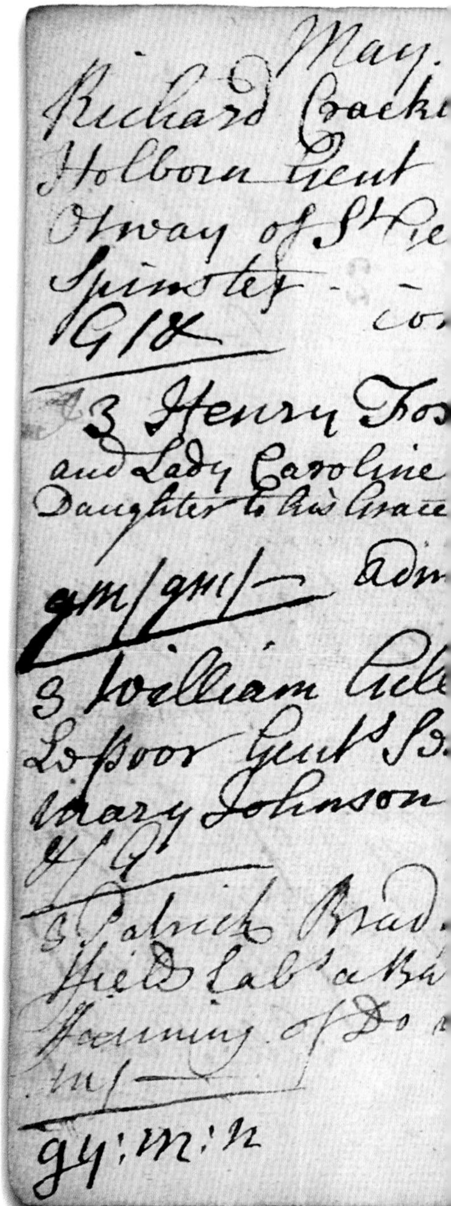
May.
Richard
Holborn Gent
Spinster
3 Henry
and Lady Caroline
3 William
Mary Johnson

taken place. The validity of a marriage, of a wife's claims on her husband, and the legitimacy of any heirs for inheritance, could turn on whether the marriage could be proved in the records – and people would pay for that proof. Registers were kept by the clergy, with a second register often kept by the Marriage House (which might be a good deal easier to locate than a wayward clergyman). Freelance register keepers were also available, and so people who wanted to be sure that they could prove the marriage later could record it several times over. On the other hand, entries could be slipped into registers in return for a bribe. Some registrars deliberately keep their books untidy, all the better for adding names at a later date.

But some of the marriages recorded are indeed the stuff of romantic fiction. The register shown here – one of more than three hundred in the National Archives – was kept by the Reverend William Dare. His scrappy notebook records the weddings as they were conducted on 2 May 1744, and the elegant register on page 112 is his neat transcript. The grandest of the eight couples married by him that day was 'The Hon$^{rble}$ Henry Fox Esq, a bachelor' and 'Lady Caroline Lenox, Daughter to His Grace the Duke of Richmond'. Lady Caroline was twenty-one, Henry Fox a politician eighteen years her senior, and they were marrying in the face of their parents' disapproval. Their marriage, though, was to be a happy one. In time, the couple's home became a centre of society and their four children included a future general and a radical Member of Parliament.

The Rules of the Fleet couldn't last. The risk of muddle about inheritance, and confusion about what did and did not constitute a legal marriage, meant it was never going to survive in the property-conscious eighteenth century. Pressure for reform also came from the Church, which of course was losing money to irregular marriages. The situation was finally regularised in 1754, when 'An Act for the Better Preventing of Clandestine Marriage' came into force, obliging residence in the parish of marriage, and the reading of banns of marriage several times in the weeks before a wedding. The Act was heralded, naturally, by a final rush of clandestine marriages.

The year 1754 did not quite mark the end for eloping couples and romantic storylines. The Marriage Act did not apply in Scotland. In the 1770s, a new road was built to the obscure Scottish village of Graitney, just across the border with England. Gretna Green, as it became known, was on course to become the world's favourite destination for lovers who liked to keep their weddings irregular.

# *The* LAD *that is* BORN TO BE KING
## Declaration of Flora MacDonald

# 1746

*Speed, bonnie boat, like a bird on the wing,*
*Onward! the sailors cry;*
*Carry the lad that is born to be King*
*Over the sea to Skye.*
*'The Skye Boat Song'*, 1870s

ABOVE: *Bonnie Prince Charlie. The Young Pretender was hunted across Scotland, but was never betrayed.*
OPPOSITE: *The first page of the statement of 'Miss MacDonald . . . prisoner for assisting the eldest son of the Pretender . . . '*

BONNIE PRINCE CHARLIE attracted romantic myths. This is our record of the best known: the moment when the young Prince, hunted by the English Army, was protected by a stranger, a beautiful young woman who disguised him as her maid and carried him across the water to the Isle of Skye. This is the declaration of that woman, Flora MacDonald, written just three weeks after the events it describes.

The Bonnie Prince – Charles Edward Stuart – was the grandson of James II of England and VII of Scotland. James succeeded his brother Charles II to the throne in 1685. It was bad enough that James was a Catholic, but when he introduced Acts of Toleration towards Catholics and religious non-conformists, it was too much for the English establishment. In 1688, a delegation invited James's daughter, Mary, and son-in-law, William of Orange, to invade England and take the throne, and James promptly fled to France. William and Mary were crowned the following year, but many secretly believed that James was their true king. These supporters came to be called the Jacobites (the name comes from 'Jacobus', the Latinised form of 'James').

The Jacobites were a strange mix. On the one hand, many were ultra-conservative. They supported James because, for good or ill, he was God's anointed king, and you can't gainsay God. On the other, followers were often anti-establishment. If you did not like the ruling powers, you could transfer your loyalty to the 'true' king in exile. Jacobites adopted secret symbols. They might decorate their possessions with oak leaves (a reference to Charles II's famous escape from Roundhead troops, by hiding in an oak tree) and white roses. If the King was toasted, they might hold their claret glass over their water glass, because they were secretly toasting the 'King-over-the-water'. There were Jacobite songs with secret meanings, at least one of which is still popular today, the carol 'Oh Come All Ye Faithful', which some think celebrates the birth of Bonnie Prince Charlie in 1720. The Jacobite cause became the Arthurian myth of its day – if only the King-over-the-water would return, then all would be well . . .

Copy of the Declaration of Miss[31] Mac Donald.

49E

Appl Cross Bay, July ye 12: 1746.



Miss Mc Donald, Daughter in Law of Mc Donald of Milton in Sky, being, by General Campbell's Order, made Prisoner for assisting the eldest Son of the Pretender in his Escape from South Uist, & asked to declare the Circumstances thereof, Says, That about Six Weeks ago, she left her Father in Law's House at Armadach in Sky, & went South to see Some Friends.

Being asked, "if she had any Invitation from "those who persuaded her to do what she "afterwards ingaged in for the young Pretender "or any Body else, before she left Sky; answerd "in the Negative, and Says that at the time of her leaving Sky, she did not know where the young Pretender was, but only heared He was Some where on the long Island: that she Stay'd at (what they call) a Sheilling of her Brothers, on the Hills, near Ormaclait, the House of Clan Ronald; and that, about the 21st of June, O Neil, or as they called him Nelson, came to where she Stay'd, & proposed to her, that as he heared she was going to Sky, that the young Pretender should go with her

32 217

him, taking with them the Woman's Apparel furnished by Lady Clan Ronald, he was dressed in. Here they heard of General Campbell's being come to South Uist, & that Capt. Fergusone was within a Mile of them. When they got this Information, they were just going to Supper. But then went off very precipitately, & sat up all Night at a Sheilling call'd Closchinisch.

Saturday, June the 25th the Cutter and Wherreer, which attended General Campbell having got from Bernera, near the Harris, through to the East Side of the long Island, & passing not far from them, put them again into great Fears, least any Body should land there. However, they continued there 'till about 9 at Night, when the young Pretender, Miss MacDonald, & one Mac Achran, with five Men for the Boat's Crew, imbarked & put to Sea, Lady Clan Ronald having provided Provisions for the Voiage.

The 29th about 11 in the Morning they got to Sky, near Sir Alexander Mac Donald's House. Here Miss Mac Donald and Mac Achran landed, leaving the young Pretender in the Boat, they went to Sir Alexander Mac Donald's House; and from thence, Miss Mac Donald



211

Miss MacDonald sent for one Donald Mac Donald, who had been in the Rebellion, but had delivered up his Arms some time ago. She employ'd this Person to procure a Boat to carry the young Pretender to Rasay, after acquainting him with their late Voyage & where she had left the young Pretender. Miss Mac Donald stay'd & dined with Lady Margaret Mac Donald; but Mac Donald & Mac Achran returned to the Boat, to inform what was done.

Miss Mac Donald being asked why Rasay was pitched upon for the young Pretender to retreat to; she answered that it was in hopes of meeting Rasay himself, with whom he was to consult for his future Security.

After Dinner, Miss Mac Donald set out for Portree, it being resolved that they should lodge there that Night; but on the Road overtook the young Pretender & Mac Achran. They had been joined by Mac Donald of King's bury. She told them she must call at Kingsbury's House, & desired they would go there also. Here, Miss Mac Donald was taken sick, & therefore with the other two, was desired to stay all Night, which they agreed to. She had a

Left and above: *Flora's statement records how the Prince's female 'disguise' just attracted attention. She persuaded him to change into his own clothes.*

There were various Jacobite plots, risings and invasion attempts down the years, but the most serious came in 1745. The deposed king, James II, was long dead, and his son, James Frances, had declared himself to be James III of England and VIII of Scotland and had been formally recognised as such by France, Spain and the Pope. His son, Charles Edward – Bonnie Prince Charlie to his supporters, the 'Young Pretender' to his enemies – was in his mid-twenties, handsome and haughty. Charles received word from the Scottish Highlands that certain clans would rise to support him if he arrived with French troops. In the event, Charles arrived in Scotland virtually alone, but managed nevertheless to gather support. He enjoyed remarkable success and his army reached as far south as Derby; but the Jacobite army eventually retreated and was defeated at Culloden Moor near Inverness. Charles had picked a bad place to fight, on marshy ground that bogged down his men's famous Highland charge and made them sitting ducks for English artillery. As the battle went to pot, Charles fled the field. It was every man for himself.

The next five months were a mixture of romance and horror. The victorious English hunted down Jacobite rebels, killing suspects and burning farmsteads, but the Prince stayed one step ahead of them. Arisaig, Scalpay, Stornaway – the Prince criss-crossed Scotland's west coast and the Hebrides, never once betrayed in spite of a £30,000 bounty on his head. He was hiding on the island of Benbecula when he met Flora MacDonald.

*At this time, he appeared in woman's clothes, his face being partly concealed by a hood or cloak.*

Samuel Johnson later described Flora as 'a woman of soft features, gentle manners, kind soul and elegant presence'; and a portrait shows her handsome face and level gaze. Asked why she had helped Charles, Flora replied that she would have helped anyone in his position of distress. She was visiting her brother and on her way to Skye when she was told that Charles was in hiding in the nearby hills. She agreed to take him with her, dressed as her maid and travelling under the name Betty Burke. A government ship cruised menacingly past Benbecula, convincing the pair that they needed to move fast. This was the famous crossing:

*Saturday, 25 June, the Cutter and Wherrier, which attended General Campbell having got from Bernera, near the Harris, through to the last side of the long island, & passing not far from them, put them again into great fears, lest anybody should land there. However, they continued there till about 9 at night when the young Pretender, Miss MacDonald and one MacAchran, with five men for the boats crew, embarked & put to sea, Lady Clan Ronald having provided provisions for the voyage. The 29th about 11 in the morning they got to Skye.*

A beautiful couple, a hunted prince, Scottish mists, a beautiful island – the poetic muses must have been having fits. At Skye, the Prince hid among the rocks while Flora found help. Flora's declaration shows that Charles's choice of disguise was probably a mistake. She, the Prince and a companion stayed at the house of MacDonald of Kingsbury:

*At this time, he appeared in woman's clothes, his face being partly concealed by a hood or cloak. Being asked, if while they were at Kingsbury's house, any of the family enquired who the disguised person was: answers, that they did not ask; but that she observed the people of the family whispering as if they suspected him to be some person that desired not to be known and from the servants she found they suspected him to be MacLeod of Bernera, who had been in Rebellion. But being pressed to declare what she knew or believed of Kingsbury's knowledge of his guests, owns, that she believes he must suspect it was the young Pretender.*

Flora had better sense than the Prince:

*30 June, Miss MacDonald set out on horseback from Kingsbury's house for Portree, having first desired the young Pretender might put on his own clothes somewhere on the road to Portree, as she had observed that the other dress made him the more suspected.*

Charles eventually boarded a French frigate and by the autumn was back in France. He would spend the rest of his life in exile. When his father died in 1766, even the Pope declined to recognise Charles as king. A late portrait shows the beautiful young Prince turned blotchy, bitter, defeated. Jacobite hopes were dead.

The Skye boatmen gossiped about the mysterious Betty Burke (Flora had been right about that dress), and Flora was turned over to the authorities. She made this declaration in typically forthright style, before being briefly imprisoned in the Tower of London. She later married a captain in the British Army and emigrated to North Carolina to fight for the Loyalists, before returning to Skye, where she died in 1790. But it was in that brief overnight journey that she would be immortalised.

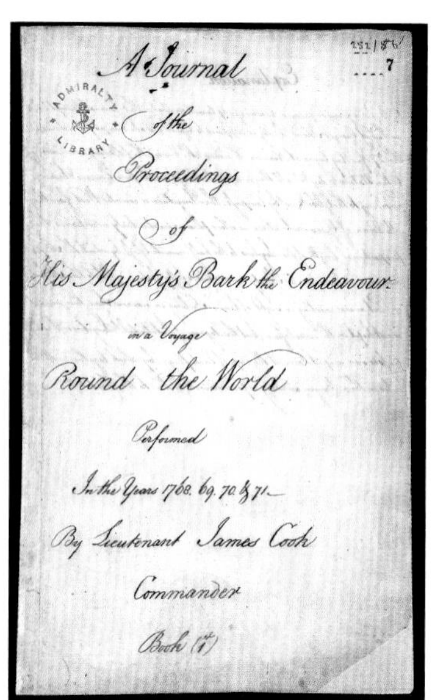

A Journal
of the
Proceedings
of
His Majesty's Bark the Endeavour
in a Voyage
Round the World
Performed
In the Years 1768, 69, 70 & 71
By Lieutenant James Cook
Commander
Book (1)

# FIRST CONTACT
## Captain Cook's Journals

## 1770

LEFT: *The National Archives holds Captain Cook's journals from his voyages of exploration; here is the one from his voyage on the* Endeavour.

CAN YOU PREDICT the future from what has happened in the past? Sometimes you find uncanny templates that are repeated, and repeated, and repeated again. The National Archives holds Captain Cook's journals of his voyages of exploration, and the page opposite describes his first contact with Australian Aborigines a few days after he had reached the eastern coast of Australia. The encounter follows a pattern that would become familiar down the years.

Cook was a Yorkshireman, the son of a farm labourer. He first tasted life at sea by working on coal boats along the English coast, then joined the merchant navy and progressed through the ranks before joining the Royal Navy. He had a talent for cartography, and he was put to surveying the coastline of Newfoundland. He produced a map so accurate that it was used well into the twentieth century.

Cook was the right man at the right place, arriving on the scene just as British overseas exploration was becoming less about derring-do and more about serious science. In 1766, Cook was engaged to ferry a shipload of scientists to Tahiti to observe the transit of Venus across the face of the sun, as part of a wider experiment to calculate the distance from the earth to the sun. Cook was then to explore the South Pacific and seek out the legendary *Terra Australis* (Land of the South). Cook found New Zealand and mapped its coastline, before heading westwards. On 19 April 1770, he sighted Australia for the first time.

Cook turned north and ten days later sailed into Botany Bay, named by him for the quantity of plants gathered there by two botanists on his ship. But plants were not all that the Europeans found.

Aboriginal Australians had had the continent to themselves for some 50,000 years, possibly arriving from Africa via southeast Asia. More than 400 distinct aboriginal peoples have been identified across the continent. The tribe who lived around Botany Bay was the Gweagal, or 'fire clan'. They were a settled tribe, living well off the region's fertile soil and rich sea life. They usually went about naked, their skin sometimes decorated with a sacred white clay. For weapons they used ground stone axes and bone-tipped spears. Cook's journal takes up the story:

OPPOSITE: *This page records the very first encounter between Captain Cook and Australian Aborigines, when he took a small boat ashore at Botany Bay. It was not a success. Even the Polynesian guide couldn't speak the language and the local tribespeople were suspicious of these strangers.*

# East Coast of New Holland

April 1770. Sunday 29

Botany Bay

In the PM Wind Southerly clear weatr with which we stood into
the Bay & Anchd under the So Shore about 2 Miles within the Entrance in 6 fam
the South Point bearing S E & the No Point Et, saw as we came in on both Points
of the bay several of the Natives & a few Hutts Men Women & Children on the So
Shore abreast of the Ship to which Place I went with the Boat accompanied by Mr Banks, Dr Solander & Tupia. as we approached the Shore they
all made off except 2 Men who seem'd resolv'd to oppose our Landing as
soon as I saw this I order'd the Boats to lay upon their Oars in order to Speak
to them but this was to little Purpose for neither us nor Tupia could under
stand one Word they said, We then threw them some Nails beads &c. ashore
which they took up & seem'd not ill Pleased in so much that I thought that
they Beckoned to us to come ashore but in this we were Mistaken for
as soon as We put the Boat in, they again Came to oppose us upon which I
fir'd a Musquet between the 2 which had no other effect than to make them
retire back where bundles of their Darts lay & one of them took up a Stone & threw
at us which caused my firing a second Musquet load with small Shott
& altho' some of the Shott struck the Man yet it had no other Effect than to
make him lay hold of a Shield or Target to defend himself, immediately
after this we landed which we had no sooner done than they throw'd 2
Darts at us this obliged me to fire a third Shott soon after which they
both made off, but not in such haste but what we might have taken one
but Mr Banks, being of Opinion that the Darts were Poison'd made me
cautious how I advanced into the Woods. we found here a few small
Hutts made of the Bark of Trees, in one of which were 4 or 5 small Children
with whom we left some strings of beads &c. a Quantity of Darts lay abt
the Hutts these we took away with us, 3 Canoes lay upon the beach the
worst I think I ever saw they were about 12 or 14 feet long made of one piece
of the Bark of a Tree drawn or tied up at each end & the Middle kept
open by Means of Pieces of Sticks by way of Thwarts; after Searching
for Fresh Water without Success except a little in a Small hole dug in the
Sand we Embarqued & went over to the No Point of the bay were in coming
in we saw several People but when we now landed there were no
body to be seen, we found here some Fresh Water which came trickling
down & stood in Pools among the Rocks but as it was troublesome to come
at I sent a Party of Men ashore in the Morning to the place were we first
landed to dig holes in the Sand ~~[illegible]~~ but searching more narrowly than we had done they found a small Stream ~~[illegible]~~
of fresh Water more than sufficient to Water the Ship, the Strings of beads &c. we
had left with the Children last Night were found laying in the Hutt this

April 1770
Botany Bay

morning Probably the Natives were afraid to take them away after breakfast we sent some Empty Casks ashore & a party of men to cutt Wood & I went my self in the Pinnace to sound & explore the bay, in the doing of which I saw several of the Natives but they all fled at my approach, I landed in 2 places one of which the People had but just left, as there were Small fires & fresh Muscles broiling upon them here likewise large heaps of the Largest Oyster Shells I ever saw

Monday 30 As soon as the Wooders & Waterers were come onb.d to Dinner 10 or 12 of the Natives came to the Watering place & took away their Canoes that lay there but did not offer to touch any one of our Casks that had been left ashore & in the afternoon 16 or 18 of them came boldly up to within 100 Yards of our People at the Watering place & there made a Stand. Mr Hicks who was the Officer ashore did all in his Power to entice them to him by Offering them presents &c. but it was to no Purpose all they seem'd to want was for us to be gone, after staying a short time they went away they were all Arm'd with Darts & wooden swords. the Darts have each 4 Prongs & pointed with fish bones, those we have seen seem to be intended more for striking fish than offensive Weapons, neither are they Poisoned as we at first thought after I had return'd from sounding the bay I went over to a Cove on the No. side where in ~~with~~ 3 or 4 Hauls with the Sean we caught above 300 Pounds weight of fish which I caused to be equally divided among the Ships Company. In the A.M. I went in the Pinnace to sound & explore the No. side of the Bay where I neither met with inhabitants or any thing re=markable, Mr Green took the Suns Meridian Alt.de a little within the So. Entrance of the Bay which gave the Lat.de 34:0 S.

Tuesday 1 Gentle breezes Northerly In the P.M. 10 of the Natives again Visited the Watering place I being onb.d at this time went immediately ashore but before I got there they were going away, I followed them alone & unarm'd some distance along shore but they would not Stop until they got farther off than I choose to trust my self, these were Arm'd in the same Manner as those that came yesterday, In the evening I sent some hands to haul the Sain but they caught but a very few fish, A little after sun rise I found the Var.n to be 11.3 E.t last Night Forby Sutherland Seaman departed this Life in the A.M. his body was buried ashore at the Watering place which occasioned my calling the So. Point of this bay after his Name

This morning a Party of us went ashore to some Hutts not far from the Watering place where some of the Natives are daily seen, here we left several Articles such as Cloth, looking Glasses, Combs, beads &c.

Opposite: *For some days Cook lay at anchor in Botany Bay. The Gweagal kept a wary distance.*
Right: *This is a letter in which Cook requests the listed mathematical instruments for his voyage on the* Endeavour *(dated 8 July 1768).*

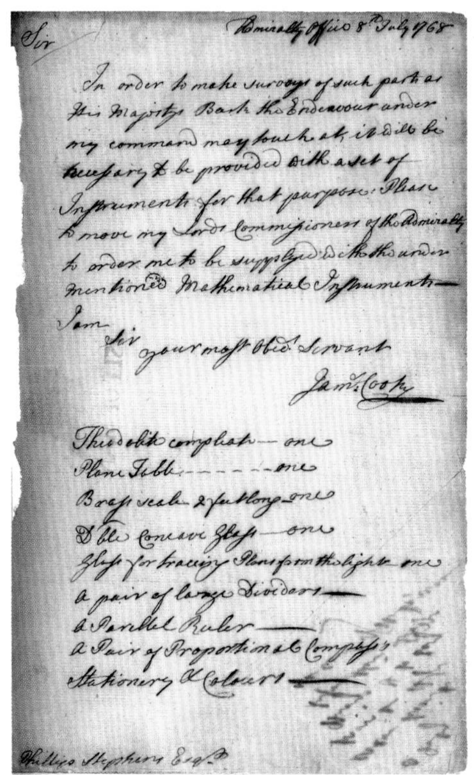

Admiralty Office 8th July 1768

Sir

In order to make surveys of such parts as His Majesty's Bark the Endeavour under my command may touch at, it will be necessary to be provided with a set of Instruments for that purpose. Please to move my Lords Commissioners of the Admiralty to order me to be supplyed with the under mentioned Mathematical Instruments —

I am
Sir your most Obed.t Servant
Jam.s Cook

Theodolite compleat — one
Plane Table — one
Brass scale 2 feet long — one
Dble Concave Glass — one
Glass for tracing Plans from the light — one
A pair of large Dividers —
A Parallel Ruler —
A Pair of Proportional Compasses
Stationery & Colours —

Phillips Stephens Esq.r

*April 1770, Sunday 29th 'Botany Bay'. The wind southerly clear, with which we entered the Bay …* [we] *saw as we came on both points of the Bay several of the natives and a few huts men, women with children on the shore abreast of the ship to which place I went with the boat accompanied by Mr Banks, Dr Solender and Tupia* [Cook's Polynesian guide]. *As we approached the shore they all made off except 2 men who seemed resolved to oppose our landings as soon as I saw this I ordered the boat to lay upon their Oars in order to speak to them but this was of little purpose for neither us nor Tupia could understand one word they said. We then threw them some nails, beads &c, ashore which they took up and seemed not ill pleased in so much that I thought that they beckoned to us to come ashore but in this we were mistaken for as soon as we put the boat in they again came to oppose us upon which I fixed a musket between the 2 which had no other effect than to make them retire back where bundles of their darts lay. One of them took up a stone and threw at us which caused my firing a second musket load with small shot and although some of the shot struck the man yet it had no other effect than to make him lay hold of a shield or target to defend himself. Immediately after this we landed which we had no sooner done than they throw'd 2 darts at us. This obliged me to fire a third shot soon after which they both made off but not in such haste but what we might have taken one but Mr Banks, being of the opinion that the darts were poisoned made me cautious. Now I advanced into the woods, we found here a few small huts made of the bark of trees, in one of which were 4 or 5 small children with whom we left some strings of beads &c. A quantity of darts lay about the huts those we took away with us. Three canoes lay upon the beach, the worst I think I ever saw … after searching for fresh water without success except a little in a small hole dug in the sand we embarked and went over to the northern point of the bay where in coming in we saw several people but when we now landed there were nobody to be seen.'*

So, first the Europeans attempted to bribe the Gweagal with a bag of nails, then they shot at them. This was not a good start.

Cook anchored in the bay for eight days. The Gweagal went about their daily affairs, fishing from their canoes, cooking on the shoreline, walking on the beach, all the time keeping a cautious distance from the Europeans. Cook then headed north, charting Australia's eastern coast. He carried with him a bundle of Gweagal spears, which you can see today in Cambridge University's Museum of Archaeology and Anthropology. Having reached Australia's northern tip, Cook struck out for England, via Jakarta and the Cape of Good Hope.

The Gweagal came away from this first contact not too bruised. The real horror would come eighteen years later. Eleven British ships returned to Botany Bay, carrying over 1,500 men and women, including 736 convicts. Within weeks, smallpox, chickenpox, influenza and measles were devastating the tribe.

# LONGMAN *and* LUKEY: MUSIC PIRATES

## Bach Chancery Proceedings

ABOVE: *Johann Christian Bach, musician, composer, and the first man in Britain to take action in the Courts against music piracy.*

# 1773

OPPOSITE: *The music pirates' defence is written in legalese, but is remarkably similar to modern equivalents.*

SINCE THE EARLIEST years of the internet, the owners of copyright in films, TV and music have fought with hip young downloaders, typified by websites such as Napster, Grokster and Pirate Bay. This document comes from a case that is the godfather of those modern battles. This is music piracy, eighteenth-century style.

Johann Christian Bach was the youngest son of the more famous Johann Sebastian Bach. He was music master to Queen Charlotte, wife of George III, and a composer of operas and arias. He is best known for a popular concert series at Vauxhall Pleasure Gardens.

Bach had composed a pair of sonatas for the harpsichord, but found that they had been copied by a publishing partnership called Longman & Lukey. Copying like this was endemic, and since composers made their real money from patronage and performance, no one had challenged the practice. But Bach was not having it. He decided to sue.

This document is Longman & Lukey's defence. It is written in near-impenetrable legalese, but what they have to say is remarkably similar to their web-based descendants: '[We] do not know have not heard nor do believe ... whether any and what [copyright] licence ... was ... granted by his present Majesty to him said Johan Christian Bach.' (Copyright? Belonging to this fellow? We don't know anything about that.) 'For anything they may be these defendants or either of them respectively know to the contrary the said J.C. Bach might compose and write a certain musical composition for the harpsichord called a sonata' (... maybe he did write a tune ...) 'But whether such sonatas were in the same as hereinafter mentioned these defendants know not' (... but don't ask if this one was by him, we don't know, and anyway ...) 'On or about the month of December last one Adolphus H. Hummel late of Hafson Street, Soho, a very intimate acquaintance of the said complainant J.C.Bach ... applied to them these defendants ... and informed them these defendants that the said complainant J.C. Bach has made him a present of the two harpsichord sonatas.' (... Bach gave them to his friend, Hummel, who gave them to us, see?)

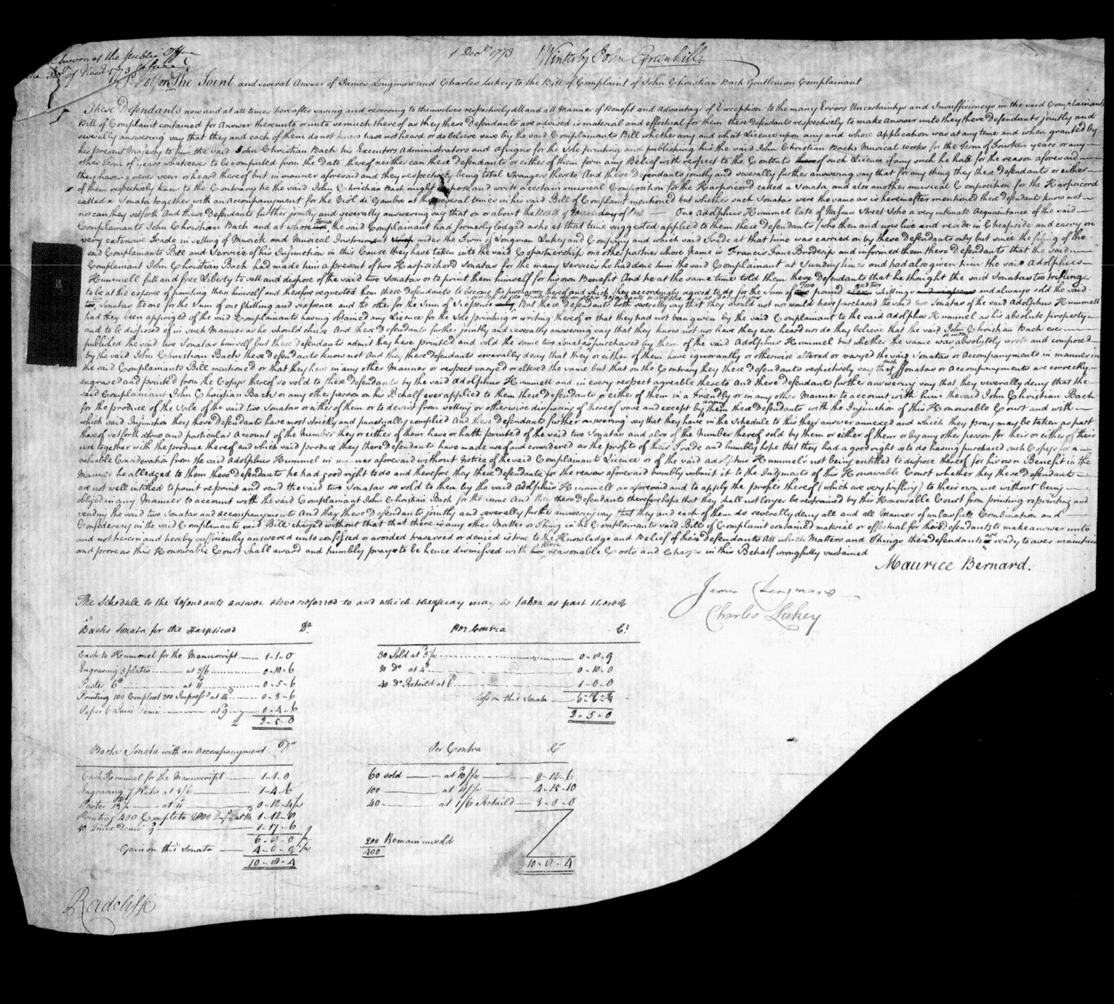

Longman & Lukey were trying to muddy the facts but, that aside, there was a serious point of law to be decided. Did the 1710 Statute of Anne, the world's first public copyright law, cover music publishing? The court held that it did. Longman & Lukey were sunk.

Parallels of experience between the twenty-first and eighteenth centuries continued after the trial. When the pirate website Napster was injuncted by the US courts in 2001, it transformed itself into a successful website from which you can now legally download licensed music. Longman & Lukey settled the case against them and made up with Bach. A few years later they were publishing his works, this time with permission. Not only that, but they began to wield copyright law themselves, attacking other publishers who copied their work. There is nothing new under the sun.

# 'LIFE, LIBERTY *and the* PURSUIT *of* HAPPINESS'
## US Declaration of Independence

## 1776

ABOVE: *Thomas Jefferson, the young representative of Virginia, who drafted the US Declaration of Independence.*
OPPOSITE: *After its soaring opening, most of the Declaration is a list of grievances against George III.*

On 4 July 1776, America declared its independence from Britain. The signed Declaration is the jewel in the crown of the US National Archives. It is the centrepiece of a marbled and muralled rotunda, flanked by American flags, its title picked out in letters carved in stone and gilded in gold. The day that the Declaration was adopted is an American national holiday.

Britain has a copy. It sits in a corner of the National Archives' small museum, marked with a white label – the ultimate 'Dear John' letter.

America's War of Independence was prompted by a series of British Acts that imposed taxes on its colony, as Britain scrabbled for money after its Seven Years' War with the French (known in America as the French and Indian War). The taxes provoked bitter resentment. The American colonies were not represented in Parliament, and 'No Taxation Without Representation!' became their rallying cry.

Protesting American militias enjoyed early successes against the British colonial army, but by 1776 things were not looking good. An armada of forty-five British ships sailed the Atlantic and dropped anchor off New York. Thousands of experienced troops began to disembark, ready to take on America's rag-tag army of merchants and farm boys. Ninety miles south, at the Second Continental Congress in Philadelphia, politicians from each of the thirteen American states took a step designed to stir the souls of their men – a declaration of national independence.

The Declaration's second paragraph opens with one of the most potent and enduring sentences ever written, a defining statement of American identity: 'We hold these truths to be self-evident, that all men are created equal, that they are endowed by their Creator with certain unalienable Rights, that among these are Life, Liberty and the pursuit of Happiness.' The words were drafted by Thomas Jefferson, the 33-year-old representative of Virginia. 'Life, Liberty and the pursuit of Happiness' is a phrase that Jefferson most likely drew from the English philosopher John Locke, who had written about 'life, liberty and estate [i.e. property]'. Jefferson's 'pursuit of Happiness' fills Locke's crabby phrase with light.

# IN CONGRESS, JULY 4, 1776.

# A DECLARATION

## BY THE REPRESENTATIVES OF THE

# UNITED STATES OF AMERICA,

## IN GENERAL CONGRESS ASSEMBLED.

WHEN in the Courſe of human Events, it becomes neceſſary for one People to diſſolve the Political Bands which have connected them with another, and to aſſume among the Powers of the Earth, the ſeparate and equal Station to which the Laws of Nature and of Nature's God entitle them, a decent Reſpect to the Opinions of Mankind requires that they ſhould declare the cauſes which impel them to the Separation.

WE hold theſe Truths to be ſelf-evident, that all Men are created equal, that they are endowed by their Creator with certain unalienable Rights, that among theſe are Life, Liberty, and the Purſuit of Happineſs—That to ſecure theſe Rights, Governments are inſtituted among Men, deriving their juſt Powers from the Conſent of the Governed, that whenever any Form of Government becomes deſtructive of theſe Ends, it is the Right of the People to alter or to aboliſh it, and to inſtitute new Government, laying its Foundation on ſuch Principles, and organizing its Powers in ſuch Form, as to them ſhall ſeem moſt likely to effect their Safety and Happineſs. Prudence, indeed, will dictate that Governments long eſtabliſhed ſhould not be changed for light and tranſient Cauſes; and accordingly all Experience hath ſhewn, that Mankind are more diſpoſed to ſuffer, while Evils are ſufferable, than to right themſelves by aboliſhing the Forms to which they are accuſtomed. But when a long Train of Abuſes and Uſurpations, purſuing invariably the ſame Object, evinces a Deſign to reduce them under abſolute Deſpotiſm, it is their Right, it is their Duty, to throw off ſuch Government, and to provide new Guards for their future Security. Such has been the patient Sufferance of theſe Colonies; and ſuch is now the Neceſſity which conſtrains them to alter their former Syſtems of Government. The Hiſtory of the preſent King of Great-Britain is a Hiſtory of repeated Injuries and Uſurpations, all having in direct Object the Eſtabliſhment of an abſolute Tyranny over theſe States. To prove this, let Facts be ſubmitted to a candid World.

HE has refuſed his Aſſent to Laws, the moſt wholeſome and neceſſary for the public Good.

HE has forbidden his Governors to paſs Laws of immediate and preſſing Importance, unleſs ſuſpended in their Operation till his Aſſent ſhould be obtained; and when ſo ſuſpended, he has utterly neglected to attend to them.

HE has refuſed to paſs other Laws for the Accommodation of large Diſtricts of People, unleſs thoſe People would relinquiſh the Right of Repreſentation in the Legiſlature, a Right ineſtimable to them, and formidable to Tyrants only.

HE has called together Legiſlative Bodies at Places unuſual, uncomfortable, and diſtant from the Depoſitory of their public Records, for the ſole Purpoſe of fatiguing them into Compliance with his Meaſures.

HE has diſſolved Repreſentative Houſes repeatedly, for oppoſing with manly Firmneſs his Invaſions on the Rights of the People.

HE has refuſed for a long Time, after ſuch Diſſolutions, to cauſe others to be elected; whereby the Legiſlative Powers, incapable of Annihilation, have returned to the People at large for their exerciſe; the State remaining in the mean time expoſed to all the Dangers of Invaſion from without, and Convulſions within.

HE has endeavoured to prevent the Population of theſe States; for that Purpoſe obſtructing the Laws for Naturalization of Foreigners; refuſing to paſs others to encourage their Migrations hither, and raiſing the Conditions of new Appropriations of Lands.

HE has obſtructed the Adminiſtration of Juſtice, by refuſing his Aſſent to Laws for eſtabliſhing Judiciary Powers.

HE has made Judges dependent on his Will alone, for the Tenure of their Offices, and the Amount and Payment of their Salaries.

HE has erected a Multitude of new Offices, and ſent hither Swarms of Officers to harraſs our People, and eat out their Subſtance.

HE has kept among us, in Times of Peace, Standing Armies, without the conſent of our Legiſlatures.

HE has affected to render the Military independent of and ſuperior to the Civil Power.

HE has combined with others to ſubject us to a Juriſdiction foreign to our Conſtitution, and unacknowledged by our Laws; giving his Aſſent to their Acts of pretended Legiſlation:

FOR quartering large Bodies of Armed Troops among us:

FOR protecting them, by a mock Trial, from Puniſhment for any Murders which they ſhould commit on the Inhabitants of theſe States:

FOR cutting off our Trade with all Parts of the World:

FOR impoſing Taxes on us without our Conſent:

FOR depriving us, in many Caſes, of the Benefits of Trial by Jury:

FOR tranſporting us beyond Seas to be tried for pretended Offences:

FOR aboliſhing the free Syſtem of Engliſh Laws in a neighbouring Province, eſtabliſhing therein an arbitrary Government, and enlarging its Boundaries, ſo as to render it at once an Example and fit Inſtrument for introducing the ſame abſolute Rule into theſe Colonies:

FOR taking away our Charters, aboliſhing our moſt valuable Laws, and altering fundamentally the Forms of our Governments:

FOR ſuſpending our own Legiſlatures, and declaring themſelves inveſted with Power to legiſlate for us in all Caſes whatſoever.

HE has abdicated Government here, by declaring us out of his Protection and waging War againſt us.

HE has plundered our Seas, ravaged our Coaſts, burnt our Towns, and deſtroyed the Lives of our People.

HE is, at this Time, tranſporting large Armies of foreign Mercenaries to compleat the Works of Death, Deſolation, and Tyranny, already begun with circumſtances of Cruelty and Perfidy, ſcarcely paralleled in the moſt barbarous Ages, and totally unworthy the Head of a civilized Nation.

HE has conſtrained our fellow Citizens taken Captive on the high Seas to bear Arms againſt their Country, to become the Executioners of their Friends and Brethren, or to fall themſelves by their Hands.

HE has excited domeſtic Inſurrections amongſt us, and has endeavoured to bring on the Inhabitants of our Frontiers, the mercileſs Indian Savages, whoſe known Rule of Warfare, is an undiſtinguiſhed Deſtruction, of all Ages, Sexes and Conditions.

IN every ſtage of theſe Oppreſſions we have Petitioned for Redreſs in the moſt humble Terms: Our repeated Petitions have been anſwered only by repeated Injury. A Prince, whoſe Character is thus marked by every act which may define a Tyrant, is unfit to be the Ruler of a free People.

NOR have we been wanting in Attentions to our Brittiſh Brethren. We have warned them from Time to Time of Attempts by their Legiſlature to extend an unwarrantable Juriſdiction over us. We have reminded them of the Circumſtances of our Emigration and Settlement here. We have appealed to their native Juſtice and Magnanimity, and we have conjured them by the Ties of our common Kindred to diſavow theſe Uſurpations, which, would inevitably interrupt our Connections and Correſpondence. They too have been deaf to the Voice of Juſtice and of Conſanguinity. We muſt, therefore, acquieſce in the Neceſſity, which denounces our Separation, and hold them, as we hold the reſt of Mankind, Enemies in War, in Peace, Friends.

WE, therefore, the Repreſentatives of the UNITED STATES OF AMERICA, in GENERAL CONGRESS, Aſſembled, appealing to the Supreme Judge of the World for the Rectitude of our Intentions, do, in the Name, and by Authority of the good People of theſe Colonies, ſolemnly Publiſh and Declare, That theſe United Colonies are, and of Right ought to be, FREE AND INDEPENDENT STATES; that they are abſolved from all Allegiance to the Britiſh Crown, and that all political Connection between them and the State of Great-Britain, is and ought to be totally diſſolved; and that as FREE AND INDEPENDENT STATES, they have full Power to levy War, conclude Peace, contract Alliances, eſtabliſh Commerce, and to do all other Acts and Things which INDEPENDENT STATES may of right do. And for the ſupport of this Declaration, with a firm Reliance on the Protection of divine Providence, we mutually pledge to each other our Lives, our Fortunes, and our ſacred Honor.

*Signed by* ORDER *and in* BEHALF *of the* CONGRESS,

JOHN HANCOCK, PRESIDENT.

ATTEST.
CHARLES THOMSON, SECRETARY.

38

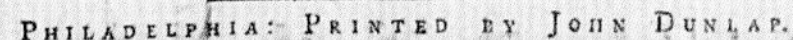
PHILADELPHIA: PRINTED BY JOHN DUNLAP.

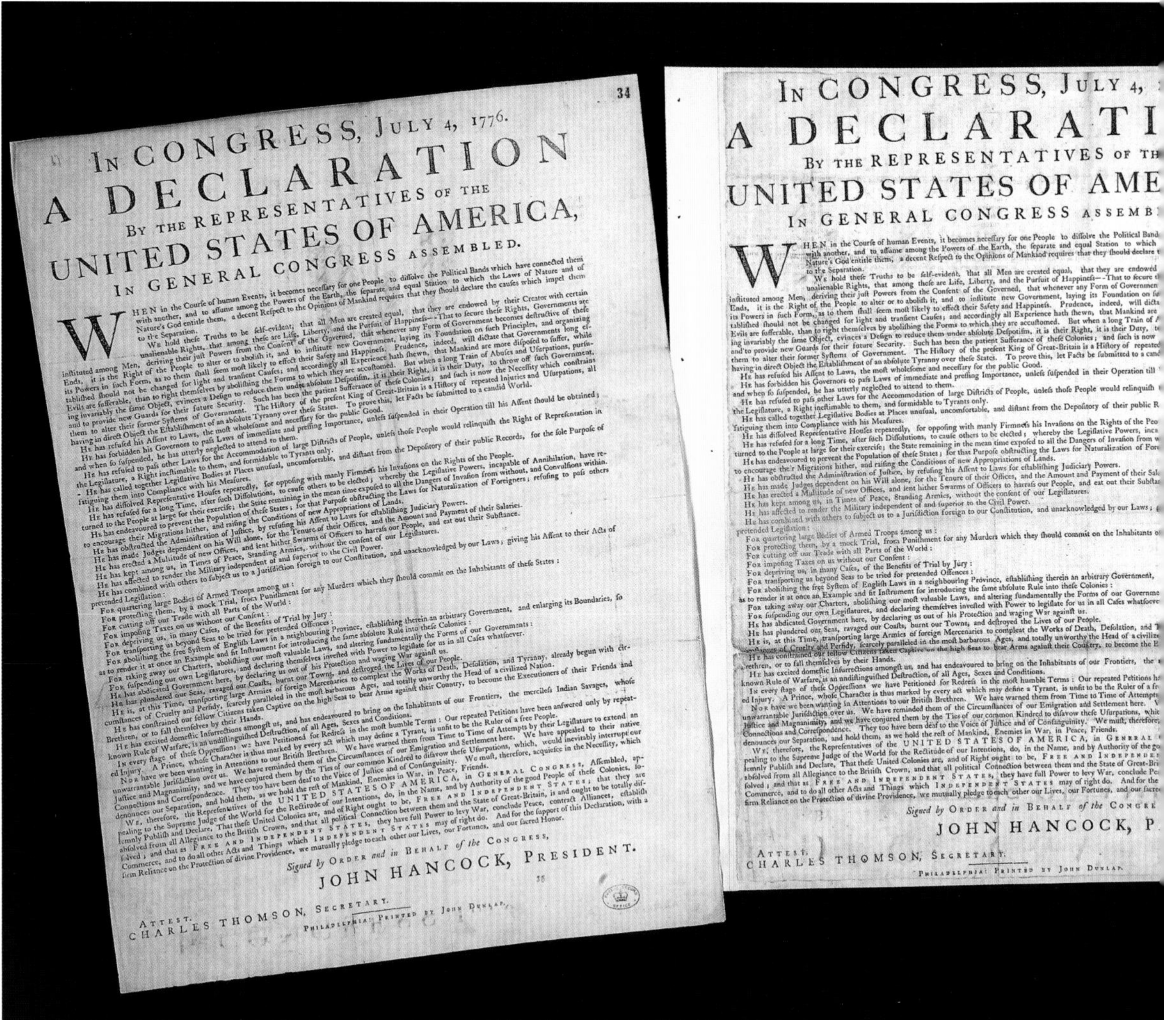

IN CONGRESS, JULY 4, 1776.

A DECLARATION

BY THE REPRESENTATIVES OF THE

UNITED STATES OF AMERICA,

IN GENERAL CONGRESS ASSEMBLED.

Signed by ORDER and in BEHALF of the CONGRESS,

JOHN HANCOCK, PRESIDENT.

ATTEST.
CHARLES THOMSON, SECRETARY.

PHILADELPHIA: PRINTED BY JOHN DUNLAP.

After this soaring start, the rest of the Declaration is a little disappointing. It says that the people have a right to abolish any government that does not achieve these ends, and then sets out the ways in which the king of Great Britain has fallen short: 'a history of repeated injuries and usurpations, all having in direct object the establishment of an absolute Tyranny over these States'. What follows is a charge sheet against George III, a list of grievances dating back a decade or more. The Declaration culminates in the dissolution of America's ties with Great Britain.

For all of the boldness of the Declaration, the final sentence betrays anxiety: 'And for the support of this Declaration, with a firm reliance on the protection of divine Providence, we mutually pledge to each other our Lives, our Fortunes, and our sacred Honor.' If the Declaration was going to survive, the Patriots knew that they were going to need God's grace, and one another.

After two days of debate (in which a quarter of Jefferson's original draft, which condemned slavery, was deleted), the Declaration was ratified by Congress. That evening, the words were rushed to the offices of a printer, twenty-nine-year-old Irish immigrant John Dunlap, who spent much of the night typesetting and

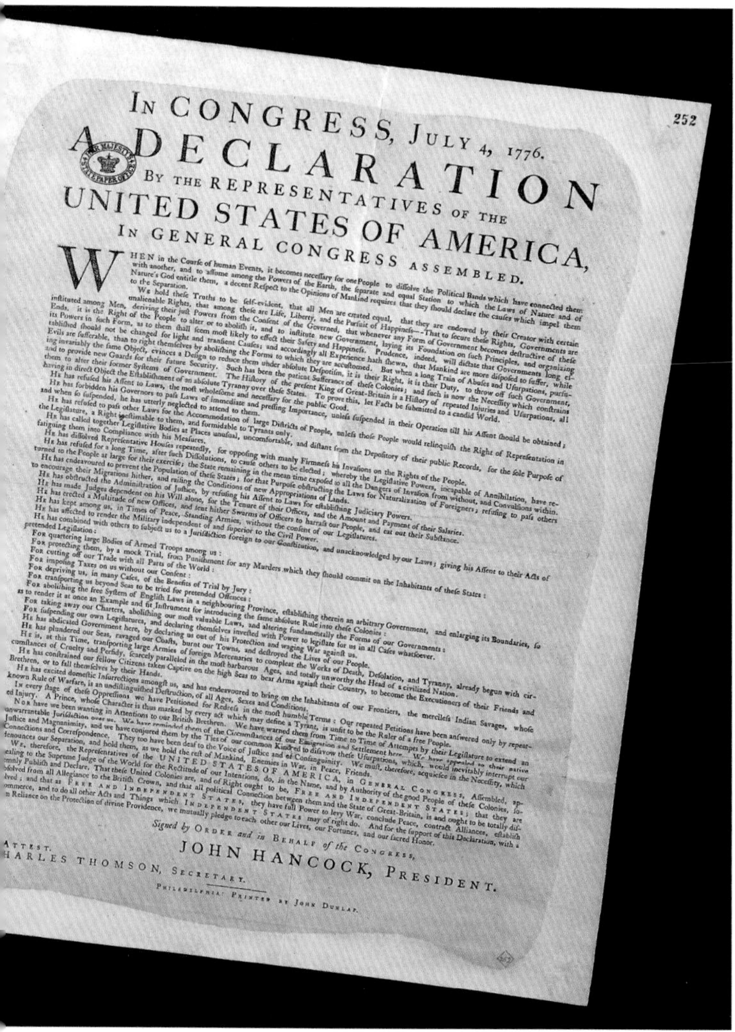

IN CONGRESS, JULY 4, 1776.

A DECLARATION

BY THE REPRESENTATIVES OF THE

UNITED STATES OF AMERICA,

IN GENERAL CONGRESS ASSEMBLED.

Signed by ORDER and in BEHALF of the CONGRESS,

JOHN HANCOCK, PRESIDENT.

ATTEST.

CHARLES THOMSON, SECRETARY.

PHILADELPHIA: PRINTED BY JOHN DUNLAP.

*'And for the support of this Declaration, with a firm reliance on the protection of divine Providence, we mutually pledge to each other our Lives, our Fortunes, and our sacred Honor.' If the Declaration was going to survive, the Patriots knew that they were going to need God's grace, and one another.*

ABOVE: *Three of the twenty-six 'Dunlap Broadsides' known to exist are in the UK's National Archives, the ultimate 'Dear John' letters. It is not known how each of these made its way across the Atlantic.*

running off around 200 copies. These 'Dunlap Broadsides' were quickly distributed across America. As British troops massed on Staten Island, Washington had one read out to his troops in New York, to loud cheers. Soldiers and townspeople were inspired to pull down a gilded statute of King George that stood in the middle of the city. They mounted its head on a spike.

The Declaration was first and foremost a rallying cry for Americans, but nevertheless three of the Broadsides found their way to the British, crossed the Atlantic, and now lie in the National Archives. Wouldn't you love to have seen the reaction of the first British readers? Was it sorrow that this would now be a war without compromise? Amusement at the presumption of these uppity colonials? An indifferent shrug? In any case, the Declaration had been made, and it would change the world.

JAN
TEERLINK,
TE VLISSINGEN.
Protea cynaroides

# *The* LETTERS *that* NEVER ARRIVED

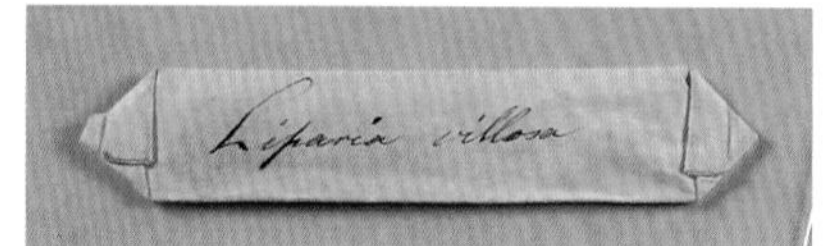


## Documents Captured in the Anglo-Dutch Wars

## 1780s *and after*

THESE DOCUMENTS ARE pregnant with possibilities. They are 'prize papers': British, American, Spanish and Dutch letters captured from ships on their way from America to Europe, and delivered to the Prize Court of the British Admiralty. Most of them have never been opened, but those that have afford glimpses into people's day-to-day lives. There are business letters, love letters, humdrum commerce, simple letters home. Many of the addresses they were being sent to still exist today.

One such envelope was sending home seeds, thirty-two different species in forty small packets stored in a red, leather-bound notebook. The seeds were collected by Jan Teerlink, a Dutch merchant, during a trip to the Dutch East Indies and China in 1803. On his return journey, with a cargo of tea and salt, his vessel *Henriette* was captured by the British Navy. All documents on board, including his notebook, were seized and in time wound up in the National Archives. Two hundred years later the seeds were sent to Kew Gardens, where three of the thirty-two species were germinated successfully. The 200-year-old flora comprise a type of Acacia, a yellow-flowered shrub called *Liparia villosa* and a stunning pin-cushion-like flower called *Leucospermum.*

What of those letters that haven't been opened, though? Their 200-year-old seals are still firmly in place. Some seem to be brief notes, others are very thick. What might they contain? The National Archives is full of such secrets.

OPPOSITE AND ABOVE: *Jan Teerlink's captured notebook contains neatly labelled little packets of the seeds he had collected at the Cape of Good Hope, where his ship stopped off on the way back from a trading voyage to the Dutch East Indies.*

*Two hundred years later the seeds were sent to Kew Gardens, where three of the thirty-two species were germinated successfully.*

Aan de wel Edele Groot Achtbare Heeren

Den Heere Representant van Zyne Doorlugtigste Hoogheid & Bewindhebberen van de Edele Generale Geoctroyeerde nederlandsche Westindische Comp^e. ter Respective Kamer

Op de Maze

Per het Schip d' Elisabeth & Sophia Schipper Jan Rontgen D.G.G.

Originele ~~Duplicaat~~ de dato primo February 1781

2 paar witte Kousen
1 wit Hemt
1 royyen zeildoeck

Waarde en Veel Geagte Zoon

hebbe met veel blijdschap Ue brief van 10 deeze
in goede welstand ontvangen hebbe daar uit
Ue welstand verstaan wat ons aanbetreft Ue moeder
zusters en al de vrinde zijn alle nog in een
volmaakte welstand ik heb zedert de tijd van
Ue vertrek na zee zeer ongerust geweest alzoo
wij bevonde dat de wind niet lang oost bleef
en ik dus wel kon begrijpe dat het niet
mogelijk was en door het dikke weer de
hoofden te kunne krijgen en daar op starke
uit de ZW. NW begon te waaijen en door het
hooge water dat het zwaar weer in zee moest
weesen dat ons heel ongerust maakten gen
gelijk ik merk uit Ue schrijve het inderdaad
geweest is hebbe menigmaal gebeeden dat godt
Ue alle mogt behoeden gelijk als gij en wij
reede van dankbaarheid hebben voor zijn godde-
lijke bewaaring tot dus verre wensche dat die
die godt die Ue alle tot dus verre bewaard heeft
Ue alle verders wil bewaaren en geleijde op de
groote wateren hebbe verstaan uit Ue brief
dat Ue gaarne iets tot een verversnapering hadde
zulle al wat te krijgen is Ue zende maar
most

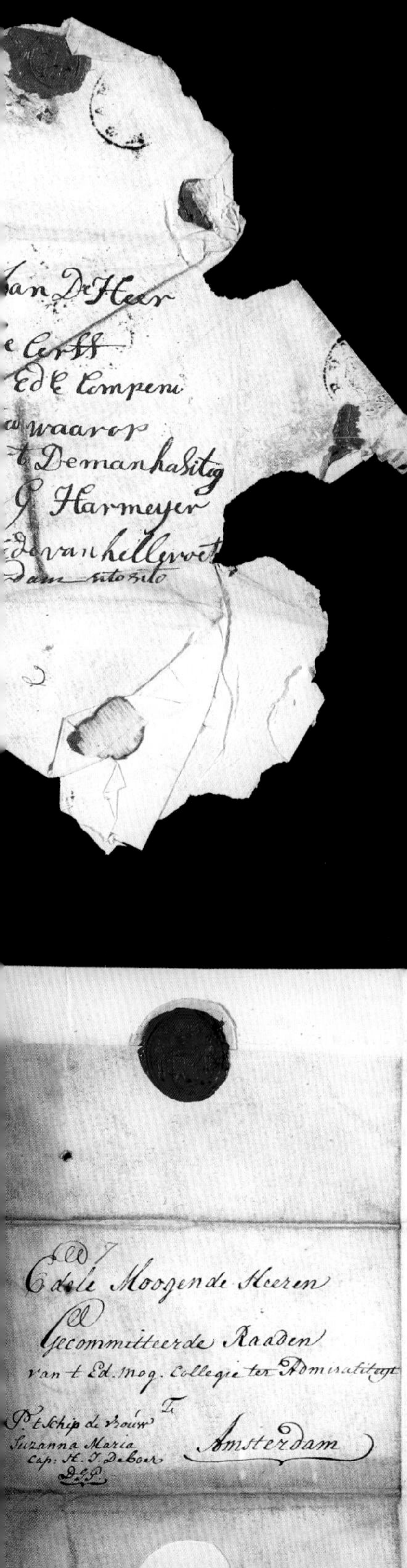

Edele Moogende Heeren
Gecommitteerde Raaden
van t Ed. Mog. Collegie ter Admiraliteyt
Te
Amsterdam
P. t Schip de Vrouw
Suzanna Maria
Cap: H. J. De Boer

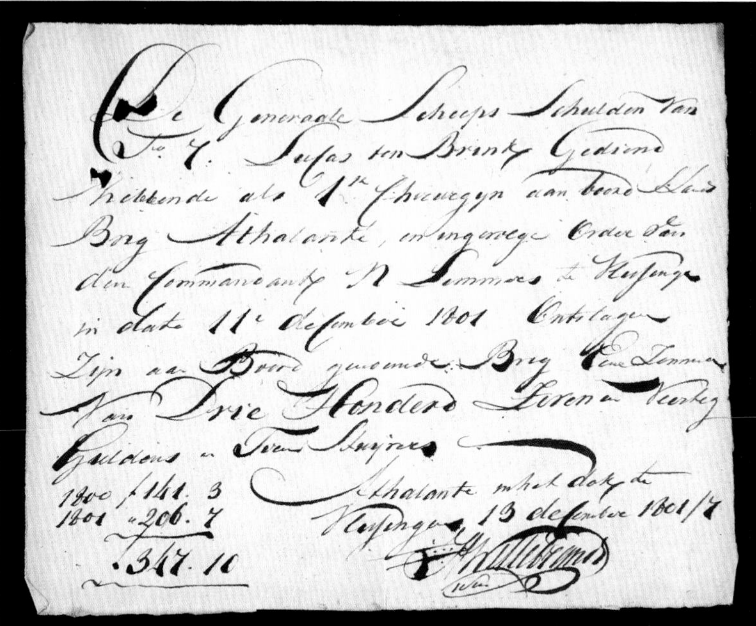

De Generaale Scheeps Schulden van ... Lucas ten Brink Gediend hebbende als 1e Chirurgyn aan boord 's Lands Brig Athalante, en ingevolge Order van den Commandant N. Lemmers te Vlissingen in date 11e december 1801 Ontslagen Zijn aan Boord genoemde Brig Eene Somma van Drie Honderd Zeven en Veertig Guldens en Tien Stuyvers

1800 f 141. 3
1801 „ 206. 7
347. 10

Athalante in het dok te Vlissingen 13 december 1801

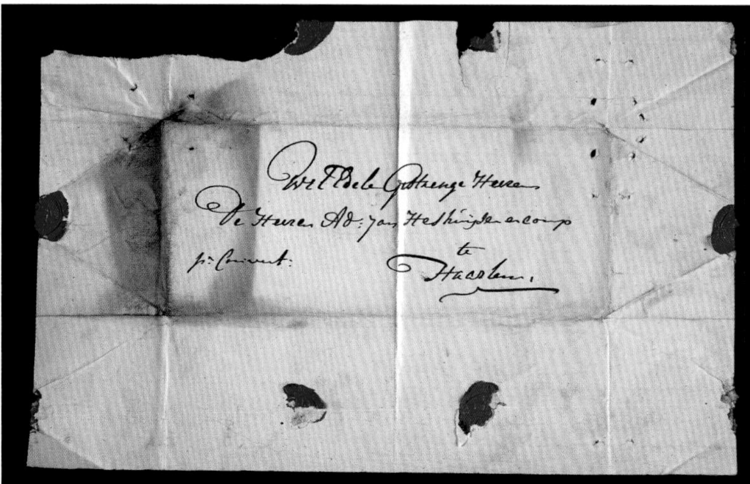

Wel Edele Gestrenge Heeren
De Heeren Ad: van Heshuijsen en comp
p. Couvert
te
Haarlem

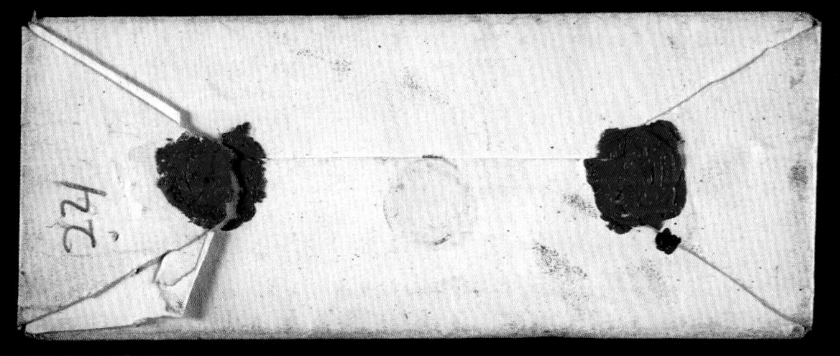

*The captured letters are to addresses, many of which still exist. They are the ordinary stuff of life – business letters, news, complaints, family. Many have never been opened and so still bear their seals.*

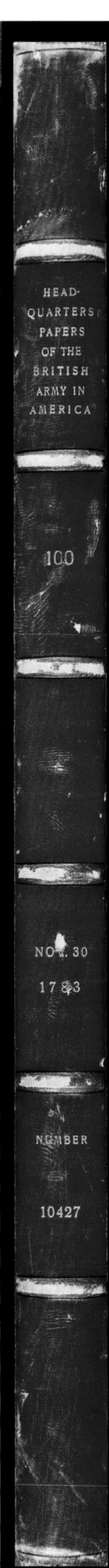


# *On the* EDGE *of* FREEDOM
## The Book of Negroes

LEFT: *The Book of Negroes was compiled in New York in 1783 – Black Loyalists seeking freedom in Nova Scotia.*

1783

IN THE AMERICAN WAR of Independence, Negro slaves were weapons. First the British, and later the Americans, issued declarations that any slave from the other side who deserted to them would be granted their freedom. The intention was to undermine the enemy economically, while providing practical help to their own war effort. Some 20,000 slaves escaped to enlist with the British. Most were non-combatants, but fighting groups included the Black Pioneers and a feared commando unit, the Black Brigade.

After the war was won, America wanted its slaves back. The treaty that ended the war included an agreement that the British Army would withdraw 'without causing any Destruction, or carrying away any Negroes or other Property of the American inhabitants'. Some Black Loyalists were abandoned to re-enslavement. But British leaders in America tried to honour their promise of freedom, by evacuating to Nova Scotia any Black Loyalists who were not claimed by their former masters.

So it was that this book came to be made, in New York, between 23 April and 30 November 1783. It is the list of around 3,000 Black Loyalists applying to be transported to their new lives. It gives each person's name, age, physical description, status, and sometimes their owner's name and place of residence.

Alongside the names and occupations, you can see some cruel last-minute challenges, as slave owners demanded the return of their property. It is difficult to imagine what life would have been like for the people taken this way – not only re-enslaved, but enslaved as runaways and traitors.

Those who made it to Nova Scotia could be allotted tools and parcels of land (smaller and of poorer quality than those given to white settlers, inevitably), or they might make a living from hunting, fishing or in domestic service. Many formed small settlements, the largest of which was Birchtown, which

OPPOSITE: *The opening page of the book quotes the US–British treaty, which forbade 'carrying away any Negroes or other Property'. Former slave owners brought many cruel, last-minute challenges to emigration by Black Loyalists. Some of the people on these pages were on the brink of freedom, but found themselves being led back to slavery.*

10427 (1)

Head Quarters New York 15th April 1783

Orders

It is the Commander in Chiefs Orders that the following Extract from the Seventh Article of the Provisional Treaty between Great Britain and the United States of America be strictly attended to and complied with by all Persons whatsoever under his Command

"And his Britannic Majesty shall, with all convenient Speed,
"and without causing any Destruction, or carrying away
"any Negroes, or other Property, of the American Inhabitants,
"withdraw all his Armies, Garrisons, and Fleets, from the said
"United States, and from every Post, Place, and Harbour, within the
"same; leaving in all Fortifications the American Artillery that
"may be therein, and shall also order and cause all the Archives,
"Records, Deeds, and Papers, belonging to any of the said States,
"or their Citizens, which in the Course of the War may have fallen
"into the Hands of his Officers to be forthwith restored and
"delivered to the proper States and Persons to whom they belong"

All Masters of Vessels are particularly cautioned, at their Peril, not to commit any Breach of the above Article

The Commander in Chief has been pleased to appoint Captain Chads, of the Royal Navy, Captains Gilfillan and Armstrong, Assistant Deputy Quarter master General on his Part, and expresses his Obligations to Hopkins and Parker Esquires, that they have, at his Request, undertaken, until proper Persons shall be authorized by Congress, to attend on the Part of America, to superintend all Embarkations and see that the above Stipulations are strictly observed:- Three of those

*The freed slaves founded what is now the capital of Sierra Leone, Freetown. Many descendants of the people in this book still live in Freetown, and in Nova Scotia.*

became home to 1,500 to 2,000 free souls formed by five companies of the Black Pioneers.

Most of the names on these pages are part of the anonymous masses of history. But we do know the next part of the story of one of the people listed: 'Lydia', a 'maid servant' from South Carolina. This is Lydia Jackson, who went on to settle in Manchester, Nova Scotia. She was persuaded by one Henry Hedley to join his household as a maid. After a few days he demanded money for her board, which of course she could not pay. Hedley then demanded that she repay the 'debt' by becoming his indentured servant. Lydia agreed to service of one year but Hedley tricked her again by having her unwittingly sign a thirty-nine-year indenture, effectively re-enslaving her. He then sold her for £20 to a Dr Bulman. She became pregnant, quite possibly by Bulman himself. Bulman stamped on her as she lay on the ground, eight months pregnant, and she lost the baby. But Lydia was resourceful. She eventually escaped into the woods and made her way to Halifax, where she joined a group led by John Clarkson, to whom she told her story.

Clarkson was leading a group of 1,100 former slaves to form a new colony in Sierra Leone. In 1792, together with half the population of Birchtown, Lydia set sail. The freed slaves founded what is now the capital of Sierra Leone, Freetown. Many descendants of the people in this book still live in Freetown, and in Nova Scotia.

| Vessels Names and their Commanders | Where Bound | Negros Names | Age | Descriptio[n] |
|---|---|---|---|---|
| Ship Hope | St Johns River | Jack Hyde | 50 | Almost past |
| Robt. Peacock Mr. | | Dick | 33 | Stout Fell |
| Ship Sovereign | St Johns River | Corn. Moss | 30 | Do. likely |
| Wm. Steward Mr. | | Thos. Brinkerhoof | 34 | Very short |
| | | Peter Bean | 32 | Likely fello |
| | | Math. Gillman | 46 | Stout short |
| | | George Black | 40 | Stout fellow |
| | | Betsy Black | 35 | Ordinary |
| | | Wm. Black | 11 | Fine boy |
| | | Sam | 30 | Stout |
| | | Luke Spencer | 25 | Do. |
| | | Abigail his Wife | 26 | Stout Wench |
| | | Bill Pigott | 28 | Stout fellow |
| | | Pompey Chase | 28 | Do. |
| | | John Vince | 36 | Do. B |
| | | Dean | 20 | Stout squat |
| Ship Ann & Elizabeth | Port Roseway | Peter Johnson | 35 | Stout fellow |
| Ben. Fowler, Mast. | | Judith Johnson | 27 | Ordinary |
| | | Thos. Danvers | 45 | Do. |
| | | Sarah Cross | 34 | Stout squat |
| | | Henry Spencell | 38 | Slender fel |
| | | Jno. Dunham | 25 | Do. |
| | | Jack Smith | 25 | Do. |
| | | Venus | 23 | Do. |
| | | Sam: Drayton | 40 | Stout Fellow |
| | | Cath. Drayton | 40 | Ordinary W |
| | | Dinah Edmonds | 34 | Do. |
| | | Thos. Edmonds | 5 | small Boy |
| | | John Rogers | 29 | Stout fellow |
| | | Henry Mayfield | 33 | Do. |
| | | Hannah his Wife | 23 | Stout Wench |
| | | Bill Browne | 24 | Stout Fello |
| | | Dinah his Wife | 23 | Lusty squat |
| | | Tom | 40 | Sickly Man |
| | | Nancy his Wife | 40 | Slim Wench |
| | | Charles | 21 | Stout B |
| | | Prince Fraction | 25 | Do. blind Le |
| Ship Montague | Port Roseway | Wm. Woodhouse | 48 | Tall & Wo |
| Robt. Wilson Mr. | | Jenny Powell | 45 | Stout Wench |
| | | Benj. Philips | 40 | Tall Slim |

RIGHT: *The book lists the applicants' names, ages, occupations and general remarks. The former slaves were hoping for a new life, independence and freedom in Nova Scotia.*

(38)

| Claimants — ames | Places of Residence | Names of the Persons in whose Possession they now are | Remarks |
|---|---|---|---|
| | | John Ketchum | Formerly Slave to Joseph Hyde, Fairfield New England left him 6 Years past G.B.C |
| | | Capt. Peacock | Do. to Jno. Jones Savannah left him 5 Y. past, Indented for 7 Years with sd. Captn. |
| | | Capt. Ed. Ellison | Do. to Dan: Moore Woodbridge N. Jersey left him 7 Years ago G.B.C. |
| | | James Petters | Do. to Corn. Boggard near Hackinsack N. Jersey left him 5 Years past G.B.C |
| | | James Travess | Do. to David Davis White Plains left him 2 Years past say he has since been Sold by his Mis. to sd. Travess |
| | | Hilliard | Do. to Major Gillman Plasto N. England left him abt. 3 Years past |
| | | Jonn. Ketchum | Do. to Jos. Portress, Peterburg Virga. left him 4 Years past G.B.C |
| | | Do. | Do. to Do. Do. |
| | | Do. | Do. to Do. Do. |
| | | James Sayre | Do. to Henry Bracy, Great Bridge Virga. left him abt. 2 Years ago G.B.C |
| | | Dr. Stevens | Do. to Oliver Spencer, Elizabeth Town N. Jersey left him 5 Years ago Do. |
| | | Do. | Served her Time out with Jos: Graham of Boston |
| | | Geo: Harding | Formerly Slave to Gabriel Jones, Augusta Coy. Virginia left him 8 Years ago |
| en Chace | River St. Johns | Reuben Chace | Property of Reuben Chace as pr. Bill of Sale from Jacob Sharp of Boston |
| | | Capt. Stewart, St. Jovery | Free born at Fonta Bell Barbadoes |
| | | Geo: Harding | Formerly Slave to Jno. Scull Philadelphia left him 4 Years ago |
| | | Stepn. Shakespeare | Says he got his freedom from Selvn. Brindly Quaker N. Jersey that he has liv'd in New York ye. 6 Years past G.B.C |
| | | Do. | Formerly Slave to Garret Sangston, Shrewsbury left him 3 Years past G.B.C |
| | | Archd. Clarke | Do. to Thos. Brown Savannah left him 5 Years past G.B.C |
| | | Do. | Says she was born free, at Tappan, serv'd her time to Ja. Reckman N. York Island |
| | | Stepn. Nirron | Formerly Slave to B. Benson N. York Isld., that Benson left him on ye. Landing of ye. British Troops on N. York Island |
| | | Nathl. Hannah | Do. to Ja. Dunham of Augusta left him 5 Years past G.B.C. |
| | | Edwd. Hannah | Do. to Wm. Smith Charles Town left him abt. 5 Years past |
| | | Do. | Do. Do. Do. |
| | | Do. | Do. to Mr. Drayton near Charles Town left her before ye. Siege of Charles Town |
| | | Do. | Do. Do. Do. |
| | | Stepn. Shakespeare | Do. to Mr. Edmonds Charles Town left him 5 Years past |
| | | Do. | Do. Do. |
| | | Andw. Gibson | Do. to Capt. Rogers, Brig Dispatch who went to England & left him free |
| | | Alexr. Watson | Free born in Mr. Philipse's House of Philips Manor G.B.C.P |
| | | Do. | Do. in Jno. Closters N. Jersey |
| | | Nichs. Brown | Formerly Slave to Jacob Arnold Morris Town N. Jersey left him 3 Years ago |
| | | Do. | Born free her Mother an Indian, served her time with Edmd. Palmer who lived & was hang'd at Pecks Kill for being a Tory |
| | | Thos. Hartley | Formerly Slave to Henry Smith Char. Town S.C. who died soon after it was taken by ye. British left no Heirs |
| | | Do. | Do. to Widow Lott of Do. who she says gave her free before she died 11 Years ago |
| | | Do. | Do. to Charles Elliott of Do. who died about 1½ Years ago |
| rigler | Port Roseway | Edwd. Trigler | Property of Edwd. Trigler purchas'd from Ja. Stokes of New York |
| | | James Rose | Formerly Slave to Wm. Woodhouse Princess Ann Virginia, left Virga. 6 Years past by Proclamatn. |
| | | Do. | Served with Capt. Torrill M. Town Virga. left him 6 Years past, no Slave |
| | | Robt. Fox | Formerly Servt. to Geo: Philips Middletown Connecticut, left him 6 Years past by Proclamn. |

# Newgate continued.

## Sentenced to Africa

| | | | | age | Sen[tence] |
|---|---|---|---|---|---|
| Middlesex Prisoners | Ap. Sess: 1787 | ✓96 | Hannah Pleasants Jones | 22 | 7 ye[ars] |
| | Sep. Sess: 1787 | ✓97 | Ann Yeomans | 28 | do |

## Capital Convicts respited on Condition

| | | | | |
|---|---|---|---|---|
| Apl. Sess: 1787 | ✓98 | Mary Himes al: Potten | 30 | 7 ye[ars] |
| | ✓99 | Hester Thornton | 18 | Life |
| July Sess: 1787 | ✓100 | Mary Chafey | 23 | 7 yea[rs] |
| | ✓101 | Sarah Young | 18 | do |
| Sep. Sess. 1787 | ✓102 | Ann Steel | 25 | Life |
| Feby Sess 1788 | ✓103 | Lydia Jones | 30 | do |
| | ✓104 | Elizth. Smith | 16 | do |
| Apl. Sess. 1788 | ✓105 | Cathe. Heyland | 34 | do |
| May Sess: 1788 | ✓106 | Mary Hook | 18 | 7 ye[ars] |
| June Sess: 1788 | ✓107 | Elizth. Goldsmith | 23 | do |
| Septr. Sess: 1788 | 108 | Elizth. Shakespear | 29 | Life |
| Jan: Sess: 1789 | ✓109 | Mary Wade | 11 | do |
| | ✓110 | Jane Whiting | 14 | do |
| | ✓111 | Mary Hounset | 25 | 7 yea[rs] |

# TEN YEARS OLD – TRANSPORTED *for* LIFE

## Records of Mary Wade

### 1788

RIGHT: *Sydney Cove, where the earliest convicts from Britain first arrived in Australia, painted in 1794.*

IN 1788, MARY WADE was just another tough little London street urchin, earning a few pennies for her family by sweeping pavements and begging. But on 5 October, she did something that would change her life forever. In Treasury Yard, Westminster, Mary and her fourteen-year-old friend Jane Whiting accosted seven-year-old Mary Phillips. Treasury Yard was an amenity that housed public latrines and a water pump, and Mary Phillips had been sent to fill a bottle with water. Whiting and Wade broke her bottle, bundled her into a public toilet, and stripped her of her clothes. They told her not to cry, but to wait in the toilet while a friend fetched another bottle. They then went directly to a pawnbroker's shop, where they got 18 pence for the dress.

Another child reported Wade and Whiting, and they were arrested and tried together at the Old Bailey in January. The copy of proceedings shows Wade as a confused little girl – one minute saying that she wished she hadn't done it, the next that she wished she'd thrown Mary Phillips down the toilet. But there seems to have been little doubt that she had committed the crime. The jury returned a guilty verdict. Wade and Whiting were sentenced to hang.

Eighteenth-century law was inflexible. Wade's crime was theft with assault, the punishment was death, and that was that. But this inflexibility was balanced, to some degree, by the royal prerogative of mercy. At the end of each court session, judges would write to the Home Secretary with a list of convicts whose sentences they recommended commuting, usually to transportation. In the 1780s, almost 60 per cent of prisoners sentenced to death were spared in this way. The National Archives holds a copy of the judge's report for 1789, which recommended that Wade and Whiting be transported for life. Britain had used to transport its criminals to America, but hadn't been able to do so since the War of Independence (see page 126). But as one transportation destination closed, another opened up: Australia.

Three months after they had been sentenced, the two little girls were brought from the filthy cells of Newgate Prison to the Bar. The Recorder of London informed them that they were not going to die. Instead, they would join a fleet of ships setting sail for New South Wales.

OPPOSITE: *Mary Wade is listed, third from the bottom, as having her capital sentence commuted to transportation for life. Although the list is headed 'sentenced to Africa', their destination was Australia. The journey would take almost a year.*

12

My Lord

In obedience to the Kings commands signified to me by your Lordship, I have reviewed the cases of the several female convicts, whose names you transmitted to me, and which I had before reported to his Majesty. To several of them I have annexed the conditions which were mentioned in council at the times of the respective reports. Of the others, where I had no memorandum but of a general Respite, I have annexed such conditions, as appeared to me best proportioned to the degrees of their several offences; and I beg leave humbly to recommend them all to his Majesty's pardon, on the several conditions set opposite to their names. If the Pardons are received in time, sentence of transportation shall be passed upon them, at the Sessions which begins on Wednesday next; after which they may be sent off whenever

What would Wade have felt at that moment? Relief that she would not hang, for sure. But she may have been hoping for a prison sentence in England, or at least for a limited transportation, perhaps for seven or fourteen years. Transportation for life meant that she would never see her family again. Several convicts offered transportation insisted on the death penalty rather than undergo the terrors of the year-long voyage and the uncertainties of the New World. This was, after all, only the second convict fleet to be sent to Australia.

In fact, Wade's life improved when she boarded the *Lady Juliana* on the Thames. She was the youngest of 237 female convicts on the ship, each of whom got a dry, warm bed and adequate food. When they set sail from England, the women were allowed to wear their own clothes and were allotted tasks. Crew members each took a 'wife' from among the convicts (so many babies would be born on the voyage that a birthing tent had to be set up on deck), and life was co-operative and relaxed. There was one woman who

ABOVE: *The National Archives contains many applications for royal mercy, many of them heart-rending. This letter to the Home Secretary recommends clemency for several female convicts who had been sentenced to hang.*

13

Gertrude Mary Thomas, and goods
val. 22s of John Thomas Esqr.

sentenced to be transported 7 years.

The things were kept in a locked garrett in the house, which was let ready furnished to Colonel Cathcart, with whom the prisoner lived servant, and the locks had been broken. The case was not such, as would have induced me originally to recommend any mitigation of her sentence; But being assured both by the late and present Sheriffs, that her conduct in the gaol has been exemplary, which it seems expedient to encourage in the prisoners, and she having suffered imprisonment for a year and half, I beg leave humbly to recommend her to the Kings mercy for a free pardon.

I have the honour to be with great Respect
My Lord your Lordships most obedt
Humble Servt

17th April. 1789 J Adair

regularly created trouble, but it turned out that she was only misbehaving in order to get herself locked in the hold, where she had discovered a supply of poorly stored liquor. She mended her ways after the captain locked her in an empty barrel on deck instead.

The *Lady Juliana* took Wade to some of the most exotic parts of the world as it picked up supplies for the colony – Santa Cruz, Rio de Janeiro, Cape Town. The little girl finally stepped onto Australian soil almost a year after leaving England, when the ship docked at the bottom of the Governor's garden in Sydney Cove. The National Archives holds the list that was made of the convicts at their departure. Wade was just twelve years old when she arrived at her destination.

Mary Wade turned out to be a true Australian pioneer. She would have her share of hardship, labour and poverty, but in due course she met and married a convict from the third fleet, a furniture maker from Bermondsey called Jonathan Brooker. They were together for nearly thirty years, and owned a farm of some sixty-five acres in an area of outstanding natural beauty. Mary Wade had twenty-one children and lived to the age of eighty-two. Her funeral was held in a church built on land donated by one of her sons. Today, thousands of Australians can trace their family back to her. What a legacy that little girl was to have.

# MUTINY *on the BOUNTY*
## Lieutenant Bligh's Journal

LEFT: *Signature of William Bligh, Lieutenant in charge of the* Bounty.

1789

IT MUST HAVE BEEN an uncomfortable experience for Lieutenant William Bligh to write this journal. In it, he had to admit that he had been captured by his men, tied to a mast, and then set adrift. This is the record of the most famous mutiny in history.

Bligh was a Cornishman who had worked his way steadily through the ranks of the Royal and merchant navies. In 1789, he was asked to take command of the *Bounty* on an expedition sponsored by the Royal Society. The ship was to go to Tahiti, pick up a cargo of live breadfruit trees, and carry them to the West Indies to see if they could become a new source of food on the slave plantations. Two days before Christmas, the *Bounty* set sail for Tahiti with forty-six men on board. Several had sailed with Bligh before, including one of the mates, Fletcher Christian.

It was a tough voyage. First they headed west across the Atlantic to sail around Cape Horn, but after spending a month battling storms at the Cape they gave up and headed westwards across great expanses of ocean. It was a full ten months before they arrived in Tahiti.

The popular image of Bligh is that he was a cruel and capricious man, who drove his men beyond endurance. The ship's log shows that he was actually quite sparing of punishment. He ran a tight ship, careful of the diet of his men and insistent on cleanliness – exactly the sort of behaviour that kept people alive on a difficult trip like this one. His chief failing was a whip-like tongue, with which he would lash any man who did not meet his own high standards. One victim of his contempt on the voyage was the sailing master, Fryer, whom he demoted and replaced with Fletcher Christian. Mr Christian, from Cockermouth in Cumberland, was Bligh's junior by ten years, and had sailed with Bligh twice before. Film portrayals of Christian have been kind. But this dark-skinned, dark-haired young man was, in some ways, a bit wet. He may also have been promoted beyond his ability. Soon he, too, was being regularly humiliated by Bligh's acid words.

If the journey had been hell, Tahiti was heaven – which was the second problem. The breadfruit plants were not ready to be transported, and needed five months of growth before the ship could set sail again. Five months of dry land, plentiful

OPPOSITE: *The moment of the mutiny. Just before dawn, Fletcher Christian and other mutineers entered Bligh's cabin, tied him up and 'threatened* [him] *with instant death' if he uttered a word. He shouted but all the loyal officers were confined in their cabins.*

# Remarks Tuesday 28th April 1789 at Sea

Light Winds and Cloudy Wr. – Wind NE E and ESE.

I kept near the Ozodoo untill 5 O'Clock this afternoon in hopes to have had some Cannoes off but I saw none. I therefore directed my Course to the West and went to the Southward of Tofoa. – Mr Fryer the Master had the first Watch. Mr Peckover the Gunner the Middle, and Mr Christian one of the Mates the Morning Watch – This was the tour of duty for the Night. –

Just before Sun rise Mr Christian, Mate, Chas. Churchill Ships Corporal, John Mills Gunners Mate and Thomas Burkitt, Seaman, came into my Cabbin while I was asleep and seizing me tyed my hands with a Cord behind my back and threatned me with instant death if I spoke or made the least noise. I however called so loud as to alarm every one, but the Officers found themselves secured by Centinels at their Doors. – There were four Men in my Cabbin and three outside Viz. Alexr Smith, Jno Sumner and Matw Quintal. – Mr Christian had a Cutlass in his hand the others had Musquets and Bayonets. I was forced on Deck in my Shirt, suffering great pain from the violence with which they had tied my hands – I demanded the reason for such a violent act, but I recieved no Answer but threats of instant death if I did not hold my tongue. – Mr Hayward & Hallett were in Mr Christians Watch, but had no Idea that any thing was doing untill they were all armed. – The Arms were all Secured so that no one could get near them for Centinels. – Mr Elphinstone the Mate was secured to his Birth. – Mr Nelson Botanist. Mr Peckover Gunner – Mr Ledward Surgeon & the Master were confined to their Cabbins, as also Mr Jno Samuel, (Clerk) but who from finesse got leave to come upon Deck. – The Fore Hatchway was guarded by Centinels, the Boatswain and Carpenter were however allowed to come on Deck where they saw me standing abaft the Mizen Mast with my hands tied behind my back, under a Guard with Christian at their Head. –

Observations.. Sextants.. Time Keeper or any of my Surveys or drawings.—

The Mutineers were now hurrying every one into the Boat, and the most of them being in, Christian directed a Dram to be served to each of his Crew.— I was now exceedingly fatigued, and unhappily saw I could do nothing to effect the Recovery of the Ship. every endeavor was threatened with death, and the following People were now in the Boat.—

John Fryer . . . . . . Master
Thos. Denmn. Ledward . . . Surgeon
x David Nelson . . . . Botanist
Willm. Peckover . . . . Gunner
Willm. Cole . . . . Boatswain
Willm. Purcell . . . . Carpenter
x Willm. Elphinstone . . . . Masters Mate
Thos. Hayward . . . . Midn.
John Hallett . . . . Midn.
x John Norton . . . . Qur. Master
x Peter Linkletter . . . . Qur. Master
Lawce. Lebogue . . . . Sail Maker
John Smith . . . . Ab
x Thos. Hall . . . . Ab
Geo: Simpson . . . . Qur. Masters Mate
Robt. Tinkler . . . . Ab
x Robt. Lamb . . . . Ab
John Samuel . . . . Clerk —

There remained on board as Pirates and under Arms

Fletcher Christian . . . . Masters Mate
Peter Heywood . . . . Midn.
George Stewart . . . . Midn.
Edwd. Young . . . . Midn.

Charles Churchill .......... Ships Corporal

John Mills .......... Gunners Mate

James Morrison .......... Boatsns Mate

Thos. Burkitt .......... Ab

Mathew Quintal .......... Ab

John Sumner .......... Ab

John Millward .......... Ab

Willm. Mickoy .......... Ab

Heny. Hilbrant .......... Ab

Willm. Muspratt .......... Ab

Alexr. Smith .......... Ab

John Williams .......... Ab

Thos. Ellison .......... Ab

Isaac Martin .......... Ab

Richd. Skinner .......... Ab

Mathew Thompson .......... Ab

Willm. Brown .......... Botanists Assistant

Michl. Byrne .......... Ab

Joseph Coleman .......... Armourer

Chas. Norman .......... Carpenters Mate

Thos. McIntosh .......... Dos. Crew

— In all 25 Hands and the most able Men on board the Ship —

This is briefly the Statement of the Case. — The Officers were called and forced into the Boat while I was under a Guard abaft the Mizen Mast, Christian holding me by the Bandage that secured my hands with one hand and a Bayonet in the other. The Men under Arms round me had their Peices cocked which so enraged me against those ungratefull Wretches that

PREVIOUS PAGES: *Bligh's list of men forced into the boat, and those who remained on board, shows a split of twenty to twenty-five. The punishment for mutiny was death – the twenty-five knew there was no going back.*

359 357

Description of the Pirates

| | Age | |
|---|---|---|
| Fletcher Christian | 24 | Masters Mate 5.9 High. Blackish or very dark brown Complexion. Dark Brown Hair. Strong Made. A Star tatowed on his left Breast. and tatowed on the backside His Knees stand a little out and he may be called a little Bow legged, He is subject to Violent perspiration, particularly in his hands so that he Soils any thing he handles. — |
| Geo: Stewart | 23 | Midshipman — 5.7. High Good Complexion, Dark Hair Slender Made, Narrow chested and long Neck. A Star tatowed on the left Breast and One on the left Arm with a heart and darts. — Tatowed on the backside. — Small Face and black Eyes. — |
| Peter Heywood | 17. | Midshipman — 5.7. High Fair Complexion, light Brown Hair — well proportioned. — very much tatowed & on the Right leg is tatowed the Legs of Man as the impression on that Coin is. — At this time he had not done growing and Speaks with the Manks or Isle of Man Accent. |
| Edw^d Young | 22 | Midshipman 5.8 High. Dark Complexion and rather a bad look, Dark brown Hair. Strong made, has lost several of his Fore teeth, and those that remain are rotten. — A Small Mole on the left side of the throat and on the Right Arm is tatowed a Heart and Dart through it with E:Y underneath and the date of the Year 1788 or 1789. — |
| Chas. Churchill | 30 | Ships Corporal 5.10. High. Fair Complexion, short light brown Hair. Top of the Head Bald. Strong Made. The Fore Finger of his left hand Crooked and his hand shews the mark of a Severe Scald. Tatowed on Several places of his Body, Legs and Arms — |

food, easy living and beautiful women. It was no wonder the crew did not want to leave. But Bligh managed to get both breadfruit and crew back on board and in early April they set sail again, travelling west. They had been at sea a little over three weeks when, as he reports, Bligh had a rude awakening:

*Just before Sun rise Mr. Christian, Mate, Charles Churchill, Ships Corporal, John Mills, Gunners Mate and Thomas Burkitt, Seaman, came into my Cabbin while I was asleep and seizing me tyed my hands with a cord behind my back and threatened me with instant death if I spoke or made the least noise. I however called so loud as to alarm everyone, but the Officers found themselves secured by Centinels at their Doors – There were four men in my Cabbin and three outside viz. Alexander Smith, John Sumner and Matthew Quintal. Mr. Christian had a Cutlass in his hand, the others has Musquets and Bayonets. I was forced on Deck in my shirt, suffering great pain from the violence with which they had tied my hands and I demanded the reason for such a violent act, but received no answer but threats of instant death if I did not hold my tongue.*

*Mr Hayward & Hallett were in Mr Christian's Watch, but had no idea anything was doing until they were all armed. The arms were all secured so that no one could get near them for Centinels. Mr Elphinstone, the Mate, was secured to his berth. Mr Nelson, Botanist, Mr Peckover, Gunner, Mr Ledward, Surgeon & the Master were confined to their Cabbins, as also Mr John Samuel (Clerk) but who from finese got leave to come upon Deck. The Fore Hatchway was guarded by Centinels, the Boatswain and Carpenter were however allowed to come on Deck when they saw me standing aloft the Mizen Mast with my hands tied behind my back, under a Guard with Christian at their Head.*

Bligh's report lists the names of the mutineers and the names of those who remained loyal. The division was roughly half and half, and seems almost random: John Fryer, the Master, was loyal, Fletcher Christian, the

Age 358 (360)

Jas. Morrison 28 Boats.n Mate – 5. 8 High. Sallow Complexion, Long Black Hair, Slender Made. has lost the use of the upper joint of the Fore finger of the Right hand – Tatowed with a Star under his left Breast, and a Garter round his left Leg with the Motto of Honi soit qui mal y pense. and has been Wounded in One of his Arms with a Musquet Ball. —

John Mills 40 Gunners Mate. 5. 10. Fair Complexion, Light Brown Hair Strong Made Raw Boned. – A Scar in his Right Arm pit Occasioned by an Abcess. —

Jnº Millward 22 Ab. – 5. 5 High. Brown Complexion, Dark Hair, Strong Made, very much tatowed in different parts of the Body. and under the pit of the Stomach with a Taoomy or Breast plate of Otaheite. —

Matw Thompson 40 Ab – 5. 8 High – Very dark Complexion, Short black Hair. Slender Made. and has lost the joint of the Great Toe of his Right Foot and is tatowed in several places of his body. —

Willm Mickoy 25 Ab – 5. 6 High. Fair Complexion, Light Brown Hair, Strong Made, A Scar where he has been Stabbed in the Belly, and a Small Scar under his Chin. is Tatowed in different parts of the Body. —

Matw Quintal 21 Ab – 5. 5. High. Fair Complexion, Light Brown Hair, Strong made, Very much tatowed on the backside and Several other places. —

Jnº Sumner 24 Ab – 5. 8 High. Fair Complexion, Brown Hair, Slender Made, a Scar upon the left Cheek and tatowed in several places. —

Thos. Burkitt 26 Ab – 5. 9. High – Fair Complexion, very much pitted with the Small Pox – Brown Hair. Well made and very much tatowed. —

Isaac Martin 30 Ab. – 5. 11. High. Sallow Complexion Short brown Hair, Raw Boned. tatowed with a Star on his left Breast. —

Opposite and left: *Bligh's journal includes descriptions of each of the 'Pirates', starting with Fletcher Christian. The group sailed to Tahiti, where some remained and were later captured. The others sailed on and found Pitcairn Island, which they made their home.*

Master's Mate, mutinied (note that Bligh has carefully forgotten that he had switched their roles); David Nelson, the Botanist, was loyal, William Brown, the Botanist's Assistant, mutinied; and so on.

The mutineers cast the loyalists adrift with food, water and sixty bottles of wine. Now began the less well known, but no less extraordinary, part of Bligh's adventure. He first navigated to a nearby island, but they were attacked by the islanders. Since they had no weapons, and Bligh and his crew were afraid that they would get a similar reception at every native island, they therefore embarked, without maps or compass, on a voyage to the European settlement at Timor, a distance of over 4,000 miles. *En route* they lost part of their provisions and were chased by cannibals, but forty-seven days later, at the limit of their endurance, they made it. It is a testament to Bligh that he did not lose a man during this amazing act of seamanship.

The mutineers did well, too, at least at first. They sailed back to their beloved Tahiti. Some chose to remain there, and were eventually captured. Christian and eight other crewmen set off to find a haven where the Royal Navy would not find them, accompanied by a group of Tahitian men and women. They stumbled across the tiny island of Pitcairn, which had been misplaced on the Navy's map. They burnt and sank the *Bounty*, to further avoid detection. At first life was good, but conflict broke out in a toxic mixture of sex (men fighting over women) and drink (one mutineer managed to construct a still). Christian and four other Europeans were killed on a day of fighting in September 1793. By then, though, he had fathered a number of children. Many of the island's current inhabitants are descended from Fletcher Christian.

Bligh's report did not go down too badly. He was cleared at a court martial, and embarked on a second breadfruit expedition to Tahiti and the West Indies – successfully this time.

# *A* WORLD *before* WHITE MEN

## Maori Map

## 1793

Above: *A Maori chief, with traditional facial markings, from a late-eighteenth-century drawing.*

THIS MAP OF New Zealand was drawn by a Maori priest, at a time when Maoris had had virtually no contact with Europeans. It is an almost pure insight into how Aboriginal New Zealanders saw their world, before contact with Europeans changed it forever.

When the first fleet of convict ships arrived in Australia, a small party was sent to colonise Norfolk Island under the command of Lieutenant Philip Gidley King. Norfolk Island lies between Australia and New Zealand and was thought a promising place to grow flax for sail-making. One day, King's ship came across a canoe carrying two Maoris, a priest called Tuki (written as Toakee or Tooke Titter a Nue on the map) and his companion Woodoo. Hoping that the Maoris would teach his men how to make linen from flax, King captured the two and had them carried to Norfolk Island. As it turned out, using flax was regarded as women's work in Maori culture and neither had a clue how to do it, but they nevertheless ended up sharing the Lieutenant's home for six months. King asked Tuki to draw a map of New Zealand, which he did in chalk on the floor. King transcribed the map and sent it to England.

The map shows both of New Zealand's islands, which at the time were mostly covered in forest. Tuki came from the North Island, the right-hand one of the two landmasses. He had only heard of the South Island, and so naturally made the North the bigger of the two. But the unknown South Island is the more vivid in Tuki's imagination. It includes a 'lake where stones for hatchets are got' and a 'tree about which Tuki and Wodoo tell some wonderful stories, which they say the T'Souduckey people [a South Island tribe] had told them of'.

The North Island had its own myths. Running left to right (south to north) across the middle of the island is a dotted path marked as 'Ea hei no none'. This is the path along which the spirits of the Maori dead would pass to Revenga Wairua (now Cape Reinga), from where they would go over the water to Hawaiki, their spiritual home. Hawaiki is a fascinating ethnological clue. The Maori were originally Polynesians, arriving in New Zealand around 1280. Hawaiki in Maori mythology was both the land of the dead, and the land from which their ancestors had first travelled to find this new island. The Maori had never forgotten where they came from.

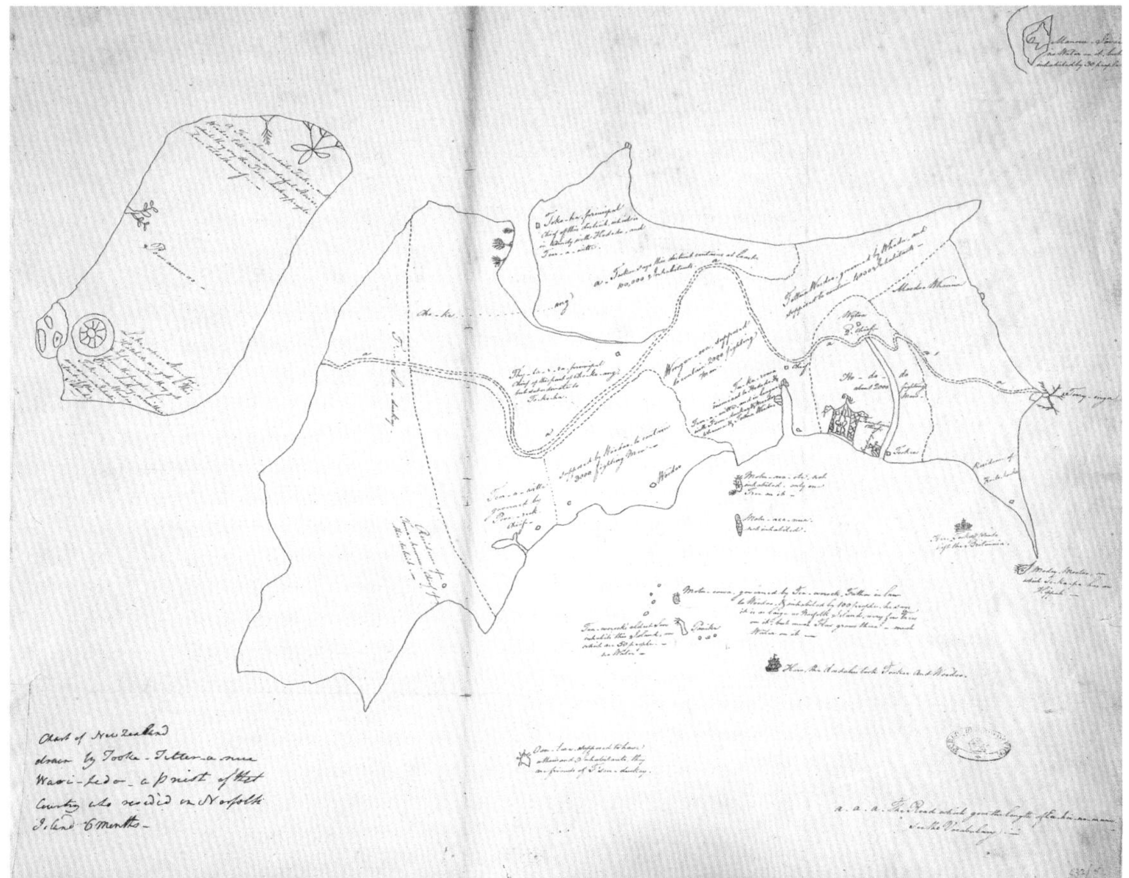


ABOVE: *Tuki's map shows New Zealand's South Island to the left, the North Island to the right. The double-dotted line shows the path of the souls of the dead. The writing marks out local tribes and notes their various strengths.*

The map also shows a detailed knowledge of the island's tribes, their chiefs, alliances and strengths: 'Chok k e ang a-Tooksa says this district contains at least 10,000 inhabitants' (this is around modern day Hokinga; later settlers in New Zealand tended to adopt the Maoris' place names); 'Won go rooa [modern day Whangaroa District] supposed to contain 2,000 fighting men'; 'Tu ka rowa inimical to Hododo & Teer a weete in league with T'Souduckey and Moodo Whenua Whenua & Settua Woodoo'. Structures are marked, possibly Wharnuis (literally 'Big Houses'), which were centres for Maori communities, meeting places and ceremonies, each marked with the name of their controlling chief. King may have prompted Tuki to set out the strength of resistance that Europeans might meet in New Zealand, but be that as it may, Tuki was very familiar with the territories, tribes and threats of the North Island.

In time, King released the two men – you can see it by the little ship on the right, '*Toakee* and Woodoo left the *Britannia*'. He sent the map to the colonial office, comparing it favourably with Cook's chart and describing the men, their customs and language. The northernmost of the tribes on Tuki's map traded piecemeal with the Europeans, who introduced them to muskets and potatoes. They used the potatoes as provisions to travel further south, and the muskets to attack the tribes they found there. Mission stations began to be established on the Island in the 1820s. The world, and way of thinking, portrayed on this map would soon be gone.

# RATIFICATIONS

OF THE TREATY OF
AMITY, COMMERCE AND
NAVIGATION, BETWEEN

# HIS BRITANNIC MAJESTY,

AND THE
UNITED STATES OF AMERICA,
OF NOVEMBER 19TH 1794.
SIGNED AT PHILADELPHIA,
AUGUST 14TH

1795.

AND OF THE
EXPLANATORY ARTICLE,
OF MARCH 15TH 1798.
SIGNED AT PHILADELPHIA,
JUNE 7TH

1798.

# *The* TREATY *of* FRIENDSHIP

## Britain–US Treaty of Amity, Commerce and Navigation

## 1795

ABOVE: *John Adams, second US president, who ratified the Treaty of Amity with Britain.*

THIS LITTLE TREATY declares perpetual 'amity', friendship, between the United States and Britain. Simple enough – but what a whirl it caused. The treaty prompted the coming of age of American political parties, the founding of the US Navy, and key principles both of international and US constitutional law. It also gave America time to gather its strength for war with its perpetual friend.

In the years that followed the American War of Independence (see page 126), Britain behaved like an ex-husband stalking his former wife. Britain maintained forts on American soil, restricted America's ability to trade with its other colonies, captured its shipping, impressed its sailors into British service, and argued about the position of its border with Canada. But the ex-husband began to feel something worse than rejection. It was the fear that America might fall into the arms of an old flame. France, which had supported America in her War of Independence, was in the grip of its own revolutionary struggle, and a European war seemed likely. Britain did not want its former colony falling in with its old enemy. It was time to normalise relations.

The Treaty of Amity was negotiated over several months in London by US Chief Justice John Jay and British Foreign Secretary Lord Grenville. Many loose ends were tied up. British forts in America would be vacated; Britain agreed to pay compensation for having interfered with American shipping, and granted America trading rights with England and the East Indies; a court of arbitration was set up to determine the position of the US–Canada border (a new and important legal precedent for resolving international border disputes). In return, America agreed to maritime policies that were distinctly anti-French. That was Britain's condition: if you want to be friends with me, you have to hate my enemy.

OPPOSITE: *The Britain–US Treaty of Amity caused a storm in America. American politics crystallised into pro- and anti-treaty parties. Fifteen years later, the friends were at war again.*

American Republicans loathed the treaty. They saw the French as their new nation's natural allies, even more so now that the French were busy setting up a similar (albeit more guillotine-heavy) republic to their own. They resented the fact that the treaty was silent on the impressing of American sailors, and on another complaint, the failure by Britain to pay compensation for liberated slaves (see page 134). Resistance to the treaty among American Republicans mobilised what had been a loose gathering of like-minded individuals into a proper political network,

*The implication behind the motion was that the President's instructions were partisan and improper. Washington dug his heels in, emphatically refusing to disclose his instructions to Jay.*

tory article: Now therefore, I John Adams, President of the United States of America, having seen and considered the said explanatory article, do, in pursuance of the aforementioned advice and consent of the Senate, ratify, accept and confirm the same, as it is set forth in this instrument of Ratification.

For the greater testimony and validity I have caused the Great Seal of States of America to be hereto Given under my Hand at the City of Philadelphia, this Seventh Day of June in the Year of our Lord one thousand seven hundred and ninety-eight, and of the Independence of the United States of America, the Twenty-second.

John Adams.

By the President of the United States of America,

Timothy Pickering Secretary of State.

with local Republican branches set up in a co-ordinated campaign of protest. Political battle lines became far sharper as public figures sorted themselves into pro-treaty and anti-treaty groups.

The treaty squeaked through a Senate vote and George Washington signed it on 18 August 1795. The furious Republicans now tried another tack. They introduced a motion that the President should submit to the House a copy of the instructions that he gave to Jay, when he was negotiating the treaty. The implication behind the motion was that the President's instructions were partisan and improper. Washington dug his heels in, emphatically refusing to disclose his instructions to Jay. This was the exercise of a second important precedent, the division between US executive freedom (Washington's right, as President, to instruct Jay as he chose) and US legislative authority (the Senate's right to pass laws, but not to manage the President).

The French took the treaty no better than the Republicans. They began to prey on US shipping. Washington was succeeded as president by John Adams, who argued that America should found a navy to protect its shipping, and expand its army to guard against French raids.

Republicans accused Adams of exaggerating the threat of war in order to build up armed forces and impose tyranny. But they then shot themselves spectacularly in the foot. Adams, wanting to stabilise

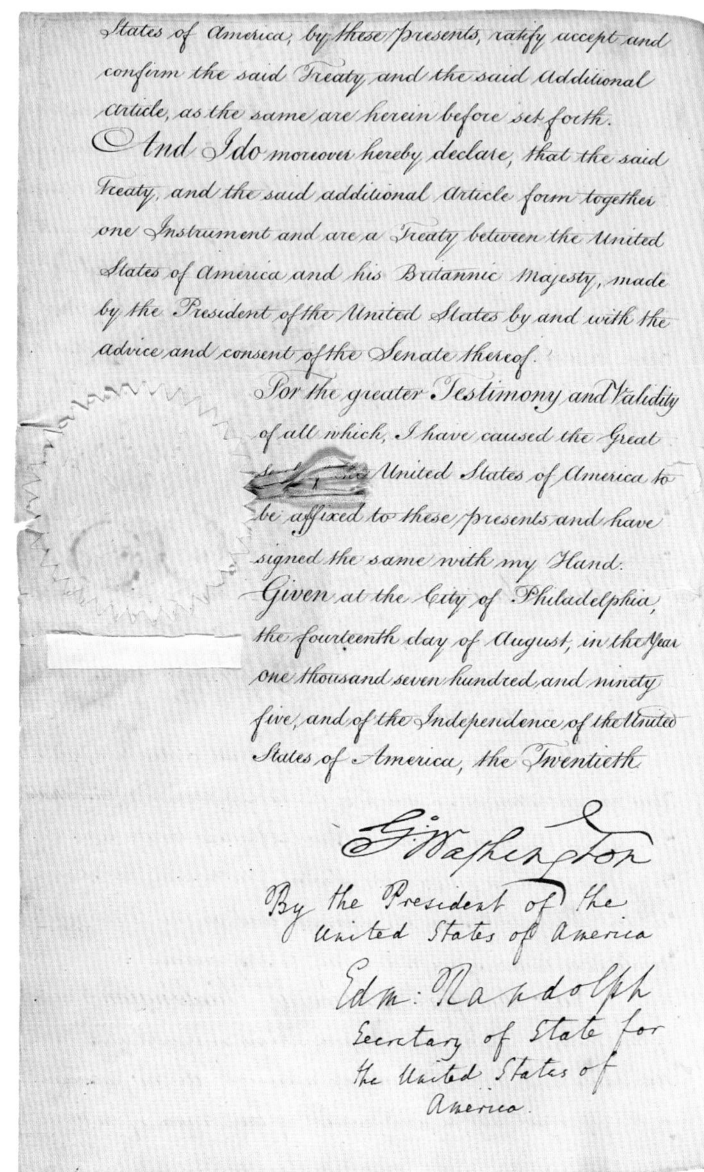

States of America, by these presents, ratify accept and confirm the said Treaty, and the said Additional Article, as the same are herein before set forth.

And I do moreover hereby declare, that the said Treaty, and the said additional Article form together one Instrument and are a Treaty between the United States of America and his Britannic Majesty, made by the President of the United States by and with the advice and consent of the Senate thereof.

For the greater Testimony and Validity of all which, I have caused the Great [illegible] United States of America to be affixed to these presents and have signed the same with my Hand.

Given at the City of Philadelphia, the fourteenth day of August, in the Year one thousand seven hundred and ninety five, and of the Independence of the United States of America, the Twentieth.

G:o Washington

By the President of the United States of America

Edm: Randolph
Secretary of State for the United States of America.

Opposite and left: *The copy of the Treaty of Amity bears the signatures of both George Washington and John Adams, first and second presidents of the United States of America.*

relations with the French, sent a reconciliation commission to France. When months of negotiations failed to bear fruit, the Republicans began to suspect that this reconciliation commission was a sham, and loudly demanded to see the negotiators' reports to the President. When Adams duly released the papers, they showed that the French Foreign Minister, Charles Maurice de Talleyrand, had demanded a personal bribe of some £50,000 before he would even begin to negotiate. The papers recorded the startled American negotiators responding to the demand with, 'No, no, not a sixpence!' This tale of American probity in the face of French corruption became a proud toast for the young nation: 'Millions for Defence, but not one cent for Tribute!' Adams's popularity skyrocketed and Congress accepted his defence proposals, authorising the construction of three frigates and the establishment of a marine corps. For the first time, America had a navy.

The Treaty of Amity was saved, too, as John Adams felt able to confirm it in 1798. The National Archives' copy of the treaty bears the signatures of both Washington and Adams.

So the Treaty of Friendship survived. But it wouldn't last. Britain couldn't resist the temptation to interfere with US shipping and internal affairs, and fifteen years after John Adams signed it, the two countries were at war again. Friendship can be tricky.

# *The* REAL SCARLET PIMPERNEL

## Secret Border Passes

## 1798

*They seek him here, they seek him there,*
*Those Frenchies seek him everywhere.*
*Is he in heaven? – is he in hell?*
*That demmed, elusive Pimpernel!*

BARONESS ORCZY,
*The Scarlet Pimpernel*, 1908

THE SCARLET PIMPERNEL is one of fiction's great secret heroes. Baroness Orczy's tale, set in the 1790s, concerns Sir Percy Blakeney, friend to the Prince Regent, one of the wealthiest men in Britain, and outwardly a buffoon. But his buffoonery is merely a cover! For Sir Percy is in fact the dashing Scarlet Pimpernel, who saves brave aristocrats from the cruel guillotine of the French Revolution and smuggles them to safety in England. A man of a thousand disguises, taker of impossible risks, he is known only by the small, red flower with which he signs his messages – a scarlet pimpernel.

Prime candidate for the title of the 'real' Scarlet Pimpernel is a Frenchman, Louis Bayard. Bayard came from a family of passionate royalists. In 1795, at the age of just nineteen, he sought employment from what was in effect the British Secret Service. The Revolution and Terror just across the Channel had prompted Britain to set up new surveillance networks, with magistrates organised to keep an eye on revolutionary activity at home, and a new Alien Office keeping an eye on the activities of non-Britons. William Wickham, Superintendent of Aliens and an important government spymaster, took Bayard on as a courier, but the Frenchman soon enjoyed a far more dramatic role. By 1798, Bayard controlled several networks of spies on the Continent, enjoyed thirty-one aliases, and was briefing British ministers. He seemed to be able to appear at will, on either side of the Channel.

Entwined with the story of Orczy's fictional Pimpernel is the story of Sir Peter Blakeney's French wife, Marguerite St Juste, a former actress in Paris. Marguerite dazzles London society with her wit and beauty, but

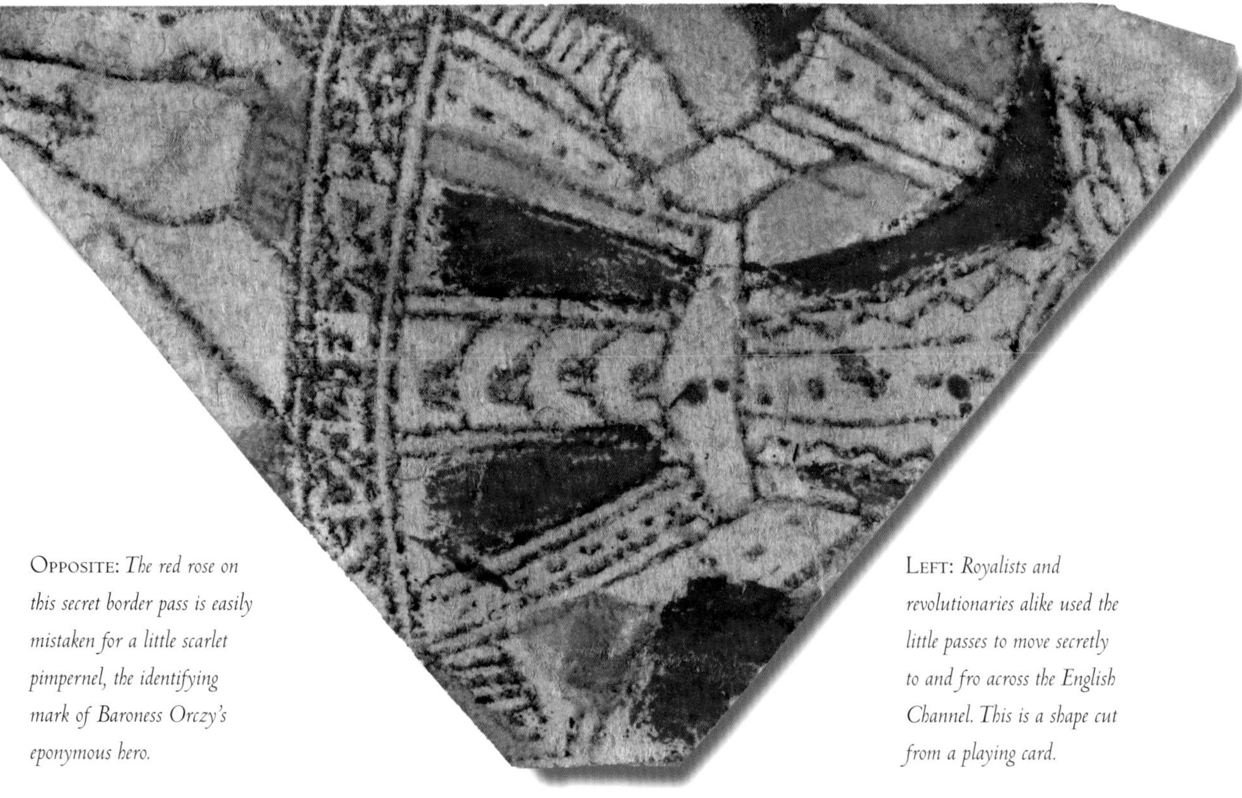

Opposite: *The red rose on this secret border pass is easily mistaken for a little scarlet pimpernel, the identifying mark of Baroness Orczy's eponymous hero.*

Left: *Royalists and revolutionaries alike used the little passes to move secretly to and fro across the English Channel. This is a shape cut from a playing card.*

is unaware of her husband's secret persona until the end of the book, when all is revealed. Bayard had his own Marguerite, who was also a former actress in Paris, a fellow spy known successively as *Madame Mayer* and *Madame Sablonière*. The hub of Bayard and Mayer's activities in Britain was an eating house that they ran together in Leicester Square (then Leicester Fields) called *Les Étrangers*, a home-from-home for scheming French émigrés.

*La Sablonière* was implicated in another striking parallel with the life of the fictional Pimpernel. British and French authorities closely monitored movements across the Channel. In order to slip across the border, a secret scheme was set up, the hub of which quite possibly was *Les Étrangers*. An agitator or spy carrying one of these triangular pieces of card could present it, together with a golden guinea, to certain corrupt border officials. He or she could then cross without passport or registration. Bayard and Mayer were by now double agents, and royalists and revolutionaries alike seem to have made use of these cards. The design on the card is meant to be a rose – but, of course, it bears a striking resemblance to a scarlet pimpernel.

When the scheme was discovered in 1798, Mayer and Bayard were forced to leave Britain for Paris. A good double agent to the last, Mayer quickly ingratiated herself with the French authorities by denouncing British agents to them. Bayard and Mayer continued their clandestine career together until Napoleon's coup in 1804. Mayer then returned to her native Strasbourg, while Bayard changed his name and disappeared.

The idea that there might be a real person behind Baroness Orczy's breathless prose seems too silly for words. But she was herself an aristocrat and refugee, from Hungary, and it is far from impossible that her story was inspired by memories and stories that she heard from other refugee aristocrats in her youth. Either that, or else these scraps of paper show that truth can have uncanny parallels with fiction.

London. Pub. by Benbow. Sep — 1820 corner of St. Clement's Church Y.d Strand.

THE BLANKET HO

A New Farce, now Performing with thundering and unbounded

# 19TH CENTURY

## Anonymous Letter from the Workers to the Gentry *to the* Marquis of Queensbury's Card

LEFT: *Satirical cartoon of George, Prince Regent, being bounced by the 'Ladies of the Metropolis'.*

# ‘WE WILL FIGHT *for* IT’

## Anonymous Letter from the Workers to the Gentry

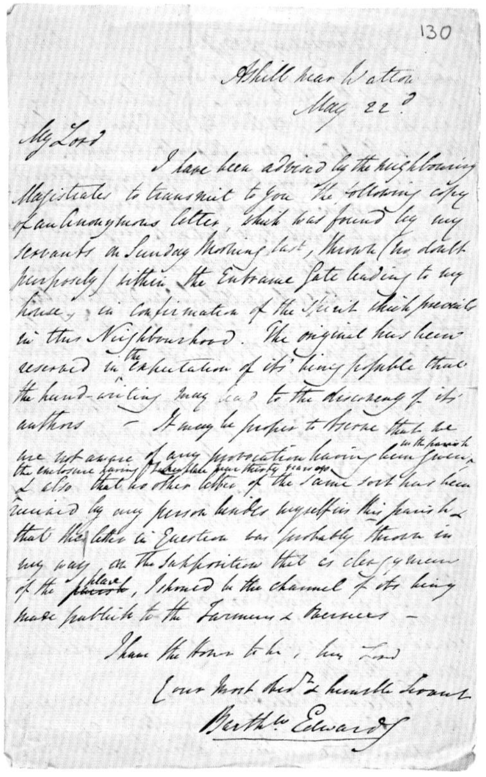

130

Ashill near Watton
May 22d

My Lord

I have been advised by the neighbouring Magistrates to transmit to you the following copy of an anonymous letter, which was found by my servants on Sunday Morning last, thrown (no doubt purposely) within the Entrance Gate leading to my house, in confirmation of the Spirit which prevails in this Neighbourhood. The original has been reserved in the expectation of its being possible that the hand-writing may lead to the discovery of its authors – It may be proper to observe that we are not aware of any provocation having been given in the parish, the enclosure having taken place near thirty years ago, & also that no other letter of the same sort has been received by any person besides myself in this parish, & that this letter in Question was probably thrown in my way on the supposition that as clergyman of the ~~parish~~ place, I should be the channel of its being made publick to the Farmers & Owners –

I have the honor to be, My Lord

Your most obedt & humble Servant

Barthw Edwards

ABOVE: *Letter notifying the authorities about the receipt of a threatening message from local workers.*

OPPOSITE: *‘To the Gentlemen of the Parish’. The letter was from one group to another, from the workers to the gentry.*

# 1816

IT MUST HAVE BEEN terrifying to receive this anonymous, threatening letter. It was intended to make the recipients, a handful of comfortable gentleman landowners in the remote rural parish of Ashill in Norfolk, feel that they were surrounded by invisible enemies. The letter shows a process that was going on all over Britain, one of the many trickles of injustice and resentment that fed into a stream of protest, and which in time would feed into the powerful river of the labour movement. But reading the letter today, it seems more than just a threat. In it, you can see minds at work, as local workers assess what is happening to them, what is being said to them, what their strength is – and come to some logical conclusions.

Conditions in the first decades of the nineteenth century were crushing. A series of bad harvests coincided with a significant increase in the population. From 1815, around 250,000 more men were dumped onto this saturated labour market, as they returned from the Napoleonic Wars. Meanwhile, that ancient and vital resource of the labouring classes, common land on which to graze their few livestock, was evaporating before their eyes, as Parliament enclosed more and more of it for private use.

The letter starts with a statement of the anonymous workers' suffering:

*To the Gentlemen of the Parish of Ashill, Norfolk*
*This is to inform you that you have by this time brought us under the heaviest burden and into the hardest yoke we ever knowed, it is too hard for us to bear ...*

To the Gentlemen of the Parish of Ashill, Norfolk

This is to inform You that you have by this time brought us under the heaviest burden & into the hardest Yoke we ever Knowed; it is too hard for us to bear; you have oftentimes blinded us saying the fault was all in the Place-men of Parliament, but now you have opened our eyes, we know they have a great power, but they have nothing to do with the regulation of this parish.

You do as you like, you rob the poor of their Commons right, plough the grass up that God send to grow, that a poor man may not feed a Cow, Pig, Horse, nor Ass; lay muck & stones on the Road to prevent the grass growing. If a poor man is out of work & wants a day or two's work you will give him 6 per week & then a little man that does not employ a labourer at all, must help to pay for your work doing, which will bring them chargeable to the parish. There is 5 or 6 of you have gotten all the whole of the Land in this parish in your own hands & you would wish to be rich & starve all the other part of the poor of the parish: If any poor man wanted any thing, there you will call a Town meeting about it, to hear which could contrive to piss him the most, which have caused us to have a County Meeting, to see if we cannot gain some Redress —

Gentlemen, these few lines are to inform you that God Almighty have brought our blood to a proper Circulation, that have been in a very bad state a long time, & now without an alteration of the foresaid, we mean to circulate your blood with the leave of God. And we do not intend to give you but a very short time to consider about it, as we have gotten one or two of the head, on our side. There was 2 cows & an ass feeding on the road last Saturday & there was 2 farmers went to the keepers & said they would pound them, if they did not drive them away; one of them candidly went home, got a plough & horses & ploughed the grass up that grew on the road.

We deem the Miller to be full as big a rogue as you farmers, for if the wheat raise 1 per coomb, he will then raise 2d per stone; so we shall drive the whole [illegible] & knock down the mill, set fire to all beggarly s[illegible]ens houses & stacks as we go along; we shall n[illegible] begin in the Night.

And the first man that refuse to join the Combination shall suffer death in a moment, or the first person that is catched saying any thing against the same, shall suffer death. we have had private ambushers rounders for some time, and by this time you will find it is coming to a point.

Take notice that this is a private letter wrote at this time, but we fear it will be too public for your profits; so we wish to prepare yourselves ready for action; for we intend to have things as we like; you have had a good long turn. We have counted up that we have gotten about 80 of us to 1 of you; therefore should you govern so many to 1? No: we will fight for it & if you gain the day, so be it.

Swinco, Fokelee Moocher Blown

It seems that the Ashill gentlemen had been blaming the suffering in the parish on the actions of Parliament in London. This was no longer going to wash:

*... you have oftentimes blinded us saying the fault was all in the Place-men of Parliament; but now you have opened our eyes, we know they have a great power, but they have nothing to do with the regulation of this parish.*

The writers were coming to see local gentry as active contributors to their suffering. They were stripping the writers of their common land, and ancient rights:

*You do as you like, you rob the poor of their Commons right, plough the grass up that God sent to grow, that a poor man may not feed a Cow, Pig, Horse nor Ass; lay muck and stones on the road to prevent the grass growing.*

They come to the injustice of the fact that the land belonged to a few families, while the majority suffered:

*There is 5 or 6 of you have gotten all the whole of the Land in this parish in your own hands and you would wish to be rich and starve all the other part of the poor of the parish.*

The scales have now fallen from their eyes – or, as they better put it, their previously still blood has started circulating properly – and they want to induce the same effect in their masters:

*Gentlemen, these few lines are to inform you that God Almighty have brought our blood to a proper circulation, that have been in a very bad state a long time and now without an alteration of the foresaid, we mean to circulate your blood with the leave of God.*

The implications of the numerical imbalance between the local 'haves' and the 'have-nots' is not lost on the writers, and in the last line of the letter they spell it out:

*We have counted up that we have gotten about 60 of us to 1 of you; therefore, should you govern so many to 1? No.*

A striking point in the letter is that although it is threatening, it is not revolutionary. The tone is local – local people who knew the local gentlemen – with underlying relationships between the writers and the recipients that may have gone back generations. They were not asking for the earth. But they were determined.

*We will fight for it, and if you gain the day, so be it.*

The letter will have been passed to the local magistrate and on to the Home Office, and so it came to the National Archives. Three years later, on the other side of the country, the Peterloo Massacre took place. A public meeting in Manchester of 60,000 to 80,000 people demanding political reform was charged by government cavalry, killing fifteen and injuring 700. Twenty-two years later, the Chartists met on Kersal Moor in Lancashire to demand universal male suffrage. Thirty-three years later the Communist Manifesto urged the workers of the world to cast off their chains. Revolution would grow from thoughts like these.

OPPOSITE: *As economic pressures on the poor were made worse by the behaviour of the gentry, the thought processes shown in this letter will have been repeated all over the country.*

# SATIRE *and* SEDITION
## Satirical Cartoons

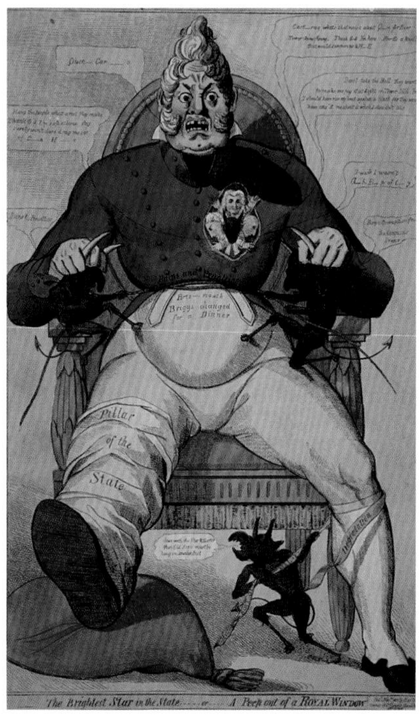


ABOVE: *The satirist's main target was the elderly dandy, George, the Prince Regent. Here, he is shown as suffering from gout and his belly is squeezed by imps while his lackeys hide in his heart.*

# 1820

SATIRICAL CARTOONS WERE a popular focus of protest and hilarity from the eighteenth to the early nineteenth centuries. These prints were bought by a government agent and studied for possible prosecution, before being stored in the Archives. Having barely seen daylight for nearly 200 years, they retain every bit of their colourful, boisterous malice.

Those shown here concern the idiotic Prince of Wales, soon to be George IV, and in particular his disastrous relationship with his wife, Caroline, Princess of Brunswick. The couple had been disappointed in each other from the start. Heavily in debt, George was forced to marry an eligible princess as a condition of Parliament increasing his allowance. Caroline was plump and vulgar, and on first meeting her the gallant Prince turned and called for a glass of brandy. Caroline in turn confided that her husband-to-be was 'nothing like as handsome as his portrait', and 'very fat'.

The couple managed to produce one daughter, Princess Charlotte, but for years led comfortably separate lives. However, when George was appointed Prince Regent in 1811 during the madness of his father George III, Caroline found herself increasingly isolated. She left England for Italy and the Mediterranean, determined to be 'a happy, merry soul'. George is said to have drunk a toast that she might never return to England.

But return she did. When Charlotte died in November 1817, George lost his only legitimate heir, and was determined to divorce his wife. He could not do so without compelling grounds, but he saw his opportunity in certain rumours that were reaching England, that

OPPOSITE: *George has removed his three-feathered crown (symbol of the Prince of Wales) and is admiring himself wearing the king's crown, when he is startled by the image of Caroline, wearing the queen's crown.*

**REFLECTION.**

To be, or not to be??

Pubd. Feby. 11 1820 by S W Fores 50 Piccadilly London–

Above: *Caroline and George, their pots bubbling on a fire fuelled by the notorious green bags, the crown hanging precariously between them. The cartoon suggests that each is as bad as the other.*

Caroline had taken as a lover one of her servants, Bartolomeo Pergami. George sent three commissioners to Milan to gather evidence, which was submitted to Parliament in two green bags. In a process that gave every appearance of grubby voyeurism, the green bags were opened and examined in secret by fifteen peers. A week later, the Government introduced a Bill to dissolve the marriage and remove Caroline from any claim to be queen. The passage of the Bill involved, in effect, a trial of the Princess, with witnesses called and cross-examined, and with Parliament acting as jury and judge. The public was agog.

The cartoons show how sophisticated political satire had become. The caricatures are peppered with oblique jokes that assume that readers are familiar with the matters and personalities satirised. The cartoon on page 163, 'Reflection: to be or not to be', concisely sets the scene, with fat-arsed George startled by the looming reflection of his wife. The one above is unusually even-handed. George and Caroline are two pots, the caption, 'The kettle calling the pot ugly names', suggesting that each is as unattractive as the other (George's affairs and sybaritic tastes were common knowledge). George's words are barely coherent, his hatred for his wife sputtering like an over-boiling pot: 'hiss hiss out hiss hiss the devil be gone you dirty grecepot.' The crisis for the throne is illustrated by the crown that floats between the couple. The cartoon is filled with knowing references. The green bags burning beneath the pair are the green bags that carried the evidence from

Above: *Victory for Caroline. When the divorce bill was abandoned, Caroline was portrayed as a ship running down George and scattering his supporters.*

George's sordid commission; the *Bergoni* pear tree is a reference to Pergami; the 'bit of wood and broomstick' is a reference to Henry Brougham (pronounced 'broom'), Caroline's advocate in Parliament.

The Bill passed in the House of Lords, but there was little prospect that it would pass a hostile House of Commons, and it was dropped. The cartoon above celebrates Caroline's victory. The King had escaped the turmoil by taking a cruise on his ship, the *Royal George*, and the drawing 'The Queen Caroline running down the Royal George' sees the great and powerful sent flying. It had become a badge of radical pride to take the Queen's side as a woman wronged by George and his aristocratic toadies, and the figures tumbling in Caroline's surf are all establishment figures, recognisable by the words put into their mouths: the Duke of Wellington ('this is worse than the grapeshot at Waterloo'), Lord Liverpool, the Prime Minster ('this pool goes against my liver'), the Lord Chancellor, Lord Eldom ('Oh my wool sack'), and the Home Secretary Lord Sidmouth ('this will be a cooling draft and purge our foul stomachs'). The knowing jokes are there again. Henry Brougham is represented by the broomstick he is holding. The words '*no mi recordo*' are spoken by one of the Princess's servants, Theodore Majocchi. He had provided lurid details of Caroline and Pergami's relationship, but in cross-examination seemed to lose his memory, responding '*no mi recordo*' ('I don't recall') more then 200 times. '*No mi recordo*' became a national joke.

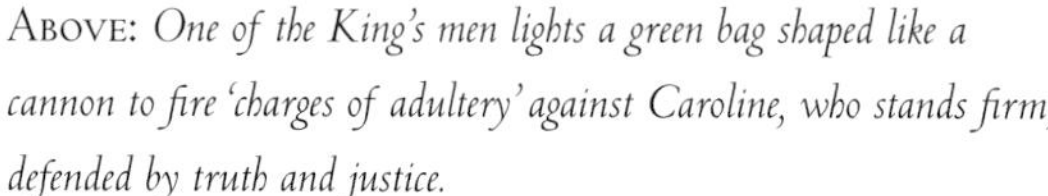

ABOVE: *One of the King's men lights a green bag shaped like a cannon to fire 'charges of adultery' against Caroline, who stands firm, defended by truth and justice.*

ABOVE: *Two members of the King's commission to investigate Caroline cook up a 'Royal Hash' made from 'Rakings of Italy'. George's face hovers in the steam from the cauldron.*

Caroline's story had an unhappy end. For all that she had defeated the passage of the Bill, it was plain that the Pot was as unattractive as the Kettle. The following year, Caroline made an undignified attempt to enter Westminster Abbey for George's coronation (to which she was not invited), and was jeered by the crowds. That night she fell ill, and died less than three weeks later. Caroline had asked to be buried with the inscription 'Here lies Caroline, the injured Queen of England', but she never got her wish. She was buried in the cathedral of her native Brunswick under an inscription that gave thanks to God for the King of Britain. She must have been spinning.

The golden age of satirical prints came to an end following the accession of Queen Victoria. An eighteen-year-old girl was harder to satirise than the preposterous George and his lackeys. Newspapers displaced the old print shops in providing caricature sketches, but perhaps took more care not to risk offending their readers and their households. The decline was lamented by William Thackeray in 1840, who recalled the old prints, populated 'with grinning, fantastical imps and merry, harmless sprites ... the sainted Caroline ... the Dandy of Sixty [George]. How we used to believe in them! To stray miles out of the way on holidays in order to ponder for an hour before that delightful window [a print shop] in Sweetings's Alley.' Satire in newspapers now consisted of 'polite points of wit which cause one to smile in a quiet, gentlemanlike way'. Something had been lost.

*... populated 'with grinning, fantastical imps and merry, harmless sprites ... the sainted Caroline ... the Dandy of Sixty [George]. How we used to believe in them! To stray miles out of the way on holidays in order to ponder for an hour before that delightful window [a print shop] in Sweetings's Alley.'*

# *The* RAILWAYS *are* COMING
## Stephenson's Patent for a Steam Engine

## 1822

ABOVE: *The Rocket, designed by George and Robert Stephenson – a stage in the evolving design of the steam engine, which would change the world.*

GEORGE STEPHENSON IS known as the 'Father of Railways'. He was the inventor of locomotives that ran with flanged wheels on rails, builder of the first railway run without animal power, and of the first purpose-built railway passenger carriage. He was involved in building railways between Liverpool, Manchester, Leeds, Derby and Birmingham. Perhaps his most enduring fame is associated with The Rocket, the speedy locomotive on which he collaborated with his son Robert. Shown overleaf is Stephenson's patent to an improved steam engine, filed seven years before The Rocket. The machine that Stephenson describes contained two chambers (marked D and C on the drawing) which would alternately fill with steam and are divided by a moving plunger (g). When the first chamber filled, the steam pressure would force the plunger to slide away, making the first chamber bigger and the empty chamber smaller. When the plunger reached a certain point, it would trigger a jet of steam into the second chamber and the release of steam from the first, and the plunger would be pushed in the other direction. One-way valves (a and b) would open or close accordingly. The same thing happened in reverse and so the plunger moved back and forth. As shown in the patent, the plunger could be attached to cranks to turn wheels, which provided power for the locomotive.

Locomotives were not uncontroversial – the Duke of Wellington opposed them on the grounds that he did not want the lower classes moving around – but soon, railways were being laid over Britain, and great tracts of London were cleared to make way for them. Food standards improved, as fresh food could be moved quickly from country to town. Suburbs were born, as people no longer needed to live so close to work. Boats powered by steam engines roared across the sea at unheard-of speeds. The hard-to-access interiors of the United States and other great continents were opened up. Engineering took a great leap forward, as the colossal power of these engines was used to dig and lift and build.

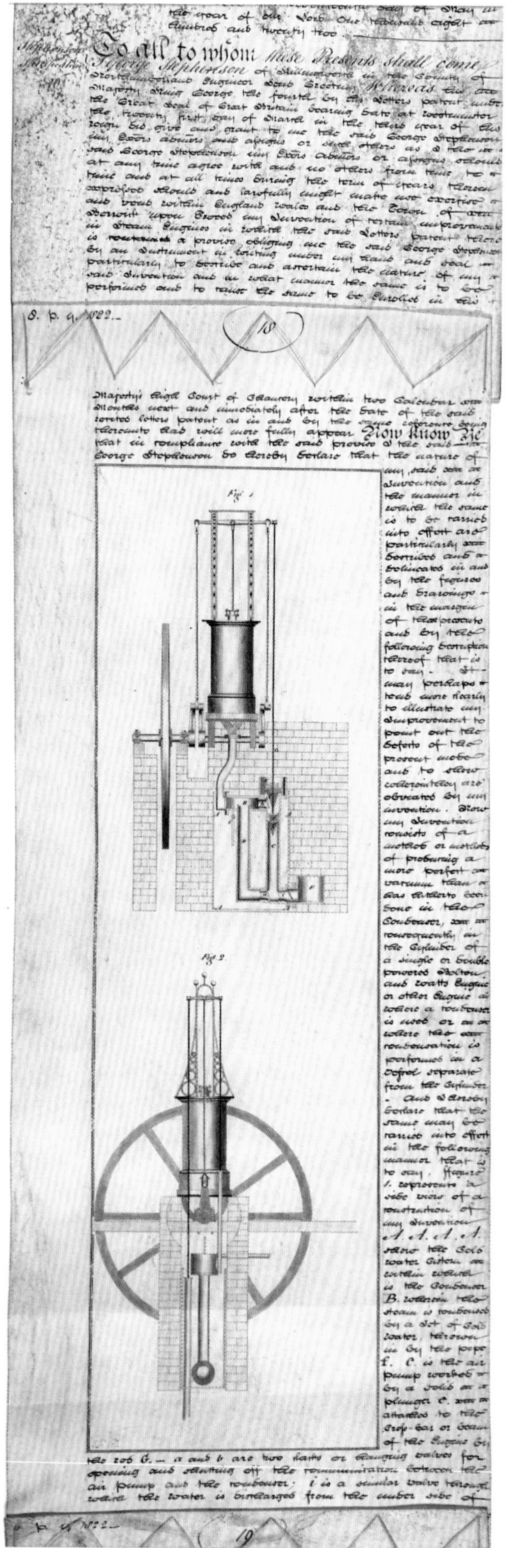

Left: *The elegant drawings that illustrate Stephenson's patent.* Right: *The written description of Stephenson's invention, which also sets out the scope of his monopoly. He says that his invention consists of a method of creating an improved vacuum in an engine, using cooling water.*

*Locomotives were not uncontroversial – the Duke of Wellington opposed them on the grounds that he did not want the lower classes moving around – but soon, railways were being laid over Britain, and great tracts of London were cleared to make way for them.*

If the patent captures the elegance and simplicity of Stephenson's design, it also expresses his eye for its commercial possibilities. Patents are state-sanctioned monopolies. Their purpose is to encourage inventors to expose their inventions to the public gaze, in return for which the state grants the inventor a monopoly over using and exploiting that invention for a period of time. This patent therefore enabled Stephenson, for a limited period, to stop others copying his invention, and gave him a head-start in commercialising it. Stephenson's patent is the capitalist seed of a capitalist explosion.

opening and shutting off the communication between the air pump and the condenser; i is a similar valve through which the water is discharged from the under side of



the plunger into the hot well F and o is a loose wooden cover on the top of the air pump for discharging the water and air from the upper side of the plunger into the hot well E. The communication pipe D is made to project a little into the Condenser so that a part of the condensing water is made to flow upon the plunger in its descent and which ought to be sufficient to occupy the space between the wooden Cover o. and the plunger, when the latter is at the summit of its ascent, this space would otherwise contain air or vapour of the same density with the external atmosphere, and which would materially injure the purity of the vacuum in the Condenser g. g. are inverted Cones respectively fixed to the under side of the wooden Cover o, and plunger e, which prevent the abrupt contact with the water in the ascending and descending stroke of the piston or plunger. To obtain a perfect vacuum in the condenser of a steam Engine is a desideratum of great value as the want of it lessens the effect of the Engine whilst every little approximation towards it increases the effect without in the least adding to the cost or expense of working the Engine. The method of condensing the steam in a vessel separate from the Cylinder, is generally considered an invention of the ingenious Mr. Watt, and has since his improvements undergone little or no alteration, this method is effected by means of a vessel distinct from the Cylinder and called the Condenser, into which the steam is allowed to flow at every half stroke of the double powered Engine and at every whole stroke of a single powered Engine and is condensed by a jet of cold water; which water, together with the air that unavoidably penetrates the packing and joints, or is extricated from the water is pumped out by means of an air pump, the construction of the air pump and condenser on Bolton and Watt's principle being so well known it will be unnecessary to enter into a minute description of them only it may be necessary to state that the air pump and condenser are supposed to stand near each other with a communication between them at the bottom shut off occasionally by a hanging valve. I shall proceed to consider the action of this apparatus immediately after the condensation is effected by the jet of cold water entering into the condenser; this water will then fill the communication pipe and ascend to a certain height within the Condenser above which the air and some steam remaining uncondensed will be resting; suppose the air Bucket begins to ascend, a vacuum will be formed beneath it and the water pressed upon by the elasticity of the air and vapour in the Condenser is impelled through the hanging valve to follow the Bucket in its ascent. Now as the air from its inferior specific gravity will not descend through the water it is evident, that the water must be forced out of the Condenser until the air obtains a passage along the roof of the communication pipe until it comes perpendicularly beneath the column of water in the air pump where it will by its specific levity ascend through the water and occupy a space immediately underneath the valves of the air Bucket and will when the Bucket has gained its full ascent be discharged in the next stroke of the Engine through the upper valve into the hot well. It follows then that the air or other steam in the Condenser will always be of that elasticity which is required to support a column of water corresponding with the size of the air pump and the quantity of injection water used; hence the vacuum is always found to be far from perfect But this is not the only imperfection in this mode. In steam Engines where the Bucket moves with great velocity as in winding Engines, the sudden impulse of the Bucket upon the water in descending soon

S. p. 4. 1822.-

20

destroys that accuracy and nicety requisite in this part of the steam Engine and still further tends to render the vacuum imperfect. I shall now explain the operation in my invention.

is not the only imperfection in this mode. In steam Engines where the Bucket moves with great velocity as in winding Engines, the sudden impulse of the Bucket upon the water in descending soon



destroys that accuracy and nicety requisite in this part of the steam Engine and still further tends to render the vacuum imperfect. I shall now explain the operation in my invention. When the condensation is effected, the water by its superior gravity will immediately fall to the bottom of the Condenser, the air and vapour resting upon the upper part. Suppose in this situation the plunger to be at the bottom of the pump and beginning to ascend leaving a vacuum below it the water in the condenser will flow down and along the communication pipe, through the valve a, and follow the plunger so far in its ascent until it (the water) finds its equilibrium with that remaining in the condenser. On the return of the plunger the valve a. shuts and the valve i. opens and the water is forced into the hot well F. and as the plunger descends a vacuum is made above it, the valve b. then opens and allows the air and elastic vapour to occupy the space above the plunger which in its reascent shuts the valve b. and discharges the whole through the loose Cover o. into the hot well E. Here then it will be seen that the air or vapour having no obstruction in entering the vacuum above the plunger except what arises from the resistance of the hanging valve b. which is made to move very freely the vacuum must be considerably more perfect than the mode heretofore used and will approximate very nearly to that of the Barometer. Hence then my Invention consists of a method of discharging the air and water from the Condenser by the action of a double pump in such a manner that the air in its escape from the condenser meets with scarcely any sensible obstruction from the condensing water; the air and water being so distinctly separated that the discharge of the former is effected chiefly by the ascent and the discharge of the latter by the descent of the plunger. In the annexed drawings I have shewn my apparatus with its application to a steam Engine where the air pump is made to work the whole length of the stroke of the Engine which together with the action both in the ascent and descent will proportionably reduce the size of my air pump. It is well known the present apparatus cannot be applied to work the whole length of the stroke of the Engine without proportionably decreasing the purity of the vacuum but in my invention the increased length of stroke increases the purity of the vacuum and further proves the superiority of the present Invention An Engine on my plan may from its simplicity of construction be removed and erected upon a smaller space and at considerably less expense than has hitherto been done *In witness* whereof I have hereunto set my hand and seal the eighteenth day of May in the year of our Lord One thousand eight hundred and twenty two. ——

*George Stephenson* (L.S.)

*Signed Sealed and Delivered* (being first duly stamped) in the presence of ——

—— *Thomas Carr Newcastle* ——

—— *Markh. Jobling his Clerk.* ——

Carr Extra — *And be it remembered* that on the eighteenth day of May in the year of our Lord 1822 the aforesaid George Stephenson came before our said Lord the King in his Chancery and acknowledged the Specification aforesaid and all and every thing therein contained and specified in form above written and also the Specification aforesaid was stamped according to the tenor of the Statute made for that purpose ——

*Inrolled* the twenty first day of May in the year of our Lord One thousand eight hundred and twenty two. ——

| 1822 | | s | d |
|---|---|---|---|
| Sept 11 | Wm Telling | 2 | 2 ½ |
| 12 | Jas Corner | 1 | 4 |
| 13 | Wm Telling | 1 | 1 ½ |
| 14 | Jas Corner | 1 | 0 ½ |
| 15 | Wm Telling | 2 | 7 |
| 16 | Jas Corner | 1 | 7 ½ |
| 17 | Wm Telling | 1 | 9 ½ |
| 18 | Jas Corner | 1 | 4 |
| 19 | Wm Telling | 1 | 2 ½ |
| 20 | Jas Corner | 2 | 1 |
| 21 | Wm Telling | 1 | 2 |
| 22 | Jas Corner | 1 | 9 |
| 23 | Wm Telling | 1 | 1 |
| 24 | Jas Corner | | 8 ½ |
| 25 | Wm Telling | 4 | 9 ½ |
| 26 | Jas Corner | 1 | 6 ½ |
| 27 | Wm Telling | 1 | 1 |
| 28 | Jas Corner | 1 | 5 |
| 28 | Recd from the Leather Sellers Compy 4/- in mony and 2/6 in Bread divided as above | 6 | 6 |
| 29 | Wm Telling | 2 | |

| 1822 | | | |
|---|---|---|---|
| October 1 | Recd from the Sadlers Compy the Sum of divided as above | 2 | 6 |
| Sept 30 | Jas Corner | 1 | 10 |
| October 1 | Wm Telling | 2 | 4 |
| 2 | Jas Corner | 2 | 3 |
| 3 | Wm Telling | 1 | 3 |
| 4 | Jas Corner | 1 | 5 ½ |
| 5 | Wm Telling | 2 | 7 ½ |
| 6 | Jas Corner | 2 | 1 ½ |
| 7 | Wm Telling | 2 | 2 |
| 8 | Jas Corner | | 11 |
| 9 | Wm Telling | 1 | 1 |
| 10 | Jas Corner | 1 | 6 |
| 11 | Wm Telling | 1 | 11 |
| 12 | Jas Corner | 2 | 3 |
| 13 | Wm Telling | 1 | 4 |
| 14 | Jas Corner | | 10 |
| 15 | Wm Telling | 1 | ½ |
| 16 | Jas Corner | | 11 |
| 17 | Wm Telling | 1 | 2 ½ |
| 18 | Jas Corner | 1 | |
| 19 | Wm Telling | 1 | 4 |

| 1822 | | | |
|---|---|---|---|
| Octor 20 | Jas Corner | 1 | 3 |
| 21 | Wm Telling | | 7 ½ |
| 22 | Jas Corner | | 8 |
| 23 | Wm Telling | 1 | 3 |
| 24 | Jas Corner | 1 | 3 |
| 25 | Wm Telling | 1 | 4 |
| 26 | Jas Corner | 1 | 7 |
| 27 | Wm Telling | 1 | 9 ½ |
| 28 | Jas Corner | 1 | 4 |
| 29 | Wm Telling | 1 | 4 |
| 30 | Jas Corner | 1 | 11 |
| 31 | Wm Telling | 1 | 1 ½ |
| Nober 1 | Jas Corner | 1 | 6 ½ |
| 2 | Wm Telling | | 6 ½ |
| 3 | Jas Corner | 1 | 7 |
| 4 | Wm Telling | 3 | 3 |
| 5 | Jas Corner | 1 | 10 |
| 6 | Wm Telling | 1 | 7 ½ |
| 7 | Jas Corner | 1 | 1 |
| 8 | John Stones | 1 | 6 |
| 9 | Jas Corner | 1 | 7 |

| 1822 | | | |
|---|---|---|---|
| Nov 8 | Cash recd for 3 Half Years Dividends on £600. £3 p Cent Red: due Octr 1822 | 27.-.- | |
| | Deduct Proctors Bill for Fees to obtain Adminis | 9.5.3 | |
| | Expences of Admin &c | 3.15.- | |
| | Mrs Fisher | 13.0.3 | |
| | Bal: | 13.19.9 | |
| | 1/3 to Fund | | 4.13.3 |
| 10 | Wm Telling | | 1 7 ½ |
| 11 | Jas Corner | | 1 8 |
| 12 | Wm Telling | | 2 1 ½ |
| 13 | Jas Corner | | 1 |
| 14 | Wm Telling | | 1 7 ½ |
| 15 | Jas Corner | | 1 5 |
| 16 | Wm Telling | | 11 |
| 17 | Jas Corner | | 1 |
| Nov 17 | Recd from the Court of Exchequer | | 6 8 |
| 18 | Wm Telling | | 1 11 |
| 19 | Jas Corner | | 7 |
| 20 | Wm Telling | | 1 3 |

# 'PRAY, REMEMBER *the* POOR DEBTORS'

## The Begging Grate Book

## 1822–1829

RIGHT: *The tap-room (drinking room) of the Fleet Prison. Life inside was comfortable, if you could afford it.*

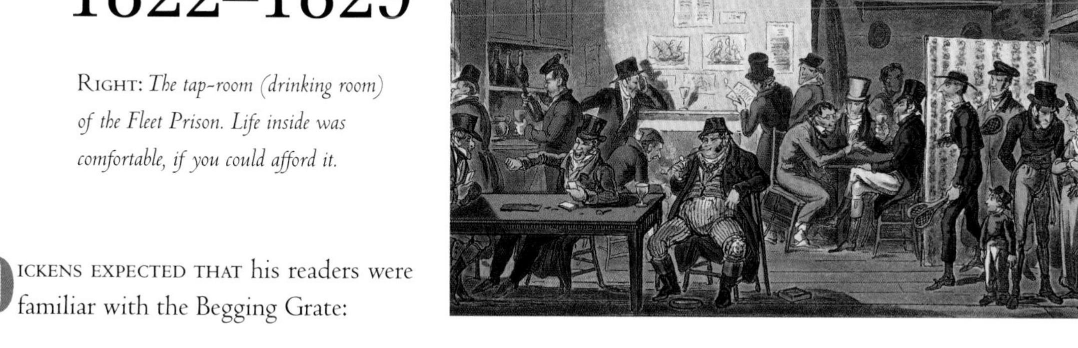

DICKENS EXPECTED THAT his readers were familiar with the Begging Grate:

*Most of our readers will remember, that, until within a very few years past, there was a kind of iron cage in the wall of the Fleet prison, within which was posted some man of hungry looks, who, from time to time, rattled a money box and exclaimed in a mournful voice, 'Pray, remember the poor debtors; pray, remember the poor debtors.'*

CHARLES DICKENS, *The Pickwick Papers*, 1837

This small volume, known as the Begging Grate Book, is the Fleet prison's record of these men 'of hungry looks'. The Fleet was a debtor's prison and it was surprisingly easy to end up there. A creditor would swear an affidavit to the debt, which was lodged with the court. The court would then issue a *Capias Ad Satisfaciendum*, or Ca.sa., instructing the sheriff to detain the debtor and return him to court on a set day. The debtor would be taken to a 'sponging house', a private house of detention, where he might have a week or so to send pleas for cash to pay the debt, 'sponging' from family and friends. If he couldn't, or wouldn't, find the money he owed, prison awaited – the Marshalsea, the King's Bench or the Fleet.

OPPOSITE: *A place at the Begging Grate was desirable for the poorest debtors. Here you see a pair, William Telling and James Cournet, working the grate in strict rotation, together with an account of the amount of money they had been given each day.*

The Fleet held about 300 debtors and their families. For some, life inside was comfortable. Many debtors carried on their trade from inside prison, and they would lay on their own entertainment. They could play at fives, skittles or tennis (the Fleet had a racquets court). There was a bake house, and a tap room that sold wine and beer. The buildings were relatively new, and accommodation was in single or shared rooms, for which you could rent home comforts, such as a carpet, chairs and a kettle.

But life was not comfortable for the poorest of the debtors, the men at the Begging Grate. What does this book tell us about them? One is that, at a certain level, a position at the Grate was desirable. From January 1823, the only face you

RIGHT: *In December 1823 there were three man at the Grate: Howarth, Harvey and Hopgood. The amounts the men made were pathetic. On Christmas Day 1823, Harvey made one shilling and four pence. This could be supplemented by larger corporate gifts – included here are donations from the Leather Sellers Company, the Sadlers Company and the Archbishop of Canterbury.*

*You too could end up on the wrong side of those bars, fighting your fellow prisoners to spend a day pleading for pennies from passers by. So pay up!*

would have seen at the Grate each day was that of one William Telling. Telling may have been a bruiser, jealously guarding his spot, because when he disappears in March – released or dead, the book doesn't say – his place is immediately taken by a pair of men, Howarth and Potter, who worked the Grate in strict rotation for the next three months. When Potter disappears, the duopoly is broken and other names – Mansfield, Harvey, Willis, Wood, Dark – appear. Who knows what negotiations, fights, threats and bribes went on behind the Grate to secure that coveted place? But, at the same time, the book records the pathetic sums of money that the men received. On Christmas Day 1823, for example, Harvey made just one shilling and four pence.

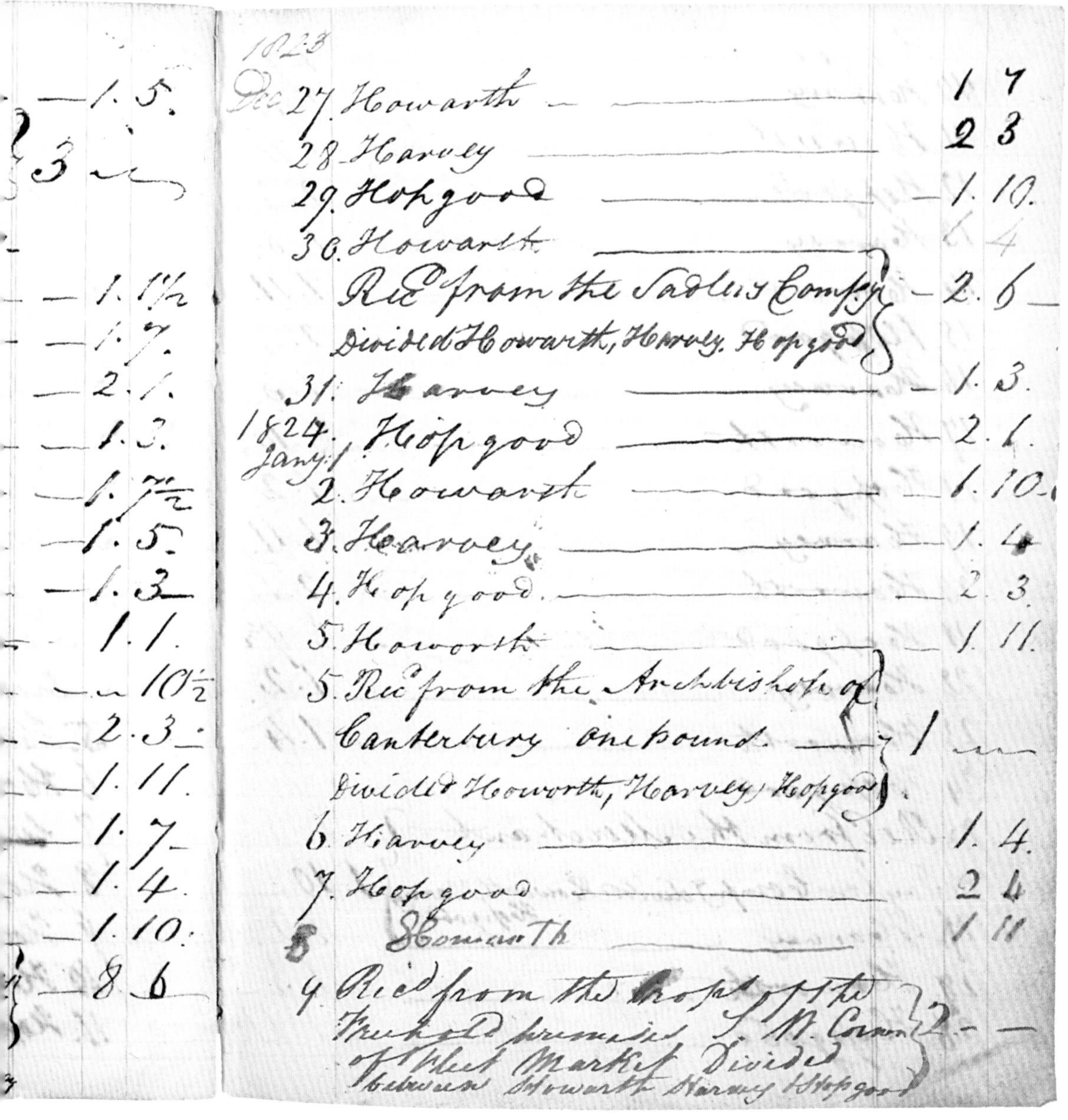

1823

Dec 27 Howarth — 1 7
28 Harvey — 2 3
29 Hopgood — 1. 10.
30 Howarth
Recd from the Sadlers Compy — 2. 6 —
Divided Howarth, Harvey, Hopgood
31 Harvey — 1. 3.
1824 Jany 1 Hopgood — 2. 1.
2 Howarth — 1. 10.
3 Harvey — 1. 4
4 Hopgood — 2. 3.
5 Howarth — 1. 11.
5 Recd from the Archbishop of Canterbury one pound — 1 —
Divided Howarth, Harvey, Hopgood
6 Harvey — 1. 4.
7 Hopgood — 2 4
8 Howarth 1 11
9 Recd from the Prop[rietors] of the Freehold premises Mr. Corner of Fleet Market Divided between Howarth Harvey & Hopgood 2 —

Imprisoning people for debt reduced their chances of earning the money that would get them out of jail, and the stupidity of this vicious circle eventually caught up with the debtor's prisons. Public opinion turned against them, helped on its way by Dickens's vivid descriptions. The Begging Grate was sealed up. The Fleet closed in 1846, and imprisonment for debt was abolished in 1869.

But individual punishment had never been the primary purpose of the Fleet, any more than the Begging Grate had been set up to help debtors help themselves. Their purpose was to deter others. The Grate was a living tableau, warning those outside of the perils of unpaid debt. You too could end up on the wrong side of those bars, fighting your fellow prisoners to spend a day pleading for pennies from passers by. So pay up!

# *The* WORKHOUSE
## Protest Poster

## 1830s

ABOVE: *The Lambeth Workhouse School, in south London. The school housed and educated pauper children, and was home to several hundred young inmates.*
OPPOSITE: *This polemical poster against the Poor Law Act shows many impoverished and destitute people being barred from relief by the warden, while those inside are shaved, chained and humiliated.*

THIS HOME-MADE PRINT is a vivid protest against one of Britain's most despised institutions: the workhouse. Within high, barbed walls, men and women are shaven like convicts. They are forced to work, smashing bones with giant hammers. Entire families are manacled to the walls, or are hung by their hands or feet. Emaciated children work at unpicking ropes. The workhouse master whips a terrified inmate, while behind him a fat parson forces a man to pull his cart like a horse.

The print (or perhaps poster) was distributed in a local popular protest. It will have been discovered and sent to a local magistrate, who in turn will have sent it to the Home Office. The poster is polemic – even at their worst, there is no evidence that any inmate of a workhouse was hung from the walls – but it shows the depth of loathing for these new institutions. A long-lasting loathing, too. The jokey threat to boisterous children that if they didn't quieten down they would be sent to the workhouse was still current among my grandparents' generation.

Since the sixteenth century, responsibility for those too ill, young or old to work had lain with the parish, paid for by a rate levied on the wealthier parishioners. Some parishes maintained a central poor-house. But most administered poor relief in an *ad hoc* and relatively sympathetic way.

Between 1801 and 1830 the general population increased by two-thirds, and the parish system came under severe strain. In 1832, a Royal Commission was set up to look at reform. The Commission recommended two principles for a new Poor Law. First, relief should be available only in a workhouse. Parishes would no longer be allowed to tailor their poor relief to the needs of the recipient. Second, paupers should be eligible for admittance only when their conditions were worse than those of the poorest labourer outside. Relief would be available for the destitute only.

By 1849, there were 427 workhouses in England and Wales, and 67 more were under construction. Some were well organised and humane. Others were horrible. Food was minimal and bad, and the work was dull

# The New Poor Law

## with a description of the new Workhouses

Look at the Picture — See

INTERIOR OF AN ENGLISH WORKHOUSE UNDER THE NEW POOR LAW ACT.

*The worst – or at least, the worst recorded – was the workhouse at Andover in Hampshire. The workhouse master was a former soldier, Colin McDougal, a drunken, cruel bully with an equally vicious wife. Paupers, including children as young as ten, were put to work crushing the bones of horses and dogs to make fertiliser, which they did using a heavy iron rammer in a tub.*

and hard. Couples and families were split up from each other as a matter of course, with men, women and children housed in separate blocks. Some workhouses were built to a 'panopticon' design, with paupers housed in buildings that radiated from a central hub where the workhouse master lived, so that inmates could be kept under constant surveillance.

Radicals described workhouses as 'pauper bastilles'. These institutions were more than a response to poverty: they were a form of class war, which explains much about this print. What did the protesters hope to achieve? The people to whom the poster was directed, at or below the poverty line, might have known the inside of the workhouses themselves, or at least known someone who had been in one. They knew that people were not hung from the walls. But they knew that misery and humiliation might be heaped upon the inmates inside. If the poor were not actually in chains, the poster is saying, they might as well be.

The worst – or at least, the worst recorded – was the workhouse at Andover in Hampshire. The workhouse master was a former soldier, Colin McDougal, a drunken, cruel bully with an equally vicious wife. Paupers, including children as young as ten, were put to work crushing the bones of horses and dogs to make fertiliser, which they did using a heavy iron rammer in a tub. McDougal kept the paupers half-starved, and despite the stench ('Pretty ripe, in the summer,' one pauper reported), the inmates gnawed at the gristle and rotting marrow in their tubs. A complaint by one of the guardians resulted in a question in Parliament, investigation by the Poor Law Commission, and detailed reporting by *The Times*. Embarrassing details emerged. Some of the guardians had been lining their pockets, buying the crushed bones at a knock-down price; the chairman of the board of guardians had not visited the workhouse in five years.

The Poor Law system was at its worst in these early decades. By the end of the century, workhouses were largely occupied by the old, the incapable or the very young (Charlie Chaplin was a young inmate of the Lambeth workhouse, when his mother was incapacitated by mental illness). The abolition of the workhouses came about with the increase of the franchise, and the corresponding rise of the welfare state. In 1834, the voteless poor formed a weak underclass. By 1930, free school meals and old-age pensions were provided, and the National Insurance scheme had been instituted. Some workhouses were demolished. Others survive as hospitals, convalescent homes or, in the case of the Andover workhouse, luxury apartments.

# *The* BATTLE *against* DISEASE

## Cholera Documents

## 1832–1866

CHOLERA WAS THE first new plague of the Victorian era. Reactions to it are an object lesson in how people respond to new threats, even today: quack solutions, serious-minded investigations, resistance by vested interests, and a high moral tone.

Cholera had long been endemic in southeast Asia, emigrating westwards as global trade increased. The disease reached England in 1831, probably through the port at Sunderland. Symptoms were, and are, terrible diarrhoea and vomiting, leading to extreme dehydration. The loss of fluid wrinkled sufferers' skin and turned it a leaden blue colour (hence cholera's nickname, the 'Blue Horror') and seemed to shrink their eyes. The disease was known as the 'Indian Cholera', and part of its terror lay in this outward changing of its victims into something foreign and unknown. No one understood what caused it, or how to cure it.

TO EMIGRANTS.

CHOLERA.

CHOLERA having made its appearance on board several Passenger Ships proceeding from the United Kingdom to the United States of America, and having, in some instances, been very fatal, Her Majesty's Colonial Land and Emigration Commissioners feel it their duty to recommend to the Parents of Families in which there are many young children, and to all persons in weak health who may be contemplating Emigration, to postpone their departure until a milder season. There can be no doubt that the sea sickness consequent on the rough weather which Ships must encounter at this season, joined to the cold and damp of a sea voyage, will render persons who are not strong more susceptible to the attacks of this disease.

To those who may Emigrate at this season the Commissioners strongly recommend that they should provide themselves with as much warm clothing as they can, and especially with flannel, to be worn next the Skin; that they should have both their clothes and their persons quite clean before embarking, and should be careful to keep them so during the voyage,—and that they should provide themselves with as much solid and wholesome food as they can procure, in addition to the Ship's allowance to be used on the voyage. It would, of course, be desirable, if they can arrange it, that they should not go in a Ship that is much crowded, or that is not provided with a Medical Man.

By Order of the Board,

S. WALCOTT,
SECRETRAY.

*Colonial Land and Emigration Office,*
*8, Park Street, Westminster,*
*November,* 1853.

ABOVE: *A notice to emigrants, following the appearance of cholera among passengers on several ships sailing between the UK and America. The disease was poorly understood – cleanliness and warm clothing are the main requirements in the notice.*

Enter the quacks. A second cholera epidemic flared up in 1848. A number of remedies were filed with the Patent Office, including a 'design for the chemical sanitary belt and cholera repellent by Thomas Drew, Chemist, Plymouth' (see document on page 180). The belt was intended to be soaked in chemicals (doubtless provided by Dr Drew) and then tied around the belly. Quacks like pseudo-science, and they also like to dress themselves in the respectable clothes of official-sounding guidance. 'The Prevention of Cholera' leaflet on page 178 also dates from the second epidemic, and was designed to look like a government poster, with its 'Remedies recommended by Government'. Cholera belts were clearly in fashion, since they come in at number 15 on the list of cures, but of course the only sure-fire way of avoiding the disease is Dr Lenac's anti-cholera tincture. No prizes for identifying the man behind the leaflet. It is easy to make fun of these 'cures' and the gullible souls who bought

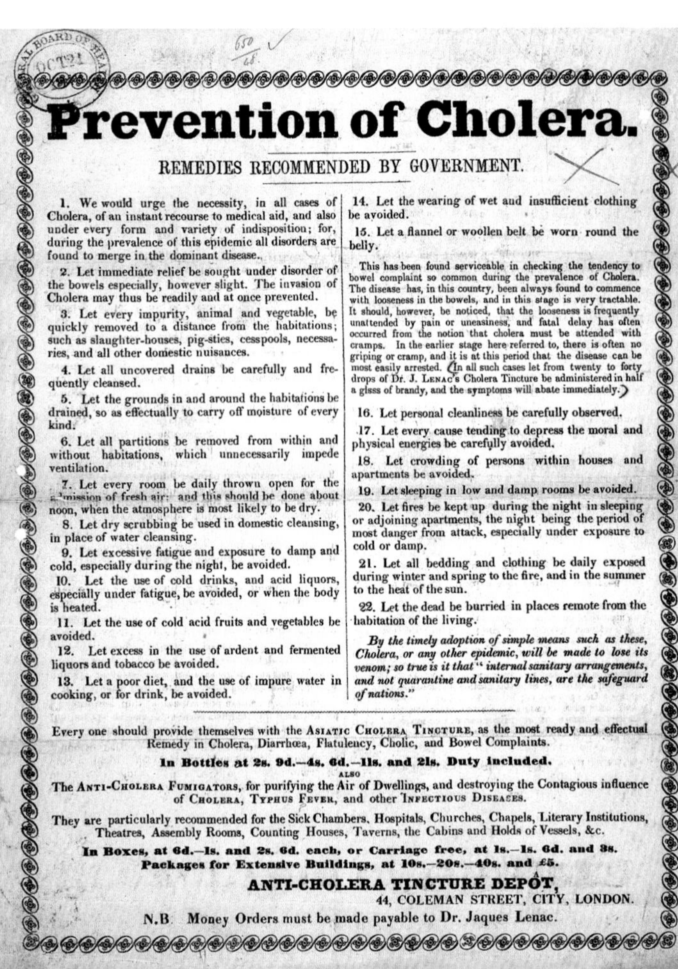

# Prevention of Cholera.

REMEDIES RECOMMENDED BY GOVERNMENT.

1. We would urge the necessity, in all cases of Cholera, of an instant recourse to medical aid, and also under every form and variety of indisposition; for, during the prevalence of this epidemic all disorders are found to merge in the dominant disease.
2. Let immediate relief be sought under disorder of the bowels especially, however slight. The invasion of Cholera may thus be readily and at once prevented.
3. Let every impurity, animal and vegetable, be quickly removed to a distance from the habitations; such as slaughter-houses, pig-sties, cesspools, necessaries, and all other domestic nuisances.
4. Let all uncovered drains be carefully and frequently cleansed.
5. Let the grounds in and around the habitations be drained, so as effectually to carry off moisture of every kind.
6. Let all partitions be removed from within and without habitations, which unnecessarily impede ventilation.
7. Let every room be daily thrown open for the admission of fresh air; and this should be done about noon, when the atmosphere is most likely to be dry.
8. Let dry scrubbing be used in domestic cleansing, in place of water cleansing.
9. Let excessive fatigue and exposure to damp and cold, especially during the night, be avoided.
10. Let the use of cold drinks, and acid liquors, especially under fatigue, be avoided, or when the body is heated.
11. Let the use of cold acid fruits and vegetables be avoided.
12. Let excess in the use of ardent and fermented liquors and tobacco be avoided.
13. Let a poor diet, and the use of impure water in cooking, or for drink, be avoided.
14. Let the wearing of wet and insufficient clothing be avoided.
15. Let a flannel or woollen belt be worn round the belly.

This has been found serviceable in checking the tendency to bowel complaint so common during the prevalence of Cholera. The disease has, in this country, been always found to commence with looseness in the bowels, and in this stage is very tractable. It should, however, be noticed, that the looseness is frequently unattended by pain or uneasiness, and fatal delay has often occurred from the notion that cholera must be attended with cramps. In the earlier stage here referred to, there is often no griping or cramp, and it is at this period that the disease can be most easily arrested. (In all such cases let from twenty to forty drops of Dr. J. Lenac's Cholera Tincture be administered in half a glass of brandy, and the symptoms will abate immediately.)

16. Let personal cleanliness be carefully observed.
17. Let every cause tending to depress the moral and physical energies be carefully avoided.
18. Let crowding of persons within houses and apartments be avoided.
19. Let sleeping in low and damp rooms be avoided.
20. Let fires be kept up during the night in sleeping or adjoining apartments, the night being the period of most danger from attack, especially under exposure to cold or damp.
21. Let all bedding and clothing be daily exposed during winter and spring to the fire, and in the summer to the heat of the sun.
22. Let the dead be burried in places remote from the habitation of the living.

*By the timely adoption of simple means such as these, Cholera, or any other epidemic, will be made to lose its venom; so true is it that "internal sanitary arrangements, and not quarantine and sanitary lines, are the safeguard of nations."*

Every one should provide themselves with the Asiatic Cholera Tincture, as the most ready and effectual Remedy in Cholera, Diarrhœa, Flatulency, Cholic, and Bowel Complaints.

**In Bottles at 2s. 9d.—4s. 6d.—11s. and 21s. Duty included.**

ALSO

The Anti-Cholera Fumigators, for purifying the Air of Dwellings, and destroying the Contagious influence of Cholera, Typhus Fever, and other Infectious Diseases.

They are particularly recommended for the Sick Chambers, Hospitals, Churches, Chapels, Literary Institutions, Theatres, Assembly Rooms, Counting Houses, Taverns, the Cabins and Holds of Vessels, &c.

**In Boxes, at 6d.—1s. and 2s. 6d. each, or Carriage free, at 1s.—1s. 6d. and 3s. Packages for Extensive Buildings, at 10s.—20s.—40s. and £5.**

**ANTI-CHOLERA TINCTURE DEPÔT,**
44, COLEMAN STREET, CITY, LONDON.

N.B. Money Orders must be made payable to Dr. Jaques Lenac.

Left: *A series of quack remedies dressed up to look like an official document.*

Above: *Letter from the Middlesex Coroner with observations on the circumstances surrounding an outbreak in 1853.*

Opposite: *A polemic against the Public Health Act, an 'un-English attack upon your rights and liberties'.*

them, but the fear of an unknown disease, and people prepared to cash in on that fear, has not changed. A 1989 study of health-food shops in the Houston area found 30 out of 41 offering a 'cure' for AIDS.

The shock of cholera prompted others to undertake more systematic investigation. The most famous example is Dr John Snow, now regarded as the father of epidemiology, who analysed information about cholera deaths in Soho and found them clustered around a particular water pump. Snow was convinced that the disease was carried in water – it later emerged that the water source for the pump was contaminated by an old sewage cistern – and he persuaded the parish council to remove the handle on the pump. The outbreak ceased almost at once. A similarly astute observation was made by Dr William Duncan in Liverpool. Duncan's letter to the Liverpool authorities points out that cholera outbreaks were flaring up around workhouses that took in newly arrived Irish migrants, who, he postulated, were bringing the disease in from infected areas in Ireland. But the masters of the busy port of Liverpool did not want to see its traffic from Ireland diminished, and dismissed Duncan's suggestion.

Although germ theory (the idea that disease is caused by germs) was still a few decades away from acceptance, the authorities understood that cholera was linked to insanitary living. On the second cholera

# A FEW BLESSINGS

OF THE

# Public Health Act!

Ratepayers! The Public Health Act has now been in force here three months—What are the blessings which are to be conferred upon you by it? Why, look at the following List of

## *Pains and Penalties*

which are to be levied upon you under that Blessed Act if you contravene its provisions, and this List, remember, is extracted from the Notices just issued by the Local Board.

**If you dare** to drain your own premises without the consent of the Board of Health, you will be fined **£5!!**

**If you dare** to build a house without giving notice to the Local Board, and obtaining their most gracious permission to do so, you will be fined **£50!!**

**If you dare** to construct a house according to your own convenience, but contrary to their orders and regulations, you will be fined **£50!!**

**If you dare** to carry on the trade of a Butcher without registering your house at the Board of Health before the 7th of November, you will be fined **£5!!** *and* **10s.** *a day* for neglecting to do so!

**If you dare** to carry on the trade of a Tallow Chandler, Soap Manufacturer, or other low "offensive" business, without the gracious permission of the Board of Health, you will be fined **£50!!** *and* **10s.** *a day* for continuing to do so!

**If you dare** to keep a "common" Lodging-house without registering it at the Board of Health, you will be fined **£2!!** and

**If you dare** to refuse the minions of the Board of Health to ransack your house between the hours of 11 and 4 in the day, you will be fined **£2!!**

**If you dare** to "injure or displace" the stones in the street, or if your horse and cart dare to knock down a post, you will be fined **£5!!** *and* **5s.** *a day for not repairing them!!*

**And for fear that neighbours will not inform against one another, and in order to give you the full benefit of the "Blessings" of the Public Health Act, certain Officers are provided to enforce the above Pains and Penalties. What is the next blessing to be conferred upon you? Why WATER from Ormesby or Norwich at your expense—Water for the Malster to make much out of little—Water for the monopolising Brewers to make a little more profit out of the Poor Man's pot of beer—and the whole to be paid for with 7s. 6d. Rates!!!**

**But will you wait for all these Blessings? Will you not rather on Saturday next, send to the right about the aristocratic clique of Brewers and Malsters who dare to bring this curse upon you—and Vote for those who will manfully resist this un-English attack upon your rights and liberties.**

MEALL, PRINTER, QUAY, OPPOSITE THE BRIDGE, YARMOUTH.

*Cholera Instructions, No. 6.*

SANITARY DEPARTMENT, GLASGOW, 1866.

# PLAIN DIRECTIONS

## FOR THE PEOPLE.

*(For Distribution by District Visitors.)*

THE bearer of this brief Address is charged to represent to the people of the district in which he visits, what things are necessary to be done in view of an epidemic of Cholera, and, if possible, so done as to prevent the epidemic from visiting Glasgow at all.

There are some causes of the disease that can only be removed by the authorities. There are others where the authorities can do but little, unless every man and woman will give assistance in keeping the evil from their own door. The Visitor who carries this paper to you is requested to take care that you are properly informed of your own duty in this matter, and, at the same time, to bring under the notice of the authorities whatever they can do for your safety. You will surely not fail to give a friendly welcome to one who comes to you so purely for your own good. Here are a few only of many cautions to be thought over carefully in Cholera times. See if there is anything in them that is not according to reason.

ABOVE: *A genuine public health leaflet, issued in Glasgow during the cholera epidemic of 1866. The leaflet adopts a high moral tone about the need for cleanliness.*

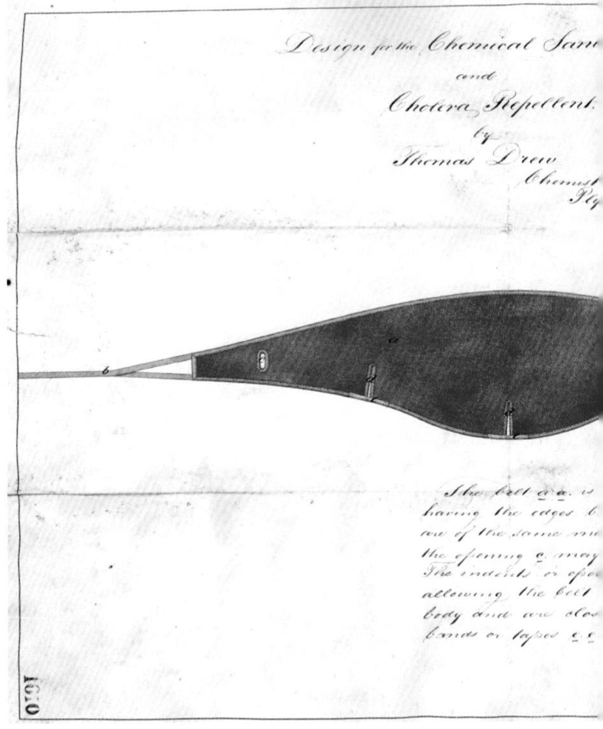


outbreak of 1848, the Public Health Acts were introduced. The Acts authorised the institution of Boards of Health, to control and co-ordinate water supply, sewage and so on, in the areas under their control. Not everyone was happy with this solution, of course. The pamphlet on page 179, 'A Few Blessings of the Public Health Act', was circulated in Great Yarmouth prior to a vote there on whether to institute a local Board of Health. It sets out claims about the 'Pains and Penalties which are to be levied upon you under that Blessed Act'. The pamphlet argues that the power of the Boards was an abuse of traditional English liberties.

The document above, 'Plain Directions for the People', is a genuine publication, issued by the Glasgow Board of Health in response to an outbreak in 1866. It makes for worrying reading. Suffer from the slightest stomach upset and you should contact the authorities. The document adopts the high moral tone that often accompanies pronouncements on public health. Just as syphilis, or more latterly AIDS, was interpreted as being a consequence of immoral lifestyles, cholera was interpreted as a consequence of the dirty habits of the poor. Human nature does not change.

ABOVE: *A patent to a 'sanitary belt and anti-cholera repellant'. The belt had to be soaked in chemicals, which were, of course, available from the patent holder.*

*Cholera Instructions, No. 1.*

# SANITARY DEPARTMENT, GLASGOW, 1866.

## INSTRUCTIONS

FOR

## DISTRICT VISITORS IN TIME OF CHOLERA,

OR WHEN CHOLERA IS THREATENED.

1. To go from house to house, systematically, but without raising alarm.

2. To observe defects of external cleansing, in closes, courts, common stairs, &c., and report to the Sanitary Office, 59 College Street, or to the Inspector specially appointed for the District.

3. To observe if the night-soil has been regularly and properly removed; otherwise, to report as above.

4. To use personal influence as to the cleansing and ventilation of common stairs and lobbies; and, in cases of gross neglect, to give notice as above.

5. To urge upon the inhabitants the frequent opening of windows, both by day and by night; and to see that windows are constructed in accordance with the law, *which requires that at least one-third of them be made to open.* It is greatly to be preferred, but not required by law, that the opening of every window should be *from the top.*

6. To urge the use of whitewash in dirty or dark houses. Orders for the materials may be had *gratis* on application at the Sanitary Office, and will be furnished either to District Visitors or directly to poor applicants.

7. To urge, in the strongest manner, as being one of the greatest securities against disease, *the most careful attention to cleanliness of person, clothing, and bedding.* Children especially should be washed from head to foot *at least once a day.* Bedclothes should be regularly spread out and aired *every morning;* and body-clothing removed and aired *every night.*

8. To explain the danger of using tainted water. All water for drinking to be taken direct from the main, *i.e.*, from the pipe or fountain on the stair or in the close, *not* from a cistern in the house, or from a pitcher or other large vessel standing in a close room. Where the sources of water-supply are at all doubtful, it is a proper caution to use water only after boiling, or in the shape of infusions, *e.g.*, tea, coffee, &c., which have been made with boiled water.

9. To recommend strongly that plain wholesome food be alone used; nothing tainted or long kept, or that has been put away in dirty closets or in ill-ventilated and ill-kept shops, or fingered by dirty hands. Hands and face should always be washed before eating; and all vessels in which food is kept or served, together with all knives, spoons, &c., employed at table, should be carefully cleansed and kept clean, so that nothing injurious may get into the food, either at meal times or otherwise. The rule of life in Cholera times is to eat and drink nothing unclean or decidedly unwholesome; but, also, *not* to restrict the diet unreasonably, nor to vary from what has been found to agree.

10. To recommend more than usual caution as regards the use of strong drinks of every kind, and the most strict watchfulness against all excess. It is certain that drunkards, and even habitual tipplers (who are not, strictly speaking, drunkards), fall in large numbers in all Cholera epidemics. It is at least very probable that every glass of whisky taken increases the risk. District Visitors will make their own application of these results of medical experience.

---

*In all cases of Diarrhœa, or of serious derangement of the stomach or bowels resembling Cholera, persons should be recommended to go to bed, to keep quiet and warm, and to send instantly for medical advice.*

RIGHT: *Instructions to visitors to Glasgow 'in time of cholera', 1866. By now, the approach to cholera was much more systematic and organised.*

# *The* FIGHT *for* DEMOCRACY

## Chartist and Anti-Chartist Posters

### 1839

RIGHT: *'Not So Very Unreasonable!!! Eh?'* Punch *cartoon (1848) about the last and largest of the petitions for the People's Charter.*

THE POSTER OPPOSITE IS preserved in The National Archives, retaining all its vivid colours as well as the urgency that it would have conveyed in the spring of 1839, when it was fixed to a wall in Carlisle. The poster is advertising a mass meeting of Britain's first national working-class movement for political reform – the Chartists.

Workers' groups had existed before the Chartists, but they tended to be disparate, campaigning for better living or working conditions on a local scale. Then in 1838, a group of six MPs and six working men wrote and published the 'People's Charter'. The Charter called for six simple reforms:

1. A VOTE FOR ALL MEN OVER 21
2. A SECRET BALLOT
3. NO REQUIREMENT THAT MPs SHOULD OWN A MINIMUM AMOUNT OF PROPERTY
4. A SALARY FOR MPs
5. CONSTITUENCIES OF EQUAL SIZE
6. PARLIAMENTARY ELECTIONS ONCE EACH YEAR

The injustices in the political system are plain from the demands. Voting for Parliament was effectively denied to working-class men. Even if they could have voted, the ballot was not secret, and so it was easy for local bosses to intimidate their workers into voting the way they wanted. MPs were unsalaried and had a minimum property qualification, and so the role was denied to anyone but the well-off, while disparities in the size of constituencies meant that small constituencies could smother the voice of larger ones. The idea of annual (as opposed to the then seven-year) elections was to stop elected MPs from getting into their seats and then defying the wishes of their electors.

The People's Charter is striking for being, to modern eyes, so obviously fair and reasonable. It is also striking for being concerned solely with process and system. The Chartists were not demanding, for example, better pay. They had recognised that so long as they campaigned for nothing more than better

OPPOSITE: *This vivid poster advertises a Chartist meeting 'on the sands' at Carlisle. It urges 'Peace, Law, and Order!!!' but also contains a veiled threat.*

# PEACE, LAW, AND ORDER!!!

"For a Nation to be Free 'tis sufficient that she wills it."

# A GREAT PUBLIC MEETING

WILL TAKE PLACE

# ON THE SANDS,

## ON WHIT TUESDAY, MAY 21ST, AT FOUR O'CLOCK,

For the purpose of adopting such measures as may be deemed expedient under the present circumstances of the country, for securing, as early as possible, the full enjoyment of the principles of the

# PEOPLE'S CHARTER.

# DR. J. TAYLOR,

AND SEVERAL OTHER

***Delegates from the Convention***

**OF THE WORKING CLASSES, AND OTHERS, WILL BE PRESENT.**

**The PEOPLE are requested to assemble on the SANDS**

**It is particularly requested that no persons come to the meeting Armed with any offensive weapons of any description whatever, so that no advantage may be taken of them by the authorities. Let the people be firm and determined; let their mien be bold and erect, like men engaged in a holy and righteous cause; at the same time watchful and circumspect; nor allow themselves to be goaded into the slightest breach of the peace, so that their Enemies may not have an opportunity of persecuting them, and *retarding the progress of Liberty.***

***It is hoped that the* MASTER MANUFACTURERS *will see* THE PROPRIETY OF ALLOWING THEIR WORKPEOPLE TO ATTEND *the* MEETING, so that any UNPLEASANT COLLISION BETWEEN THEM may be *avoided.***

Members of the Radical Association are informed that the QUARTERLY MEETING of that body will take place on Monday evening, the 27th of May, at 8 o'clock, in the Theatre, for the purpose of choosing Office Bearers, &c. when a statement of the accounts will be read, and a report of the progress of the cause in Carlisle and neighbourhood. *Admission to all parts of the house One Penny.*

**By Order of the Committee of the**
**CARLISLE RADICAL ASSOCIATION.**

HENRY LOWES, PRINTER, ENGLISH-STREET.

# V.  R.



# Illegal Assemblies, &c.

# PUBLIC CAUTION

**WHEREAS**, by Her Majesty's Proclamation issued on the 3rd day of May instant, for the **SUPPRESSION** of **ILLEGAL ASSEMBLIES**, Justices of the Peace, Sheriffs, Under-Sheriffs, and all other Civil Officers are commanded to use their utmost endeavours to Discover, Apprehend, and Bring to Justice the Offenders; and also to Prevent, Put Down, and Suppress all **UNLAWFUL MEETINGS**:

And Whereas, a **CERTAIN MEETING** has been Called by Placard, to be Held within this Borough, at the **STANLEY ARMS INN**, at Seven o'Clock, this Evening, which Meeting, if not Illegal in its commencement, may become so:

Now, therefore, We, the Justices of the Peace, acting in and for the said Borough of Stockport, in order to Warn all of Her Majesty's Peaceable Subjects of the danger of Attending such a Meeting, do Hereby Give this **PUBLIC NOTICE**, that if, by the Exhibition of Weapons, or Fire Arms, or if by excitements to Physical Force, or if by any Procession of the Parties the Peaceable Inhabitants of Stockport are put in Fear, or any other Breach of the Peace takes place, and such Assembly becomes Illegal, it is our determination to Suppress and Disperse the Meeting or Assemblage, to Apprehend the Principals and Parties engaged therein, and to deal with such Parties according to Law:

**And all Innkeepers and others are hereby ordered to abstain from having in their Houses Seditious Meetings, and from acting contrary to the Law, by allowing Parties for Illegal Purposes to Assemble therein.**

**Given under our Hands at Stockport aforesaid, this 9th day of May, 1839.**

R. PENDLEBURY, Mayor,
S. DAVENPORT,
JAMES NEWTON,
W. B. WORTHINGTON,

JOHN SLACK,
APELLES HOWARD,
P. E. MARSLAND.

*Court House, Stockport.*

THOMAS KING, PRINTER 8, BRIDGE-STREET, STOCKPORT.

OPPOSITE: *This anti-Chartist poster deploys the full weight of public authority to deter people from attending a Chartist meeting at the pub.*

*The Charter struck a chord. Workers' groups united behind it, and local groups sprang up to promote it.*

working conditions they would be perpetual beggars, forever holding out pleading hands to men of power. But if the system itself was changed – if all men could have a say in how things were run – then better conditions would naturally follow.

The Charter struck a chord. Workers' groups united behind it, and local groups sprang up to promote it. For the first time, and in short order, Britain found itself with a mass working-class movement.

The poster on page 183 was probably disseminated by James Arthur, a Carlisle bookseller whose shop was a centre for Chartist activity in the town. Its author was clearly anxious to avoid giving the authorities any excuse to cause trouble. It asks the public not to bring weapons to the great meeting. The plea is made so that 'no advantage may be taken of them by the authorities', who will try to goad them into breaching the peace and so give themselves the opportunity to persecute the protestors. Still, the poster shows the organisers issuing a veiled threat to employers, asking that they allow their workers to attend, in order to avoid any 'unpleasant collision' between them.

The authorities rose to the challenge. Although the great mass of Chartists were peaceful, there were occasional outbreaks of violence, which allowed the Government to portray the movement as dangerous, and to try to suppress its meetings. The poster opposite was rushed out by the doughty justices of Stockport. It has the authority of the state, the letters 'V. R.' on either side of the imposing royal arms stand for Victoria Regina, Queen Victoria. This weight of authority is directed towards a meeting at a pub, the Stanley Arms Inn, at seven o'clock that evening. The poster is loaded with threat: if the assembly is not actually illegal, it 'may become so'; it may involve 'the Exhibition of Weapons, or Fire Arms'; it may put people 'in Fear', in which case the justices intend to arrest … the Parties engaged therein'. It would have taken a brave soul indeed to attend after that.

In 1839 and 1842 Parliament ignored large Chartist petitions – the second containing some three million signatures – and more violence ensued. James Arthur was convicted of participating in Chartist disturbances in Manchester (his second conviction; his first, rather splendidly, was for being drunk and disorderly at a temperance meeting). In 1848, the Chartists tried yet another petition and a massed rally in Kennington. An estimated 150,000 people attended in support, while an astonishing 100,000 opponents were drafted in as special constables to 'police' the rally – strong proof of the Government's success in alarming the wider population about the threat of Chartism. But in Carlisle, at least, Chartist agitation had already run out of steam. Meetings had been poorly attended and James Arthur turned his focus to his business. The Kennington rally got nowhere. Chartism seemed to have failed.

But it hadn't. As the threat of violence receded, simple reasonableness prevailed. Twenty-five or so years after this poster was put up, the 1867 Reform Act doubled the size of the electorate. Secret ballots were introduced five years after that. Annual elections were never introduced (thank goodness), but otherwise every single one of the Chartists' demands would become law in time.

# *The* GREATEST SHOW *on* EARTH

## Exhibitor Tickets for the Great Exhibition

## 1851

Right: *The Crystal Palace, 1,851 feet (564 metres) long and tall enough to cover the park's trees.*

Below: *The Great Exhibition was to be the greatest show on Earth. No one had attempted a global exhibition before.*

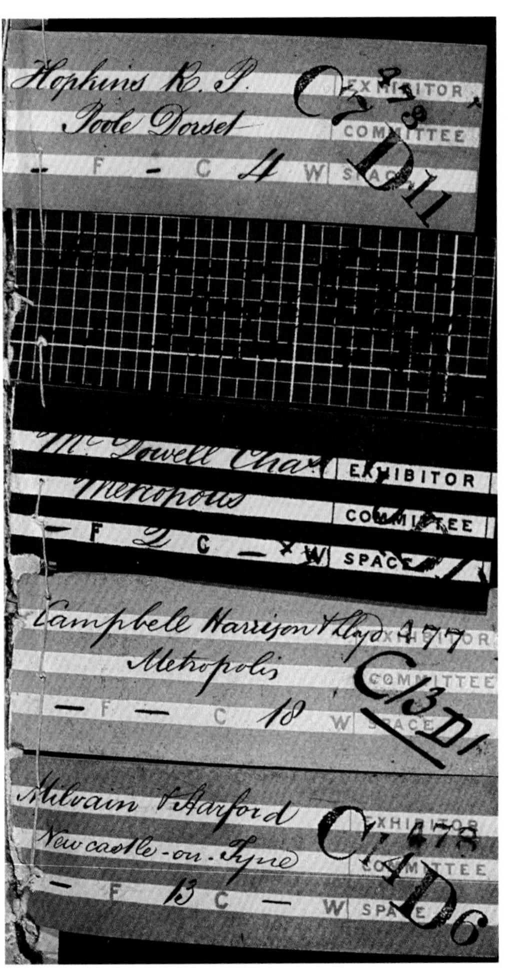


Documents need not be weighty to be delightful. Ephemera – objects that are so insignificant that most end up as rubbish – can be deeply evocative. Few of these little tickets have survived, but in 1851, they would have entitled you to exhibit at the greatest show on Earth: the Great Exhibition.

Up until this point in time, exhibitions had been associated with the French. The Revolution had swept away aristocratic patronage, and French artists found that exhibitions were a good way to reach new markets. French industry had followed suit and begun to put on exhibitions of elegant new products to attract buyers.

But the Great Exhibition was far more ambitious than its predecessors. It was to be international, a showcase both for Britain and for the world. It would be ideological, encouraging free trade over protectionism. Prizes would be awarded in the spirit of healthy competition. It would be educational. Bits of it might even be fun.

A vast plate-glass palace, 1,851 feet (564 metres) long, was built to house the Exhibition in London's Hyde Park. The day of the opening, 1 May, was declared a national holiday, and 300,000 people gathered to witness the ceremony. The Archbishop of Canterbury led the people in prayer, and the palace filled with the sound of the 'Hallelujah Chorus'. When Queen Victoria declared the Exhibition open, guns were fired, trumpets sounded and

RIGHT: *Exhibitors came from across Britain and from around the world, and their tickets show the names of the firms, their hometowns and the stand allocated to them. The exhibitor tickets on these pages are for companies from Poole, Newcastle, Brighton, Edinburgh and 'Metropolis' (London).*

the exhibits were uncovered. A crystal fountain at the heart of the Palace began to tinkle with Eau De Cologne, filling the air with its scent.

What would you have seen when you walked through the doors? The Palace was high enough to enclose one of Hyde Park's elms, and its long arms stretched away on either side. Flowers and palm trees grew in its natural light. First port of call for many was the Queen's Koh i Noor diamond, all 186.5 carats of it, exhibited in a metal cage that was locked to the floor. The diamond exuded an aura of exotic mystery, and visitors found it extraordinary to be close to an object of such value.

You might then turn to the country exhibits. Tuscany, Spain, Turkey, Sardinia, Brazil, Switzerland, China, India, France, Austria and Belgium were all represented. Some of the country displays were prophetic. Russia had sent heavy symbols of power, vast chunks of malachite and jasper and huge iron castings. The American display, in contrast, was rather sparse (Her Majesty pronounced it 'not very interesting'), but it was dominated by new labour-saving devices, sewing machines and automatic harvesters. You might also have noted the significance of a tea set, made entirely from Californian gold.

Some exhibits depended for their effect on scale. You could have looked through a 20-foot (6-metre) long telescope, containing the largest refractor in the world. You could have listened to a gigantic organ of 4,500 pipes. British metalwork was celebrated by an ornate penknife that held eighty blades. You could have contemplated Britain's resources, in the form of eight 16-tonne blocks of coal.

Other exhibits showed how new technology could work for the good. From the world of medicine there were glass eyes, an artificial hand, and an 'artificial leech' for drawing blood. For the arts, there was a bust of Shakespeare, cast in a new-fangled material called concrete. Religious visitors could visit the dancing light

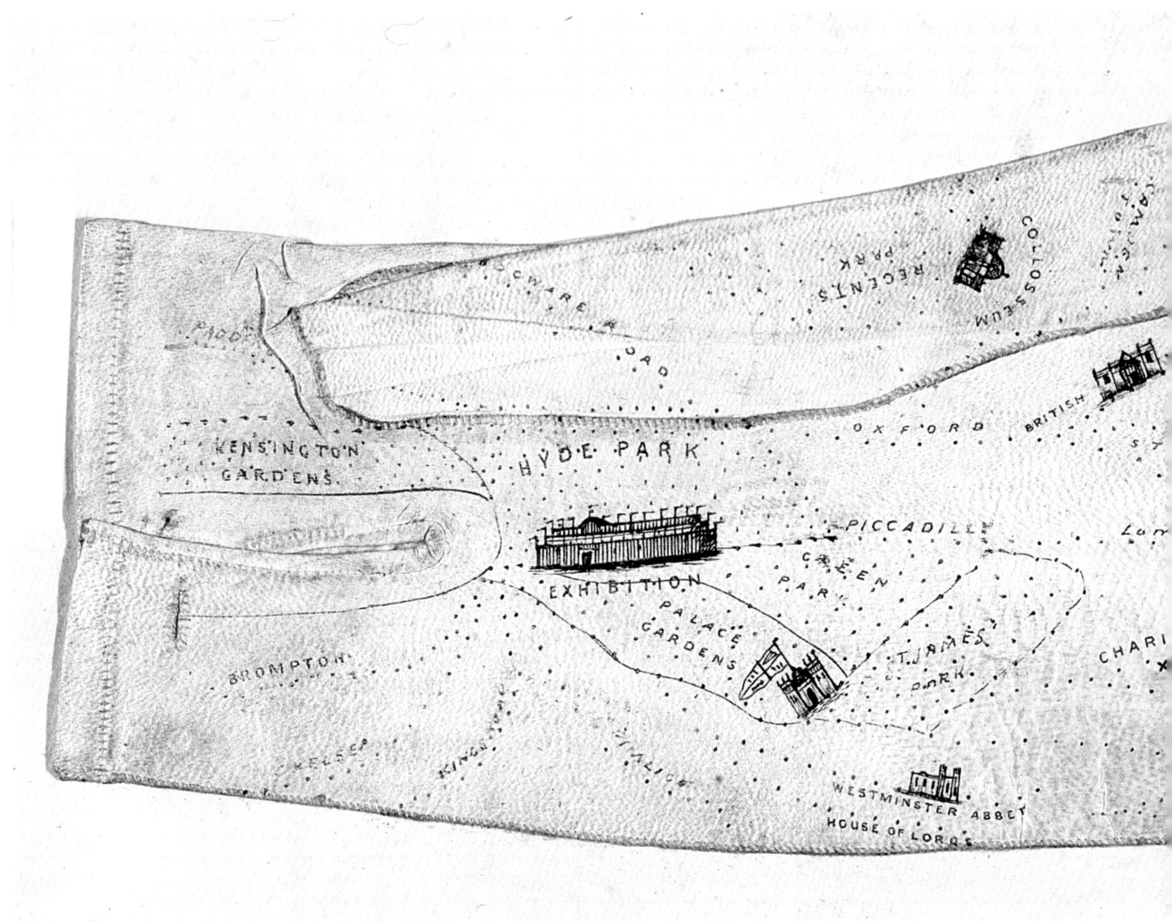


of the stained-glass gallery, or view a medieval-style altar created with a new patent carving mechanism. The Exhibition's aims were God's aims.

Some of the names present are familiar today. There were guns from Colt, tobacco from Lambert & Butler, food from Fortnum & Mason. The latest Ordnance Survey map, of Lancashire and Yorkshire, was on display. Wilkinson & Sons showed off its swords, including one encrusted with jewels. Goodyear produced a giant rubber boat.

Other exhibits were simply bonkers. There was champagne made from rhubarb; an ornate drinks decanter that was too heavy to pick up; a barometer powered by leeches; a piano with four keyboards for playing by four people; an alarm bedstead that would wake you up by upending you into the middle of your bedroom (where, the catalogue said, a bath of cold water could be positioned – very Wallace and Gromit). And if, after all that, you felt the call of nature, you could make use of the world's very first public convenience, for a price of one penny.

Nothing escapes controversy, and the Exhibition was no different. Some foreign visitors complained of a British bias towards the superiority of its products. Many writers visited and praised the Exhibition – Charlotte Brontë, Dickens, Tennyson, Lewis Carroll – but Karl Marx objected to its capitalist fetishism of commodities. Certainly, the Exhibition gave plenty of opportunity for exploitation. A whole world of souvenir products was

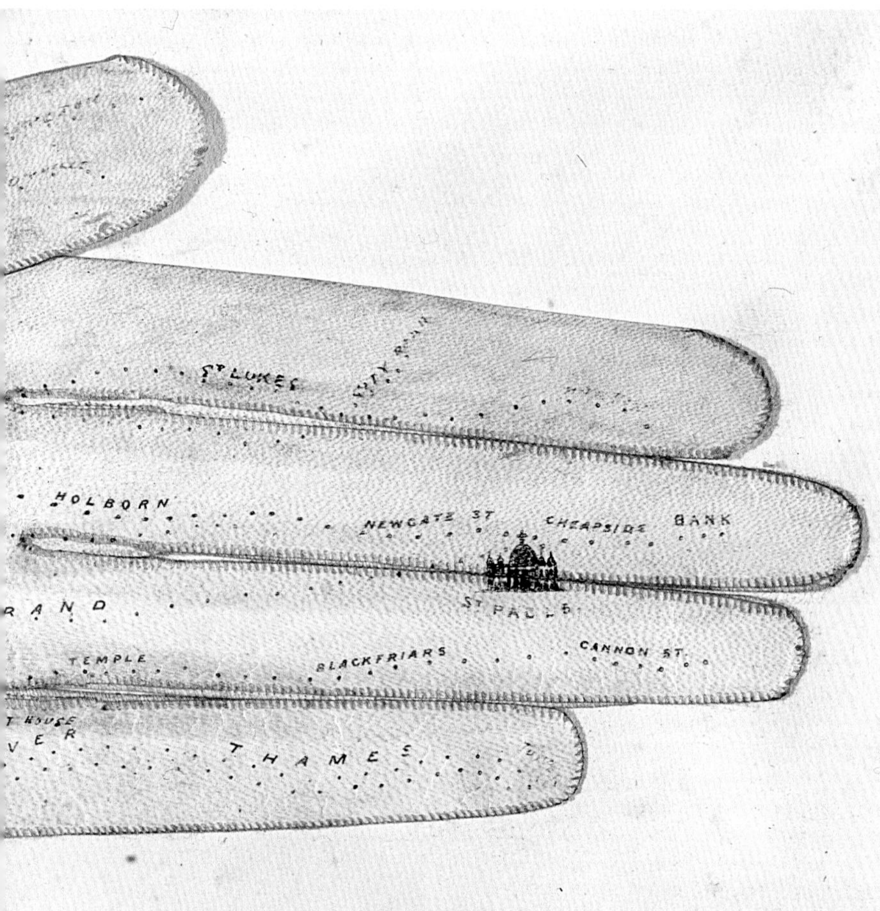


LEFT: *This lady's glove is one of thousands of exhibition-themed souvenirs. The dotted lines – from the Thames, St Paul's Cathedral, Westminster Abbey, the British Museum, the Coliseum – all converge on the Crystal Palace.*

made for the Exhibition, such as a glove, also in The National Archives, on which a map of London was drawn, with the Crystal Palace in the palm. London businesses cashed in on the tourist boom. Ancillary 'exhibitions' were opened, including venues where you could sample cuisine from around the world, and Exhibition-themed shows were staged everywhere from established theatres to the upstairs rooms in pubs. Images of the Crystal Palace were stamped on saleable items from household utensils to tourist knick-knacks. Six million tickets to the Exhibition were sold, to one quarter of the population. The Exhibition made a colossal profit, and the money was used to purchase eighty-six acres of land in South Kensington, now home to the Victoria and Albert Museum (where you can still see exhibits from the Exhibition), the Science Museum, the Natural History Museum, the Royal Albert Hall, Imperial College and the Royal College of Music. The Albert Memorial, in which a catalogue of the Exhibition rests on the knee of Albert's gilt bronze statue, stands next to its original site.

The Exhibition closed in October 1851. The Crystal Palace was dismantled and reassembled in southeast London, where it continued to be a popular venue (even keeping up with the times as a home for speedway racing), before sadly burning down in 1936. But the rest of the world had noticed. An economic boom in the years that followed the Exhibition was, rightly or wrongly, attributed to its effect. Exhibitions inspired by the Great Exhibition of 1851 were mounted from Sydney to Paris to Chicago and today's International Expos are their direct descendants.

"A"
MAP TO ILLUSTRATE
THE CHARGE OF THE LIGHT CAVALRY AT THE BATTLE OF BALAKLAVA OCT. 25, 1854.
Reservoir
FEDUKINE HEIGHTS
To Traktir Bridge
Tchernaya R.
Aqueduct
Bridge
Position of Light Brigade when they retired
Russian Cavalry intercepting retreat of Lt. Brigade
Russian Cavalry support'g Guns
Russian Battery
Position of Light Brigade when first line entered the Russian Battery
French Cavalry (Chasseurs d'Afrique)
Line of Charge
Position of Light Brigade previous to Charge
17th Lancers
11th Hussars
13th Lt. Dragoons
4th Lt. Dragoons
8th Hussars
Heavy Brigade in support
Woronzoff Road
Redoubt No. 4
Redoubt No. 3
Redoubt No. 2
Redoubt No. 1
Redoubt No. 5
Canrobert's Hill
To Kamara
EXPLANATION
BRITISH
RUSSIANS
FRENCH
SCALE OF 1 MILE

# INTO *the* VALLEY *of* DEATH

## Reports of the Charge of the Light Brigade

### 1854

Right: *Musical score, 'Charge of the Light Brigade'. Hundreds galloped to their deaths, in obedience to a fumbled order.*

One of the most iconic moments in British military history is described in these reports – the Charge of the Light Brigade. During a battle of the Crimean War, a fumbled order sent 661 cavalry rushing straight at the enemy guns, resulting in 292 killed, wounded or captured. These reports, by the man who gave the order, and the man who received it, both honour the gallant dead – and descend into finger-pointing about who was responsible.

The Crimean War began in 1853, when the bellicose Russian Empire took advantage of a dispute between Catholic and Orthodox Christians in Jerusalem to go to war with its weak neighbour, the Ottoman empire, with which it shared borders to the west and east of the Black Sea. The war prompted the intervention the following year of Britain and France, who wanted to curb the ambitions of the increasingly belligerent Russians. The allies' target was Sevastopol, Russia's naval base to the north of the Black Sea, the capture of which would put an end to Russian naval power there.

British and French forces landed around 31 miles to the north of Sevastopol and marched south. Having succeeded in their first engagement with the Russians in a battle around the River Alma, they laid siege to the port. On 17 October, the allies subjected Sevastopol to a massive bombardment from the heights above the city and from the Black Sea fleet. The city did not break, but the Russians decided that they needed to respond with direct action. They decided to try to take Balaclava, a small port 12½ miles to the south of Sevastopol, which was the British supply base for the siege.

Opposite: *A map that illustrates the charge – Fediukhin Heights at the top, the ridge of the Causeway Heights running from bottom left. Between them lies the 'Valley of Death'. The Light Brigade was positioned to the left, the Russian guns to the right.*

Russian forces advanced to the Balaclava valley, which ran east to west, just to the north of the port. They took up positions on the northern slopes of the valley, known as the Fediukhin Heights, and at the eastern end. British defences sat on a spine of land that ran along the middle of the valley, known as the Causeway Heights. The defences comprised a line of six small redoubts, each carrying two or three twelve-pounder guns and guarded by Ottoman Turks.

641

Cathcart, to move forward, and take advantage of any opportunity to regain the heights; and, not having been able to accomplish this immediately, and it appearing that an attempt was making to remove the captured Guns, the Earl of Lucan was desired to advance rapidly, follow the Enemy in their retreat, and try to prevent them from effecting their object.

In the meanwhile the Russians had time to reform on their own ground with

209

642

Artillery in front and upon their flanks.

From some misconception of the instruction to advance, the Lieutenant General considered that he was bound to attack at all hazards, and he accordingly ordered Major General the Earl of Cardigan to move forward with the Light Brigade.

This order was obeyed in the most spirited and gallant manner. Lord Cardigan charged with the utmost vigour, attacked

Behind the Causeway Heights were stationed the 92nd Highland Infantry Brigade, the cavalry division of Lord Lucan (of which the Light Brigade and Heavy Brigade formed part), and Royal Marines, around 5,000 men, against 60,000 Russians.

On 25 October, the Russians bombarded and then stormed the redoubts, taking the eastern four in the line. Russian cavalry hurtled down towards Balaclava port, but was beaten back by the original 'thin red line' of British redcoats, just two men deep, which let fly three rallies and caused the Russian cavalry to veer off and then retreat. After further fierce fighting the Russian cavalry withdrew to the eastern end of the north valley. Balaclava was saved.

Now came the fumbled order.

From his position on the Heights at the west end of Balaclava, the British Commander in Chief, Lord Raglan, could see the retreating Russians removing British guns from the captured redoubts along the Causeway Heights. Raglan had fought Bonaparte under the Duke of Wellington, who supposedly had never lost a gun, and the prospect of this capture was unbearable. He sent orders to Lord Lucan: 'Lord Raglan wishes the cavalry to advance rapidly to the front – follow the enemy and try to prevent the enemy carrying away the guns.'

What Raglan's order did not explain was, which enemy and which guns? From where Lucan and his cavalry were standing, at the western end of the valley looking east, they could see three sets of guns: the captured

643

a battery which was firing upon the advancing squadrons, and having passed beyond it, engaged the Russian Cavalry in its rear; but there his Troops were assailed by Artillery and Infantry as well as Cavalry, and necessarily retired, after having committed much havoc upon the Enemy. They effected this movement without haste or confusion, but the loss they have sustained has, I deeply lament, been very severe in Officers, Men, and horses, only counterbalanced by the brilliancy

of the attack, and the gallantry, order, and discipline which distinguished it, forming a striking contrast to the conduct of the Enemy's Cavalry which had previously been engaged with the heavy Brigade.

The Chasseurs d'Afrique advanced on our left, and gallantly charged a Russian Battery, which checked its fire for a time, and thus rendered the British Cavalry an essential service.

I have the honor to inclose copies of Sir Colin Campbell's

ABOVE: *The report of the charge from the British Commander-in-Chief, Lord Raglan. He describes 'some misconception of the order to advance' but praises the gallantry of the men. The report is relatively sanguine, but hard questions would soon be asked about who was responsible.*

guns on the Causeway Heights to the right, Russian guns on the Fediukhin Heights to the left, and straight ahead, at the far end of the valley, more Russian guns, which were protecting the main Russian force.

Lucan decided that Raglan meant him to take the far end of the valley, and ordered the Light Brigade to advance. As they broke into a trot, the first Russian shells exploded. What followed was carnage. Cannonballs, grapeshot and musket fire rained down from the Fediukhin and Causeway Heights to their left and right, and from the cannons straight ahead. Encircled in this blaze of fire, horses and men fell in every direction. The following lines of cavalry had to swerve round the dead and wounded of the first line, as terrified horses careened about.

But they made it. Within a few minutes the Light Brigade had ridden into the 'mouth of the volcano', as one of its corporals later put it, and were in among the Russian gunners and then the Russian cavalry beyond them. The Russians were panicked by this disciplined, relentless force, and their forward lines turned and slammed into the lines behind them, before the entire mass stampeded away.

The exhausted men of the Light Brigade turned and retraced their route along the valley, again under fire from left and right, straggling back in twos and threes. Of the estimated 661 men who started the

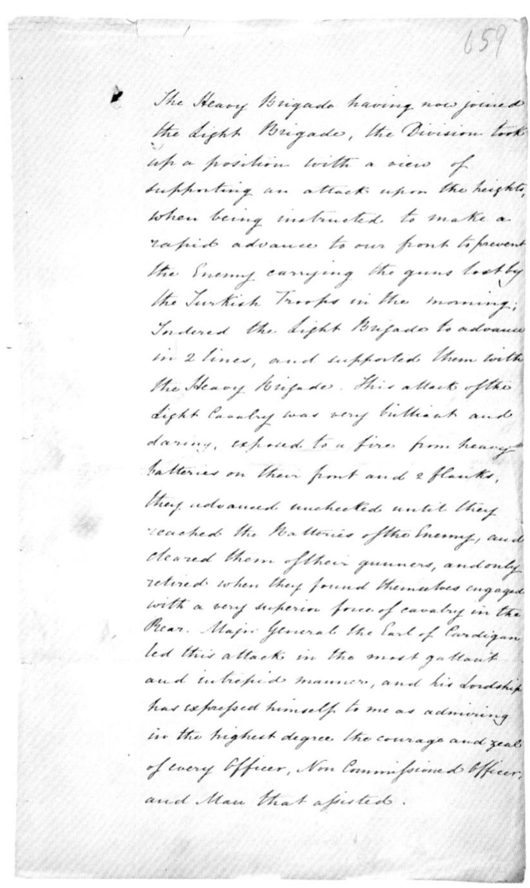

659

The Heavy Brigade having now joined the Light Brigade, the Division took up a position with a view of supporting an attack upon the heights, when being instructed to make a rapid advance to our front to prevent the Enemy carrying the guns lost by the Turkish Troops in the morning; I ordered the Light Brigade to advance in 2 lines, and supported them with the Heavy Brigade. This attack of the Light Cavalry was very brilliant and daring, exposed to a fire from heavy batteries on their front and 2 flanks, they advanced unchecked until they reached the Batteries of the Enemy, and cleared them of their gunners, and only retired when they found themselves engaged with a very superior force of cavalry in the Rear. Major General the Earl of Cardigan led this attack in the most gallant and intrepid manner, and his Lordship has expressed himself to me as admiring in the highest degree the courage and zeal of every Officer, Non Commissioned Officer, and Man that assisted.

LEFT: *The report of Lord Lucan, who had overall command of the British cavalry. He is definite that Raglan ordered a rapid advance. Historians still debate responsibility. All that is clear today is that neither commander had made sure that there was no misunderstanding.*

charge, 113 had been killed, 134 wounded and 45 taken prisoner.

Raglan's report of the charge was written three days afterwards, on 29 October. He describes 'some misconception of the order to advance', but said that when Lucan ordered the advance, 'The order was obeyed in the most spirited and gallant manner'.

The report crossed with Lucan's written the day before. Lucan was definite regarding his orders: '... when being instructed to make a rapid advance to our front to prevent the enemy carrying the guns lost by the Turkish Troops in the morning, I ordered the Light Brigade to advance in 2 lines ... The attack of the Light Cavalry was very brilliant and daring ...' Disquiet about what had actually happened prompted Raglan's second report, written in December. This time he is scathing: 'not only did the Lieu General [Lucan] misconceive the written instruction that was sent to him, but there was nothing in that instruction which called upon him to attack at all hazards, or to undertake the operation, which led to such a brilliant display of gallantry on the part of the Light Brigade ...'

Historians still debate what went wrong that day, and cite these documents in evidence. All that is really clear is that neither Raglan nor Lucan had made sure that there was no misunderstanding.

Within two months of the charge, Tennyson's famous poem captured perfectly the combination of tragic mistake with heroic sacrifice:

*Theirs not to reason why,*
*Theirs but to do and die:*
*Into the valley of Death*
*Rode the six hundred.*

*'... when being instructed to make a rapid advance to our front to prevent the enemy carrying the guns lost by the Turkish Troops in the morning, I ordered the Light Brigade to advance in 2 lines ... The attack of the Light Cavalry was very brilliant and daring ...'*

# DR BARRY'S SECRET
## Doctor's Report

LEFT: *Portrait of Dr James Barry around 1815, shortly after joining the British Army Medical Corps.*

## 1865

WHEN HE RETIRED in 1864, Dr James Barry could look back on more than fifty years of successful medical practice. After studying medicine at Edinburgh University, he had become an apprentice at St Thomas's Hospital in London, and in 1813 joined the British Army Medical Corps. His work as an army surgeon took him all over the world – South Africa, Jamaica, Corfu, the Crimea, Canada. He had a special talent for organising hospitals, even upbraiding Florence Nightingale on the cleanliness of her wards (Nightingale described him as 'a brute'). By his retirement, he had risen to the rank of Inspector General of Army Hospitals.

But James Barry had a secret. It was a secret that would have stayed hidden forever, were it not for the letter shown on pages 197 and 198.

James Barry was a woman.

The letter was written in 1865, shortly after Barry's death, by his own doctor, Dr D. R. McKinnon. Dr McKinnon is writing to the Registrar General, Major George Graham, to report his conversation with the woman who had laid out Barry's body after his death in his rooms overlooking London's Cavendish Square:

*Sir,*

*I beg to acknowledge receipt of your letter of the 23rd August respecting the death of Inspector General Dr James Barry.*

*I had been intimately acquainted with that gentleman for a good many years, both in the West Indies and in England and I never had any suspicion that Dr Barry was a female.*

*I attended him during his last illness, and for some months previously for bronchitis, and the affection causing his death was diarrhoea produced apparently by errors in diet.*

*On one occasion after Dr Barry's death, I was sent for to the office of Sir Charles McGregor, and there the woman who performed the last offices for Dr Barry was waiting to speak to me.*

*She wished to obtain some perquisites of her employment which the lady who kept the lodging house in which Dr Barry died had refused to give her.*

*Amongst other things she said Dr Barry was a female and that I was a pretty Doctor not to know this and that she would not like to be attended by me. I informed her that it was none of my business whether Dr Barry was a male or a female – and that I thought it as likely he might be neither, viz an imperfectly developed man.*

Victoria by the Grace of God of the United Kingdom of Great Britain and Ireland Queen Defender of the Faith &c.
To Our Trusty and well beloved James Barry, Esquire, M.D. Greeting
We do by these Presents Constitute and Appoint you to be Inspector General of Hospitals, with local rank
from the 25th of September 1857 You are therefore carefully and diligently to discharge the Duty of Inspector General of Hospitals by doing and performing all and all manner of Things thereunto belonging. And you are to observe and follow such Orders and Directions from Time to Time as you shall receive from Us or any your superior Officer according to the Rules and Discipline of War. Given at our Court at Saint James's the Thirtieth day of September 1857 in the Twenty first Year of Our Reign.

War Office.

By Her Majesty's Command.

James Barry Esq. M.D.
Inspector General of Hospitals
with local rank

LEFT: *The Queen's commission, appointing Barry to the post of Inspector General of Army Hospitals.* OPPOSITE: *The letter from Dr McKinnon to the Registrar General that reveals Dr Barry's secret.*

*She then said that she had examined the body and that it was a perfect female and farther that there were marks of her having had a child when very young. I then enquired how have you formed this conclusion? The woman pointing to the lower part of her stomach, said from marks here I am a married woman, and the mother of nine children I ought to know.*

*The woman seemed to me to think that she had become acquainted with a great secret and wished to be paid for keeping it. I informed her that all Dr Barry's relatives were dead and that it was no secret of mine, and that my own impression was that Dr Barry was a Hermaphrodite.*

*But whether Dr Barry was male, female or a hermaphrodite I do not know, nor had I any purpose in making a discovery as I could positively swear to the identity of the body as being that of a person whom I had been acquainted with as Inspector General Hospitals for a period of eight or nine years.*

As word spread of the dead doctor's secret, many claimed that they had known all along. Don't they always? People pointed to Barry's physical appearance. He was only five feet tall, and wore elevated boots. He was known to pad out his shoulders with towels. He preferred to wear the Army's full dress uniform, perhaps to cover his curves. A fiery red-head, Dr Barry would quickly challenge you to a duel if you mocked his high-pitched voice or peculiar manner of riding a horse. And then there was his unusually close relationship with Lord Charles Somerset, Governor at the Cape of Good Hope when Dr Barry was posted there in 1816. Somerset provided Barry with apartments at his residence, and rumours about the nature of their friendship prompted an investigation by a Royal Commission. Barry and Somerset were exonerated of any 'unnaturalness'. But at the height of his friendship with Somerset, Barry appeared to leave South Africa for a year, saying that he was going to work in Mauritius. No records of a stay in Mauritius have been found. Dr McKinnon reported that marks had been found on Barry's body of an apparent pregnancy. Perhaps Barry had spent the year hidden away, pregnant with Somerset's child, which may have been still-born or given for adoption.

Copy

18913
3

Recruiting Department
25 Duke St. Westmins[ter]
24th August 186[5]

Sir

I beg to acknowledge the receipt of your letter of the 23 August respecting the death of Ins[pector] General Dr James Barry

I had been intimately acqu[ainted] with that gentleman for a good m[any] years, both in the West Indies, & [in] England, and I never had any suspic[ion] that Dr Barry was a female

I attended him during hi[s] last illness, and for some months previously for bronchitis, & th[e] affection causing his death was diarrhœa produced apparently by errors in diet.

On one occasion after Dr Barry's death, I was sent for to [the] Office of Sir Charles McGregor, & the[re] the woman who performed the la[st] offices for Dr Barry was waiting to speak to me.

She wished to obtain som[e] perquisites of her employment which the Lady who kept the lodging house in which Dr Ba[rry] died had refused to give her

Amongst other things s[he] said Dr Barry was a female & [that] that I was a pretty Doctor not [to]

know this & that she would not like to be attended by me. I informed her that it was none of my business whether Dr Barry was a male or a female – & that I thought it as likely he might be neither, viz an imperfectly developed man.

She then said that she had examined the body & that it was a perfect female & farther that there were marks of her having had a child when very young. I then enquired how have you formed this conclusion. The woman pointing to the lower part of her stomach, said from marks here. I am a married woman, & the mother of nine children & I ought to know.

The woman seemed to me to think that she had become acquainted with a great secret & wished to be paid for keeping it. I informed her that all Dr Barry's relatives were dead, & that it was no secret of mine, & that my own impression was that Dr Barry was a Hermaphrodite.

But whether Dr Barry was male, female, or hermaphrodite I do not know, nor had I any purpose in making the discovery

as

18913

Memorandum of the Services of Dr. James Barry Inspector General of Hospitals -

I entered the Army as a Medical Officer under the age of fourteen years and served first at the Cape of Good Hope about thirteen years attached to the personal Staff of the late General Lord Charles Somerset on whose resignation I was promoted to the rank of Staff Surgeon and sent to the Mauritius, I served there about eighteen months and was recalled in consequence of the serious illness of Lord Charles Somerset upon whose death I proceeded to Jamaica and served under Sir Willoughby Cotton during the Rebellion and the burning of the Plantations by the Negroes, I was in Medical charge of the Troops employed on that service the Inspector General remaining at Head Quarters.

Thence I was ordered to St Helena as Principal Medical Officer and subsequently to the Windward and Leeward Islands and did Duty at Antigua and Trinidad, and for several months was in Medical charge of the Troops in the Command during the absence of the Inspector General and when relieved was thanked

OPPOSITE: *Dr McKinnon's letter, reporting that the woman who had laid out Dr Barry's body said that she was 'a perfect female', and bore marks of a pregnancy.*
LEFT: *Memorandum by Dr Barry describing his career in the Army. He twice mentions Lord Charles Somerset, with whom he may have had a child.*

Recent research has pieced together Barry's early life. She was christened Margaret Ann Bulkley in County Cork, Ireland. Margaret Ann's uncle was James Barry, a distinguished professor of painting at the Royal Academy. When her uncle died in 1806, he left a legacy that enabled Margaret Ann and her mother to move to London, where the girl took lessons from a physician, Edward Fryer, and conceived her ambition to become a doctor. This was impossible, of course. Women could not even attend university, let alone join one of the professions. And so, in 1809, she changed sex. In order not to attract attention, she must have made the switch when she and her mother left London to catch a boat to Edinburgh, where she was to enrol at the university. Shortly before leaving, behind closed curtains, she must have cut her hair and changed her clothes, before lowering her head and stepping outside for the first time as a man. When she and her mother arrived at the boat, she was travelling as her mother's nephew, and shared the name of her supposed father, James Barry.

And so Margaret Ann Bulkley became Britain's first female qualified doctor and surgeon. You feel a little sorry that she did not reveal herself while she was still alive. Around the time that Barry retired, pioneering women like Elizabeth Blackwell in the US and Elizabeth Garrett Anderson in the UK were just beginning to push open the closed doors of the medical profession. What impact might it have had if a surgeon so distinguished, so brave and dedicated, had revealed that he was a woman? But Barry never wanted to be a figurehead. She simply wanted to practise medicine. And perhaps that is her best memorial: a pioneering reformer in hygiene and hospitals; a fine surgeon; and a respected member of her profession, whatever her sex.

# *The* WELSH PILGRIM FATHERS
## Embarkation List of the *Mimosa*

ABOVE: *Photograph of the Welsh settlers in Patagonia, 1890. After a miserable start, the settlers learned to work the land, and life improved.*

**1865**

OPPOSITE: *The embarkation agreement simply records the emigrants' destination as Nuevo Bay, Patagonia. They were ill-equipped for such a hostile land.*

THE VOYAGE OF the *Mimosa* is as famous and totemic in Wales and Argentina as the voyage of the *Mayflower* is in England and America. This crew list and itinerary, completed and signed shortly before the voyage, records the 153 idealistic Welsh emigrants who, two months later, would be dumped in an isolated bay in South America and left to fend for themselves in the middle of winter.

Like the Pilgrim Fathers on the *Mayflower*, the travellers on the *Mimosa* were driven by religious faith, and religious resentment. They were Welsh non-conformists, bitterly opposed to laws that forced them to pay for the upkeep of the established Church as well as their own, and yearning to practise their faith in peace and freedom. But they had another motive, too, one that gives their voyage enduring significance in Wales. The British Government of the time believed that if a single language were used throughout the British Isles, greater unity among its people would result – the favoured language being, of course, English. The Government made it difficult to speak or use Welsh in any official or legal context. If religion had been the only driver for the voyage, one option might have been to follow the, by now, relatively well-travelled path to the United States. But the Welsh non-conformists noticed that emigrants to the US almost invariably ended up speaking English. To preserve their language, these linguistic refuseniks were going to have to get themselves as far away from English speakers as they could.

A pair of surveyors were sent to Patagonia, a place so remote that it barely appeared on the charts. The surveyors returned to Wales in a state of wild enthusiasm. This, they said, was the Welsh Promised Land. Encouraged by the reports, on 28 May 1865, the group boarded the tea clipper *Mimosa* in Liverpool port. The crew list gives the names of the sailors running the ship, and shows how summarily the emigrants were to be offloaded before the ship headed on to its next destination: 'The several persons whose names are hereto

Liverpool. 22                                                                                                   1

(AC) 2824
SANCTIONED BY THE BOARD OF TRADE, MARCH 1865. IN PURSUANCE OF 17 & 18 Vict. c. 104.

# AGREEMENT AND ACCOUNT OF CREW.

(FOREIGN-GOING SHIP.)

Executed in 2 Folio.

Engagement Fee ... £1 10 0
Discharging Fee ... £1 10 0

* Any Erasure, Interlineation, or Alteration in this Agreement will be void, unless attested by some Superintendent of a Mercantile Marine Office, Officer of Customs, Consul, or Vice-Consul, to be made with the consent of the persons interested.

| Name of Ship. | Official Number. | Port of Registry. | Port No. and Date of Register. | Registered Tonnage. | Nominal Horse-power of Engines (if any). | Managing Owner: Name. | Managing Owner: Address. (State No. of House, Street, & Town.) | Master: Name. | Master: No. of Certificate. | Master: Address. (State No. of House, Street, & Town.) |
|---|---|---|---|---|---|---|---|---|---|---|
| Mimosa | 1973 | Lpool | 314 19/7/53 | 409 | | Henning Kitley & Co. | Lpool | G. Pepperell | 20991 | 45 Upr. Warwick St. Lpool. |

Scale of Provisions to be allowed and served out to the Crew during the Voyage.

| | Bread lb. | Beef lb. | Pork lb. | Flour lb. | Peas pint. | Tea oz. | Coffee oz. | Sugar oz. | Water qts. |
|---|---|---|---|---|---|---|---|---|---|
| SUNDAY | 1 | 1½ | — | ½ | — | ⅛ | ½ | 2 | 3 |
| MONDAY | 1 | — | 1¼ | — | ⅓ | ⅛ | ½ | 2 | 3 |
| TUESDAY | 1 | 1½ | — | ½ | — | ⅛ | ½ | 2 | 3 |
| WEDNESDAY | 1 | — | 1¼ | — | ⅓ | ⅛ | ½ | 2 | 3 |
| THURSDAY | 1 | 1½ | — | ½ | — | ⅛ | ½ | 2 | 3 |
| FRIDAY | 1 | — | 1¼ | — | ⅓ | ⅛ | ½ | 2 | 3 |
| SATURDAY | 1 | 1½ | — | — | — | ⅛ | ½ | 2 | 3 |

SUBSTITUTES.[4]

1 oz. of Coffee, or Cocoa, or Chocolate, may be substituted for ¼ oz. of Tea. Molasses for Sugar, the quantity to be one-half more. 1 lb. of Potatoes or Yams, ½ lb. of Flour or Rice, ⅓ pint of Peas, or ¼ pint of Barley, may be substituted for each other. When Fresh Meat is issued, the proportion to be 2 lbs. per man per day, in lieu of Salt Meat, Flour, Rice, and Peas. Beef and Pork may be substituted each for the other.

[4] Here any stipulation for changes or substitution of one article for another may be inserted.

N.B.—The Board of Trade do not interfere as to the quantities of provisions to be supplied.

The several Persons whose names are hereto subscribed, and whose descriptions are contained below, and of whom 8 are engaged as Sailors, hereby agree to serve on board the said Ship, in the several capacities expressed against their respective Names, on a Voyage from[1] Liverpool to Nuevo Bay (Patagonia) and any ports and places in the Atlantic Pacific and Indian Oceans (thence to a port for orders and to the Continent if required) and back to a final port of discharge in the United Kingdom, term not to exceed 2 years.

And the said Crew agree to conduct themselves in an orderly, faithful, honest, and sober manner, and to be at all times diligent in their respective Duties, and to be obedient to the lawful Commands of the said Master, or of any Person who shall lawfully succeed him, and of their Superior Officers, in everything relating to the said Ship and the Stores and Cargo thereof, whether on board, in boats, or on shore: in consideration of which Services to be duly performed, the said Master hereby agrees to pay to the said Crew as Wages the Sums against their Names respectively expressed, and to supply them with Provisions according to the annexed Scale: And it is hereby agreed, That any Embezzlement or wilful or negligent Destruction of any part of the Ship's Cargo or Stores shall be made good to the Owner out of the Wages of the Person guilty of the same: And if any Person enters himself as qualified for a duty which he proves incompetent to perform, his Wages shall be reduced in proportion to his incompetency: And it is also agreed, That the Regulations authorized by the Board of Trade, which in the paper annexed hereto are numbered[2] 1622

are adopted by the parties hereto, and shall be considered as embodied in this Agreement: And it is also agreed, That if any Member of the Crew considers himself to be aggrieved by any breach of the Agreement or otherwise, he shall represent the same to the Master or Officer in charge of the Ship in a quiet and orderly manner, who shall thereupon take such steps as the case may require: And it is also agreed, That[3] the Crew shall consist of Mate, Carp., Std., Cook, 6 Seamen, 2 Ords. and 3 Boys. No Grog allowed.

In witness whereof the said parties have subscribed their Names hereto on the days against their respective Signatures mentioned.

Signed by George Pepperell Jnr Master, on the 23 day of May, 1865.

[1] Here the Voyage is to be described and the places named at which the Ship is to touch, or if that cannot be done, the general nature and probable length of the voyage is to be stated.

[2] Here are to be inserted the numbers of any of the Regulations for preserving Discipline (Form R) issued by the Board of Trade, which the parties agree to adopt. If any of them are so adopted, a Copy of the Regulations is to be kept annexed to the Agreement.

[3] Here any other stipulations may be inserted to which the parties agree, and which are not contrary to Law.

[5] The Authority of the Owner or Agent for the allotments mentioned below is in my possession.

S. Cuukins [?]
Superintendent.

[5] This is to be filled up if such an authority has been produced.

PARTICULARS OF ENGAGEMENT. / PARTICULARS OF DISCHARGE, &c.

| Reference No. | Signature of Crew. | Age. | Town or County where born. | Nos. of Certificates (if any). | Ship in which he last served: Name, Official No., or Port she belonged to, or Nature of Employment. | Date of Discharge from such Ship. | Place of Discharge from such Ship. | Date of joining this Ship. | Place of joining this Ship. | In what Capacity engaged, and if Mate or Engineer, No. of his Certificate. | Time at which he is to be on board. | Amount of Wages per Calendar Month, Share, or Voyage. | Amount of Wages advanced on Entry. | Amount of Monthly Allotment. | Signature or Initials of Superintendent, Consul, or Officer of Customs. | Date of leaving this Ship, or of Death, Maiming, or Hurt. | Place. | *Cause. | Amount of Forfeitures to Owner. | Amount of Fines payable to Superintendent. | Contributions to Merchant Seamen's Fund: Period. | Contributions to Merchant Seamen's Fund: Amount. |
|---|---|---|---|---|---|---|---|---|---|---|---|---|---|---|---|---|---|---|---|---|---|---|
| 1 | George Pepperell Jnr (The Master to sign first.) | 25 | Dartmo. | | Same | | | | | Master. | | £ | | | J.C. | | | Remains | | | | |
| 2 | John Connes [?] | 39 | Coffman [?] | | La Zingari Lpool | Jan | Lpool | 23 May | Lpool | Mate C 26111 | 24 May 8 A.M. | 6 0 0 | 6 0 0 | 3 0 0 | J.C. | 23/11/65 | Lpool | Discharge | | | | |
| 3 | Matthew Henry Burgess | 24 | Macclesfield | RV2 9714 | Lookout do | Feb | do | do | do | 2 Mate C 30038 | 24 May | 4 0 0 | 4 0 0 | | J.C. | 23/11/65 | do | do | | | | |
| 4 | Robert Coulrose [?] | 33 | Durham | | D Harrison Lpool | Jan | Lpool | do | do | Carp | 24 May | 5 10 0 | 5 10 0 | 2 10 0 | J.C. | 21/11/65 | do | do | | | | |
| 5 | James Fish [?] | 22 | Blackpool | | Mimosa do | Apl | do | do | do | Stew | 24 May | 3 0 0 | 3 5 0 | | J.C. | 21/11/65 | do | do | | | | |
| 6 | John + Smith | 39 | Wilmington | | Parana Wford [?] | Mar | do | 25 do | do | Cook | 25 May 2 P.M. | 3 0 0 | 3 0 0 | | J.C. | 21/11/65 | do | do | | | | |
| 7 | Alexander Tolaie [?] | 33 | Troon | | C Barter Ldon | May | Lpool | 23 do | do | AB | 24 May | 2 15 0 | 2 15 0 | | J.C. | 21/11/65 | do | do | | | | |
| 8 | Owen + Williams | 24 | Anglesea | | Baroda Lpool | do | do | do | do | AB | 24 May | 2 15 0 | 2 15 0 | | J.C. | 21/11/65 | do | do | | | | |
| 9 | Lars Petterson | 33 | Sweden | | Ayrshire Lass Wrecked | | | do | do | AB | 24 May | 2 15 0 | 2 15 0 | | J.C. | 21/11/65 | do | do | | | | |
| 10 | Joseph + Leonard | 27 | Guernsey | | Mary Smith Guoch [?] | May | London | do | do | AB | 24 May | 2 15 0 | 2 15 0 | | J.C. | 21/11/65 | do | do | | | | |

* If any Member of the Crew enters Her Majesty's Service, the name of the Queen's Ship into which he enters is to be stated under the head of "Cause of leaving the Ship," and if he is a Royal Naval Volunteer his Certificate must be given to the Commanding Officer for transmission to the Registrar General of Seamen.

## INSTRUCTIONS TO MASTERS.

Upon the arrival of the Ship at any Foreign Port where there is a British Consular Officer, or at any Port in any British Possession abroad, the Master is bound under a *Penalty of Twenty Pounds* to deliver within forty-eight hours of the Ship's arrival (if the Ship remains forty-eight hours at the Port, and is not a Passenger Ship), to the Consular Officer, or the Chief Officer of Customs, the Agreement, and all Indentures and Assignments of Apprenticeships. These the Officer will keep during the Ship's stay at the Port, and will, within a reasonable time before the Ship's departure, return them to the Master, with a Certificate endorsed hereon stating when they were delivered and returned.

Within forty-eight hours after the Ship's arrival at her final port of destination in the United Kingdom, or upon the discharge of the Crew, whichever first happens, the Master is to deliver to the Superintendent of the Mercantile Marine Office the Agreement with a list of the Crew and Official Log Book, and Accounts of the Wages and Effects of any Seaman or Apprentice who has died on board during the Voyage, whether he formed part of the Crew or not; and must hand over to the Superintendent of the Mercantile Marine Office any effects remaining unsold, together with the balance of wages or other monies belonging to any such Seaman or Apprentice. The Master should also deliver to the Superintendent of the Mercantile Marine Office the Certificates (Mates, E 1, or R V 2) of any Seaman who has died or deserted during the Voyage, unless the same have been delivered up to a Consul or Officer in a British Possession abroad. Upon these being done, the Superintendent of the Mercantile Marine Office will give a Certificate for the purpose of Clearance.

The statement of the conduct, character, and qualifications of each member of the Crew formerly entered by the Master in the old List C. is to be entered in future in the Official Log Book as required by the 282d section of the Merchant Shipping Act.

## ACCOUNT OF APPRENTICES ON BOARD (IF ANY).

| Christian and Surnames of the Apprentices at length. | Ages. | Registry of Indenture: Date of | Registry of Indenture: Port of | Registry of Assignment: Date of | Registry of Assignment: Port of | Date. | Place. | Cause. |
|---|---|---|---|---|---|---|---|---|
| Colin Walker Hardwicke | 15 | 9 Nov/61 | London | | | | | |
| Henry Cannon | 15 | 20 Mar/63 | Lpool | | | | | |
| Thomas Creswell Wayntaff [?] | 14 | 5 June/62 | do | | | | | |

(Date, Place, and Cause of leaving this Ship, or of Death, Maiming, or Hurt. To be filled up by Master when the occurrence referred to takes place, or at the end of the Voyage.)

I declare to the truth of the entries in this Agreement and Account of Crew, &c.
Delivered to the Superintendent of the Mercantile Marine Office at Liverpool on the 25 day of November 1865

Geo. Pepperell Jnr Master.

LONDON: PRINTED BY GEORGE EDWARD EYRE AND WILLIAM SPOTTISWOODE, PRINTERS TO THE QUEEN'S MOST EXCELLENT MAJESTY.

RIGHT: *This letter from the emigrants, sent not long after their arrival, shows the desperate state that they had got into. Eventually, though, they would win through.*

In 7472/66

New Bay and Chupat River
Patagonia.

To your Honour and Excellency the Governor

We beg to call your attention to our present state and circumstances, and humbly desire on our behalf your merciful feelings, and Christian efforts to sympathies with the few natives of the British Government in our present state in Patagonia, the intended land to establish the Welsh Colony. Before we departed from our native land, Great Britain, the Council of this movement published in several news-papers and hand-bills, that, Patagonia was pointed out as the most convenient, best, and peculiar land to establish the Welsh Colony – and guaranteed to every three persons one hundred acres of land, 5 Horses, 10 Cows, 20 Sheep, seed for the ground, proper articles for farming, and plenty of food to live on till the harvest season.

According to that statement and good promise, several of the Welsh nation were strongly convinced and fully persuaded to enter this great undertaking, with great hopes of meeting every thing all right in this noble land which was reported so favourably by the Leaders of this important and false movement.

When we arrived in this Colony we
expected

> *'... we had nothing there to keep us alive for many weeks only a few biscuits, barely two of them to each person a day and at last a small cup of water mixed with tea ... many of our friends are wearing their last clothing and nothing to depend on but the bare skin towards the winter season.'*

subscribed, and whose descriptions are contained below, and of whom eight are engaged as sailors, hereby agree to serve on board the said Ship, in the several capacities expressed against their respective names, on a voyage from Liverpool to Nuevo Bay (Patagonia) ...' Two months later, on 28 July 1865, the *Mimosa* did indeed sail into Nuevo Bay. She dropped off her passengers, and sailed on.

Another document in the National Archives picks up the story. This is a petition to an English governor, written the year after arriving. As the emigrants pecked at Patagonia's unpromising winter soil, several panicked. Led by their minister, sixteen wrote a petition in pitiful terms:

*When we arrived in this colony we expected that every preparation was made to receive according to what was published, but to our wonder after a long sailing, there was nothing in short to comfort the whole party but the open air day and night, and many of this party have been in great need of food ... we had nothing there to keep us alive for many weeks only a few biscuits, barely two of them to each person a day and at last a small cup of water mixed with tea ... many of our friends are wearing their last clothing and nothing to depend on but the bare skin towards the winter season.*

The concluding petition shows how hunger and cold can trump idealism:

*... and according as we are situated, we are applying to you, as a governor of an English colony to sympathise with us to move us to the Falkland Islands. For God's sake have mercy upon us to bring us to British liberty.*

Over time, things improved for the emigrants, particularly when they learned irrigation and started eating local produce. (When they first arrived, the immigrants had been forbidden by their ministers to eat any food not described in the Bible. In nineteenth-century Patagonia, this would have been tricky.) A little over ten years later, the colony was strong enough to send congratulations to Queen Victoria on her Golden Jubilee. Many emigrant parties followed from Wales, and further colonies and towns were founded. The last major migration from Wales took place in 1911.

For decades, therefore, the local language in this part of South America was Welsh. When the Argentinian authorities required that Spanish be taught in schools, about 400 people left in protest (they wound up in Canada, the world's first community of Welsh-Patagonian-Canadians).

Today, Welsh is still taught in local schools, and there remain some older people who favour Welsh over Spanish. Although Welsh has become less current in the region, in local names – Diego Jones is a favourite – the legacy of the *Mimosa* emigrants lives on.

# WITNESS *to a* MASSACRE

## Letters from Dr Livingstone

LEFT: *David Livingstone, missionary and explorer. Livingstone's tales of the people, animals and landscapes of Africa transformed ideas about the Dark Continent.*

## 1871

THE FIRST LETTERS written by David Livingstone after he had been found in the heart of Africa by Henry Stanley and greeted with the famous 'Dr Livingstone, I presume?' are the product of two extraordinary stories – Livingstone's explorations and Stanley's attempts to find him. But above all, they show that Livingstone cared nothing for famous phrases or tales of daring. He wanted to tell the world about a massacre.

David Livingstone was the son of a door-to-door tea salesman from Lanarkshire, from whom he inherited a profound sense of Christian duty. He went to work as a missionary in the south of Africa. When his mission closed, he spent four years walking from Cape Town through the Kalahari desert and then across Africa, a distance of some 4,000 miles. When he finally arrived home, he wrote a book about his experiences, *Missionary Travels*. His vivid, warm descriptions of the people, animals and landscapes he had encountered transformed ideas about the Dark Continent. Livingstone used his fame to expose the filthy realities of the slave trade. His writing was to slavery what Dickens' writing was to poverty: by describing vividly what they had seen, both had a profound impact on public opinion.

This time, Livingstone was in Africa to search for the source of the Nile. The longest river in the known world was not fed by known rains or water sources, and yet its great waters never shrivelled. Ancient writers decorated the mystery with tantalising romance. Herodotus pictured the source as a group of vast fountains; Ptolemy believed that it lay in a mountain range that he called the Mountains of the Moon. The mystery would seem easy enough to solve – go to the Nile and head upstream – but every expedition had been defeated by the scale and difficulty of the task. In 1865 the President of the Royal Geographical Society persuaded Livingstone to try to find it.

Livingstone believed that the source was a chain of lakes which started farther south than had previously been thought. In April 1866, Livingstone and his convoy landed on the banks of the Rovama River. They spent the next four months slogging through dark bamboo forests and mangrove swamps to reach Lake Nyassa. The map on page 206 shows their route to that inland sea.

By the following spring, Livingstone was in real trouble. Rebellious porters had deserted, taking with them supplies and vital medicines. As the party pressed on

OPPOSITE: *Livingstone's description of the Nyangwe massacre. The slavers shot into the crowd, and then shot the men and women in the water, who were trying to swim away.*

with guns and felt inclined to reprove them
for bringing them into the market place but
refrained by attributing it to ignorance in new
comers. They began to fire into the dense crowd
around them - another party down at the canoes
rained their balls on the panic struck multitude
that rushed into these vessels. All threw away
their goods - the men forgot their paddles. The
canoes were jammed in the creek and could
not be got out quick enough: so many men
and women sprang into the water = the women
of the left bank are expert divers for oysters and
a long line of heads showed a crowd striking
out for an island a mile off - to gain it they
had to turn the left shoulder against a current
of between a mile & a half to two miles an hour
Had they gone diagonally with the current though
that would have been three miles many would
have gained the shore - It was horrible to see
one head after another disappear - some calmly
others throwing their arms high up towards the
great Father of all and going down = some of
the men who got canoes out of the crowd
paddled quick with all their arms to help their friends = three took
people in till they all sank together = one man
had clearly lost his head for he paddled a canoe
which would have held fifty people straight
up stream - nowhere = The Arabs estimated
the loss at between 400 & 500 souls = Dugumbe
sent out some of his men in one of thirty canoes
which the owners in their fright could not
extricate, to save the sinking. One lady refused
to be taken on board because she thought
that she was to be made a slave - but he
rescued twenty one and of his own accord
sent them next day home - many escaped
and came to me and were restored to their
friends - When the firing began on the terror
stricken crowd at the canoes Tagamoio's band
began their assault on the people on the West of the
river and continued the fire all day - I counted
seventeen villages in flames and next day
six - Dugumbe's power over the underlings is
limited but he ordered them to cease shooting -
those in the market were so reckless they shot
of their own number - Tagamoio's crew came back
next day in canoes shouting and firing off
their guns as if believing they were worthy of
renown

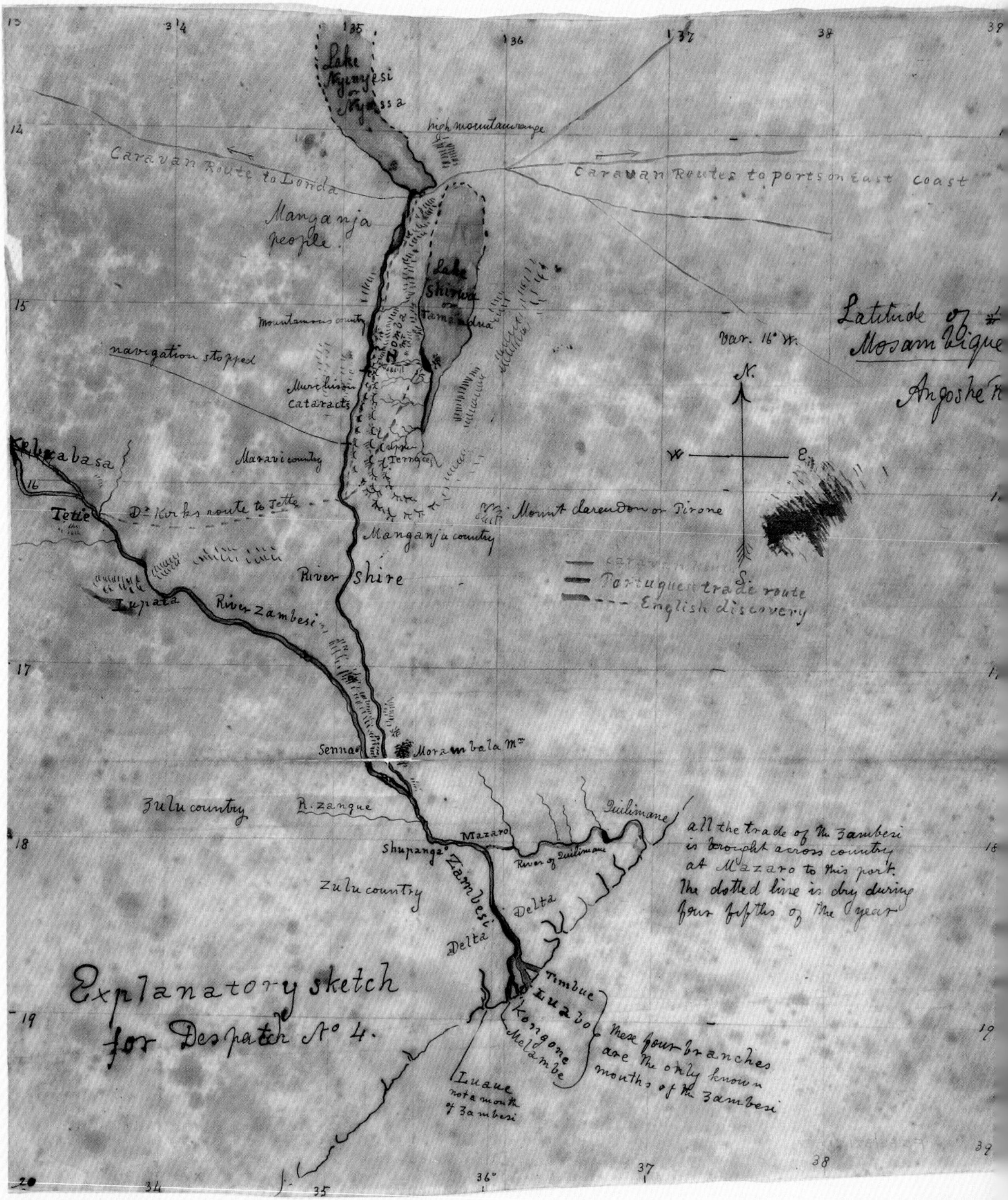

Explanatory sketch for Despatch No 4.

Lake Nyinyesi or Nyassa

high mountain range

Caravan Route to Londa

Caravan Routes to ports on East coast

Manganja people

Lake Shirwa or Tamandua

Mountainous country

navigation stopped

Zomba

Murchison Cataracts

Terraces

Maravi country

Kebrabasa

Tette

Dr Kirk's route to Tette

Mount Clarendon or Pirone

Manganja country

River Shire

Lupata

River Zambesi

Var. 16° W.

N.

W

E.

S.

Latitude of Mosambique

Angoshe

Caravan Route

Portuguese trade route

English discovery

Senna

Morambala Mt

Zulu country

R. Zanque

Quilimane

Mazaro

Shupanga

River of Quilimane

Zambesi

Zulu country

Delta

Delta

all the trade of the Zambesi is brought across country at Mazaro to this port. The dotted line is dry during four fifths of the year

Timbue

Luabo

Kongone

Melambe

These four branches are the only known mouths of the Zambesi

Luaue not a mouth of Zambesi

Opposite: *Livingstone's map, penned in his own hand, tracing his four-month journey from the coast to Lake Nyassa in the interior.*

*Africa whittled away at Livingstone. He endured chronic dysentery, haemorrhoids, pneumonia and rheumatic fever. He suffered bone-eating ulcers on his feet, pulled blood-sucking leeches from his skin, plucked maggots from the depths of his sores and lost most of his teeth. Close to starvation, Livingstone had to fall on the mercy of the people whom he most despised – Arab slavers.*

through dripping forests and oozing bogs it was reduced to a diet of dried corn and rats. Africa whittled away at Livingstone. He endured chronic dysentery, haemorrhoids, pneumonia and rheumatic fever. He suffered bone-eating ulcers on his feet, pulled blood-sucking leeches from his skin, plucked maggots from the depths of his sores and lost most of his teeth. Close to starvation, Livingstone had to fall on the mercy of the people whom he most despised – Arab slavers. For three and a half years, Livingstone and his tiny band (in the end, just three loyal servants) relied on the slavers for food and safety. Livingstone eventually reached a slave town at almost the dead-centre of Africa, Ujiji, which was known to the British and where he hoped to find supplies waiting for him. But the supplies had never arrived. Not only was Livingstone destitute, he was trapped. Native Africans were finally rising against the Arab slavers, and travel was intensely dangerous. Livingstone couldn't go forward, and he couldn't go back.

Henry Morton Stanley was an illegitimate boy from a Welsh workhouse who had decamped to America and managed to fight on both sides in the Civil War before discovering a talent for journalism. Stanley was prickly, pushy, gauche; a British general once described him as 'a howling cad'. But his journey to find Livingstone was his own triumph of will. Speculation over Livingstone's whereabouts had become intense and, looking for a journalistic scoop, the *New York Herald* commissioned Stanley to find him. Stanley's 700-mile walk into the heart of Africa was one-third coastal jungle, one-third savannah and desert, one-third thick rocky forest. He negotiated disease, desertions and the death of associates. But he got lucky. Word reached him that a white man had been seen in Ujiji. Word had also reached Livingstone about Stanley's approach, and this is his first report of the famous meeting:

*A vague rumour reached Ujiji in the beginning of last month, that an Englishman had come to Unyanyembe with boats, horses, men, and goods in abundance. It was in vain conjecture who this could be; and my eager enquiries were met by answers so contradictory that I began to doubt if any stranger had come at all. But, one day, I cannot say which, for I was three weeks too fast in my reckoning, my man Susi came dashing up in great excitement, and gasped out, 'an Englishman coming: see him!'; and off he ran to meet him. The American flag, at the head of the caravan, told me the nationality of the stranger. It was Henry M Stanley, the travelling correspondent of the 'New York Herald', sent by the son of the editor, James Gordon Bennett, Junior, at an expense of over £4,000, to obtain correct information about me, if living; and, if dead, to bring home my bones. The kindness was extreme, and made my whole frame thrill with excitement and gratitude.*

The meeting is mentioned in passing; the famous 'Dr Livingstone, I presume?' does not appear. Rather, Livingstone's letters focus on his discoveries, and are peppered with descriptions of the foul trade in slaves. He was particularly haunted by a horror that he had witnessed four months before – the Nyangwe massacre.

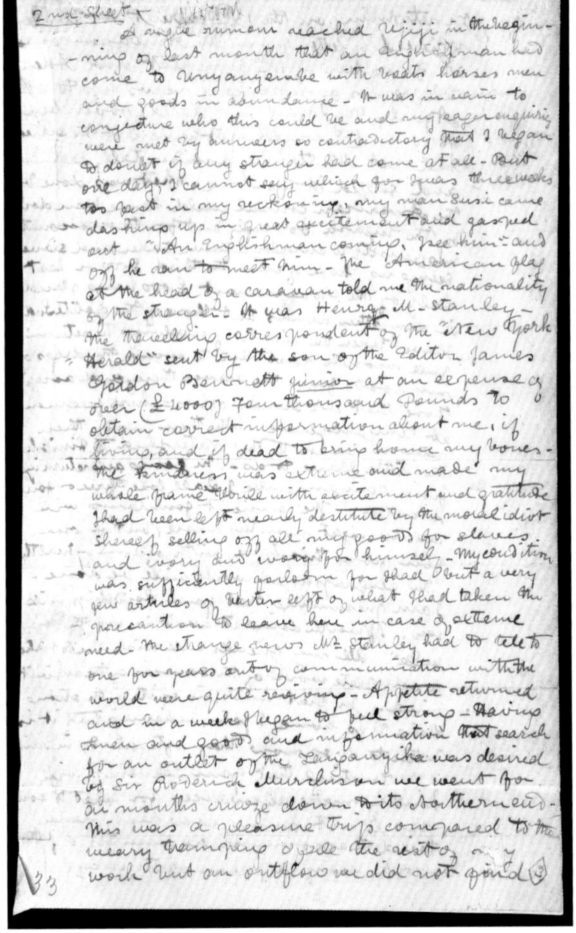

LEFT: *Livingstone's report of his first meeting with Stanley. The words 'Dr Livingstone, I presume?' do not appear.*

In March 1871, Livingstone had arrived at the village of Nyangwe on the banks of the Lualaba river. The leader of the local slavers, called Tagamoro, found his wares elsewhere, so in the village, slavers and natives mixed calmly. However, when the local chief started trading with a rival company of slavers, Tagamoio instigated a co-ordinated and ruthless attack. Livingstone writes this account of what he saw:

*I had left the market only a minute or two when three men whom I had seen with guns, and felt inclined to reprove them for bringing into the market place, but had refrained by attributing it to ignorance in new-comers; they began to fire into the dense crowd around them; another party, down at the canoes, rained their balls on the panic-struck multitude that rushed into these vessels. All threw away their goods, the men forgot their paddles, the canoes were jammed in the creek and could not be got out quick enough, so many men and woman sprang into the water. The woman of the left bank are expert divers for oysters, and a long line of heads showed a crowd striking out from island a mile off ... It was horrible to see one head after another disappear, some calmly, others throwing their arms high up towards the Great Father of all, and going down ... Some of the men who got canoes out of the crowd paddled quick, with hands and arms, to help their friends; three took people in until they all sank together. One man had clearly lost his head, for he paddled a canoe which would have held fifty people straight-up stream, nowhere. The Arabs estimated the lost at between 400 and 500 souls ... when the firing began on the terror-stricken crowd at the canoes, Tagamoio's band began their assault on the people on the west of the river and continued to fire all day. I counted seventeen villages in flames, and the next day six ... Tagamoio's crew came back next day, in canoes, shouting and firing off their guns as if believing that they were worthy of renown.*

Stanley carried these letters home, while Livingstone carried on his search for the Nile's source. It was too much. On the night of 1 May 1873 Livingstone died, half-starved and racked with disease, kneeling in prayer beside his camp bed. His heart was buried in Africa, but his faithful attendants carried his body to the coast from where it was sent to England for a state funeral in Westminster Abbey.

# *The* TICHBORNE CLAIMANT

## Tichborne Court Papers

1872

LEFT: *A cartoon of the Tichborne claimant.*
RIGHT: *The Dowager Lady Tichborne.*

THE NATIONAL ARCHIVES CONTAIN many stories that are unbelievable, but true. These documents tell a story that is just plain unbelievable. It is the tale of the Tichborne Claimant.

The story began in April 1854, when the *Bella* set off from Rio de Janeiro to sail to New York. Among its passengers was Roger Charles Doughty Tichborne, heir to the Tichborne baronetcy and estates in England. The child of a domineering French mother and an alcoholic father, Roger had grown up sickly and slight. After a stint in the Army, he had set off in search of adventure, and for some time had been roaming the interior of South America. He was now on his way back to the English-speaking world.

Six days after the *Bella* set sail, a passing ship found her longboat floating bottom-up, surrounded by the debris of a shipwreck. The *Bella* had been loaded high with coffee, and since her longboat had not been launched, the ship was presumed to have hit a squall, toppled and sunk with all hands. When news reached England, the Tichbornes were plunged into mourning – except for Roger's mother. She became convinced that Roger was not dead, but instead had been rescued and carried to Australia. She would press visitors from the colony for news of her son. She posted advertisements in the Australian press, desperately seeking him. One such advertisement found its way to a cattle town called Wagga Wagga, situated halfway between Sydney and Melbourne, where it fell into the hands of a butcher, Tom Castro. Tom wrote to the Dowager Lady Tichborne with photographs of himself, and announced that he was her long-lost son.

Tom Castro was an unlikely Roger Tichborne. Roger had been slight. Castro was fat – by the time of the trial, a staggering twenty-seven stone. Whereas Roger was fluent in his mother's French, Castro spoke no French at all. Castro had the manners of an outback butcher, and could barely spell. He was missing three front teeth, and had a tendency to drool.

And yet, and yet ... There was something in those eyes that conveyed the same sad melancholy as the eyes of the late heir. Roger had suffered from Saint Vitus' Dance, and Castro suffered from similar twitches and spasms. He too had travelled in South America and had picked up words of Spanish. He would let slip tantalising details of his young life at Tichborne. And if he remembered little beyond those details, well, that just *proved* that he was Roger, didn't it? A true imposter would have done his research. No one would have the brass neck to say that they had forgotten so much.

PREVIOUS PAGES: *Roger Tichborne (left) and Tom Castro (right). While Tichborne was slight, Castro was fat, but Castro nevertheless convinced Tichborne's mother that he was her long-lost son.*

RIGHT: *Tom Castro's declaration that he was Roger Tichborne. He would be convicted of criminal perjury.*

IN CHANCERY.

BETWEEN SIR ROGER CHARLES DOUGHTY TICHBORNE, BARONET . . . . . . . . . . *Plaintiff.*

AND

THE HONORABLE TERESA MARY JOSEPHINE DOUGHTY TICHBORNE WIDOW
THE HONORABLE WILLIAM STOURTON
RENFRIC ARUNDELL
EDWARD HOPKINS AND
ROGER JOSEPH DOUGHTY TICHBORNE AND
HENRY ALFRED JOSEPH DOUGHTY TICHBORNE (SEVERALLY INFANTS UNDER THE AGE OF 21 YEARS) . . . . . . . . . . . . . . *Defendants.*

I SIR ROGER CHARLES DOUGHTY TICHBORNE Baronet of Tichborne in the County of Southampton now residing at No. 2 Wellesley Villas Wellesley Road Croydon in the County of Surrey the above-named plaintiff make oath and say as follows—

1. I am the eldest son of the late Sir James Francis Doughty Tichborne 10th Baronet of Tichborne deceased (who under royal licence assumed the name of Doughty before that of Tichborne as hereinafter mentioned) and I am the 11th Baronet and grandson of the late Sir Henry Tichborne 7th Baronet of Tichborne now deceased.

2. The said Sir Henry Tichborne being then a bachelor intermarried in the year 1778 with Elizabeth Plowden spinster now deceased and had issue of such marriage—

(1.) Henry Joseph Tichborne now deceased his first son who was born on the 5th day of January 1779.

(2.) Benjamin Edmund Tichborne now deceased his second son who was born on the 2nd day of September 1780 and died in the year 1810 in China without ever having been married.

(3.) Edward Tichborne now deceased his third son who was born on the 27th day of March 1782 and assumed by royal licence dated the 29th May 1826 the surname of Doughty.

(4.) And the said James Francis Tichborne (deceased) his fourth son who was born on the 3rd day of October 1784 and assumed by royal licence dated the 26th April 1853 the name of Doughty in addition to and before that of Tichborne and the 4 younger children in the 2nd paragraph of my Bill of Complaint filed in the above mentioned cause in that behalf named.

3. An indenture of release (grounded on a lease for a year) dated the 28th day of January 1806 was duly made between the several parties and of or to the purport or effect set forth in the 3rd paragraph of my said bill.

4. The said Sir Henry Tichborne party to the last-mentioned indenture died on the 14th of June 1821 leaving the said Henry Joseph Tichborne also party

a 2

The Dowager Lady invited Castro to Paris. She had endured years of mockery and condescension over her insistence that her son was alive. This was her chance to prove the sceptics wrong. The moment they met, she cradled Castro's head in her thin arms, and acknowledged him as her own. She would put her remaining energy and wealth towards elevating this man to his proper place.

But hostile forces were massing. The heir to the Tichborne estates and title was Roger's young nephew, the infant Henry Tichborne. Henry's care was entrusted to a group of powerful trustees who were not about to allow a butcher from Wagga Wagga to take the inheritance. Castro applied to the courts for a declaration that he was Roger Tichborne and the rightful heir. The trustees filed a defence that he was not. For the next four years both sides gathered their evidence. Disaster hit the Claimant's camp, when the Dowager Lady Tichborne died. With her gone, Castro lost not only his star witness, but his principal source of funds. Wealthy backers donated money at massive interest against his eventual inheritance. When even that was not enough, Castro went public. 'Tichborne Bonds' were issued against a return of £100 when Sir Roger came into his estates, and were traded in pubs and markets, raising £40,000.

The case started in 1871, and newspapers reported the events in court every day. Opinion on the claim was divided along class lines. Claims like this were an obvious threat to the property-owning classes, and they loudly condemned the Claimant. This oafish colonial could not possibly be taken seriously – which was precisely the attitude that caused the working classes to love him. How dare the Judge suggest, as he had, that this could not be Roger Tichborne, because no man of breeding would swap his life for theirs?

But the evidence against the Claimant was just too great. Fearful that he was about to lose the case, the Claimant quickly withdrew it – and was immediately charged with criminal perjury. The trial was effectively re-run, only in a criminal court this time. The Claimant was found guilty of lying on oath about his identity and sentenced to fourteen years in prison. On his release the Claimant survived as a carnival curiosity, retelling his story to paying crowds. He continued to insist, to the end of his life, that he was indeed Roger Tichborne.

# CITIZEN MARX

## Karl Marx's Application for British Citizenship

## 1874

ABOVE: *'The notorious German agitator' – in his adopted country, Karl Marx enjoyed evening strolls, pub crawls and picnics on Hampstead Heath.*

IN THE NINETEENTH century, Britain's open borders were a source of national pride. *The Times* in 1858 thundered that: 'Every civilised people on the face of the earth must be fully aware that this country is the asylum of nations, and that it would defend the asylum to the last drop of its blood. There is no point on which we are prouder or more resolute ... We are a nation of refugees.' Among the refugees to whom Britain gave asylum was one Karl Marx, philosopher, economist and revolutionary socialist. Famously, Marx died a stateless exile. But, as these documents show, it was not for want of trying. This is Karl Marx's application to be British.

The Marx family – Karl (then aged thirty-one), his wife Jenny and their three young children – arrived in England in August 1849. Marx was German, and had been associated with revolutionary groups since his university days. He became a journalist and newspaper editor, and spent several years bouncing around Europe, as he provoked various ruling powers into booting him out of their countries. The year before he arrived in England, he had written the *Communist Manifesto*, in which he urged the workers of the world to unite, saying they had nothing to lose but their chains. Revolution was then sweeping Europe – revolts, it must be said, caused by disgust at the corruption of the ruling powers, rather than by anything Marx had written – and Marx was expelled from Belgium. He went to France, which in turn tried to exile him to swampy Brittany. Instead, he chose to cross the channel to the asylum of nations.

The penniless family started life in England in fashionable Chelsea, until the bailiffs caught up with them. They then had to endure six years spent impoverished in Soho. Their rooms were frightful (according to Jenny), but at least they were close to the headquarters of the Communist League, which rented rooms over a local pub. They were also close to the British Library, where Marx was to set about researching and writing his greatest work, *Das Kapital*.

Family legacies and the support of Marx's great friend Friedrich Engels allowed the family to move up in the world, first to Kentish Town, and then to 1 Modena Villas at the foot of Hampstead Heath. At a

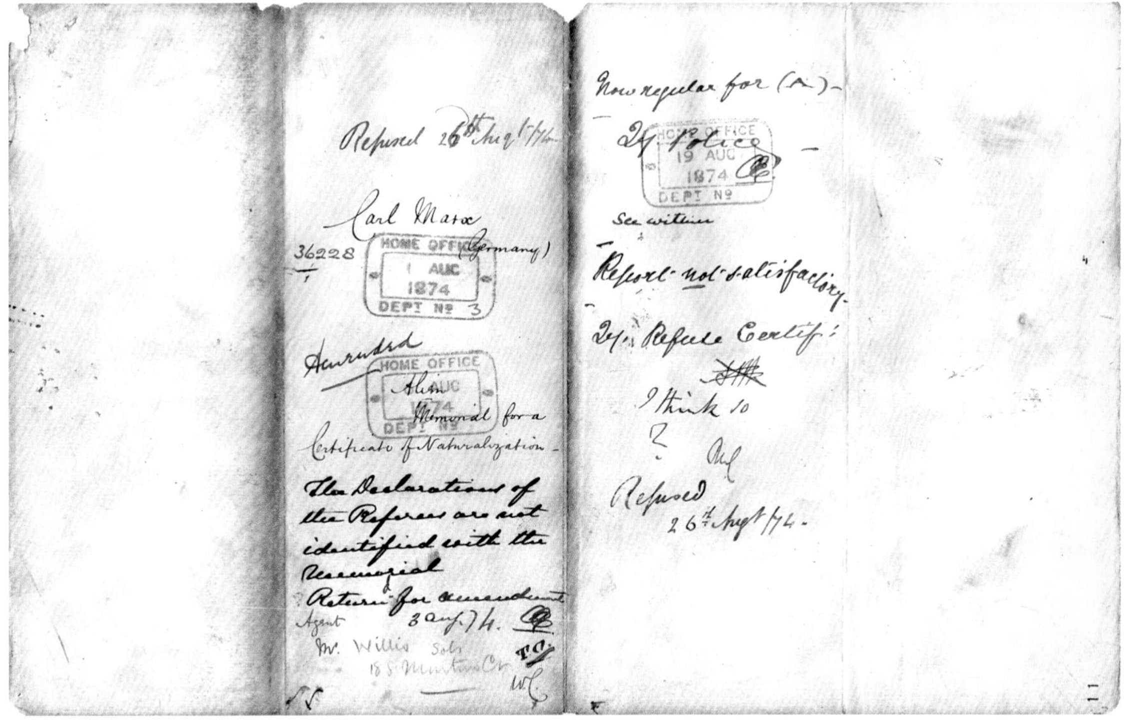

Refused 26th Aug 74

Carl Marx (Germany)

36228

HOME OFFICE 1 AUG 1874 DEPT No 3

Amended

HOME OFFICE AUG 1874 DEPT No

Memorial for a Certificate of Naturalization

The Declarations of the Referees are not identified with the Memorial
Return for amendment 3 Aug 74.

Agent Mr. Willis Solr

Now regular for (A)

HOME OFFICE 19 AUG 1874 DEPT No

Police

See within

Report not satisfactory.

Refuse Certif:

I think so

Refused 26th Aug 74.

Above: *The official rejection of Marx's application: 'Report not satisfactory'. Several inspectors concurred.*

political level, Marx found England intensely frustrating. It was baffling to him that England, the world's greatest industrial power, seemed so resistant to revolution. Marx described his adoptive homeland as the '*rock against which the revolutionary waves break, the country where the new society is stifled in the womb*'. But Marx nevertheless took on some very English habits. He would walk the streets of London for an hour after dinner, go on pub crawls (on one larky night out, he ran off with a policeman's helmet) and declaim passages from Shakespeare as he led his family onto the slopes of Hampstead Heath for Sunday picnics.

Marx's application for British citizenship was a bit of a wheeze. A heavy smoker and chronic over-worker, Marx was plagued with health problems, and he had become rather fond of spa cures. During a particularly bad bout of carbuncles and short breath, he was told that the best place for him was a particular spa in Germany. But there was a problem. If Marx stepped on to German soil, he would be arrested. The solution? To become a British citizen, and so take on the protection of the British Crown.

Anyone resident in Britain for more than a year was entitled to apply for citizenship, and applications were almost rubber stamped. Not Marx's. Someone was watching him, as the National Archives' files show. One Sergeant Reinners wrote on his form:

*He is the notorious German agitator, the head of the International Society, and an advocate of Communistic principles. This man has not been loyal to his own King and Country.*

Opposite: *Marx's application. He naturalised his name to start with a 'C', described himself as a Doctor of Philosophy, gave his profession as author and said that he emigrated 'by permission' of Prussia.*

36228

"A."

MEMORIAL
FOR CERTIFICATE
OF NATURALIZATION.

SOLD BY
EVISON & BRIDGE,
22, CHANCERY LANE.

36228

**To the Right Honorable** Richard Assheton Cross Esq. M.P.
**Her Majesty's Principal Secretary of State for the Home Department.**

The Humble Memorial of Carl Marx –
of No 1 Maitland Park Road Haverstock Hill in the County of Middlesex Doctor of Philosophy – an Alien

Shewеth

1. That your Memorialist is a natural-born subject of the Emperor of Germany but having Emigrated by permission of the Prussian Government in the year 1846 ceased to be a subject of Prussia and has not since been naturalised in any Country –

2. That your Memorialist is of the age of Fifty Six years having been born on ———— the Fifth day of May 1818 at Trèves Rhenish Prussia and is by Profession an Author

State Occupation or Profession.

3. That your Memorialist is married and has one daughter named Eleanor of the age of nineteen years – residing with him

State whether married, and whether any children under age residing with Memorialist, and their names and ages.

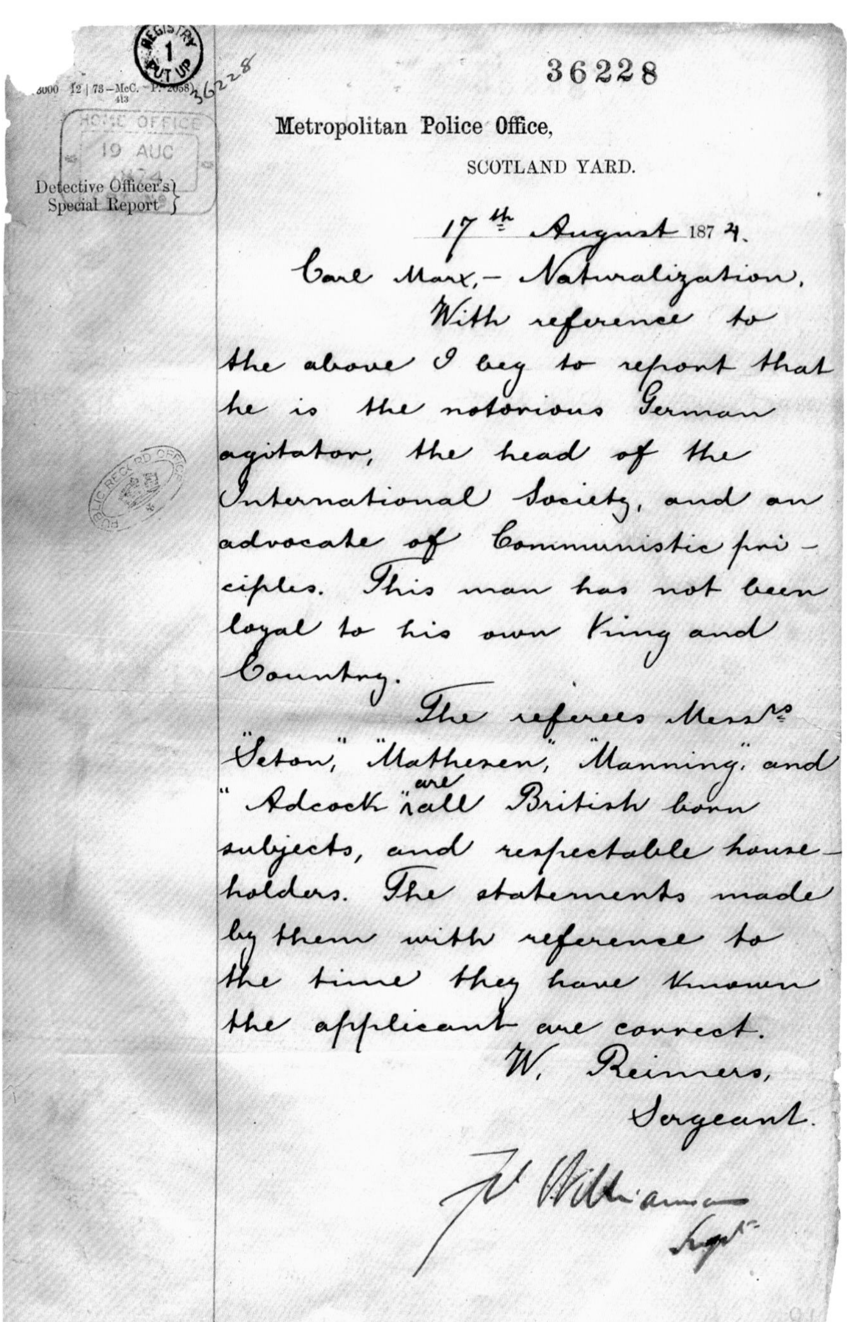

3000 12 | 73—McC. —P. 2058) 413 36228

HOME OFFICE 19 AUG 1874

REGISTRY 1 PUT UP

Detective Officer's Special Report

36228

Metropolitan Police Office,

SCOTLAND YARD.

17th August 1874.

Carl Marx,— Naturalization.

With reference to the above I beg to report that he is the notorious German agitator, the head of the International Society, and an advocate of Communistic principles. This man has not been loyal to his own King and Country.

The referees Messrs "Seton," "Mathesen," "Manning," and "Adcock" are all British born subjects, and respectable householders. The statements made by them with reference to the time they have known the applicant are correct.

W. Reimers,
Sergeant.

F. Williamson
Supt.

RIGHT: *The report that caused Marx's application to be rejected. Sergeant Reinners of the Metropolitan Police describes Marx as 'the notorious German agitator' who had 'not been loyal to his own King and Country'.*

Happily, Marx seems not to have been too worried by Britain's failure to appreciate him. He made the trip to his German spa anyway, where fellow guests were said to have been charmed by his company. He returned to England, where he died in 1883. He was buried in the cemetery in Highgate, North London, his reputation as a man 'without a state' intact. His statelessness would add to the mythology around Marx. In the long run, the British authorities did him a favour.

# *The* PRISONERS
## Photographs of Prison Inmates

# 1873

ABOVE: *Photographs of new inmates at Wandsworth prison.*

IN 1873, the authorities at Wandsworth prison adopted a new technology. As each new inmate entered the prison, they took the person's photograph.

It is rare today to see a studio portrait for which the sitter has not had a chance to tidy up or put on his or her best face. But the men and women here were just told to sit, face a particular direction, and keep still. They look as if they are barely aware of what is happening. As a result, the photographs are disarmingly natural. This is how men, women and children really looked in 1873, not how they would have liked you to see them. Some of them are unlike any faces that you would see today. All crude shaving and snaggle-teeth, they are utterly Victorian. Others, particularly the children, you half-recognise. Put them in a T-shirt and trainers, and you might pass them in the street.

The book supplements each record with personal details, such as these:

| | |
|---|---|
| Name - prison number and Aliases | Robert Thomas Hughes 5409 |
| Age | 14 |
| Height | 4ft 10¾ |
| Hair | Brown |
| Eyes | Brown |
| Complexion | Fresh |
| Where born | Lambeth |
| Married or single | Single |
| Trade or occupation | None |
| Distinguishing Marks | Scar on forehead |
| Address at time of apprehension | 29 Richmond Street, Kennington Road |
| Place & date of conviction | Lambeth – 26 April '73 |
| Offence for which convicted | Simple Larceny<br>Stg [Stealing] a watch & 3 gold rings |
| Sentence | 21 days |
| Date to be liberated | 16 May '73 |
| Intended residence after liberation | |
| Previous convictions/summary | 13 Jan '73 willfully damaging 40 Jugs – 1 Cal month or 6/- |

Description when liberated.

| | |
|---|---|
| Age (on discharge) | 11 |
| Height | 4 ft 1 3/4 |
| Hair | Brown |
| Eyes | Brown |
| Complexion | Fresh |
| Where born | Middlesex |
| Married or single | Single |
| Trade or occupation | None |
| Any other distinguishing mark | Scar on forehead and on right shoulder |

Photograph of Prisoner.



Above and opposite: *For most prisoners, this was the first, and last, time in their lives that they would be subject to the new technology of photography. The photographs are clear, and disarmingly natural. This is how people really looked in 1873. Next to each photograph is a note of that person's personal details, trade and distinguishing marks.*

The ages of the inmates range from eleven to seventy. The predominant crime is larceny (theft) usually of pathetic items – a bag of potatoes, a piece of bacon, a shawl, a basket of butter, a punnet of gooseberries. The inmates list their trades, and are either unskilled manual workers, ex-military or unemployed – former hawkers, costermongers, wood choppers, errand boys, painters, soldiers, sailors, tailors. The sentences range from twenty-one days to three or four months.

Eighty-five years earlier, the people in these photographs might have been transported (see page 139), but Australia by now objected to being a dumping ground for convicts, and punishment was being re-thought. Prison was now designed to deliver a short, sharp shock, to deter people from reoffending. A few years before these photographs were taken, the 1865 Prisons Act was introduced, which authorised the 'Silent System'. Prisoners were kept in silence and subject to long, hard labour. There was the treadmill, on which prisoners walked up rotating steps to power prison machinery, ten minutes on, five minutes off, for eight hours. Even more pointless was the crank, a handle attached to a paddle in a box of sand, which the prisoner would have to turn several thousand times each day before they would be fed. Food was deliberately dull and monotonous. Sleep was on hard boards.

Not that it seemed to have much effect on the some of these prisoners. Many are serial offenders, often for exactly the same crime. You see lists of previous convictions that simply read 'Assault–Assault' or 'Drunk–Drunk–Drunk'. The photographs are captivating, and sad.

79/4 Name, No. David Jackson 1931 26 April 73

and Aliases. Matthews

Description
Age (on discharge) — 18
Height — 5 ft 6½
Hair — Brown
Eyes — Brown
Complexion — Fresh
Where born — Surrey
Married or Single — Single
Trade or occupation — Labourer
Distinguishing marks — Scar on Left Arm & Back

Address at time of apprehension — 4 Clarks Orchard Rotherhithe.

Place and date of conviction — Surrey Sessions 6 May 72

Offence for which convicted — Larceny from the person St 7/6

Sentence — 12 Cal Mo HL

Date to be liberated — 5 May 73

Intended residence after liberation — Same

Previous Convictions
Summary
David Matthews
30 June 69 St 5 Eggs
6 Weeks HL Southwark
David Jackson
20 May 71. R O V. frequenting a certain Dock &c 3 Cal Mo HL Greenwich

By Jury

Remarks, antecedents &c.

171 / 12.2.79.

Rorkes Drift
25th January 1879

8

Sir;

I have the honor to report that on the 22nd inst I was left in command at Rorkes Drift by Major Spalding, who went to Helpmakaar to hurry on the Compy. 24th Regt. ordered to protect the ponts –

About 3.15 pm on that day I was at the ponts when two men came riding from Zulu-land at a galop, and shouted to be taken across the river – I was informed by one of them, Lieut Adendorff of Lonsdales Regt. (who remained to assist in the defence) of the disaster at Isandhlwana Camp, and that the Zulus were advancing on Rorkes Drift – The other a Carbineer rode off to take the news to Helpmakaar –

Almost immediately I received a message from Lieut Bromhead, Commdg. the Company 24th Regt. at the Camp near the Commt. Stores, asking me to come up at once –

I gave the order to inspan, strike tents, put all stores &c into the wagon, and at once rode up to the Commt. Store and found that a note had been received from the Third Column to state that the enemy were advancing in force against our post, which we were to strengthen and hold at all costs –

Lieut Bromhead was most actively employed in loopholing and barricading the store building and hospital and connecting the defence of the two buildings by walls of mealie bags and two wagons that were on the ground –

I held a hurried consultation with him and with Mr. Dalton of the Commt. (who was actively superintending the work of defence, and whom I cannot sufficiently thank for his most valuable services) entirely approving of the

# RORKE'S DRIFT
## Report of Battle

**1879**

RIGHT: *Medallion on which the British Empire, seated on a lion, runs down Zulu warriors.*

THIS ACCOUNT OF the defence of Rorke's Drift was written at the site just two days after the battle. Hundreds of dead Zulus lay round about. Wounded survivors were still being found and shot. It was written well before anyone noticed that the story could be a useful distraction from the fact that, a few days previously, the British Army had undertaken an illegal invasion and suffered a humiliating defeat; and long before anyone would feel uncomfortable with the idea of Europeans armed with guns fighting Africans armed with spears. But it is hard to resist the excitement of the tale, in which barely 100 British soldiers fought off an army of almost 4,000 Zulus, from behind defences made of grain sacks and biscuit boxes.

In 1878, the southern tip of Africa was ruled by the British. To the east, on the other side of the Buffalo River, lay Zululand. The British High Commissioner to South Africa, Sir Bartle Frere, believed that Zululand should be absorbed into British territories. The British Government refused to countenance a war with the Zulu, and so Frere decided to force the issue. On the basis of some trumped-up grievances and demands, he ordered a British invasion force to cross the Buffalo River.

Rorke's Drift was a mission station which lay half-a-mile into Zululand. As the army surged by its small house was converted into a hospital, and its church into an ammunition store, and, together with the newly built ponts across the Buffalo River, it was left in the care of thirty-one-year-old Lieutenant John Chard of the Royal Engineers, the man who would later write this report, with a token force of 100 men. Chard had a reputation as a plodder – not that it mattered. As his commanding officer said before leaving Rorke's Drift, 'I see you are senior, so you will be in charge, although of course, nothing will happen.'

The British invasion force of 5,000 had camped about six miles into Zululand, below a long rocky outcrop, Isandlwana. Reports had come in that the Zulu army was advancing from the east and so the commanding officer sent an advance force to meet it, leaving behind 1,700 men. But the reports were wrong. The Zulu army was encamped nearby, in a hidden valley. Around 10 a.m., parties of Zulu were spotted on the heights, looking down at the British camp. Suddenly, streams of fast-running Zulu warriors descended to right and left. The British troops barely had time to organise a defensive line before the Zulu slammed into it. Within half-an-hour, the camp was encircled, its defences

OPPOSITE: *The first page of the report of Lieutenant Chard, written at the site just two days after the defence of Rorke's Drift.*

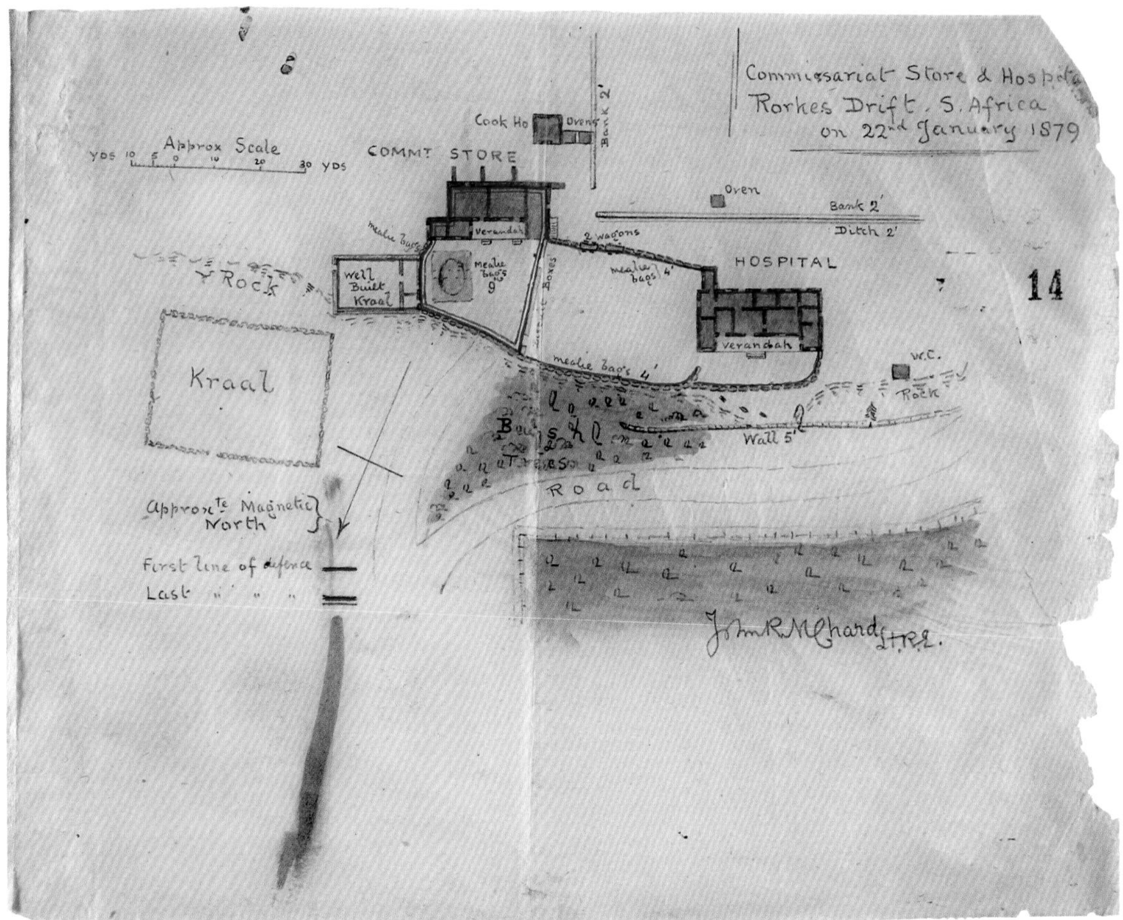


breached. Within another half-an-hour it was completely destroyed, its defenders massacred.

ABOVE: *Chard's drawing of Rorke's Drift – hospital to the right, store to the left. The red lines are the walls made of biscuit boxes and mealie bags.*

Life at Rorke's Drift had been rather comfortable since the invasion force had left. Thirty-five patients in the hospital had ailments ranging from fever to blisters, and the rest of the small force pottered about or wrote letters home.

At around 3.30 p.m., Chard was resting beside the ponts, when two survivors of Isandlwana came tearing towards the river on horseback, shouting that the Zulu were coming. Back at Rorke's Drift, news of the disaster had already reached the men. With no chance of outrunning the Zulu, they had set about building defensive walls with the only materials to hand, biscuit boxes and mealie (maize) bags. The four-foot-high defensive lines ran from the corners of the hospital to the ammunition store, with an inner retrenchment just in front of the store. Chard's report takes up the story:

*We had not completed a wall two boxes high when about 4.30pm, 500 or 600 of the enemy came in sight around the hill to our South, and advanced at a run against our South wall. They were met by a well sustained fire; but, notwithstanding their heavy loss, continued the advance to within 50 yards of the wall, when they met with such heavy fire from the wall, and cross-fire from the store, that they were checked, but taking advantage of the cover afforded by the cook-house, ovens etc kept up a heavy fire. The greater number however without stopping moved to the left around the hospital and made a rush of our north-west wall of mealie bags but after a short but desperate struggle were driven back with heavy loss into the bush around the works . . . Taking advantage of the bush, which we had not time to cut down, the Enemy were able to advance under cover, close to our wall, and in this part soon held one side of the wall, while we held the other. A series of desperate assaults were made, extending from the hospital along the wall as the bush reached, but each was most splendidly met and repulsed by our men, with the bayonet . . . All this time, the enemy had been attempting to force the hospital and shortly after set fire to its roof.*

*The garrison at the hospital defended it room by room, bringing out all the sick who could be moved before they retired . . . As darkness came on, we were completely surrounded and after several attempts had been gallantly repulsed, were eventually forced to retire to the middle and then inner wall, of the Kraal on our East. The position we then had we retained throughout. A desultory fire was kept up all night, and several assaults were attempted and repulsed; the vigour of the attack continuing until after midnight; our men firing with the greatest coolness, did not waste a single shot; the light afforded by the burning hospital being of great help to us.*

The cool, well-ordered report spares some of the terrifying drama – the desperate hand-to-hand fighting, when the biscuit-box-wall was all that separated waves of Zulu warriors from British soldiers; the men in the hospital having to hack holes in the internal walls to escape as the Zulu overwhelmed them room by room; the guns so hot with firing that the men had to rip the arms off their uniforms to make protective gloves just to hold them; the Zulu framed in the firelight of the burning hospital; the men finally trapped in their last, tiny retrenchment, as the Zulu attacked and attacked again.

The courage of the British defenders was extraordinary; so, too, was the courage of the Zulu warriors who hurled themselves into the attack in spite of seeing their companions repeatedly cut down. But the Zulu were already exhausted from Isandlwana, had not eaten for two days, and were desperately thirsty. At about 4 a.m., as the light from the burning hospital died away, they retreated into the darkness. As dawn broke, Chard and his men realised that they had survived. Later that morning, they were finally relieved.

Seventeen British troops died in the defence; 351 Zulu are recorded as having been buried, although the real number of Zulu dead could be as high as 600. Chard's report was dispatched to England, where it was reproduced by an enthusiastic press. Chard was feted as a hero, invited to meet Queen Victoria, and received rapid promotion. Eleven Victoria Crosses were awarded to the defenders, the highest for any regiment in a single engagement. The illegal invasion of Zululand and the disaster at Isandlwana could not be covered up or explained away, but Lieutenant Chard's report provided a potent distraction.

ABOVE: *The report is calm, accurate, well-ordered. Chard himself had a reputation as a plodder, and it is likely that he had more senior help with it.*

POLICE NOTICE.

TO THE OCCUPIER.

On the mornings of Friday, 31st August, Saturday 8th, and Sunday, 30th September, 1888, Women were murdered in or near Whitechapel, supposed by some one residing in the immediate neighbourhood. Should you know of any person to whom suspicion is attached, you are earnestly requested to communicate at once with the nearest Police Station.

Metropolitan Police Office,
30th September, 1888.

Printed by McCorquodale & Co. Limited, "The Armoury," Southwark.

# *The* RIPPER LETTERS
## Letters to the Police

LEFT: *A police notice, distributed to houses near the killings. The police had no leads as to the identity of the murderer.*

1888

THERE IS A DARKNESS in the story of Jack the Ripper that does not depend on the acts of one maniac. It is the reaction of members of the public. The National Archives holds a cascade of letters that were sent to the authorities, claiming to be from the killer. Distracting the police, revelling in the butchery, these letters seem to be egging the Ripper on.

The first Ripper murder took place on 31 August 1888. Mary Ann 'Polly' Nichols was found in Bucks Row in London's East End, her throat slashed and blood pooled into a gutter next to her head. She had been disembowelled. The next murder took place eight days later. Annie Chapman was found in a backyard in Spitalfields, her throat deeply severed, her body eviscerated.

On 29 September, the Central News Agency received a letter that claimed to be from the killer:

*Dear Boss, I keep on hearing the police have caught me but they wont fix me just yet. I have laughed when they look so clever and talk about being on the right track ... I saved some of the proper red stuff in a ginger beer bottle over the last job to write with but it went thick like glue and I cant use it. Red ink is fit enough I hope. Ha ha. The next job I do I shall clip the lady's ears off and send to the police officers just for jolly wouldnt you. Keep this letter back till I do a bit more work then give it out straight. My knife's so nice and sharp I want to get to work right away if I get a chance. Good luck. Yours truly, Jack the Ripper. Dont mind me giving the trade name.*

ABOVE: *A 'self-portrait' of Jack the Ripper, accompanied by a taunt: '10 more and up goes the sponge' i.e. ten more killings and I stop.*
OPPOSITE: *The police were deluged with letters claiming to be from the killer. Some are written in an elegant hand, some are scrawls, some use blood-red ink, some have drawings. Almost all are signed Jack the Ripper. The public was identifying with the murderer.*

The night after the police received this letter, the murderer struck twice. Elizabeth Stride was found in Berner Street with her throat cut. Forty-five minutes later, a second body was found a short

To Dear old Boss
from Jack the Ripper

E. F. G.—In England and Wales there is one policeman to every seven hundred and seventy-five people.

---

Notice
I. Jack the Riper
Will Pay Shortly
a Visit to your
Residence or
your City Shop
Truly yours
Jack Riper

---

every body no's me
TRADE MARK

PS. I give you a good
chance to cach me, so have a
try. Signed
Catch me who can or
Jack Sharpe

---

Sam Jack
the
ripper
Catch me
if you can

---

16/11/88 brown paper wrapper
games reports
To the Supt
I know you are look
ing for me everywhere but you
will never find me. I am chiefly
in Hampstead Rd & Tottenham
court Rd. Why I passed a Policeman
yesterday & he didnt take no
notice of me. Its no use you
putting up those bills you wont
find no partner. I'm on the other
side I do it by myself. I'm not
in any fishing smacks as you
call them, I'm a private
Gentleman.
NB
Look out for me on Saturday
I intend to do some more
murders. No one wont get
no 1600 pounds

---

2

25 Sept. 1888.

Dear Boss
I keep on hearing the police
have caught me but they wont fix
me just yet. I have laughed when
they look so clever and talk about
being on the right track. That joke
about Leather Apron gave me real
fits. I am down on whores and
I shant quit ripping them till I
do get buckled. Grand work the last
job was. I gave the lady no time to
squeal. How can they catch me [illegible]
I love my work and want to st[illegible]
again. You will soon hear of me
with my funny little games. I
saved some of the proper red stuff in
a ginger beer bottle over the last job
to write with but it went thick
like glue and I cant use it. Red
ink is fit enough I hope ha. ha.
The next job I do I shall clip
the lady's ears off and send to the

---

I live in George St. very
comfortably. I'm 30 years
old tall [illegible]
if you cant find me your
a lot of fools. ~~Yours the~~
Yours Truly
Joe the catsmeat man
& woman hunter

Heres my
photo I'm
considered
a very
handsome
Gentleman

Look
out old
Charlie
Warren

193

I was not codding
dear old Boss when
I gave you the tip
you ll hear about
saucy Jacky's work
tomorrow double
event this time
number one squealed
a bit couldnt
finish straight
off. had not time
to get ears for
police thanks for
keeping last letter
back till I got
to work again.
Jack the Ripper

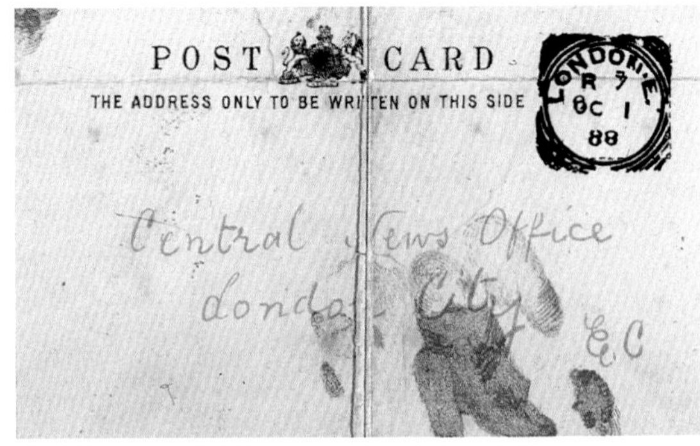


distance away in Mitre Square. Catherine Eddowes was horribly mutilated and, as before, a portion of her innards had been taken.

A second Ripper note was now received, heavily smeared with blood, and postmarked 1 October:

*I was not codding [kidding] dear old Boss when I gave you the tip, you ll hear about Saucy Jacky's work tomorrow double event this time number one squealed a bit couldnt finish straight off. had not time to get ears for police thanks for keeping last letter back till I got to work again. Jack the Ripper.*

The reference to the earlier letter and the close knowledge of the facts of the murders persuaded the police that the same person had written both letters, and that they might indeed be from the killer. In the hope that someone might identify the handwriting, the letters were published in the press, and reproduced on posters in many London police stations.

Far from producing any new leads, the publication of these letters prompted a wave of copycats, with taunting messages and promises of more murders to come. Virtually all of the letters were signed '*Jack the Ripper*'. Most adopted the language of the original two: the repetition of 'Boss', and 'ha ha', the threats to cut off parts of the victim's body, the use of red ink, the bedlam tone. Some of the letters are grammatical and well spelt, others are illiterate; some are legible, others are scrawls; some contain drawings of knives, bones or coffins. These people were giving their letters some thought.

Hoax letters were not limited to England. Facsimiles of the original letters had been published in the international press, and letters were received from France, Portugal, Ireland and the USA. One was found in a bottle, washed up on a beach in Kent. Several were not posted but were found in the street, or in one case tacked to a tree.

After a gap of five weeks the murderer struck again, with his most demented killing. On 9 November 1888, Mary Jane Kelly's body was found in her one-room dwelling place in Spitalfields. Kelly had died from a single blow to the neck, but she had then been grotesquely mutilated. This latest ghastly murder inspired a new wave of letters.

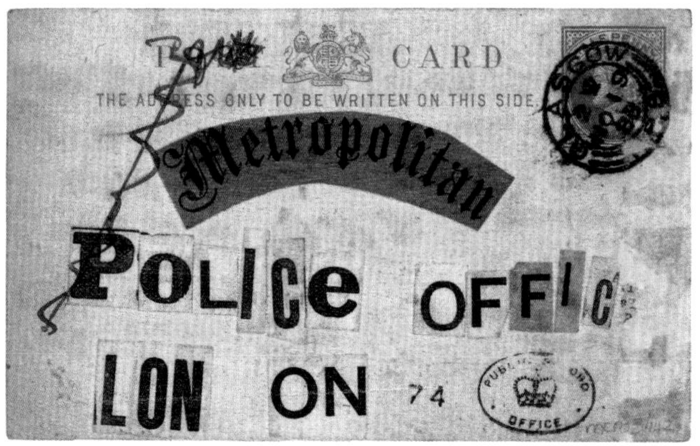

CARD
THE ADDRESS ONLY TO BE WRITTEN ON THIS SIDE.
Metropolitan
POLICE OFFIC
LON ON 74

THE WHITECHAPEL ATROCITIES.
ALL ON THE WRONG SALVAGE! I AM IN A FIRST-CLASS AT GOVAN WANTED young lady the 24th instant. BY GOD I SHALL CLEAR GLASGOW AND GOVAN AND POLLOKSHIELDS OF 16 ENGLISH WHORE LADIES AND GENTLEMEN THE LORD WILL DO HIS Guaranteed WORK BY SCUTCHER 300 Pieces
REQUIRED
NO CLUE

Opposite: *One of the two original blood-smeared letters from the 'real' Ripper. Police at the time concluded that, in fact, it had been sent by a journalist.*
Above and right: *More copycat letters from the public. They were posted, tacked to trees – one was even found in a bottle washed up on the shoreline.*

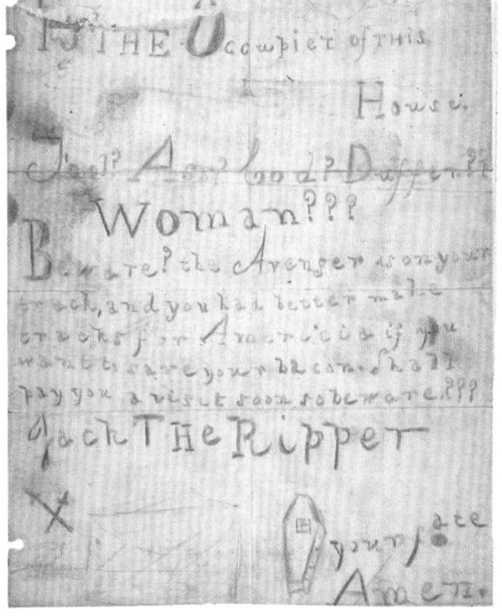

TO THE Occupier of THIS House.
Woman???
Beware? the Avenger is on your track, and you had better make tracks for America if you want to save your bacon. I shall pay you a visit soon so beware???
Jack THE Ripper
your fate
Amen.

Who wrote these appalling letters? The original letters may have come from the murderer himself, but they might equally have come from a well-informed journalist with an interest in spinning the story. The police at the time believed this to be the case, and suspected that a journalist called Tom Billing was the writer. Strikingly, the only two people caught and convicted of writing Ripper letters were both women. One, Maria Coroner, wrote her fake letters from Jack to the local police and press in Bradford, claiming to have arrived in town. She was a 21-year-old milliner and claimed to have written her letters as a joke. But she was also reportedly excited by the killings, hated prostitutes and enjoyed the panic she caused when her letter to the press was published. The other person convicted was a 14-year-old maidservant, who wrote to her master pretending to be Jack and threatening to burn down the house and murder the inhabitants. But the sheer number and variety of these letters demands more than one explanation. They could have been written by people with a grudge against the police; by men excited by the idea of killing women; by school children having a lark; by respected pillars of the community. The public was getting a thrill.

# *The* DOWNFALL *of* OSCAR WILDE

## The Marquis of Queensberry's Card

## 1895

LEFT: *Oscar Wilde, writer and aesthete, in 1882.*
RIGHT: *Exhibit envelope used by the Central Criminal Court (left); the envelope used by the hall porter (middle); the Marquis of Queensberry's card (right).*

THIS TINY CARD, with its barely legible writing, caused one of the greatest tragedies in the history of literature. It would lead to the imprisonment, public disgrace and exile of the writer Oscar Wilde. How could such a tiny scrap of paper cause such a terrible downfall?

In 1891, Oscar Wilde was aged thirty-six and already famous as a wit and writer. That summer, Wilde was introduced to a handsome young aristocrat and undergraduate from his old college, Lord Alfred Douglas. Over the course of the next year, the two men became inseparable.

Douglas was engaged in a vicious battle of wills with his father, the Marquis of Queensberry. Initially friendly towards Wilde, Queensberry became aggressive when the intimacy of his son's relationship with the older writer became apparent. By February 1895, Queensberry was looking to force a confrontation. On 14 February, he was narrowly prevented from disrupting the opening night of Wilde's greatest play, *The Importance of being Earnest*. On 18 February, Queensberry visited Wilde's London club, the Albemarle. Finding that Wilde was not there, he hastily scrawled a message on his visiting card and handed it to the hall porter, instructing him to give the message to Wilde when he was next in. The porter slipped the card into an envelope, writing the date and time of receipt on the back.

The message was intended to be a public insult, but it is difficult to tell exactly what Queensberry wrote. 'Sodomite' (homosexual) is misspelt 'so*m*domite'. When he was interviewed later, the hall porter (who was the only person to have seen the card) said that he thought that it read: 'For Oscar Wilde ponce and sodomite.' Queensberry hurriedly corrected the reading, saying that in fact the card read: 'For Oscar Wilde posing as sodomite.' These fine distinctions were to be important. To prove that someone is *posing* as a homosexual might be easier than proving that they *are* a homosexual. While, if Queensberry had written 'ponce' (i.e. pimp) and sodomite – well, Wilde was plainly no pimp. Tiny details can separate success and disaster.

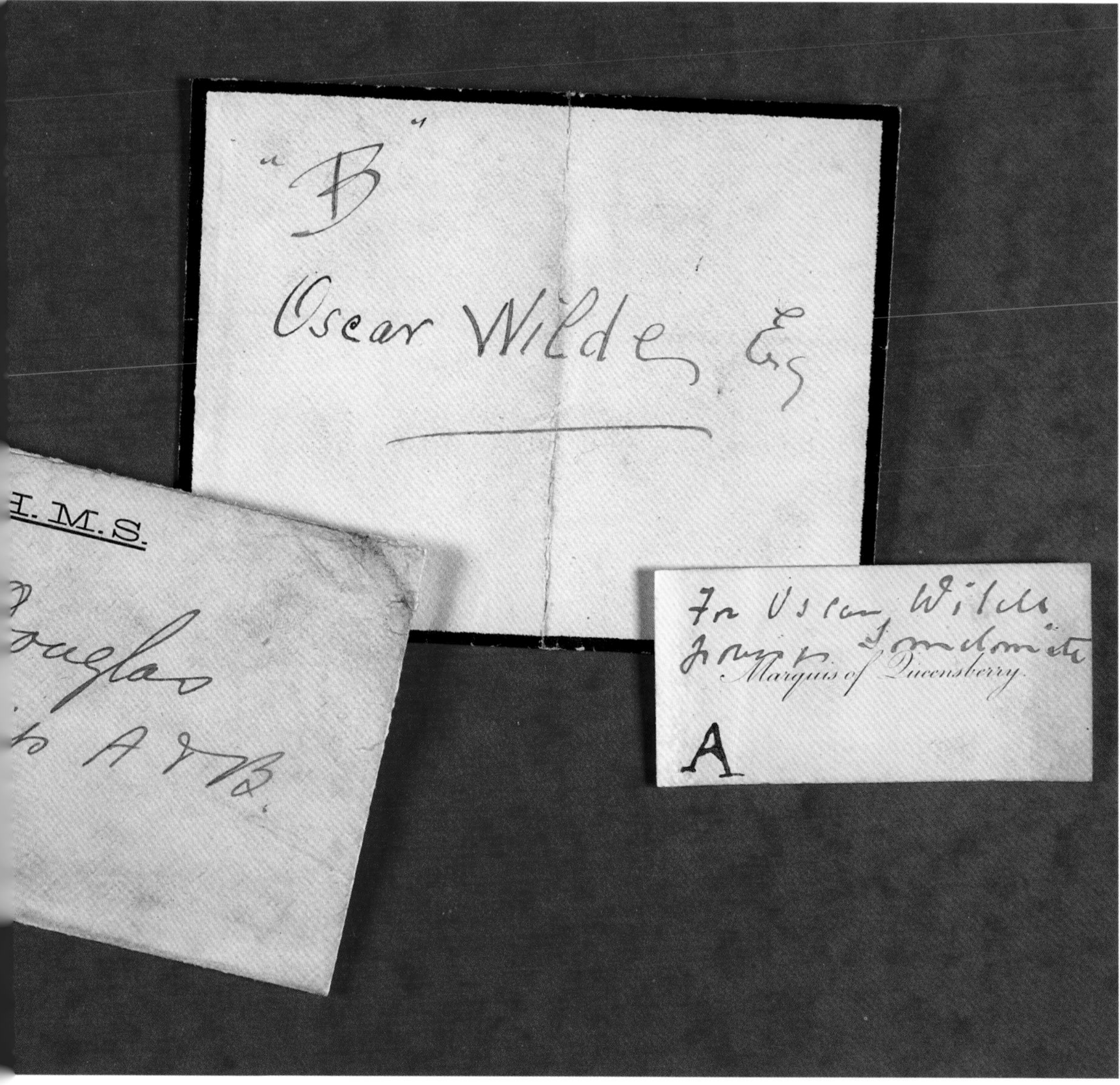


Wilde was given the card when he called into his club ten days later. He did not at first want to go to law about the insult. But Douglas saw his opportunity for a public showdown with his father, and tried to fire Wilde up.

Wilde visited his lawyers, Humphreys and Humphreys. As a lawyer, I wonder what legal advice Wilde received at this point. Did they explore with him whether he had committed any indiscretions, however small, which could be used against him (as they were)? Did they consider whether there was anything in his writings that could be misinterpreted (as it would be)? Did they ask whether he knew anyone, and in particular anyone capable of being corrupted, who might give evidence against him (as they did)? Did they suggest to Wilde that a barely legible scrawl on a tiny card that had been seen by just one other person might not be worth taking action over? Wilde may have been badly served by Humphreys and Humphreys.

# STATEMENT OF THE ACCUSED.

John Sholto Douglas
Marquis of Queensberry

(hereinafter called the Accused) stands charged before the undersigned, one of the Magistrates of the Police Courts of the Metropolis sitting at the Marlborough Street Police Court, in the Metropolitan Police District, this 9th day of March in the Year of our Lord One Thousand Eight Hundred and Ninety-five as herein before set forth, and the said charge being read to the said Accused, and the said Witnesses for the prosecution being severally examined in the presence of the said Accused, the said Accused is now addressed by Me as follows:
"Having heard the evidence do you wish to say anything in answer to the charge?
"You are not obliged to say anything unless you desire to do so, but whatever you
"say will be taken down in writing and may be given in evidence against you upon
"your trial, and if you desire to call any Witness, you can now do so."

Whereupon the said Accused
saith as follows:—

I have simply to say this that I wrote the card, simply with the intention of bringing matters to a head, having been unable to meet Mr Wilde otherwise and to save

~~Taken before me at the Police Court aforesaid, on the day and year above mentioned.~~

*Indictable Forms.* N.
Sch. II.—No. 16.
[166.]
STATEMENT
OF THE ACCUSED.

18

W B & L (256G)—39352—4000-5·94

LEFT: *The Marquis of Queensberry's witness statement, on which he has added, '. . . I wrote the card simply with the intention of bringing matters to a head . . .'* RIGHT: *The governor of Reading gaol and a prison commissioner debate whether to allow Wilde to send a letter to Douglas. Permission was refused.*

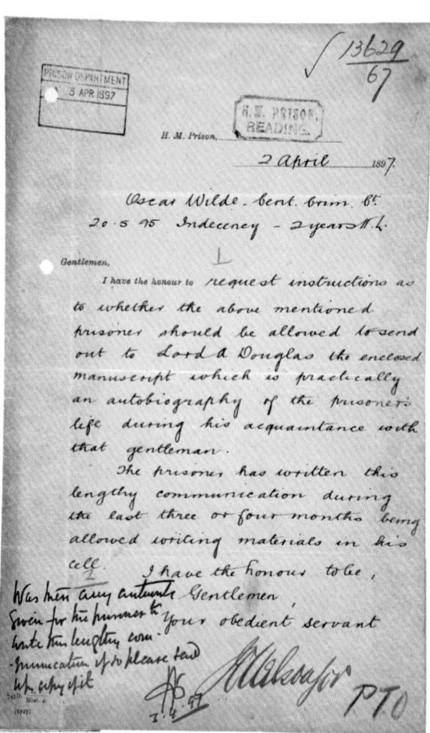

13629 / 67

PRISON DEPARTMENT 5 APR 1897

H.M. PRISON, READING.

H. M. Prison, 2 April 1897.

Oscar Wilde. Cent. Crim. Ct. 20.5.95 Indecency – 2 years H.L.

Gentlemen,

I have the honour to request instructions as to whether the above mentioned prisoner should be allowed to send out to Lord A. Douglas the enclosed manuscript which is practically an autobiography of the prisoner's life during his acquaintance with that gentleman.

The prisoner has written this lengthy communication during the last three or four months being allowed writing materials in his cell.

I have the honour to be, Gentlemen, Your obedient servant

[illegible]

Was there any authority given for the prisoner to write this lengthy communication? If so please send [illegible] copy of it

[illegible] 3.4.97 PTO

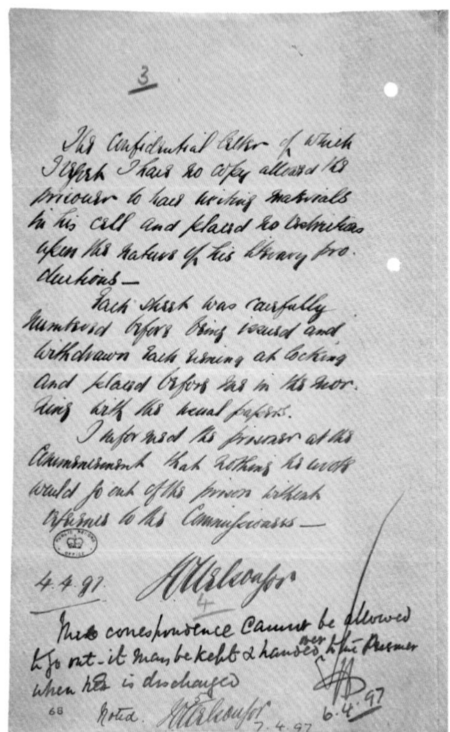

3

The Confidential letter of which [illegible] I have no copy allowed the prisoner to have writing materials in his cell and placed no restrictions upon the nature of his literary productions –

Each sheet was carefully numbered before being issued and withdrawn each evening at locking and placed before me in the morning with the usual papers.

I informed the prisoner at the commencement that nothing he wrote would go out of the prison without reference to the Commissioners –

4.4.97. [illegible]

4

This correspondence cannot be allowed to go out – it may be kept & handed over to the prisoner when he is discharged

[illegible] 6.4.97

Noted. [illegible] 7.4.97

Wilde was persuaded to take action. On 2 March, Queensberry was arrested and charged with publishing a libel against Wilde.

Relaxed and confident of their success, on 12 March, Wilde and Douglas went on holiday to the South of France. One can only imagine their reaction when they returned to find that Queensberry had pleaded justification – in other words, that the words on the card were not libellous because they were true.

While Wilde and Douglas had been away, a team of private detectives hired by Queensberry had assembled a mass of witness evidence. Wilde v. Queensberry opened on 3 April 1895. When the time came for the defence to put its case, Queensberry's barrister opened with the claim that they had located several male prostitutes each of whom had signed a statement detailing their relationship with Wilde.

None of these statements survives. Indeed, the minutes of evidence of the trial are themselves missing from the National Archives' files. Instead, the file contains a note – 'The details of this case are unfit for publication' – a piece of self-censorship that appals modern archivists as much as it frustrates historians.

Wilde quickly dropped his suit against Queensberry. Just as quickly, Queensberry's solicitor sent the incriminating evidence to the Director of Public Prosecutions. Wilde was arrested and charged with sodomy.

The Judge of the criminal trial, Mr Justice Wills, described it as 'the worst case I have ever tried'. He said that he had no doubt that Wilde was at the centre of a 'circle of corruption of the most hideous kind among young men'. Wilde was sentenced to two years' hard labour.

On his release, Wilde caught a boat to Dieppe, and never returned to Britain. After three years of impoverished exile, he died at the Hotel D'Alsace in Paris on 30 November 1900.

You find yourself looking at this little card with wonder. Did a great man's collapse really come about from something so small?

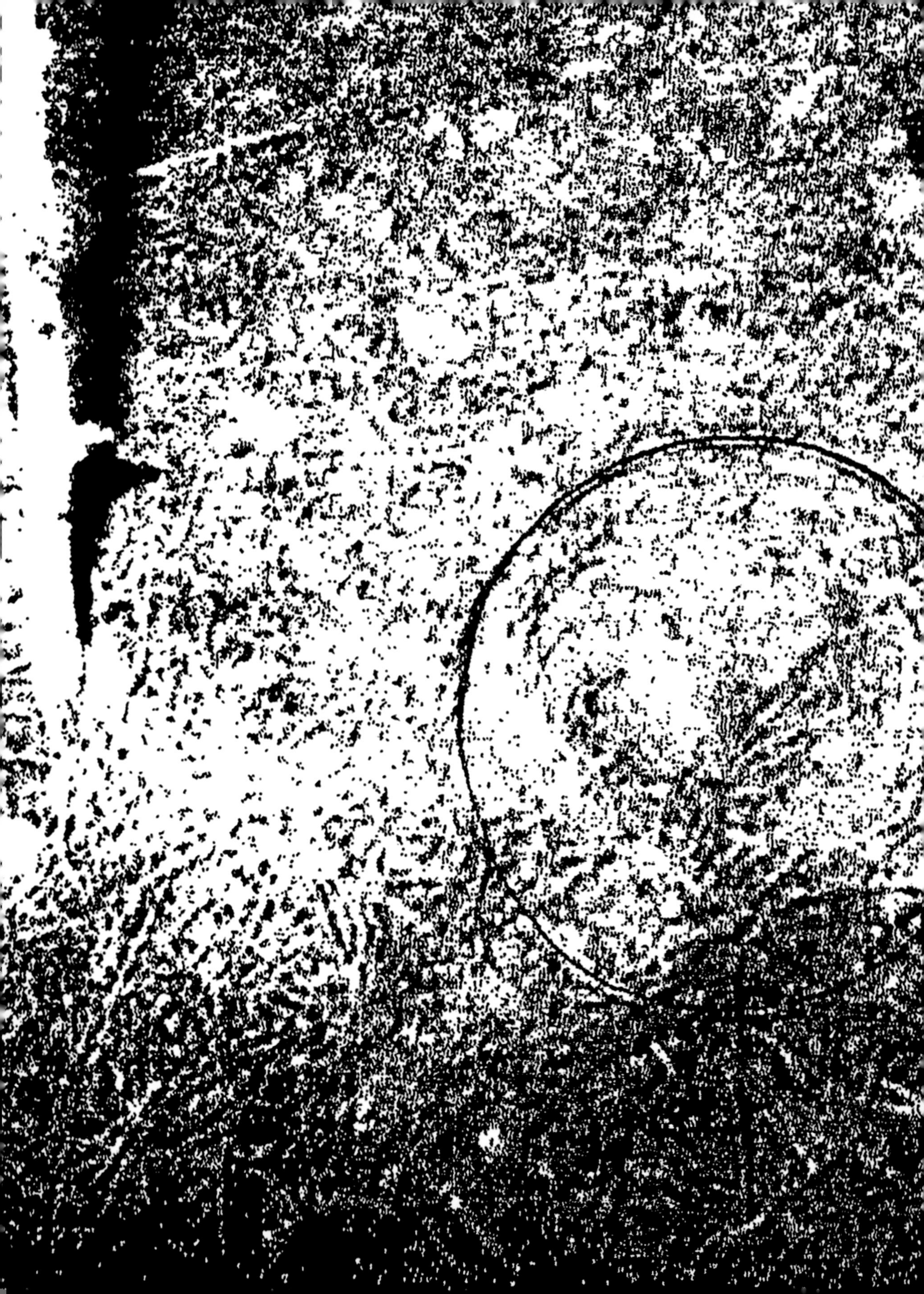

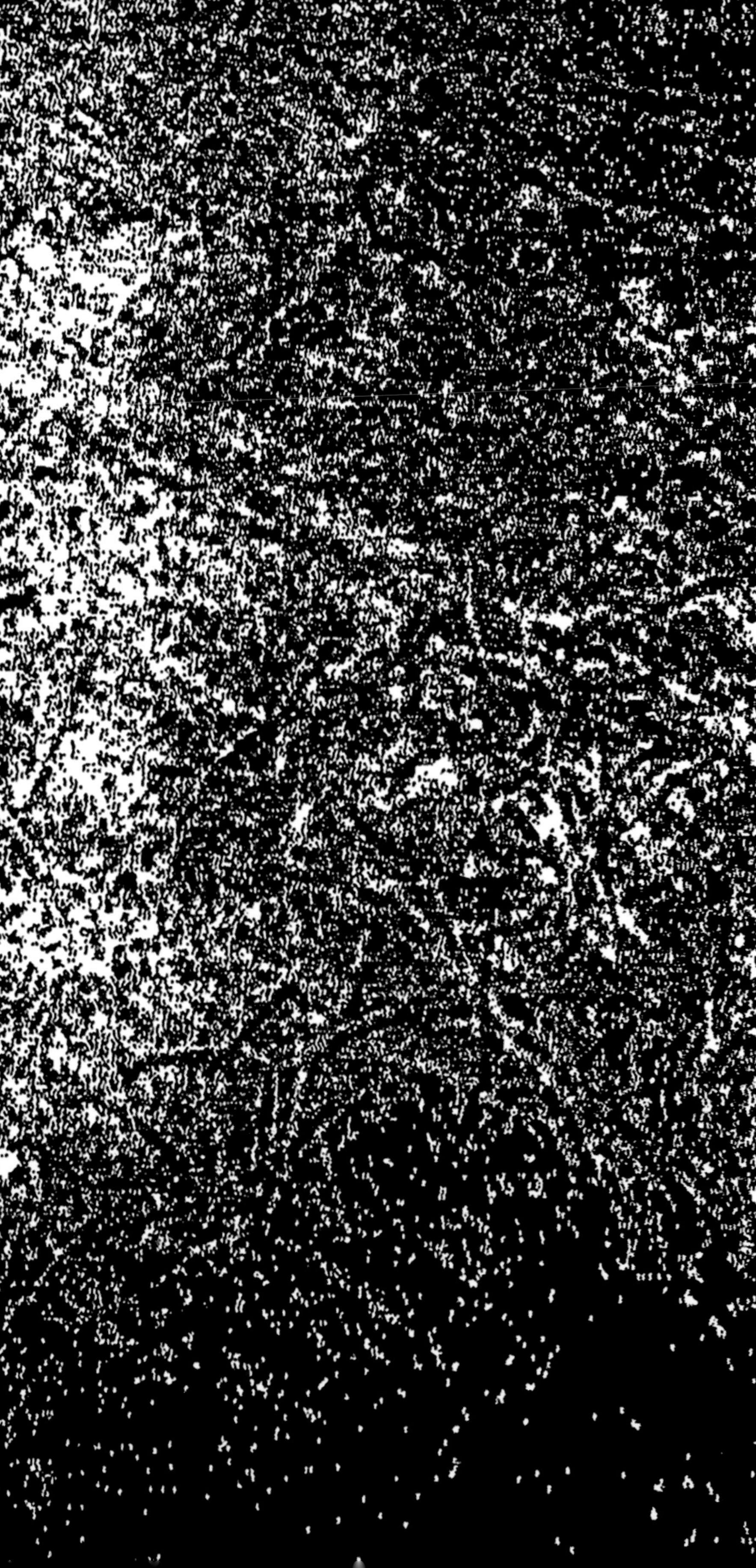

# 20TH CENTURY

## Spoiled Census Returns *to* The British X-Files

LEFT: *Photograph from the British X-files. Circled is an indentation allegedly caused by a UFO.*

# CENSUS OF ENGLAND AND WALES, 1911.

Number of Schedule 368
(To be filled up by the Enumerator after collection.)

*Before writing on this Schedule please read the Examples and the Instructions given on the other side of the paper, as well as the headings of the Columns. The entries should be written in Ink.*

*The contents of the Schedule will be treated as confidential. Strict care will be taken that no information is disclosed with regard to individual persons. The returns are not to be used for proof of age, as in connection with Old Age Pensions, or for any other purpose than the preparation of Statistical Tables.*

| | NAME AND SURNAME of every Person, whether Member of Family, Visitor, Boarder, or Servant, who (1) passed the night of Sunday, April 2nd, 1911, in this dwelling and was alive at midnight, or (2) arrived in this dwelling on the morning of Monday, April 3rd, not having been enumerated elsewhere. No one else must be included. (For order of entering names see Examples on back of Schedule.) | RELATIONSHIP to Head of Family. State whether "Head," or "Wife," "Son," "Daughter," or other Relative, "Visitor," "Boarder," or "Servant." | AGE (last Birthday) and SEX. Ages of Males. | Ages of Females. | PARTICULARS as to MARRIAGE. Write "Single," "Married," "Widower," or "Widow," opposite the names of all persons aged 15 years and upwards. | Completed years the present Marriage has lasted. | Total Children Born Alive. | Children still Living. | Children who have Died. | PROFESSION or OCCUPATION. Personal Occupation. | Industry or Service with which worker is connected. | Whether Employer, Worker, or Working on Own Account. | Whether Working at Home. | BIRTHPLACE of every person. | NATIONALITY of every Person born in a Foreign Country. | INFIRMITY. |
|---|---|---|---|---|---|---|---|---|---|---|---|---|---|---|---|---|
| | 1. | 2. | 3. | 4. | 5. | 6. | 7. | 8. | 9. | 10. | 11. | 12. | 13. | 14. | 15. | 16. |
| 1 | Estimated | | | | | | | | | | | | | OX | | |
| 2 | Louisa Burnham | Head | | 46 | Single | | | | | | | | | OX | | |
| 3 | 2 ~~[illegible]~~ do | Sister | | 48 | do | | | | | | | | | OX | | |
| 4 | 1 Maid | Servant | | 24 | | | | | | | | | | | | |
| 5 | | | | | | | | | | | | | | | | |
| 6 | | | | | | | | | | | | | | | | |
| 7 | | | | | | | | | | | | | | | | |
| 8 | | | | | | | | | | | | | | | | |
| 9 | | | | | | | | | | | | | | | | |
| 10 | | | | | | | | | | | | | | | | |
| 11 | | | | | | | | | | | | | | | | |
| 12 | | | | | | | | | | | | | | | | |
| 13 | | | | | | | | | | | | | | | | |
| 14 | | | | | | | | | | | | | | | | |
| 15 | | | | | | | | | | | | | | | | |

No Vote No Census. 020
If I am intelligent enough
to fill in this Census form
I can surely make a X
on a Ballot Paper.
Louisa Burnham
(Miss)

192 Elms Road

(To be filled up by the Enumerator.)

I certify that:— (1.) All the ages on this Schedule are entered in the proper sex columns. (2.) I have counted the males and females in Columns 3 and 4 separately, and have compared their sum with the total number of persons. (3.) After making the necessary enquiries I have completed all entries on the Schedule which appeared to be defective, and have corrected such as appeared to be erroneous.

Initials of Enumerator [illegible]

| Total. Males. | Females. | Persons. |
|---|---|---|
| | 3 | 3 |

o 1.

(To be filled up by, or on behalf of, the Head of Family or other person in occupation, or in charge, of this dwelling.)

Write below the Number of Rooms in this Dwelling (House, Tenement, or Apartment). Count the kitchen as a room but do not count scullery, landing, lobby, closet, bathroom; nor warehouse, office, shop.

I declare that this Schedule is correctly filled up to the best of my knowledge and belief.

Signature

---

| Total. Males. | Females. | Persons. |
|---|---|---|
| ~~2~~ | 4 ~~5~~ | 7 |

~~Wife Away~~
My wife unfortunately being a Suffragette put her pen through her name, but it must stand as correct. It being an equivocation to say she is away. She being always resident here & has only attempted by a silly subterfuge to defeat the objects of the Census To which as "Head" of the Family I object E. A. Maund

---


# CENSUS OF ENGLAND AND WALES, 1911.


Number of Schedule 4
(To be filled up by the Enumerator after collection.)


*Before writing on this Schedule please read the Examples and the Instructions given on the other side of the paper, as well as the headings of the Columns. The entries should be written in Ink.*

*The contents of the Schedule will be treated as confidential. Strict care will be taken that no information is disclosed with regard to individual persons. The returns are not to be used for proof of age, as in connection with Old Age Pensions, or for any other purpose than the preparation of Statistical Tables.*


| | NAME AND SURNAME | RELATIONSHIP to Head of Family. | Ages of Males. | Ages of Females. | PARTICULARS as to MARRIAGE. | Completed years the present Marriage has lasted. | Total Children Born Alive. | Children still Living. | Children who have Died. | Personal Occupation. | Industry or Service with which worker is connected. | Whether Employer, Worker, or Working on Own Account. | Whether Working at Home. | BIRTHPLACE of every person. | NATIONALITY of every Person born in a Foreign Country. | INFIRMITY. |
|---|---|---|---|---|---|---|---|---|---|---|---|---|---|---|---|---|
| | 1. | 2. | 3. | 4. | 5. | 6. | 7. | 8. | 9. | 10. | 11. | 12. | 13. | 14. | 15. | 16. |
| 1 | Edward Arthur Maund | Head | 60 | | Married | 21 | 5 | | | Company Director 994 | | Own Acc. | | Lavestock Wilts | 260 | – |
| 2 | ~~Eleanora Maund~~ (Eleanora) | ~~Wife~~ | | ~~38~~ 38 | ~~Married~~ Married | ~~21~~ 21 | ~~5~~ | ~~5~~ | ~~–~~ | | | | | ~~Shipley Yorkshire~~ | 030 | – |
| 3 | Geoffrey Richard G. Maund | Son | 17 | | Single | | | | | Bank Clerk 501 | | Worker | | Kings Langley Herts | 310. | – |
| 4 | Miele Cecily Eleanora Maund | Daughter | | 15 | Single | | | | | | | | | Rhodesia Africa | Resident 723 | – |
| 5 | Hugh Brigham Maund | Son | 14 | ~~14~~ | | | | | | | | | | Ipswich Suffolk | 201 | – |
| 6 | Annie Brown | Servant | | 29 | Single | | | | | Cook (Domestic) 010 | | 0 | | Wellington Somerset | 140 | |
| 7 | May Brice | Servant | | 26 | Single | | | | | General Servant (do) 010 | | 0 | | Wellington Somerset | 140. | |
| 8 | | | | | | | | | | | | | | | | |
| 9 | | | | | | | | | | | | | | | | |
| 10 | | | | | | | | | | | | | | | | |
| 11 | | | | | | | | | | | | | | | | |
| 12 | | | | | | | | | | | | | | | | |
| 13 | | | | | | | | | | | | | | | | |
| 14 | | | | | | | | | | | | | | | | |
| 15 | | | | | | | | | | | | | | | | |


(To be filled up by the Enumerator.)

I certify that:— (1.) All the ages on this Schedule are entered in the proper sex columns. (2.) I have counted the males and females in Columns 3 and 4 separately, and have compared their sum with the total number of persons. (3.) After making the necessary enquiries I have completed all entries on the Schedule which appeared to be defective, and have corrected such as appeared to be erroneous.


Initials of Enumerator

| Total. Males. | Females. | Persons. |
|---|---|---|
| 3 ~~2~~ | 4 ~~5~~ | 7 |


~~Wife Away~~
My wife unfortunately being a Suffragette put her pen through her name, but it must stand as correct. It being an equivocation to say she is away. She being always resident here & has only attempted by a silly subterfuge to defeat the objects of the Census To which as "Head" of the Family I object E. A. Maund



(To be filled up by, or on behalf of, the Head of Family or other person in occupation, or in charge, of this dwelling.)

Write below the Number of Rooms in this Dwelling (House, Tenement, or Apartment). Count the kitchen as a room but do not count scullery, landing, lobby, closet, bathroom; nor warehouse, office, shop.

I declare that this Schedule is correctly filled up to the best of my knowledge and belief.


13.

Signature E. A. Maund

Postal Address 8. Edith Road West Kensington W.

# *The* SUFFRAGETTES' CENSUS
## Spoiled Census Returns

## 1911

IN 1911, BRITAIN held its ten-yearly census. It came at the height of a protest movement that had been gathering strength for more than a decade – the campaign for votes for women. The suffragettes campaigned with marches, rallies and lobbying. Now the census presented them with a perfect opportunity. If you don't count enough to vote, why should you be counted? The suffragettes mobilised a mass boycott of the census. The census forms shown here include some typical suffragette responses.

A few days before the weekend of 1/2 April 1911, blank census forms were delivered to every household in Britain. Householders were meant to complete the forms with details of the people living at the residence on the night of Sunday, 2 April. Over the following days the completed forms would be collected by a small army of enumerators.

ABOVE: *1911 handbill advertising a rally for Votes For Women. The bill is printed in the suffragette colours of purple, green and white.*

It was the enumerator who filled in the details on the first of these returns, for Louisa Burnham, her sister and one servant of 192 Elms Road. Louisa herself had responded rather differently: 'No Vote No Census. If I am intelligent enough to fill in this census form I can surely make an X on a Ballot Paper.'

OPPOSITE ABOVE: *Louisa Burnham's census return, marked 'No Vote No Census'.*

OPPOSITE BELOW: *Edward and Eleanora Maud's census return, marked by Edward, 'My wife unfortunately being a Suffragette put a pen through her name.'*

The second shows a divided household. Edward and Eleanora Maud lived with their three children and two servants at 8 Edith Road, West Kensington. Eleanora has struck through her name. Edward has reinstated it, with a note of explanation at the foot of the page, in red: 'My wife unfortunately being a Suffragette [has an underlining ever expressed such exasperation?] put her pen through her name, but it must stand as correct. It being an equivocation to say she is away. She being always resident here and has only attempted by a silly subterfuge to refute the object of the census to which as "Head" of the family I object.'

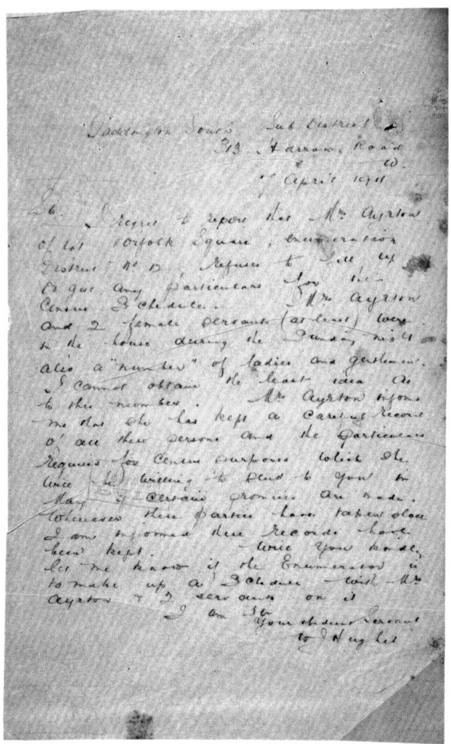

Paddington South Sub District
313 Harrow Road
W.
7 April 1911

Sir,
I regret to report that Mrs Ayrton of 101 Norfolk Square, Enumeration District No 12, refuses to fill up or give any particulars for the Census Schedule. Mrs Ayrton and 2 female servants (at least) were in the house during the Sunday night also a "number" of ladies and gentlemen. I cannot obtain the least idea as to their number. Mrs Ayrton informs me that she has kept a careful record of all these persons and the particulars required for Census purposes which she will be willing to send to you in May if certain promises are made. Wherever these parties have taken place I am informed these records have been kept. Will you kindly let me know if the Enumerator is to make up a Schedule with Mrs Ayrton & 2 servants on it

I am Sir
Your obedient Servant
W J Hughes

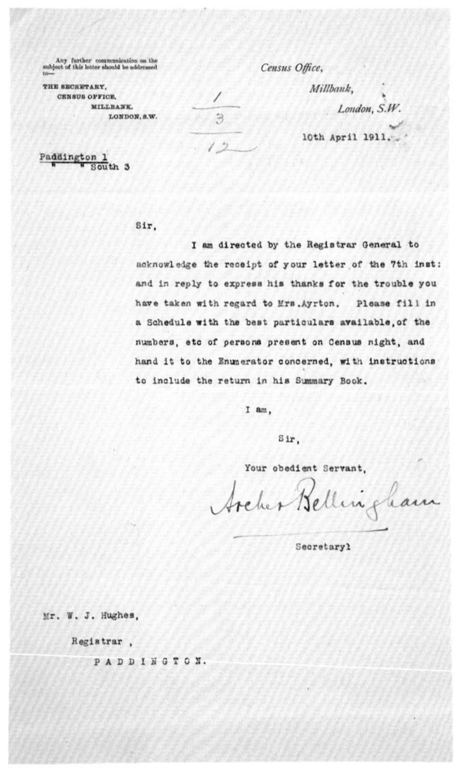

Any further communication on the subject of this letter should be addressed to—
THE SECRETARY,
CENSUS OFFICE,
MILLBANK,
LONDON, S.W.

1/3/12

Census Office,
Millbank,
London, S.W.

10th April 1911.

Paddington 1
" " South 3

Sir,

I am directed by the Registrar General to acknowledge the receipt of your letter of the 7th inst: and in reply to express his thanks for the trouble you have taken with regard to Mrs.Ayrton. Please fill in a Schedule with the best particulars available, of the numbers, etc of persons present on Census night, and hand it to the Enumerator concerned, with instructions to include the return in his Summary Book.

I am,
Sir,
Your obedient Servant,
Archer Bellingham
Secretary

Mr. W. J. Hughes,
Registrar,
PADDINGTON.

LEFT ABOVE: *The Paddington Registrar writes to the Census Office for guidance over a Mrs Ayrton, who was refusing to complete the census form.*

LEFT BELOW: *The Census Office's doughty reply: 'Please fill in a schedule with the best particulars available.'*

It may be that Eleanora's 'silly subterfuge' was to spend a night away from home to avoid the count. She may have joined other suffragettes in London who spent the night walking in Trafalgar Square, picnicking on Wimbledon Common or attending special entertainments at Aldwych skating rink. Others hid in bicycle sheds or coal cellars. Years later, a former suffragette said that she felt sorry for later generations who had not had the fun of a night out on census day.

The boycott probably had little impact on the count due, at least in part, to the work of the sturdy enumerators. They were paid by the number of completed forms they submitted, and if a return was spoiled they would do their best to complete it themselves. You can see from Louisa Burnham's return that her enumerator seems to have noted her protest, shrugged, and filled her name in anyway.

In the following years, the struggle for votes would become darker. In 1912 and 1913, after the Government broke promises of reform, window-smashing, arson, even bombings were added to the armoury of the more militant suffragettes. Since 1909, some women imprisoned for their protests had gone on hunger strike, and the authorities responded by force-feeding them through tubes. The Government tried a different tactic with the 'Prisoners (Temporary Discharge for Ill Health) Act 1913', better known as the 'Cat and Mouse Act'. Hunger strikers were allowed to starve themselves to a state of weakness, whereupon they were released, only to be rearrested on minor pretexts once they had got their strength back. But with the advent of the First World War, the suffragettes suspended their protests so that they could throw their weight behind the war effort, and when the war ended the vote was given to all men over the age of twenty-one, and to women of property over thirty. Full equality of suffrage arrived ten years later. Louisa and Eleanora counted at last.

# 'WE *are* SINKING'
## Telegrams Received from RMS *Titanic*

1912

ABOVE: *Survivors being picked up by the* Carpathia.
ABOVE RIGHT: *Jack Philips, from Godalming, radio operator on the* Titanic, *who sent these messages.*

THESE TELEGRAMS WERE sent from RMS *Titanic* as she was sinking. The largest steamer of her day, she had a swimming pool, palm court, French chefs and Italian waiters. She also had a double-bottomed skin and sixteen watertight compartments, five of which would have to fill before she risked sinking. Although her owners never claimed that their ship was unsinkable, they probably thought as much. But, famously, they had made a terrible error. Although the *Titanic* carried 2,240 passengers when she set off across the Atlantic from Southampton Dock on 10 April 1912, the capacity of her lifeboats was just 1,178.

The passengers on this maiden voyage included one of the richest men in the world, John Jacob Astor IV; mining magnate Benjamin Guggenheim; the founder of Macy's Department Stores, Isidor Straus; a member of the US Davis Cup team, Carl Behr; and Thomas Andrews, the ship's designer. But the *Titanic* was predominantly an immigrant ship. In the ship's passenger list you see entire families heading for new lives in the New World, and a preponderance of Scandinavian names.

On 14 April, the *Titanic* was warned of icebergs in the area, but she steamed on regardless. At 11.40 p.m., an iceberg was spotted straight ahead. The engines were thrown into reverse but it was too late and a series of small holes were smashed into the ship's hull.

These telegrams are exchanges between the *Titanic* and SS *Birma*, a Russian East Asiatic steamship. On the *Titanic*, Londoner Harold Bride relayed messages from the captain on the bridge, while Jack Philips worked the keys. The radio operator on the *Birma* was another young Londoner, Joseph Cannon, sailing his maiden voyage. Their first exchange was calm. ('MGY' is the *Titanic*'s call sign.)

Titanic: *We have struck iceberg sinking fast come to our assistance. Posn Lat 41 46'N. Long 50 14W. MGY*
Birma: *What is the matter with you?*
Titanic: *OK We have struck iceberg and sinking please tell captain to come. MGY*

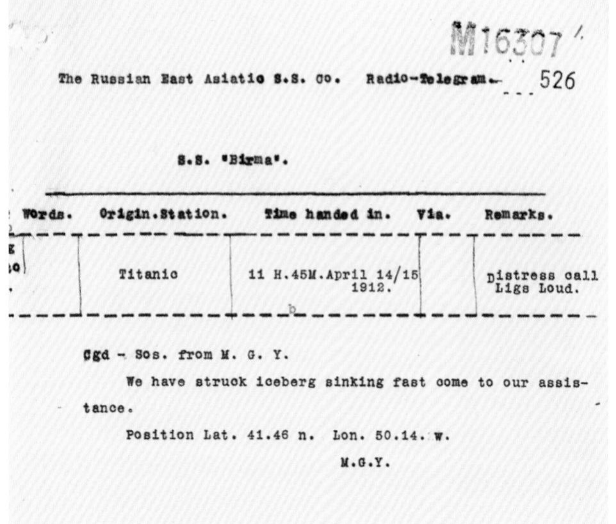

M16307 4

The Russian East Asiatic S.S. Co. Radio-Telegram. 526

S.S. "Birma".

| Words. | Origin.Station. | Time handed in. | Via. | Remarks. |
|---|---|---|---|---|
| 10 | Titanic | 11 H.45M.April 14/15 1912. | | Distress call Ligs Loud. |

Cgd – Sos. from M. G. Y.

We have struck iceberg sinking fast come to our assistance.

Position Lat. 41.46 n. Lon. 50.14. w.

M.G.Y.

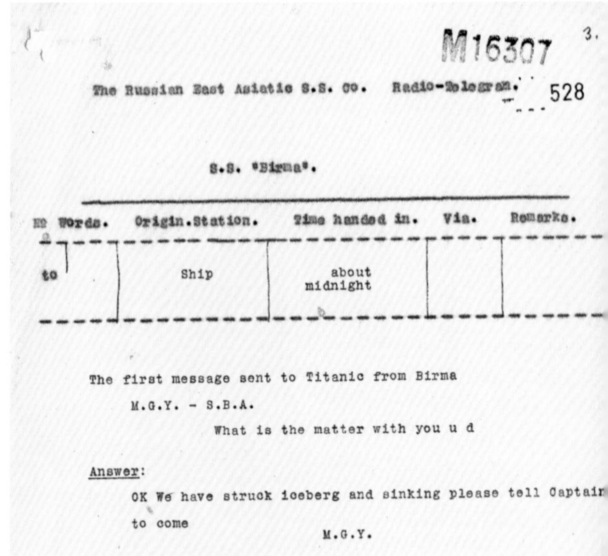

M16307 3.

The Russian East Asiatic S.S. Co. Radio-Telegram. 528

S.S. "Birma".

| No | Words. | Origin.Station. | Time handed in. | Via. | Remarks. |
|---|---|---|---|---|---|
| | to | Ship | about midnight | | |

The first message sent to Titanic from Birma

M.G.Y. – S.B.A.

What is the matter with you u d

Answer:

OK We have struck iceberg and sinking please tell Captain to come

M.G.Y.

Above: *Telegrams from the* Titanic *received by the* Birma. *Initially calm and controlled, the messages, which are open to all ships, become increasingly frantic. The* Titanic *sank thirty-five minutes after the last one was sent.*

Opposite: *The Register of Deceased Passengers; on these pages are some of those from 1st Class. The recurrence of surnames shows that whole families died together.*

The *Birma* calculated its distance from the *Titanic* and said it would be with them by 6.30 a.m. Philips responded: 'Okay OM [Old Man]'.

The next message hits like a lightning bolt: 'SOS SOS CQD [CQD is the international code for 'All stations attend distress'] We are sinking fast passengers being put into boats'.

This was an open message to all ships, as are all the messages that follow. Philips now fired messages continuously, his concentration so intense that Bride had to fix a lifebelt around his colleague while he worked. 'Women and children in boats. Cannot last much longer.' The final message at 1.45 a.m. was simply 'CQD' and 'SOS'.

The *Titanic* sank thirty-five minutes after the last message was sent. Bride helped push a collapsible boat over the side and jumped in with it. The boat capsized and he was trapped underneath, but somehow he escaped and rolled on to the edge of the upturned boat. Bride later recalled listening to the band on the deck of the *Titanic* as it played until the ship sank.

The first ship to reach the scene, the *Carpathia*, did so at 4 a.m. The *Birma*, on the other hand, found that the *Titanic* had sent it the wrong co-ordinates – some 13 miles out, with a icefield lying between it and the place where the *Titanic* had sunk. It travelled around the icefield, and shortly after midday passed the *Carpathia* heading west with some 705 survivors, including Harold Bride. With nothing more that it could do, the *Birma* carried on its way to St Petersburg.

These messages were gathered through diplomatic channels to form part of the Commission of Enquiry into the disaster, records that are as distressing now as they were in the moments that they were sent. It is not possible to be precise about the numbers of the dead, but less than one-third survived. Among the dead was Jack Philips. After sending his last message, he jumped from the ship and managed to reach the upturned boat that Harold Bride was on. But sometime in the night, exhausted, he slipped under the sea.

M16307

The Russian East Asiatic S.S. Co. Radio-Telegram. 527

S.S. "Birma".

| Words. | Origin.Station. | Time handed in. | Via. | Remarks. |
|---|---|---|---|---|
| | Ship. | | SBA | |

M.G.Y. We are only 100 miles from you steaming 14 knots be with you by 6-30 our position Lat' 40.48 N. Long. 52.13 W.

S.B.A.

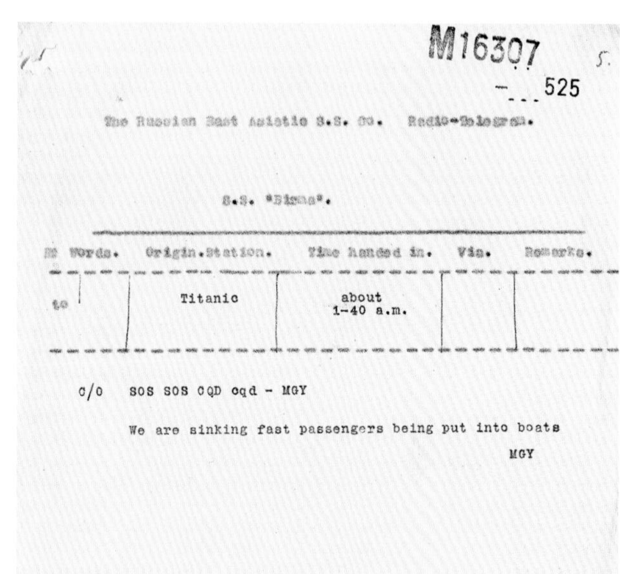

M16307

525

The Russian East Asiatic S.S. Co. Radio-Telegram.

S.S. "Birma".

| Words. | Origin.Station. | Time handed in. | Via. | Remarks. |
|---|---|---|---|---|
| to | Titanic | about 1-40 a.m. | | |

c/o SOS SOS CQD cqd - MGY

We are sinking fast passengers being put into boats

MGY

Month *June* Year 1912.

**REGISTER OF DECEASED PASSENGERS.** 43

| 1.–8. | 9. Name. | 10. Official Number. | 11. Port of Registry. | 12. Date of Death. | 13. Place of Death. | 14. Name and Surname | 15. of Deceased. | 16. Sex. | 17. Age. | 18. Rank, Profession, or Occupation. | 19. Nationality, or Birthplace. | 20. Last Place of Abode. | 21. CAUSE OF DEATH. |
|---|---|---|---|---|---|---|---|---|---|---|---|---|---|
| C Dub Sea In - W S | Titanic | 131428 | Liverpool | 15.4.12. | About Lat. 41.16 N Long 50.14 W. | | 1st Class Passengers | | | | | | Supposed Drowned |
| | | | | | | Stephen Weart | Blackwell | M | | | U.S.C. | | |
| | | | | | | J. J. | Borebank | M | | | Eng | | |
| | | | | | | John B | Brady | M | | | | Elysee Palace Hotel Paris | |
| | | | | | | E. | Brandeis | M | | | | | |
| | | | | | | Arthur Jackson | Brewe | M | | | U.S.C | | |
| | | | | | | Archibald W | Butt | M | | Major in American Army | do | | |
| | | | | | | Alexander | Cairns (Carter's manservant) | M | | | | | |
| | | | | | | Frank | Carlson | M | | | U.S.C. | | |
| | | | | | | F. M. | Carron | M | | | do | | |
| | | | | | | J. P | Carron | M | | | do | | |
| | | | | | | Howard B. | Case | M | | | do | Vacuum Oil Co. London | |
| | | | | | | T. W. | Cavendish | M | | | do | 23 Chesham Place London | |
| | | | | | | Herbert F | Chaffee | M | | | do | | |
| | | | | | | Roderick | Chisholm | M | | | Irish | Harland & Wolffe Belfast | |
| | | | | | | Walter M. | Clark | M | | | U.S.C. | c/o Amexco Rome | |
| | | | | | | George Quincy | Clifford | M | | | do | c/o Kings [illegible] Cheapside, London | |
| | | | | | | E. P. | Colley | M | | | Irish | [illegible] Rathgar Dublin | |
| | | | | | | A. T. | Compton Jr | M | | | | Hotel Dysart Paris | |
| | | | | | | John B | Crafton | M | | | U.S.C. | Victoria Hotel London | |
| | | | | | | Edward G. | Crosby | M | | | | Grand Trunk Rly. London SW | |
| | | | | | | John Bradley | Cummings | M | | | | c/o Morgan Harjes Paris | |
| | | | | | | Thornton | Davidson | M | | | U.S.C. | | |
| | | | | | | W. D. | Douglas | M | | | do | c/o Boyd Neel 1 Rue Damion Paris | |
| | | | | | | William C | Dulles | M | | | do | Hotel France & Choiseul Paris | |

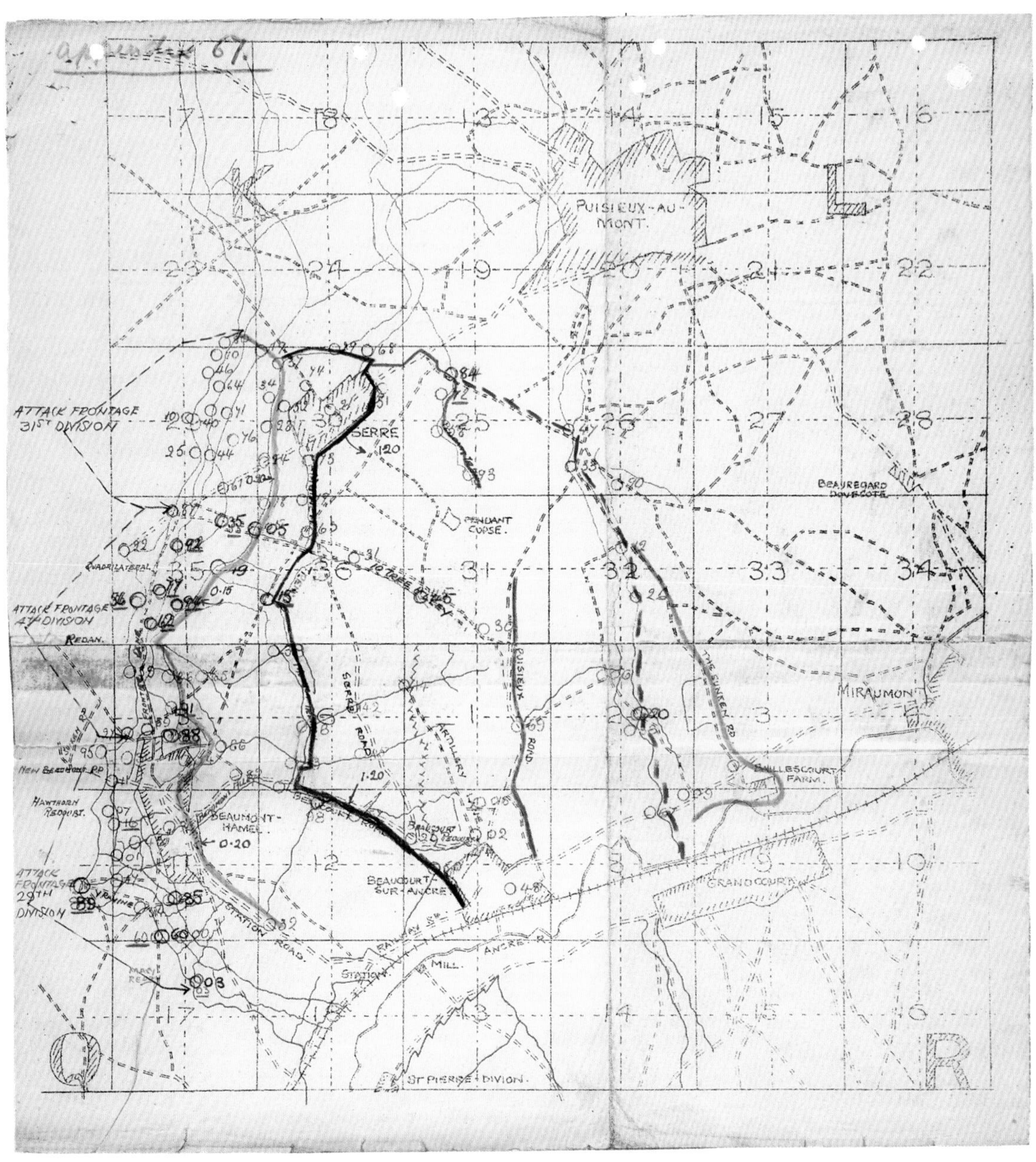


*For five days, its artillery would pound the German front lines, destroying their trenches, dugouts and barbed wire. The Army would then walk, in a steady and orderly manner, across no-man's-land to occupy the lifeless, shattered German positions . . .*

ABOVE: *A battleplan for the Somme. The thin red lines show the German trench system. The British trenches are shown far right. The thick, coloured lines are the sequence of that day's objectives.*

# *The* FIRST DAY *of the* SOMME

## Battlefield Plans and Reports

LEFT: *Remembrance Day poppy, dating from the period between the two world wars.*

## 1 July 1916

THESE ARE DOCUMENTS from the darkest day in the history of the British Army: a plan for, and minute-by-minute reports of, the first day of the Battle of the Somme. The reports show an unfolding tragedy. They also show why that first day went so horribly wrong.

The First World War started for Britain in the summer of 1914, and was meant to be over by Christmas. Instead there was stalemate, and a line of trenches that stretched continuously from the Belgian coast, across northern France to Switzerland. The British trench zone was close to the English Channel, running almost due north to south, from the town of Ypres to the River Somme. The deadlock in the trenches continued throughout 1915, and as winter drew in, the Allies – France, Britain, Russia and Italy – formed plans for 1916. They agreed on a co-ordinated attack, the British part of which would take place along a fifteen-mile stretch of trenches that ran northwards from the Somme.

The map shown here is the battleplan for the British VIII Corps, which was responsible for a three-and-a-half mile section of that front line. The British trenches are off to the far left of the plan, running north to south (top to bottom). The German trench system, shown as thin red lines, stands opposite the British trenches. The VIII Corps was made up of three main divisions, the 31st, the 4th and the 29th. The 31st, which was composed almost entirely of volunteers from Yorkshire and Lancashire, had the northernmost section of the attack, opposite the village of Serre. To the south of them was the 4th Division. The 4th Division included some of the most experienced soldiers in the British Army, regular soldiers from the campaigns of 1914 and 1915. Below them, opposite the village of Beaumont-Hamel, stood the 29th Division, which was made up of Englishmen, Scots, Irish and an enthusiastic battalion of Newfoundlanders, who had set sail from Canada the previous year.

The thick red line (marked 0.20) was VIII Corps' first planned objective of the day, and included taking Beaumont-Hamel. The thick blue line (marked 1.20) was the next objective, including the village of Serre and a German rear trench known as the Munich Trench. The thick green and brown lines were later objectives.

The British strategy was simple. For five days, its artillery would pound the German front lines, destroying their trenches, dugouts and barbed wire. The Army would then walk, in a steady and orderly manner, across no-man's-land to occupy the lifeless, shattered German positions, followed by a push further eastwards.

CONFIDENTIAL.

Instructions regarding War Diaries and Intelligence Summaries are contained in F. S. Regs., Part II. and the Staff Manual respectively. Title Pages will be prepared in manuscript.

# WAR DIARY
~~or~~
~~INTELLIGENCE SUMMARY~~
(Erase heading not required.)

Army Form C. 2118.

VIII CORPS G.S.

| Place | Date | Hour | Summary of Events and Information | Remarks and references to Appendices |
|---|---|---|---|---|
| MARIEUX. | 1916. July. 1. | 5.15am. | Fine day. Warm. Light breeze W. to S.W. 4th, 29th and 31st Divisions reported in position in their assembly trenches. Artillery programme for "Z" morning attached, carried out, also smoke barrage programme. | App. 63. App. 64. |
| | | 7.21. | Mine under HAWTHORN REDOUBT exploded. | |
| | | 7.30. | Assault launched along whole Corps front. | |
| | | 7.41. | 29th Division report enemy's front line successfully crossed and Reserve Battalion of each Brigade gone forward. | |
| | | 7.45. | 11th Brigade (4th Division) report leading lines on whole front (of Division ) are over German front line. X Corps report 36th Division have got enemy's front line on Left and Centre and 2nd line on Right. | |
| | | 7.59. | 29th Division report Innis. Fusiliers got to 0.20 line. 3 red flares sent up in BEAUMONT HAMEL. 2nd line Battalions all gone through. 36th Division taken 0.20 line. Germans are running up BEAUMONT ALLEY. | |
| | | 8.3. | Corps O.P. No. 1 reports another wave of 29th Division gone out and filed along German trenches to their left. Heavy casualties. Ulster Division have got SCHWABEN REDOUBT. | |
| | | 8.5. | 4th Division reports 11th Brigade over first two lines of German trenches. Barrage now on German old front line and NO MAN'S LAND. | |
| | | 8.27. | 31st Division forwards report of 16th Brigade R.F.A. "Infantry advancing through SERRE". | |
| | | 8.28. | Corps O.P. No. 2 reports our troops believed through BEAUMONT HAMEL which Germans are now shelling. Doubt report that our troops have reached MUNICH trench. 8.30am certain our troops not reached MUNICH trench. X Corps report 36th (Ulster) Division have got enemy's Reserve line along whole front. | |

2449 Wt. W14957/M90 750,000 1/16 J.B.C. & A. Forms/C.2118/12.

CONFIDENTIAL.

Instructions regarding War Diaries and Intelligence Summaries are contained in F. S. Regs., Part II. and the Staff Manual respectively. Title Pages will be prepared in manuscript.

# WAR DIARY
~~or~~
~~INTELLIGENCE SUMMARY~~
(Erase heading not required.)

Army Form C. 2118.

VIII CORPS G.S.

| Place | Date | Hour | Summary of Events and Information | Remarks and references to Appendices |
|---|---|---|---|---|
| MARIEUX. | July 1. | 8.35. | Corps O.P. No. 2 reports Infantry, 29th Division crossing 2nd objective. | |
| | | 8.40. | F.O.O. reports 29th Division are crossing MUNICH trench. | |
| | | 8.40. | 31st Division reports 93rd Brigade hung up in front of German 2nd line at 8.2am. | |
| | | 8.50. | 29th Division reports that they are retarding Artillery programme by 30 minutes. Held up in front line by Germans in deep dug-outs who are showing fight. | |
| | | 9.0. | Corps Reserve ordered to move to position of assembly. | |
| | | 9.0. | 31st Division report information received from two sources, that our Infantry have entered SERRE and are consolidating MUNICH trench. 93rd Brigade report Infantry held up by Machine Gun fire from direction of QUADRILATERAL and fire of field guns from right. | |
| | | 9.14. | 29th Division report 86th Brigade held up in BEAUMONT HAMEL by machine gun fire, also further south at points 16 and 89. Enemy have got up machine guns half way between points 60 and 03. Am now preparing for another attack supported by Trench Mortars and 2 Companies 88th Brigade have been warned to go through on the South. Artillery barrage on the BEAUCOURT Ridge delayed till 9.50. Doubtful about getting through by then. 2 Battalions of 87th Brigade went right through to STATION Road. Machine guns brough out by enemy are now firing into backs of these. Map with identification numbers of various points attached. | App.67. |
| | | 9.16. | O.P. No. 3 reports 1 rocket seen from Right Centre of SERRE 1.45. | |
| | | 9.33. | 29th Division report situation improving. We have cleared point 89, and Newfoundland and Essex Regiments are going straight on to clear the whole front system. | |
| | | 9.33. | O.P.No. 3 reports "Can see clearly as far as SERRE. None of our troops W. of SERRE. They are in SERRE". | |

2449 Wt. W14957/M90 750,000 1/16 J.B.C. & A. Forms/C.2118/12.

CONFIDENTIAL.

Instructions regarding War Diaries and Intelligence Summaries are contained in F. S. Regs., Part II. and the Staff Manual respectively. Title Pages will be prepared in manuscript.

# WAR DIARY
~~or~~
~~INTELLIGENCE SUMMARY~~

(Erase heading not required.)

Army Form C. 2118.

VIII CORPS G.S.

| Place | Date | Hour | Summary of Events and Information | Remarks and references to Appendices |
|---|---|---|---|---|
| MARIEUX. | July 1. | 9.50. | 4th Division report believe we are in possession of MUNICH trench from point 15 northwards, but not certain. Have moved two Brigades forward. | |
| | | 9.55. | O.P.No.3 reports ordinary white rockets sent up from N. end of SERRE. A lot of machine gun fire in SERRE but now stopped. | |
| | | 10.0. | 29th Division - message to say that Artillery barrage will not lift from BEAUCOURT Ridge till 10.20am. | |
| | | 10.0. | No. 2 O.P. - 29th Division retired off crater. Just back in our front trench. | |
| | | 10.4. | 4th Division report Somersets (10th Brigade) have captured point 15 and 11th Brigade believed to have reached MUNICH trench from Point 15 Northwards to left of this objective. Situation from Point 15 Southwards is not defined and Right of 11th Brigade appears to be held up between Points 91 and 62. | |
| | | 10.20. | 29th Division message "Artillery barrage will not lift from BEAUCOURT Ridge till 10.50am. | |
| | | 10.20. | 29th Division report several parties got through. Inniskillings got through and part of S.W.B's. Germans came out of dug-outs in front line, re-took trench and cut these troops off. Germans now got machine guns along whole front line, except crater. We have crater. In front of BEAUMONT HAMEL Germans got front line back. | |
| | | 10.25 | Corps Commander decided to postpone attack on green line. All efforts must now be directed to gaining and consolidating 1.20 line. | |
| | | 10.28. | 48th Division report advanced Headquarters established CAFE JOURDAIN, MAILLY MAILLET 9.35am. | |
| | | 10.30. | Corps Commander ordered H.A. to bombard German front line trench on 29th Division front. H.A. to lift at 12.30 and fresh attack to be made at that hour. | |



CONFIDENTIAL.

Instructions regarding War Diaries and Intelligence Summaries are contained in F. S. Regs., Part II. and the Staff Manual respectively. Title Pages will be prepared in manuscript.

WAR DIARY
~~or~~
~~INTELLIGENCE SUMMARY~~

(Erase heading not required.)

Army Form C. 2118.

VIII CORPS G.S.

| Place | Date | Hour | Summary of Events and Information | Remarks and references to Appendices |
|---|---|---|---|---|
| MARIEUX. | July 1. | 12.17pm. | 29th Division report arrangements made for fresh attack on enemy's front line from Point 03 to Point 89 and on to Point Q.10.b.78.28 at 12.30pm. | |
| | | 12.35. | Above attack postponed till 12.45pm. | |
| | | 12.30. | O.P.No.2. reports enemy bombarding front line 29th Division with heavy shrapnel. Forwards report of 4th Division that 11th Brigade has not got any partion of MUNICH trench. | |
| | | 12.40. | On receipt of situation report from 4th Division, Corps Commander wired to Fourth Army as follows "11th Brigade are on Q.5.c.5.9 - Q.5.a.3.5 - K.35.c.6.2 - K.35.a.8.1. It is reported some of the 12th and 10th Brigades are on line K.36.c.1.5 - K.36.a.6.3. 12th Brigade are attacking through 11th Brigade so as to capture 2nd objective. | |
| | | 1.17pm. | 48th Division report Division assembled MAILLY MAILLET 1.0pm. | |
| | | 1.40 | 29th Division report: From left to right, 86th Brigade practically no one left and can muster only 150 men in front line trenches, exclusive of 10% reserve - 87th Brigade have all been used up, also 2 Battalions of 88th Brigade of which leading Battalion, the Worcesters are now filling up the first line trenches opposite to Point 89 ready to attack as soon as they are fully assembled. Owing to communication trenches being blocked and number of wounded in front line there has been great delay in getting forward. Do not intend to attack until everything is ready. | |
| | | 1.45. | Corps Commander spoke to General de LISLE and told him to organise his Division for defence today, clearing his trenches of wounded and keeping 2 Battalions of 88th Brigade in hand to prepare for offensive to-morrow. | |
| | | 1.55. | 4th Division report - Rifle Brigade and Somersets now reported to be back in own front line. 8th Warwicks and portions of 12th Brigade who had pushed furthest through are almost back in our own line. General WILDING says Germans are holding their front line about Point 56. General CROSBIE has been put in charge of line from Point 56 Northward and told to hold on where he is. General WILDING told to take charge from Point 56 southward. | |

Previous pages and opposite: *The early battlefield reports record success after success. The British have taken the towns, they have reached their objectives, the Germans are running away. But none of this was real. From around midday, the reports start to record an unfolding disaster.*

As the British troops advanced, the artillery would fire over their heads, the bomb-line smashing German defences ahead of the advancing infantry line. On paper, it looks very plausible.

The VIII Corps' reports of the day itself open with the dawn, which appeared warm and fine over the packed British trenches. The first recorded action is at 7.21 a.m. Miners had tunnelled under the Hawthorn Redoubt, which stood just in front of Beaumont-Hamel, and had laid a massive charge. When it was detonated, a column of earth rose high into the air. Shock waves from the explosion knocked the men in the trenches off their feet, and created a wide crater. But by the time British troops reached the crater, they found that German soldiers had got there first.

The German front-line troops were not all dead, and their defences had not been shattered. But British High Command had been so fixated on its plan that it had failed to see the reality. This had been apparent to some men on the ground before the battle had started. A Brigade Major in 31st Division records that, the day before the battle, the Corps Commander 'was extremely optimistic, telling everyone that the wire had been blown away, although we could see it standing strong and well'.

These reports show vividly how, during the morning of the battle, British High Command continued to see the world in terms of its plan. The VIII Corps' General Staff record success after success. Within minutes of the start of the battle, the German front line is successfully crossed; Beaumont-Hamel is taken, its German defenders running away down Beaumont Alley; the infantry advances through Serre; troops reach the Munich Trench by 8.40, ahead of schedule.

None of this was real. Along this stretch of the battlefield, the German wire had not been blown away, and no one could walk through it. Beaumont-Hamel and Serre had been bombed to rubble, but far from emptying the villages of German troops, it had simply made them perfect cover for German machine guns. The Germans had been warned about the start of the attack, and were ready for it. As these reports came in, the steadily walking men from VIII Corps were being mown down by German bullets, and blasted to pieces by German artillery.

There is a terrible note here, which unknowingly records an approaching massacre. Two hours after the start of the attack, hardly a man had crossed the German wire in front of Beaumont-Hamel, and the incredulous commanders ordered two more brigades to attack. At 9.33, the reports record: '29th Division reports situation improving. We have cleared point 89, and Newfoundland and Essex Regiments are going straight on to clear the whole front system.' Ordered to get forward quickly, the Newfoundlanders rose from their reserve trench to walk the 300 yards to the British front line. German machine guns opened fire at once. As the Newfoundlanders were funnelled through gaps in the British wire, the killing intensified. In just forty minutes, 684 Newfoundlanders were killed or wounded, out of 752 who had risen up from the reserve trench. Only a few dozen even made it beyond the British wire; none reached the German front line.

CONFIDENTIAL.

# WAR DIARY

~~or~~ ~~INTELLIGENCE SUMMARY~~

*(Erase heading not required.)*

Army Form C. 2118.

VIII CORPS G.S.

Instructions regarding War Diaries and Intelligence Summaries are contained in F. S. Regs., Part II. and the Staff Manual respectively. Title Pages will be prepared in manuscript.

| Place | Date | Hour | Summary of Events and Information | Remarks and references to Appendices |
|---|---|---|---|---|
| MARIEUX. | July 1. | 2.20. | Corps Commander spoke to G.O.C., 48th Division and explained situation. Corps Reserve ordered to remain in present position for to-night and be ready to attack behind either 4th or 31st Divisions or to repulse a counter attack if directed on 143rd Brigade. Corps Commander added he had no intention of making any further attacks on 29th Division front. | |
| | | 2.50. | Report on situation telegraphed to Fourth Army, VII and X Corps and 15 Sqdn., R.F.C. | |
| | | 3.37. | 4th Division report (2.55pm) Attack of 10th Brigade ordered for 12.45pm did not take place owing to failure of 29th Division to attack and to German counter-attack against QUADRILATERAL and trenches to North. Casualties heavy and no further attack possible. | |
| | | 3.57. | 29th Division forward report of Heavy Trench Mortar Officer who saw original attack of 86th Brigade, 29th Division. He says that the moment they advanced machine guns opened fire on the leading Battalions from North side of the AUCHONVILLERS - BEAUMONT HAMEL road and practically wiped out whole Battalion. | |
| | | 4.7. | R.F.C.Observer reports as follows :-<br>__2.30.__ Line R.ANCRE to HAWTHORN REDOUBT occupied by German sentry groups.<br>__2.33.__ German front line W. of BEAUMONT HAMEL very weakly occupied, apparently by Germans. Crater at HAWTHORN REDOUBT occupied on W. edge by British troops. Crater a very large one.<br>__2.45.__ From FRONTIER LANE and trenches parallel as far as point 94 occupied by small parties, thought to be British. Flare seen K.35.c.5.8. Troops in trench from Points 77, 92, 55 occupied by small detachments of Germans. QUADRILATERAL occupied by British.<br>__2.50.__ SERRE apparently unoccupied. Line also unoccupied round here including MUNICH trench. PENDANT trench at Point 72 unoccupied. Trenches between SERRE and Mark Copse occupied by small parties of enemy. No troops visible in BEAUMONT HAMEL. No big movement in communication trenches. Aeroplane was constantly fired at along this line (returned with 40 holes in it). Was not fired at over SERRE. | |
| | | 4.27. | 31st Division report E.Lancs. are still in Serre. Durhams did not get to PENDANT COPSE but some of 4th Division did. Information obtained from a man who has been carrying bombs and has just returned. Fourth Division are now in their own front line. | |

2449 Wt. W14957/M90 750,000 1/16 J.B.C. & A. Forms/C.2118/12.

CONFIDENTIAL.

# WAR DIARY

~~or~~ ~~INTELLIGENCE SUMMARY~~ VIII CORPS G.S.

*(Erase heading not required.)*

Army Form C. 2118.

Instructions regarding War Diaries and Intelligence Summaries are contained in F. S. Regs., Part II. and the Staff Manual respectively. Title Pages will be prepared in manuscript.

| Place | Date | Hour | Summary of Events and Information | Remarks and references to Appendices |
|---|---|---|---|---|
| MARIEUX | July 1. | 7-0pm. | B.G.,G.S. visited General WANLESS O'GOWAN and made arrangements for an attack by 31st Division on enemy's line in front of SERRE at 2 am tomorrow with a view to joining up with men of the Division believed to be holding on in SERRE. | |
| | | 9.45. | Above attack at 2 am countermanded.<br>Corps Commander held a conference with Generals FANSHAWE and DE LISLE & gave orders regarding further operations. | |
| | | 11.30. | Situation 29th 4th and 31st Divisions hold our front line on the front of attack. 2 Battalions 48th Division from JOHN COPSE to HEBUTERNE. 2 Brigades 48th Division at MAILLY MAILLET. 92nd Brigade (31st Division) moving back to BUS in Corps Reserve. Line is being cleared and strengthened. | |
| | | 11.50. | Operation Order No. 3 by G.O.C., Fourth Army received. Copy attached. | App. 65. |
| | | | Notes on the battle W. of SERRE on the morning of 1st July 1916 by Brigadier General H.C.REES, D.S.O., Temporarily Commanding 94th Infantry Brigade, 31st Division.<br>Scheme for VIII Corps Offensive. | App. 66.<br>App.66a. |
| | | | Narrative of Operations of 1st July, showing situation as it appeared to G.S., VIII Corps from information received during the day (with map).<br>Narrative of Operations of 1st July compiled from reports subsequently received from Divisional Commanders (with map). C.G.L. | App. 67.<br>App.67a. |
| | July 2. | | Fine day. Situation unchanged.<br>Considerable artillery activity on both sides during night. Very quiet from 7 am to 2.30 pm on greater part of front. We bombarded enemy's trenches heavily at 3.0 and 6.30 pm. Enemy retaliation considerable.<br>VIII Corps ordered to take over line held by 36th Division (X Corps) from the left of the latter, as far as the R.ANCRE (inclusive to X Corps).<br><br>Army Commander, Reserve Army, assumes control of operations of VIII and X Corps from 7 am to-day. Advanced report centre 7.10am QUERRIEUX after that TOUTENCOURT.<br>Enemy placed Red Cross flag in centre of BEAUMONT HAMEL at 7.25am. It was removed at 11 am. | |

2449 Wt. W14957/M90 750,000 1/16 J.B.C. & A. Forms/C.2118/12.

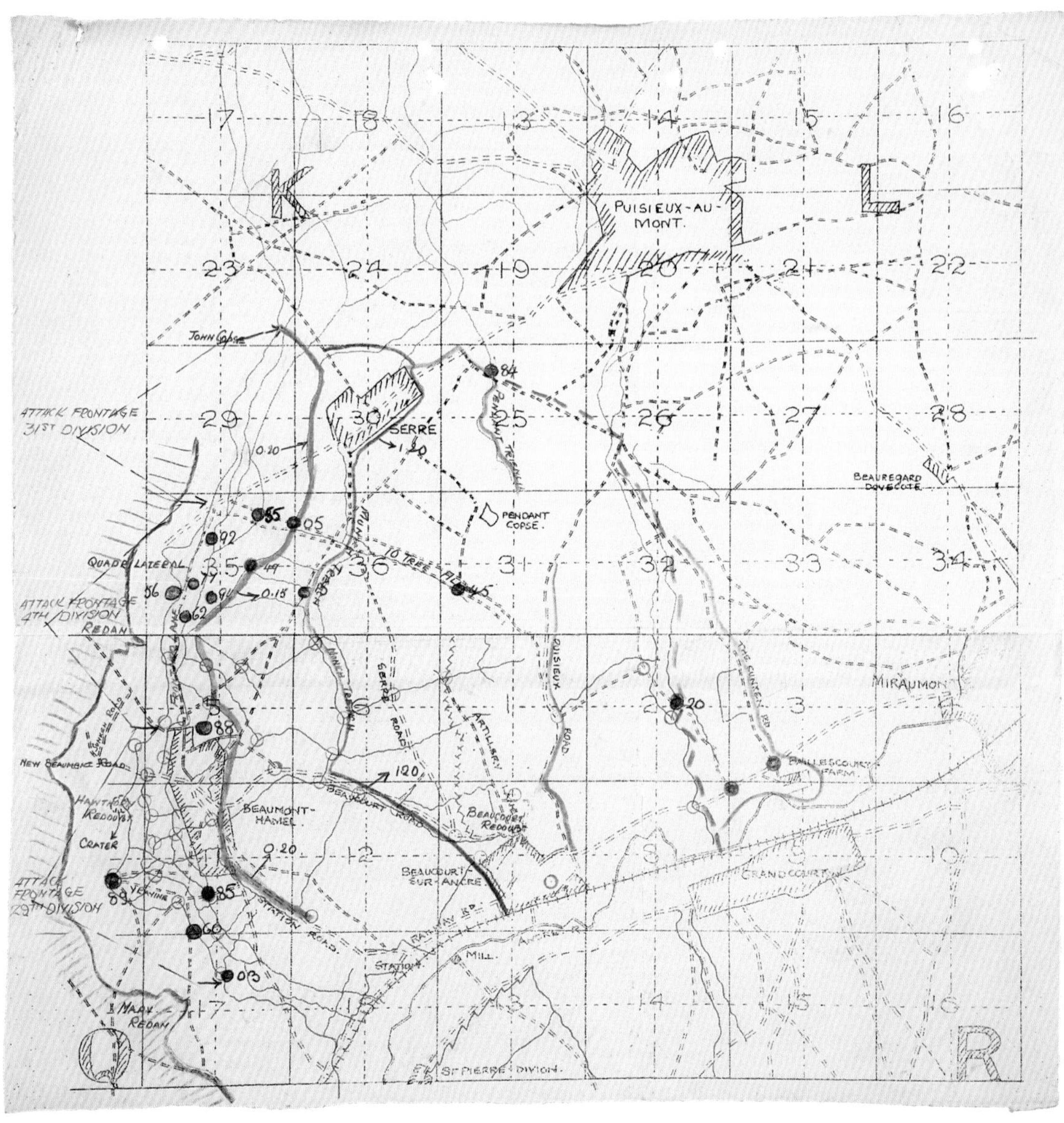


ABOVE: *After the battle, British High Command produced this map. The blue line to the left shows the final position of the British troops.*

Reality begins to break into the reports from around midday. Attacks are abandoned; the 11th Brigade was reported as having not, in fact, got to any portion of the Munich Trench; the 86th Brigade is recorded as having 'practically no one left'.

By the end of the day, VIII Corps had abandoned the attack. It had not gained an inch of ground. In the process it had lost, on that one day, 13,636 men and 662 officers. Along the whole of the British front, some 60,000 men had been killed or wounded, half of them in the first hour. What you are seeing in these documents is not only the disaster as it happened. You are also seeing why it happened: the blindness of the British High Command.

# *A* SOLDIER'S DECLARATION

## Declaration of Siegfried Sassoon

# 1917

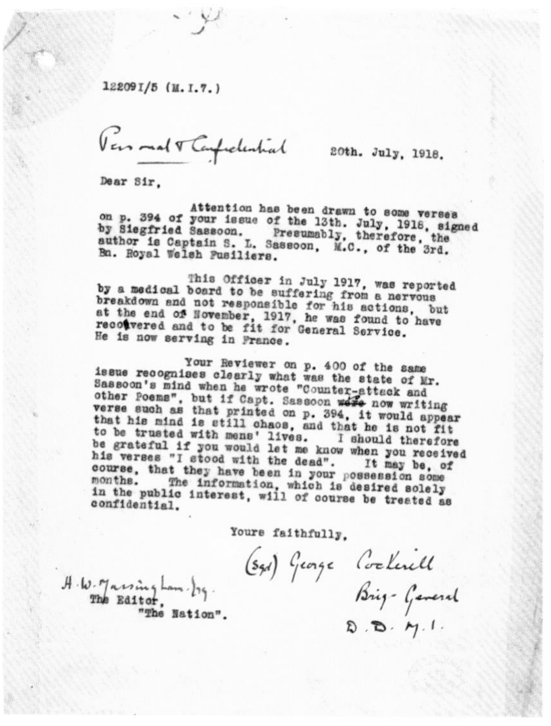

122091/5 (M.I.7.)

Personal & Confidential

20th. July, 1918.

Dear Sir,

Attention has been drawn to some verses on p. 394 of your issue of the 13th. July, 1918, signed by Siegfried Sassoon. Presumably, therefore, the author is Captain S. L. Sassoon, M.C., of the 3rd. Bn. Royal Welsh Fusiliers.

This Officer in July 1917, was reported by a medical board to be suffering from a nervous breakdown and not responsible for his actions, but at the end of November, 1917, he was found to have recovered and to be fit for General Service. He is now serving in France.

Your Reviewer on p. 400 of the same issue recognises clearly what was the state of Mr. Sassoon's mind when he wrote "Counter-attack and other Poems", but if Capt. Sassoon ~~were~~ now writing verse such as that printed on p. 394, it would appear that his mind is still chaos, and that he is not fit to be trusted with mens' lives. I should therefore be grateful if you would let me know when you received his verses "I stood with the dead". It may be, of course, that they have been in your possession some months. The information, which is desired solely in the public interest, will of course be treated as confidential.

Youre faithfully,

(Sgd) George Cockerill
Brig-General
D.D.M.I.

H. W. Massingham. Esq.
The Editor,
"The Nation".

RIGHT: *Letter of complaint from the Army to a magazine that published Sassoon's poems after he had returned to the front.*

THE CRUMPLED DOCUMENT shown on page 249 is an extraordinary find. In 1917, the poet and decorated war hero Siegfried Sassoon published a 'Soldier's Declaration', which condemned the Allies' conduct of the First World War. Overnight Sassoon found himself vilified by the press and declared insane by the Army; but in time, the Declaration would become an iconic protest against the insanity of the war. This document, found on a train, may be Sassoon's original Declaration.

Sassoon was brought up in Kent, the child of a Jewish father and Christian mother, who separated when he was young. Before the war, Sassoon had been fairly directionless – living on a small inheritance, he spent his days playing cricket, hunting and writing. He joined the British Army as the threat of war loomed and was already in service when it was declared. Sassoon was exceptionally brave, nicknamed 'Mad Jack' for his nearly suicidal actions in battle. On one occasion, he single-handedly captured a German trench, where he settled down to read a book of poetry that he had brought with him, before heading back to the British lines. In July 1916, Sassoon was awarded the Military Cross.

But Sassoon felt a growing disillusion with the war. At home on leave in 1917, he wrote and issued his 'Soldier's Declaration', which was read out in Parliament, and printed in the national press. Sassoon declared that the war, which had originally been justified as a war of defence, had been turned into a war of aggression and conquest. Sassoon did not mince his words. The war was 'evil and unjust', a 'deception', 'a callous complacency' and a 'continuance of agonies'.

There had been opposition to the war before, but never from a prominent front-line fighter. The Declaration caused a sensation, and Sassoon immediately found himself attacked from all sides. The military authorities panicked at the possibility that the Declaration would encourage protests and desertions among the troops. They claimed that he was suffering from shellshock, and was temporarily insane. But the National Archives'

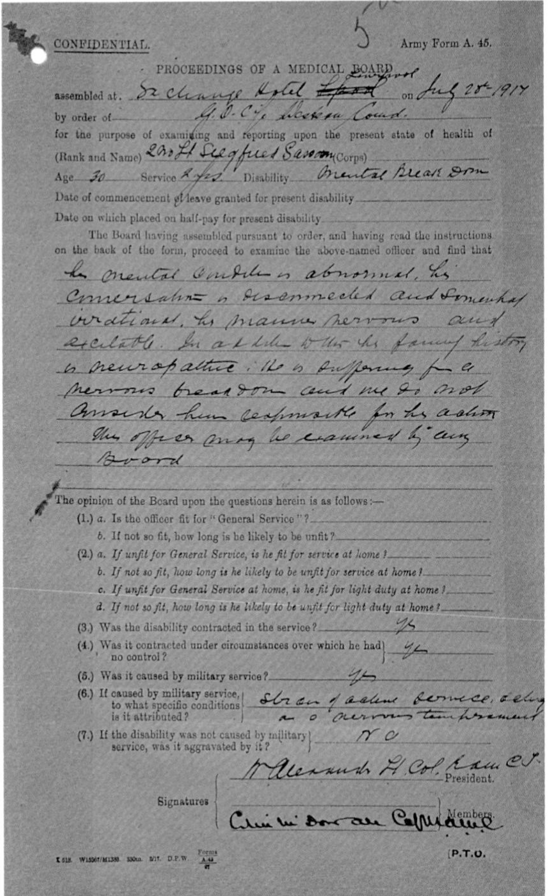

CONFIDENTIAL. Army Form A. 45.

PROCEEDINGS OF A MEDICAL BOARD

assembled at: Exchange Hotel Liverpool on July 20th 1917

by order of G.O.C. Western Command

for the purpose of examining and reporting upon the present state of health of

(Rank and Name) 2nd Lt Siegfried Sassoon (Corps)

Age 30 Service 2 yrs Disability Mental Break Down

Date of commencement of leave granted for present disability

Date on which placed on half-pay for present disability

The Board having assembled pursuant to order, and having read the instructions on the back of the form, proceed to examine the above-named officer and find that

his mental condition is abnormal, his conversation is disconnected and somewhat irrational, his manner nervous and excitable. In addition to this his family history is neuropathic. He is suffering from a nervous breakdown and we do not consider him responsible for his actions. This officer may be examined by any Board

The opinion of the Board upon the questions herein is as follows:—

(1.) a. Is the officer fit for "General Service"?

b. If not so fit, how long is he likely to be unfit?

(2.) a. *If unfit for General Service, is he fit for service at home?*

b. *If not so fit, how long is he likely to be unfit for service at home?*

c. *If unfit for General Service at home, is he fit for light duty at home?*

d. *If not so fit, how long is he likely to be unfit for light duty at home?*

(3.) Was the disability contracted in the service? Yes

(4.) Was it contracted under circumstances over which he had no control? Yes

(5.) Was it caused by military service? Yes

(6.) If caused by military service, to what specific conditions is it attributed? Strain of active service, acting on a nervous temperament

(7.) If the disability was not caused by military service, was it aggravated by it? No

Signatures: W Alexander Lt Col RAMC President.

Members.

[P.T.O.]

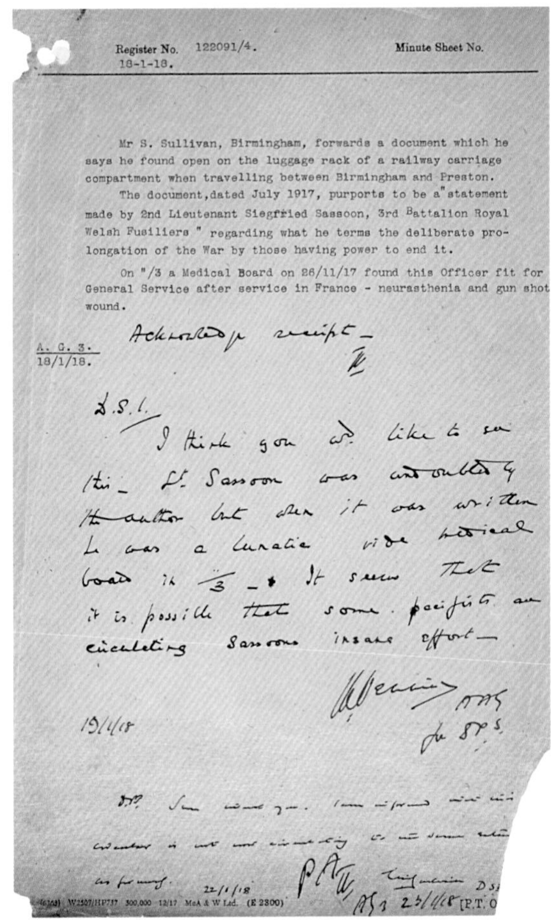

Register No. 122091/4. Minute Sheet No.
18-1-18.

Mr S. Sullivan, Birmingham, forwards a document which he says he found open on the luggage rack of a railway carriage compartment when travelling between Birmingham and Preston.

The document, dated July 1917, purports to be a "statement made by 2nd Lieutenant Siegfried Sassoon, 3rd Battalion Royal Welsh Fusiliers" regarding what he terms the deliberate prolongation of the War by those having power to end it.

On "/3 a Medical Board on 26/11/17 found this Officer fit for General Service after service in France - neurasthenia and gun shot wound.

A. G. 3.
18/1/18.

Acknowledge receipt –

D.S.I.

I think you wd like to see this – Lt. Sassoon was undoubtedly the author but when it was written he was a lunatic vide medical board in /3 – It seems that it is possible that some pacifists are circulating Sassoon's insane effort –

19/1/18

file on Sassoon is telling. He is recorded as having received a gunshot wound, but up until June 1917 there is no mention of any mental or physical ill health. Only after the Declaration was made public do allegations of insanity appear.

Sassoon was sent for treatment to the Craiglockhart War Hospital for Officers near Edinburgh, where he stayed from July to November 1917 (and befriended fellow inmate Wilfred Owen, who was also to become one of the great war poets). In November 1917, Sassoon was declared fit for service. He reported again to his reserve unit in Litherland, Liverpool, and was eventually returned to the front.

On 16 January 1918, the War Office received a note from a member of the public, Mr Sullivan, who had written: 'I am enclosing to you a circular from a luggage rack on a train from Birmingham to Preston.' Sassoon's route back to his unit makes it likely that he would have travelled on that train. It is hard to imagine what else this note would be, if it were not the original of the Declaration. Sassoon used the press to disseminate it, and there would have been no need to make or circulate individual copies. Perhaps he was throwing away his original copy of the Declaration – or perhaps it just fell out of a pocket. Either way, it is a remarkable original.

ABOVE LEFT: *Notes of the proceedings of Sassoon's medical board.*

ABOVE: *Internal government memorandum about the finding of the original document in the luggage rack on a train.*

RIGHT: *This document may be Sassoon's original 'Soldier's Declaration'.*

by

Sec. Lt. Siegfried Sassoon,

3rd Batt: Royal Welsh Fusiliers,

July, 1917.

I am making this statement as an act of wilful defiance of military authority because I believe that the war is being deliberately prolonged by those who have the power to end it. I am a soldier, convinced that I am acting on behalf of soldiers. I believe that the war upon which I entered as a war of defence and liberation has now become a war of agression and conquest. I believe that the purposes for which I and my fellow soldiers entered upon this war should have been so clearly stated as to have made it impossible to change them and that had this been done the objects which actuated us would now be attainable by negotiation.

I have seen and endured the sufferings of the troops and I can no longer be a party to prolong these sufferings for ends which I believe to be evil and unjust. I am not protesting against the conduct of the war, but against the political errors and insincerities for which the fighting men are being sacrificed.

On behalf of those who are suffering now, I make this protest against the deception which is being practised upon them; also I believe it may help to destroy the callous complacency with which the majority of those at home regard the continuance of agonies which they do not share and which they have not enough imagination to realise.

# ENDING *one* WAR, STARTING ANOTHER

## The Treaty of Versailles

## 1919

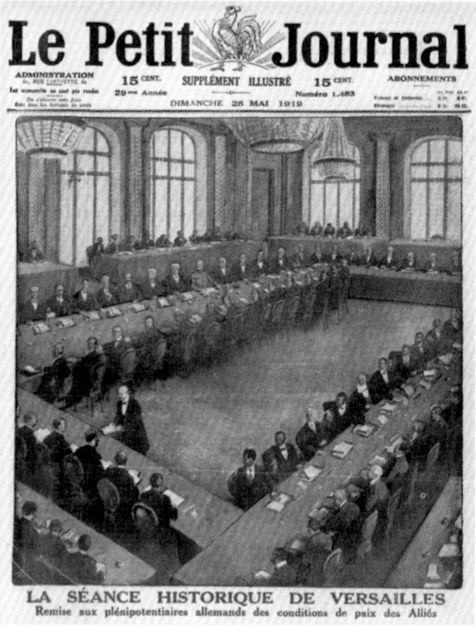
Le Petit Journal
ADMINISTRATION
15 CENT.
SUPPLÉMENT ILLUSTRÉ
15 CENT.
ABONNEMENTS
29me Année
Numéro 1.483
DIMANCHE 25 MAI 1919
LA SÉANCE HISTORIQUE DE VERSAILLES
Remise aux plénipotentiaires allemands des conditions de paix des Alliés

ABOVE: *From a French newspaper, artist's impression of peace 'negotiations' at the Palace of Versailles.*

RIGHT: *Article 231, the so-called 'Guilt Clause'.*

THE TREATY OF VERSAILLES ends one period of history, and starts another. The 'Treaty of Peace' (as it was optimistically titled) set out the terms on which the First World War was brought to an end. It also contained the seeds of the Second World War.

Fighting in the First World War ceased on 11 November 1918, when Germany signed an armistice with the Allied Powers. Over the coming months, diplomats from the Allied Powers would negotiate the Treaty, each with their own agenda and ideas about how they wanted Europe re-drawn, and Germany punished. When the winning powers concluded their negotiations, the text was, more or less, simply presented to the defeated nations to sign. The Treaty was executed on behalf of each power in the Great Hall of Mirrors at the Palace of Versailles on 28 June 1919.

The Treaty is roughly two inches thick, and runs to 440 articles. It provided for the occupation of Germany's Rhineland for fifteen years, restricted the size of the German military, and handed territory to the victorious countries. These provisions were painful enough, but the article on which they hung, and which more than any other would pitch the world back into war, was article 231, the so-called 'Guilt Clause':

*'The Allied and Associated Governments affirm and Germany accepts the responsibility of Germany and her allies for causing all the loss and damage to which the Allied and Associated Governments and their nationals have been subjected as a consequence of the war imposed upon them by the aggression of Germany and her allies.'*

The Guilt Clause entitled the Allies to try as war criminals the German Emperor, Wilhelm II, and other German leaders. Moreover, it justified the financial reparations set out in the articles that followed, which were eventually set at 269 billion gold marks (around 100,000 tonnes of gold), although the amount was halved after a couple of years. Some economists protested at the scale of the reparations – famously, John Maynard

ARTICLE 229.

Persons guilty of criminal acts against the nationals of one of the Allied and Associated Powers will be brought before the military tribunals of that Power.

Persons guilty of criminal acts against the nationals of more than one of the Allied and Associated Powers will be brought before military tribunals composed of members of the military tribunals of the Powers concerned.

In every case the accused will be entitled to name his own counsel.

ARTICLE 230.

The German Government undertakes to furnish all documents and information of every kind, the production of which may be considered necessary to ensure the full knowledge of the incriminating acts, the discovery of offenders and the just appreciation of responsibility.

## PART VIII.

# REPARATION.

---

## SECTION I.

### GENERAL PROVISIONS.

---

ARTICLE 231.

The Allied and Associated Governments affirm and Germany accepts the responsibility of Germany and her allies for causing all the loss and damage to which the Allied and Associated Governments and their nationals have been subjected as a consequence of the war imposed upon them by the aggression of Germany and her allies.

ARTICLE 232.

The Allied and Associated Governments recognize that the resources of Germany are not adequate, after taking into account permanent diminutions

102

of such resources which will result from other provisions of the present Treaty, to make complete reparation for all such loss and damage.

The Allied and Associated Governments, however, require, and Germany undertakes, that she will make compensation for all damage done to the civilian population of the Allied and Associated Powers and to their property during the period of the belligerency of each as an Allied or Associated Power against Germany by such aggression by land, by sea and from the air, and in general all damage as defined in Annex I hereto.

In accordance with Germany's pledges, already given, as to complete restoration for Belgium, Germany undertakes, in addition to the compensation for damage elsewhere in this Part provided for, as a consequence of the violation of the Treaty of 1839, to make reimbursement of all sums which Belgium has borrowed from the Allied and Associated Governments up to November 11, 1918, together with interest at the rate of five per cent. (5 %) per annum on such sums. This amount shall be determined by the Reparation Commission, and the German Government undertakes thereupon forthwith to make a special issue of bearer bonds to an equivalent amount payable in marks gold, on May 1, 1926, or, at the option of the German Government, on May 1 in any year up to 1926. Subject to the foregoing, the form of such bonds shall be determined by the Reparation Commission. Such bonds shall be handed over to the Reparation Commission, which has authority to take and acknowledge receipt thereof on behalf of Belgium.

ARTICLE 233.

The amount of the above damage for which compensation is to be made by Germany shall be determined by an Inter-Allied Commission, to be called the *Reparation Commission* and constituted in the form and with the powers set forth hereunder and in Annexes II to VII inclusive hereto.

This Commission shall consider the claims and give to the German Government a just opportunity to be heard.

The findings of the Commission as to the amount of damage defined as above shall be concluded and notified to the German Government on or before May 1, 1921, as representing the extent of that Government's obligations.

The Commission shall concurrently draw up a schedule of payments prescribing the time and manner for securing and discharging the entire obligation within a period of thirty years from May 1, 1921. If, however, within the period mentioned, Germany fails to discharge her obligations, any balance remaining unpaid may, within the discretion of the Commission, be postponed for settlement in subsequent years, or may be handled otherwise in such manner as the Allied and Associated Governments, acting in accordance with the procedure laid donwn in this Part of the present Treaty, shall determine.

ARTICLE 234.

The Reparation Commission shall after May 1, 1921, from time to time,

100

The Allied and Associated Governments on the one part and the German Government on the other part reciprocally undertake also to furnish to each other:

(1.) A complete list of those who have died together with all information useful for identification;

(2.) All information as to the number and position of the graves of all those who have been buried without identification.

PART VII.

PENALTIES.

ARTICLE 227.

The Allied and Associated Powers publicly arraign William II of Hohenzollern, formerly German Emperor, for a supreme offence against international morality and the sanctity of treaties.

A special tribunal will be constituted to try the accused, thereby assuring him the guarantees essential to the right of defence. It will be composed of five judges, one appointed by each of the following Powers: namely, the United States of America, Great Britain, France, Italy and Japan.

In its decision the tribunal will be guided by the highest motives of international policy, with a view to vindicating the solemn obligations of international undertakings and the validity of international morality. It will be its duty to fix the punishment which it considers should be imposed.

The Allied and Associated Powers will address a request to the Government of the Netherlands for the surrender to them of the ex-Emperor in order that he may be put on trial.

ARTICLE 228.

The German Government recognises the right of the Allied and Associated Powers to bring before military tribunals persons accused of having committed acts in violation of the laws and customs of war. Such persons shall, if found guilty, be sentenced to punishments laid down by law. This provision will apply notwithstanding any proceedings or prosecution before a tribunal in Germany or in the territory of her allies.

The German Government shall hand over to the Allied and Associated Powers, or to such one of them as shall so request, all persons accused of having committed an act in violation of the laws and customs of war, who are specified either by name or by the rank, office or employment which they held under the German authorities.

LEFT: *'Reparations' from Germany included loss of land and massive payments.*
ABOVE: *The section on 'Penalties' gave the Allies power to put the German Emperor on trial.*

Keynes in *The Economic Consequences of Peace* (1919) – but politicians had anticipated popular feeling at home that it should be even higher. Far from arguing that it should be lower, they had to justify the reparations to their electorates by saying that it was as high as they thought Germany was able to pay. The First World War had killed and maimed more people than any war in history. The winners sought the humiliation of the losers, and people were in no mood to take a longer view.

If only they had. The Treaty of Versailles was the source of profound resentment within Germany. Extremist parties were quick to tap into that resentment to promote their own agendas. Less than fourteen years after the Treaty was signed, the leader of one those parties, Adolf Hitler, became Chancellor of Germany. He wanted the cancellation of reparations and expansion of the armed forces, policies that were a direct reaction to the terms of the Treaty.

Following the Second World War, Germany agreed once again to pay the reparations required by the Treaty of Versailles, although payment would be made over twenty years, and postponed until such time as the country was reunified (an event then unforeseeable). The reunification of Germany in 1990 was a trigger for the payments to start again. Germany made the last reparation payment under the Treaty of Versailles on 3 October 2010.

# GIVING UP *the* CROWN

## The Instrument of Abdication

## 1936

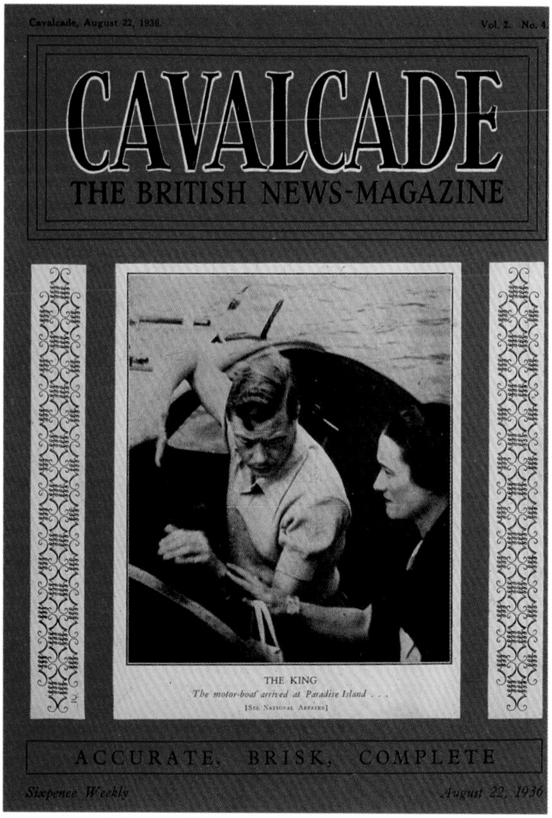

How does a king resign? Before this document, it had never happened in Britain. The institution of monarchy, which depends so much on form and precedent, had no form or precedent for abdication. They had to make it up.

Edward VIII had been a playboy prince, handsome, blond and blue-eyed. The roaring twenties had passed for him in a whirl of parties, fast cars and love affairs. Some people, including his father George V, winced at the idea that he would one day be king. Still, the Prince was charming, well travelled and possessed a genuine concern for the poor. When George V passed away in January 1936, there were high hopes for Edward's reign.

But there was a problem. In 1931, Edward had been introduced to a lively American socialite, Wallis Simpson. Wallis was about the King's age, dark haired, poised, vivacious – and twice married. Simpson's first husband had been a pilot in the US Navy, and they were married for eleven years before his drinking became too much and she left him. She had then married Ernest Simpson, a man in the shipping business, and the couple settled down in London. In 1931, they met the Prince of Wales. It was a slow-burn of a relationship, but by the end of 1934 Edward and Mrs Simpson were in love. He was determined to marry her.

This just wasn't possible. The King would be Supreme Governor of the Church of England, which at the time did not even allow divorced people to remarry while their former spouse was alive. We tend to forget today how shocking divorce still was, outside a racy metropolitan set. It wasn't just shocking for the ordinary men and women of England. Edward would rule the British Empire. How would the dominions react to their King and Emperor marrying a twice-divorced American party girl? A cabal of the Prime Minister,

Above: *Australian magazine* Cavalcade *reports on Edward VIII's summer cruise in the Adriatic, accompanied by Mrs Simpson.*

SECRET

Commissioner,

The identity of Mrs.Simpson's secret lover has now been definitely ascertained. He is Guy Marcus TRUNDLE, now living at 18 Bruton Street, W.

TRUNDLE is described as a very charming adventurer, very good looking, well bred and an excellent dancer. He is said to boast that every woman falls for him. He meets Mrs.Simpson quite openly at informal social gatherings as a personal friend, but secret meetings are made by appointment when intimate relations take place.

TRUNDLE receives money from Mrs.Simpson as well as expensive presents. He has admitted this.

Mrs.Simpson has said that her husband is now suspicious of her association with other men as he thinks this will eventually cause trouble with P.O.W.

Mrs.Simpson has also alleged that her husband is having her watched for this reason, and in consequence she is very careful for the double purpose of keeping both P.O.W. and her husband in ignorance of her surreptitious love affairs.

TRUNDLE is a married man. He was born in York on 25th April 1899 and is the son of a Clerk in Holy Orders. He was married in 1932 to Melosine Vivien Helen Mary CARY-BARNARD, the daughter of Cyril Darcy Vivien CARY-BARNARD, described as a retired General of the Tank Corps.

TRUNDLE is a motor engineer and salesman and is said to be employed by the Ford Motor Company. It is not known what salary he gets.

Prior to his association with Mrs.Simpson, TRUNDLE had an "affair" with Mrs.Fearnley Whittingstall.

TRUNDLE claims to have met P.O.W. through Mrs.Simpson.

3/7/1935.

Superintendent.

METROPOLITAN POLICE,
SPECIAL BRANCH,
SCOTLAND HOUSE,
LONDON, S.W.1.

WE HAVE NO PICK AGAINST YOU BUT WE WILL GIVE YOU A BIGGER ROW THAN MARLY. THE KING IS A ROTTEN SWINE ASKING US TO PAY FOR EMERELDS AND FINE THINGS FOR HIS UGLY WHORE WE WILL LET HIM GO TO THE PARLIMENT O.K. FOR HIS MA'S SAKE BUT IF THAT YANKEE HARLOT DOES NOT GET OUT WE WILL SMASH HER WINDOWS AND GIVE HER A HIDING. GALLACHER CANNOT GO TO AMERICA WHY SHOULD WE KEEP YANKEE DIRT. SIMON CAN TURN OUT THE SOLDIERS WE DONT CARE A DAM. WE HAVE WARNED YOU SO ARE NOT DOING THE LOW DOWN

SB

8 REGISTRY

21 OCT 1936 6.

anonymous letter which refers to Mrs Simpson, although her actual name is not mentioned

22/10/36

the Archbishop of Canterbury and the Editor of *The Times* joined forces, and told Edward that he could not marry Wallis and remain king.

So Edward renounced the throne, the first British monarch to do so. On 10 December 1936, at his home at Fort Belvedere at Windsor, Edward signed an 'Instrument of Abdication'.

You expect royal documents to be grand and gilded; the Instrument of Abdication is more like a memo. Edward's playboy signature, with its forward tilt, like speed-stripes on a racing-car, is unhesitating, determined. The 'R I' after his name stands for 'Rex Imperator', 'King Emperor', the last time Edward could use these letters. The signature of Edward's brother Albert, who would succeed Edward and become George VI, is far more diffident, the sort of slightly naïve, looping signature that you have to practise to pull off. Albert had never asked or wanted to be king. The day before, he had broken down in tears to his mother about what he was now being asked to do. As he signed, he would have been feeling distinctly queasy.

ABOVE LEFT: *A secret report, showing how closely the Government monitored the relationship between Edward and Mrs Simpson.*

ABOVE: *An anonymous letter, threatening violence against the 'Yankee harlot'.*

OPPOSITE: *The Instrument of Abdication.*

The other two signatures belong to Edward's other brothers, Henry and George. No members of the Government or Church were asked to sign. Doubtless the Government had been involved in the wording, but Edward's abdication was treated as a family affair. That comes out, too, in the way that Edward revokes the throne 'irrevocably', and not just for himself, but also for 'My descendants'. It wouldn't do for Edward to change his mind, or for one of his and Wallis's descendants to claim the throne, were they to have children.

The day after he had signed this document, Edward made a famous radio broadcast from Windsor Castle, in which he described how impossible it would have been for him to take on a king's heavy burden of

# INSTRUMENT OF ABDICATION

I, Edward the Eighth, of Great Britain, Ireland, and the British Dominions beyond the Seas, King, Emperor of India, do hereby declare My irrevocable determination to renounce the Throne for Myself and for My descendants, and My desire that effect should be given to this Instrument of Abdication immediately.

In token whereof I have hereunto set My hand this tenth day of December, nineteen hundred and thirty six, in the presence of the witnesses whose signatures are subscribed.

SIGNED AT
FORT BELVEDERE
IN THE PRESENCE
OF

Edward R I

Albert

Henry.

George.

SECRET

17th October, 1935.

Commissioner,

The association of P.W. with Mrs.Simpson continues. She was with him during his recent holiday on the Continent.

Mr.Simpson is said to have paid a short visit to Cannes during this period and to have then gone to New York on business, leaving Mrs.Simpson with P.W.

P.W. is said to have taken great pains to prevent Mrs.Simpson appearing in any Press pictures.

Mrs.Simpson was seen with P.W. at the Cafe de Paris, Coventry Street, this week.

The attached American weekly magazine, which is on sale in London, dated 23rd September, contains an article on page 20, referring to P.W. and Mrs.Simpson.

Superintendent.

THE LIFE STORY OF

MRS. WALLIS SIMPSON

The Examiner brings you the FIRST complete, authentic life story of Mrs. Wallis Simpson, the most talked-of woman in the world! It's a fascinating story . . . written by the former Nanine H. Ulman of Baltimore, who has been Mrs. Simpson's close friend since early childhood. Five thrilling installments beginning in your Sunday Examiner. Don't miss it!

BEGINS SUNDAY

IN THE

EXAMINER

BUCKINGHAM PALACE

December 14th 1938

My dear Prime Minister,

Thank you very much for your letter enclosing the précis of your conversation with my brother in Paris. I have heard from all sides that there is a strong feeling amongst all classes that my brother should not return here even for a short visit with the Duchess of Windsor. You said in your letter to me that you would keep him informed as to the state of public opinion in this country, & I think that, if you agree, this is the moment for you to write & tell him that it would not be at all

BUCKINGHAM PALACE

wise for him to contemplate such a visit. I am sure that it would be only right to let him know this decision now, before he makes any further plans for the spring. I think you know that neither the Queen nor Queen Mary have any desire to meet the Duchess of Windsor, & therefore any visit made for the purpose of introducing her to members of the Royal Family obviously becomes impossible. I think it is very important that this question should be settled as soon as possible. I am very glad that your good offices are available, as this is in

BUCKINGHAM PALACE

matter is one of such an intimate nature, that perhaps my brother would take this decision in a more friendly manner from you than from me!

Believe me

Yours very sincerely

George R.I.

OPPOSITE: *The Government's secret monitoring of the relationship included gathering reports from the overseas press.* ABOVE AND RIGHT: *Two years after the abdication, this letter from George VI to Prime Minister Neville Chamberlain says that a visit to England by the Duke and Duchess of Windsor would be 'unwise'.*

responsibility 'without the support of the woman I love'. Edward and Wallis then left for Austria. They married the following June, after Wallis's divorce had come through. During the Second World War, Edward served as Governor of the Bahamas, but otherwise the Duke and Duchess of Windsor (as Edward and Wallis were now known) spent the rest of their lives in retirement abroad.

It is almost impossible nowadays to form a neutral view on Edward. For many of my grandparents' wartime generation, he and Wallis were the selfish pair who had preferred the passing drama of romance to the solid discipline of duty. For others, Edward was a victim of the British establishment, which showed itself to be unbending, resistant to progress, and hostile to love.

# BIG BROTHER *was* WATCHING HIM

## Special Branch File on George Orwell

## 1936–1942

*There was of course no way of knowing whether you were being watched at any given moment. How often, or on what system, the Thought Police plugged in on any individual wire was guesswork. It was even conceivable that they watched everybody all the time. But at any rate they could plug in your wire whenever they wanted to. You had to live – did live, from habit that became instinct – in the assumption that every sound you made was overheard and, except in darkness, every movement scrutinised.*

George Orwell, *1984*

When he wrote these words, George Orwell did not know that he himself had been under State surveillance.

The Special Branch of London's Metropolitan Police opened a file on Orwell when he visited Wigan in 1936, collecting material for his fifth book, *The Road to Wigan Pier*. Detective Constable John Duffy of Wigan Central Police Station reported that Eric Blair (Orwell's real name) had been observed staying in a working-class district, in accommodation found for him by a member of the local Communist Party, and that he had attended a Communist meeting. DC Duffy reported that Blair was collecting data on the district, about its coalmines and factories, the numbers of its churches and public houses, and the size of its local population. All fair occupation for a writer, but in the restless 1930s it made people wonder if you were up to no good.

2891-2. ALL COMMUNICATIONS TO BE ADDRESSED TO THE CHIEF CONSTABLE.

County Borough of Wigan

Chief Constable's Office.

Wigan.

THOMAS PEY, O.B.E. CHIEF CONSTABLE

| REFERENCE | |
|---|---|
| YOURS | OURS |
| | DO/M. |

24th February, 1936.

REGISTRY 25 FEB 1936 10. A.M.

Sir,

re ERIC A. BLAIR.

I herewith enclose a copy of a Police report respecting the above named which is self explanatory.

I shall be obliged if you will cause enquiries to be made and inform me of the result in due course.

I am, Sir,

Your obedient Servant,

Chief Constable.

The Commissioner of Police of The Metropolis, New Scotland Yard, LONDON.S.W.1.

NO TRACE "R" Bch. (S.B.)

SPECIAL BRANCH REGISTRY RECEIVED 25 FEB 1936

Above: *The letter from the Chief Constable of Wigan to Scotland Yard that caused Orwell to be put under surveillance.* Opposite: *Special Branch's report on 'Eric A. Blair, alias George Orwell'. The biographical description of Orwell is good, the sources of information accurate.*

S.B. No. 1 (Plain).

Special Report }

SUBJECT Eric Arthur BLAIR @ George ORWELL.

Reference to Papers. 301/NWC/683.

M.P. 35-7382/10M B43(4)

**METROPOLITAN POLICE.**

2A

INDEXED

E SPECIAL BRANCH,

Metropolitan Police,

Scotland House,

11th day of March 1936.

With reference to the attached correspondence from the Chief Constable, Wigan, respecting Eric A. BLAIR, alias George ORWELL :-

Enquiry shews that this man's correct name is Eric Arthur Blair. He is by occupation a journalist and author, and writes under the name of George Orwell.

He was born at Motihari, Bengal, India, on 25-6-1902, his father being Richard Walmesley Blair, a former Indian Civil Servant, who on retirement settled at Southwold, Suffolk.

Blair was educated at St. Cyprian's School, Eastbourne, from September 1911 until December 1916, and for a short time in 1917 he was at Wellington College. Later in the same year he went to Eton College, and remained there until December 1921.

On leaving Eton, he applied for employment in the Indian Police Service, and in 1922 he was appointed an assistant superintendent of police in Burma. He served in this capacity until the latter part of 1927, when he returned on leave to England. Whilst on leave, he telegraphed direct to his local government in India for permission to resign his appointment, and with the authority of the Secretary of State for India, this was granted, his resignation dating from 1-1-1928. Blair gave no official reason for terminating his appointment, but he is reported to have told his intimate friends that he could not bring himself to arrest persons for committing acts which he

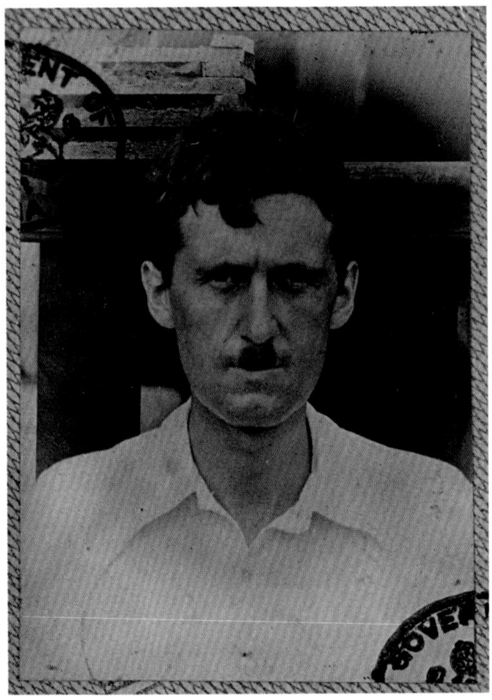

ABOVE: *Photograph of Orwell on Special Branch files. Copies of his passport photograph were made and circulated.*

2.

**All minutes to be numbered in consecutive order.** **No. 729** (Unruled).

did not think were wrong.

Shortly after resigning from the Indian Police, Blair went to France, and for some time eked out a precarious living as a free lance journalist. Whilst in Paris, he took an interest in the activities of the French Communist Party, and spent a good deal of time studying "LA Humanité". Information is not available to shew whether he was an active supporter of the revolutionary movement in France, but it is known that whilst there, he offered his services to the "Workers' Life", the forerunner of the "Daily Worker", as Paris correspondent.

During his stay in Paris, he also collected part material for a book entitled "A Down and Out in London and Paris", which he wrote under the nom de plume, G. Orwell. Under the same style, he has recently completed a book called "Burmese Days", which deals with his experiences in Burma. Both the above books are published by Victor Gollancz, Ltd., 14, Henrietta Street, W.C., a firm which specialises in Left Wing literature.

Following his stay in Paris, Blair returned to London, and spent some time living the life of a 'down and out' to obtain the necessary material to complete the book mentioned above.

In 1932, he became a master at a preparatory school known as "The Hawthorns", Church Road, Hayes, Middlesex, and remained there for a year, leaving at the end of this period to take a similar position at another preparatory school known as Fray's College, Harefield Road, Uxbridge, Middlesex. He continued as a master at this school until the end of 1933, when he became ill, principally through his experiences as a 'down and out', and for a time he was a patient at the Uxbridge and District Cottage Hospital.

On being discharged from hospital in January 1934, Blair went to Suffolk to recuperate, and gave his address

M.P.-35 6466/200m G31 (4)

The police compiled a thumbnail biography of Orwell: his birth in India, education at Wellington and Eton, work for the Indian Police Service, and then employment as a school teacher. Letters that Orwell received while he was staying in Wigan were inspected. One of these had been forwarded from an address in Hampstead, which became the next target of a Special Branch visit. The address turned out to be a book shop, 'Booklovers' Corner', run by Francis Westrope. Westrope, the officers reported, was 'known to hold socialist views and considers himself an "intellectual"' – the contempt in those inverted commas! The officers darkly reported that the name 'Booklovers' Corner' was not registered under the Registration of Business Names Act. Was it, in fact, a handling point for revolutionary material?

The truth was less exciting. Orwell's Aunt Nellie had found a job for him at Booklovers' Corner, where he worked as a part-time sales assistant. Orwell described the experience in his essay 'Bookshop Memories'. Typical customers, Orwell wrote, were 'vague-minded women looking for birthday presents for their nephews', the bestsellers were Christmas novelties and romantic fiction. Westrope was simply forwarding letters to his former employee.

Orwell's file is just one of hundreds that Special Branch generated through this edgy period, some of them with good cause. After all, it was around this time that Soviet Intelligence was – unbeknown to Special Branch, of course – recruiting men into the notorious spy ring that was later known as the Cambridge Five. Orwell's

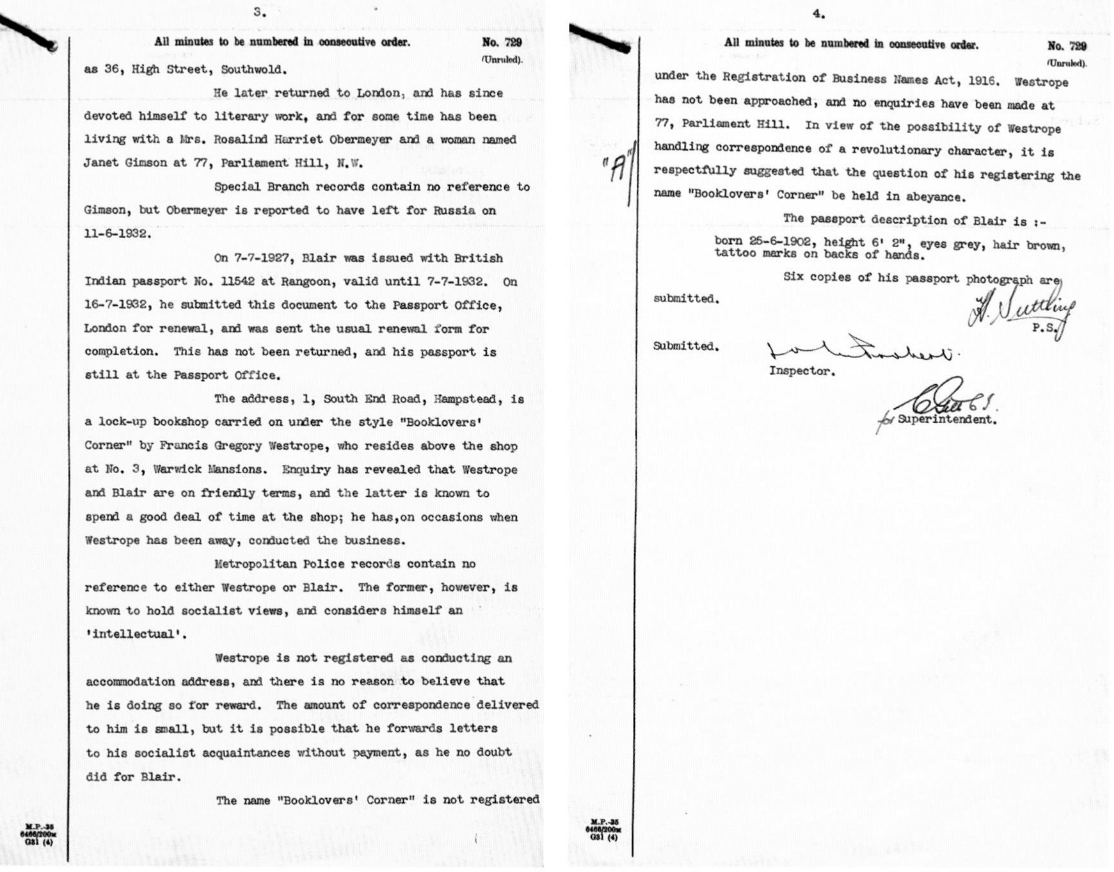

3.

All minutes to be numbered in consecutive order. No. 729 (Unruled).

as 36, High Street, Southwold.

He later returned to London, and has since devoted himself to literary work, and for some time has been living with a Mrs. Rosalind Harriet Obermeyer and a woman named Janet Gimson at 77, Parliament Hill, N.W.

Special Branch records contain no reference to Gimson, but Obermeyer is reported to have left for Russia on 11-6-1932.

On 7-7-1927, Blair was issued with British Indian passport No. 11542 at Rangoon, valid until 7-7-1932. On 16-7-1932, he submitted this document to the Passport Office, London for renewal, and was sent the usual renewal form for completion. This has not been returned, and his passport is still at the Passport Office.

The address, 1, South End Road, Hampstead, is a lock-up bookshop carried on under the style "Booklovers' Corner" by Francis Gregory Westrope, who resides above the shop at No. 3, Warwick Mansions. Enquiry has revealed that Westrope and Blair are on friendly terms, and the latter is known to spend a good deal of time at the shop; he has,on occasions when Westrope has been away, conducted the business.

Metropolitan Police records contain no reference to either Westrope or Blair. The former, however, is known to hold socialist views, and considers himself an 'intellectual'.

Westrope is not registered as conducting an accommodation address, and there is no reason to believe that he is doing so for reward. The amount of correspondence delivered to him is small, but it is possible that he forwards letters to his socialist acquaintances without payment, as he no doubt did for Blair.

The name "Booklovers' Corner" is not registered

M.P.-35 6466/200m G31 (4)

4.

All minutes to be numbered in consecutive order. No. 729 (Unruled).

under the Registration of Business Names Act, 1916. Westrope has not been approached, and no enquiries have been made at 77, Parliament Hill. In view of the possibility of Westrope handling correspondence of a revolutionary character, it is respectfully suggested that the question of his registering the name "Booklovers' Corner" be held in abeyance.

"A"

The passport description of Blair is :-

born 25-6-1902, height 6' 2", eyes grey, hair brown, tattoo marks on backs of hands.

Six copies of his passport photograph are submitted.

H. Sutting
P.S.

Submitted.

Inspector.

for Superintendent.

M.P.-35 6466/200m G31 (4)

file is remarkable only for what he did next. A few years later, this attendee of Communist meetings in Wigan wrote his devastating critique of Soviet communism, *Animal Farm,* followed by his dystopian vision of a world under surveillance, *1984.*

But there is an oddly comforting gap between Orwell's nightmare vision and the reality of surveillance in the 1930s. There were no Thought Police. It was perfectly legal to be a Communist (even an 'intellectual'). There was no wire that the police could turn on to observe suspects. Special Branch's agents peered at envelopes, but don't seem to have opened them. Evidence of the seriousness with which putting a man under surveillance was regarded is that the reports are signed in triplicate, all the way up to the level of Superintendent. And then there is the dull jobbery of the police officers themselves, getting into a twist about whether Booklovers' Corner had properly registered its name. In our digital age, Orwell's vision of the all-seeing wire is chilling. These reports champion a world that just earnestly plods along.

OPPOSITE RIGHT AND ABOVE: *The Special Branch report on Orwell pieces together his left-wing and communist connections. Orwell would go on to write a powerful critique of communism,* Animal Farm.

# *The* NOTE *that* GAVE BIRTH *to the* BOMB
## Frisch Peierls Memorandum

Above: *Mushroom cloud from an atomic bomb, exploded during US tests in the Nevada desert in 1955.*

### 1940

Opposite: *This memorandum postulated a 'super-bomb', equivalent to 1,000 tons of dynamite or the heat of the interior of the sun.*

This elegant scientific memorandum, authored in 1940 by two young scientists at the University of Birmingham, gave birth to the atomic bomb.

The memorandum is the work of Otto Frisch and Rudolf Peierls, Jewish refugees from Hitler's Germany. Frisch was a physicist who had been working with radioactivity for several years. It was he who had coined the phrase 'nuclear fission', the process by which the nucleus of an atom may split into smaller parts, for example when bombarded with subatomic particles. Working with his aunt, the scientist Lise Meitner, he was also the first to hypothesise that fission in uranium could release massive amounts of energy. At the outbreak of the Second World War, Frisch was in Birmingham and found himself unable to return to the Continent. At the university he met another Jewish refugee, Rudolf Peierls, who was Professor of Mathematical Physics. If Frisch brought a depth of knowledge to the subject, it was Peierls who brought the width. Barely thirty, the bespectacled, owlish Peierls had already made major discoveries in the fields of semiconductors, photodisintegration and statistical mechanics.

Although it was known that uranium fission produced energy, it was thought that uranium neutrons moved too quickly to create an explosion. Unless several tons of uranium were used, the neutrons would rapidly dissipate, and would not reach the necessary critical mass. Even if you could make a bomb with uranium, it would be too heavy for an aeroplane to carry. The idea was simply impractical.

The key to Frisch and Peierl's breakthrough was a known isotope of uranium, U235, in which the neutrons move more slowly. They realised that the difference in neutron speed meant that as little as one pound of U235, densely packed to reduce the surface area through which neutrons could escape, would be needed to generate a colossal explosive force.

As a scientific paper, the memorandum is a delight. You find yourself thinking, 'Ah! So *that's* how you do it! How clever!' The scientists not only solved the theoretical problem, they addressed several practical ones too.

Strictly Confidential

Memorandum on the properties of a radioactive "super-bomb".

The attached detailed report concerns the possibility of constructing a "super-bomb" which utilizes the energy stored in atomic nuclei as a source of energy. The energy liberated in the explosion of such a super-bomb is about the same as that produced by the explosion of 1000 tons of dynamite. This energy is liberated in a small volume, in which it will, for an instant, produce a temperature comparable to that in the interior of the sun. The blast from such an explosion would destroy life in a wide area. The size of this area is difficult to estimate, but it will probably cover the centre of a big city.

In addition, some part of the energy set free by the bomb goes to produce radioactive substances, and these will emit very powerful and dangerous radiations. The effect of these radiations is greatest immediately after the explosion, but it decays only gradually and even for days after the explosion any person entering the affected area will be killed.

Some of this radioactivity will be carried along with the wind and will spread the contamination; several miles downwind this may kill people.

In order to produce such a bomb it is necessary to treat a few cwt. of uranium by a process which will separate from the uranium its light isotope ($U_{235}$) of which it contains about 0.7%. Methods for the separation of isotopes have recently been developed. They are slow and they have not until now been applied to uranium, whose chemical properties give rise to technical difficulties. But these difficulties are by no means insuperable. We have not sufficient experience with large-scale chemical plant to give a reliable estimate of the cost, but it is certainly not prohibitive.

It is a property of these super-bombs that there exists a "critical size" of about one pound. A quantity of the separated uranium isotope that exceeds the critical amount is explosive; +++ The bomb would therefore be manufactured in two (or more) parts, each being less than the critical size, and in transport all danger of a premature explosion would be avoided if these parts were kept at a distance of few inches from each other. The bomb would be provided with a mechanism that brings the two parts together when the bomb is intended to go off. Once the parts are joined to form a block which exceeds the critical amount, the effect of the penetrating radiation always present in the atmosphere will initiate the explosion within a second or so.

The mechanism which brings the parts of the bomb together must be arranged to work fairly rapidly because of the possibility of the bomb exploding when the critical conditions have just only been reached. In this case the explosion will be far less powerful. It is never possible to exclude this altogether, but one can easily ensure that only, say, one bomb out of 100 will fail in this way, and since in any case the explosion is strong enough to destroy the bomb itself, this point is not serious.

We do not feel competent to discuss the strategic value of such a bomb, but the following conclusions seem certain:

1. As a weapon, the super-bomb would be practically irresistible. There is no material or structure that could be expected to resist the force of the explosion. If one thinks of using the bomb for breaking through a line of fortifications, it should be kept in mind that the radioactive radiations will prevent anyone from approaching the affected territory for several days; they will equally prevent defenders from reoccupying the affected positions. The advantage would lie with the side which can determine most accurately just when it is safe to re-enter the area; this is likely to be the agressor, who knows the location of the bomb in advance.

+++ yet a quantity less than the critical amount is absolutely safe.

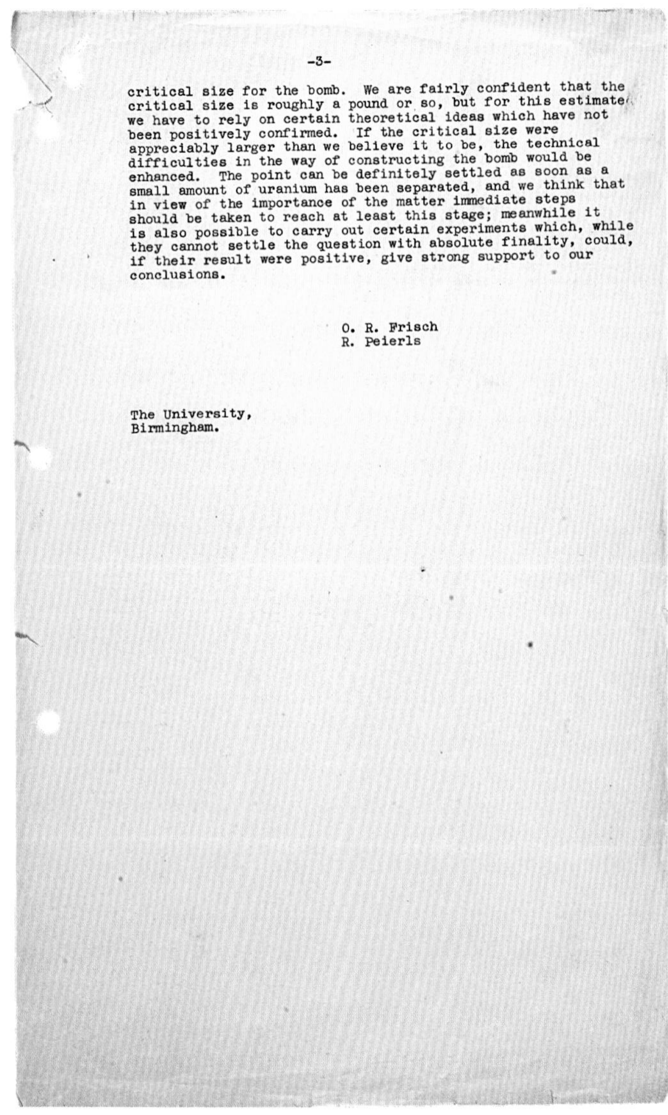

-3-

critical size for the bomb. We are fairly confident that the critical size is roughly a pound or so, but for this estimate we have to rely on certain theoretical ideas which have not been positively confirmed. If the critical size were appreciably larger than we believe it to be, the technical difficulties in the way of constructing the bomb would be enhanced. The point can be definitely settled as soon as a small amount of uranium has been separated, and we think that in view of the importance of the matter immediate steps should be taken to reach at least this stage; meanwhile it is also possible to carry out certain experiments which, while they cannot settle the question with absolute finality, could, if their result were positive, give strong support to our conclusions.

O. R. Frisch
R. Peierls

The University,
Birmingham.

RIGHT: *Frisch and Peierls put their names to the memorandum, just as one would to any scientific paper. Few papers have had the impact that this one would have.*

They proposed ways of manufacturing U235 in sufficient quantities to make a bomb, and included a safety feature. They recommended that its core should comprise two parts of U235, neither of which would be large enough to explode on its own, but which would be brought together on impact. And they addressed some of the consequences for human beings: 'The energy liberated by a five kilogram bomb would be equivalent to several thousand tons of dynamite ... the radiations would be fatal to living beings even a long time after the explosion ... effective protection is hardly possible.' Behind the smooth scientific analysis, there are hints of nervousness at what they had just made possible. The memorandum emphasises: '... it would be very important to have an organisation which determines the exact extent of the danger area ... so that people could be warned from entering it.'

Frisch and Peierls gave the memorandum to Marcus Oliphant, Professor of Physics at Birmingham. Realising its significance, Oliphant passed it to Henry Tizard, Chairman of the Committee on the Scientific Survey of Air Defence. Within a month Tizard had set up a committee know as MAUD (Military Application of Uranium Detonation) to steer further research into the idea. A year later, the committee reported that a bomb was indeed feasible. In America, Frisch and Peierls took the discovery further in the Manhattan Project. Frisch determined the mass of uranium needed to make a bomb, known as Little Boy, which Peierls assembled by hand. In August 1945, the bomb was exploded over Hiroshima.

After the war both Frisch and Peierls returned to their academic work in England, major figures whose work developed our understanding in a number of scientific fields. But nothing they did would match the impact of this little paper.

# NAZI PROPAGANDA *and the* GREATEST RAID *of* ALL

## Intercepted German Reports of the St Nazaire Raid

## 1942

ABOVE: *The* Campbeltown *hangs on the dock gates at St Nazaire. The Nazis did not know that she was primed to explode.*

THE BRITISH RAID on St Nazaire, Operation Chariot, has gone down in history as 'the Greatest Raid of All'. These documents were created in the immediate aftermath of the raid, and show the Nazi's triumph over its apparent failure. Part of the thrill in reading them is that they are like ticking bombs. When they were made, the Nazis didn't know what was just about to happen.

The port of St Nazaire is on the Loire River in France. It contained the only dry dock near the coast that was capable of running repairs to the largest German ships. Without it, the bigger ships damaged in fighting would have to limp back to Germany before they could be restored to battle strength. The objective of Operation Chariot was to destroy St Nazaire's dry dock.

A First-World-War destroyer, HMS *Campbeltown*, was loaded with 4.5 tons of explosives and primed with a delayed detonator. It was accompanied by commandos on board eighteen smaller ships. The flotilla set off from Falmouth at 2 p.m. on 26 March 1942, and reached St Nazaire in the early hours of 28 March. Under heavy fire, the *Campbeltown*, which had been flying the German flag, raised British colours, increased its speed, and smashed into the dock gates. The force was so great that the ship was carried some thirty-three feet over the gates, where it hung intact.

The commandos jumped ashore, aiming to destroy the dry dock's water-pumping and other machinery. After mixed success, they found their evacuation ships destroyed by heavy German fire. The commandos tried to battle through the town, but most ran out of ammunition and were captured.

On the morning of 28 March, therefore, the Nazis believed that the raid had failed. Goebbels' propaganda machine swung into action. The first part of this broadcast, which was intercepted by a BBC monitoring station, transcribed and sent to British Combined Operations, was recorded immediately after the commandos were captured.

V O

ABM

+19

URGENT

Cdr Ryder & COTL. Saw this. FCR SPRO

RBCT No. DIG. Cdr Ryder.

19

URGENT

ZEESEN IN ENGLISH FOR NORTH AMERICA 00.15 31.3.42

REPORT FROM THE FRONT: ST.NAZAIRE PRISONERS COME IN:

---

PRESUMABLY AN EYE-WITNESS COMMENTARY FROM THE QUAYSIDE AT ST. NAZAIRE: SOUNDS OF HEAVY FOOTSTEPS AND SHOUTING VOICES ARE TO BE HEARD IN THE BACKGROUND. AFTER THE INTERVIEWS WITH PRISONERS, THE COMMENTATOR CONTINUED ALMOST WITHOUT INTERRUPTION TO REPORT THE RESULT OF THE RAID THE NEXT DAY, INDICATING THAT THE REPORT CONSISTS OF RECORDINGS MADE ON TWO XX SEPARATE OCCASIONS)

COMMENTATOR: IT HAS BEEN A HECTIC NIGHT: THE BRITISH HAVE ATTEMPTED A RAID ON THE FRENCH COAST AT ST.NAZAIRE. BUT THE ATTEMPT WAS A FAILURE AND ALL THE EFFORTS WERE NIPPED IN THE BUD. NOW WE ARE HERE DOWN BELOW IN THE HARBOUR AND WE SHOULD EXPECT A PATROL BOAT BACK WHICH HAS BEEN OUT AT SEA DURING THIS NIGHT, AND BRINGING BACK SOME PRISONERS OF WAR WHO HAVE BEEN TAKEN OFF A SUNKEN MOTOR TORPEDO BOAT. HERE, WE EXPECT THE PRISONERS VERY SOON. THE BOATS HAVE JUST APPROACHED THE MOLE. THEY HAVE FOUGHT QUITE HARD BUT THEN GIVEN UP.

ONE OF THE TORPEDO BOATS ENTERED THE INNER HARBOUR BUT IT WAS SO SEVERELY DAMAGED THAT IT SANK BY THE STERN. THE FORWARD PART RAN UP ON SHORE AND FROM THEIR DETACHMENTS TRIED TO ENTER THE DOCKYARDS, BUT HERE THEY WERE WE

LCOMED BY TERRIFIC FIRE AND THEY BROKE DOWN. WE SEE A TREMENDOUS AMOUNT OF DEAD BRITISH SOLDIERS LYING ABOUT AND THE DAMAGE THEY HAVE DONE IS QUITE INSIGNIFICANTM AND NOW WE GO DOWN TO WATCH THE ARRIVAL OF A MOTOR PATROL VESSEL. IT COMES BACK WITH SOME SURVIVORS OF A MOTOR TORPEDO BOAT. BRITISH SOLDIERS ARE COVERED WITH BLANKETS. THEY LOOK QUITE DOWN-CAST. THEY HAVE GONE THROUGH A TREMENDOUS STRAIN. THE SKY OVER THE COAST WAS BLOOD RED LAST NIGHT AND BOATS WERE ABLAZE IN THE HARBOUR AFTER THEY HAD BEEN SHELLED BY THE ARTILLERY. THEY ARE BRINGING THE PRISONERS ASHORE NOW. HERE TWO ARE COMING. AND ANOTHER ONE. ONE WHO JUST PASSED BY HAD AN INJURED EYE WHICH WAS ALL CLOSED UP. NONE OF THEM HAD ANY SHOWS BECAUSE THEY PROBABLY THREW THEM AWAY WHEN THEY JUMPED INTO THE SEA. NOW WE HAVE THEM ALL LINED UP ON THE SHORE AND THE POLICE WILL BE TAKING THEM TO THE G'PO (SIC PRESUMABLY GESTAPO) WHERE THEY WILL FURNISH THEM WITH NEW CLOTHES AND WILL TAKE CARE OF THEIR INJURIES.

AND HERE WE HAVE A POOR CHAP IN BATTLEDRESS. HE CAN HARDLY WALK. A YOUNG GERMAN SOLDIER HELPS HIM ALONG. HE IS LEANING ON HIM. NOW I'LL HAVE A TALK WITH ONE OF THE PRISONERS, WHO HAS JUST COME FROM THE MOTOR TORPEDO BOAT.

''AND DID YOU JUMP INTO THE WATER WHEN YOU WERE HIT OR (ONE WORD) BY SHELLS?''

PRISONER:: ''NO, THE (FEW WORDS) WAS SENT AHEAD AND STRANDED: THEN SHE CAUGHT FIRE''.

COMMENTATOR: ''OH, AND THEN SHE CAUGHT FIRE. AND YOU JUMPED INTO THE WATER (UNINTELLIGIBLE COMMENT FROM PRISONER ENDING '' AND THE SHELLS BURST'') OH, I SEE, SO YOU MEAN YOU WERE DOWN IN THE ENGINE ROOM ALL THE TIME?''

OPPOSITE AND LEFT: *This transcript of the Nazi broadcast following the St Nazaire Raid was interrupted by a BBC monitoring station. The commentator gives an eye-witness account of the British prisoners as they file past.*

COMMENTATOR: *It has been a hectic night: the British have attempted a raid on the French coast at St Nazaire. But the attempt was a failure and all the efforts were nipped in the bud. Now we are here down below in the harbour and we should expect a patrol boat back which has been out at sea during this night and bringing back some prisoners of war who have been taken off a sunken motor torpedo boat. Here, we expect the prisoners very soon. The boats have just approached the Mole* [a jetty at St Nazaire known as the 'Old Mole']. *They have fought quite hard but then given up.*

*One of the torpedo boats entered the inner harbour but it was so severely damaged that it sank by the stern. The forward part ran up on shore and from their detachments tried to enter the dockyards. But here they were welcomed by terrific fire and they broke down. We see a tremendous amount of dead British soldiers lying about and the damage they have done is quite insignificant and now we go down to watch the arrival of a motor patrol vessel. It comes back with some survivors of a motor torpedo boat. British soldiers are covered with blankets. They look quite downcast. They have gone through a tremendous strain. The sky over the coast was blood red last night and boats were ablaze in the harbour after they had been shelled by the artillery. They are bringing the prisoners ashore now. Here two are coming. And another one. One who just passed by had an injured eye which was all closed up. None of them had any shows because they probably threw them away when they jumped into the sea. Now we have them all lined up on the shore and the police will be taking them to the G'PO* [sic, *presumably the Gestapo*] *where they will furnish them with new clothes and will take care of their injuries.*

The reporter is adopting a thoroughly reasonable tone. Patronising credit is granted to the conquered troops, who 'fought quite hard'. They are fellow human beings with whom listeners could sympathise, 'covered with blankets', 'quite downcast', having 'gone through a tremendous strain'. These were not bad men or cowards, they simply could not resist the 'terrific fire' of the victorious defenders. And now, because the victors are civilised men, the Gestapo would clothe the prisoners and take care of their injuries. It would be hard to think of a more chilling sentence.

PRISONER: ''NO, NO. I WASN'T. I WAS A PASSENGER ON THE MOTOR TORPEDO BOAT''.

COMMENTATOR: ''YOU WERE A PASSENGER?''

PRISONER: ''YES, I WAS BEING TAKEN BACK.

COMMENTATOR: ''OH, I SEE''.

PRISONER: ''SHE WAS HIT''.

COMMENTATOR: ''YES, I SEE. WELL, ANDHOW ARE YOU GXX FEELING NOW?''

PRISONER: ''WELL MY ARM HAS GONE.

COMMENTATOR: ''YOU MUST FEEL QUITE COLD AND SHIVERY, EH? (THE PRISONER AND COMMENTATOR THEN TALKED SIMULTANEOUSLY ABOUT THE COLD AND BLANKETS) SORRY THAT'S WARM''.

HERE COMES A STRETCHER, FOR THERE ARE PROBABLY SOME WOUNDED WHO CAN'T WALK. THERE ARE THREE SAILORS WOUNDED. THEY ARE BROUGHT FROM THE BOAT. IT IS A HARD JOB BECAUSE THE BOAT IS RATHER LOW IN THE WATER AND THE MOLE IS HIGH

AND SO WE HAVE TO USE SOME ROPES TO PULL THEM UP. WELL, ALL THE BOYS WHO CAN'T WALK, THEY HAVE TO STAND HERE. AND THERE'S A CHAP HERE (FEW WORDS) AND THE REST GO OFF. SOME OF THE BOYS ARE MAKING ANGRY FACES AT ME. WELL, IT DOESN'T FEEL GOOD, DOES IT? YOU, YOU DON'T FEEL VERY GOOD, DO YOU? YOU COME OUT ALREADY: AND THIS OTHER CHAP AND YOU. (PRESUMABLY THE COMMENTATOR WAS COLLECTING A FEW MEN ROUND HIM TO QUESTION) HOW DID YOU ACQUIRE THIS INJURY ON YOUR LEG:

The second part of the broadcast consists of cheery messages home: '*This is (Leslie) Wilcock of 56 San Domingo Road, Liverpool 5 speaking. Hello, Mum, Dad, I'm quite well; no need to worry. Cheerio.*'

Some of the exchanges are Pythonesque:

German interviewer: *'And how are you feeling now?'*
British prisoner: *'Well, my arm has gone.'*
German interviewer: *'You must feel quite cold and shivery, eh?'*

Why did the men give so much more information than their regulation name, rank and number? One of those recorded was Lieutenant Stuart Chant. He later gave an account to his superiors of the propagandists' methods, which is also in the National Archives' files. Fake Red Cross officials had visited the prisoners in hospital, he reported. The officials asked the prisoners where they were from, and told them that they could send messages home, which were then recorded with hidden microphones. But Lieutenant Chant's claims do not quite add up. Why tell someone that they can send messages home and then record them on a hidden microphone? The messages read as if the men knew full well that they were being recorded. Lieutenant Chant may have been embarrassed about the use to which the recordings were put, and was himself stretching the truth.

Above: *The German reports include interviews with prisoners. To give more than name, rank and number was a breach of regulations.*

There is a thrill nowadays in reading the triumphalist reporting, because we know what happened next. Just after noon, while the *Campbeltown* was undergoing inspection by senior German officers, the detonator finally triggered. A colossal explosion destroyed the gates and a great wall of water swept away two tankers that had been sitting in the dry dock. The dock was out of operation for the rest of the war. Operation Chariot was a victory.

# BEYOND COURAGE

## Special Operations Executive Files

## 1943–1944

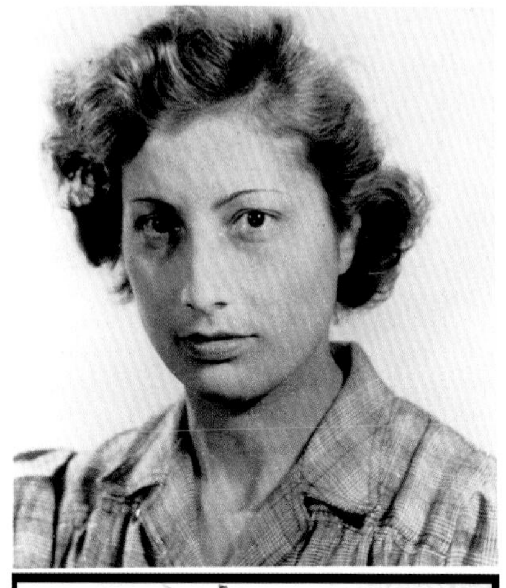


RIGHT: *Noor Khan was exotic, the daughter of an Indian mystic and an American poet, born in Moscow, raised in London and Paris.*

IN THE SPRING of 1940, Winston Churchill ordered that a secret organisation should be set up. Its cover name was the Inter Services Research Bureau, but it is known to history as the Special Operations Executive (SOE). Its mission was overseas reconnaissance, espionage and sabotage.

SOE agents operated across Europe and the Far East. In Britain, they were trained in weaponry and explosives, combat skills, demolition, telegraphy and tradecraft. They were then smuggled into the countries in which they were to operate. Many were natives of the countries to which they were sent, or at least fluent in the language. But the key qualification for SOE agents was an extraordinary degree of selflessness and bravery. If captured, they were not protected by the conventions of war. Captured agents were routinely tortured and executed.

The National Archives holds the files of many SOE agents. These documents tell the story of just one of them, Noor Khan.

Khan had a cosmopolitan background. The daughter of an Indian Muslim mystic and an American poet, she was born in Moscow and raised first in London, then Paris. When Germany invaded France, the family fled to London, where Khan joined the Women's Auxiliary Air Force (WAAF) and trained as a wireless operator. A woman with a distinctly Indian beauty, she may have been treated flippantly by her male colleagues, and was nicknamed 'Bang Away Lulu' after a bawdy song, because of her heavy Morse typing. But Khan wanted more – more for herself, more for her adopted home, and more for her Indian heritage. She wrote in a letter: 'I wish some Indians would win high military distinction in the war. If one or two would do something in the Allied Service which was very brave and which everyone admired, it would help to make a bridge between the English people and the Indians.'

Khan's knowledge of France caught the eye of someone in the know, and she was invited to train for the SOE. The first document here is an enthusiastic report from her senior officer, written using her code name, 27 X 16. Khan sounds more like best-friend material than a potential Mata Hari: 'Very feminine in character, very eager to please ... capable of strong attachments, kind hearted, emotional and imaginative.' But she was already well aware of the risks that she would be running: 'The fact that she has already given some thought to preparing her mother for the inevitable separation and cessation of correspondence shows that she has faced some, at any rate, of the implications of the job.'

Date:- 19 Apr 43
STS 52

SECRET

## Reports on Officer Students
## Report No. 22

**27 X 16**

This student, like her two F.A.N.Y. companions of the 27 X party, has thrown herself heart and soul into the life of the school. She has any amount of energy, and spends a lot of it on voluntary P.T. with the object of overcoming as far as possible feminine disabilities in the physical sense.

She is, also, very feminine in character, very eager to please, very ready to adapt herself to the mood of the company, or the tone ofthe conversation, interested in personalities, capable of strong attachments, kind-hearted, emotional and imaginative. She is very fond of her family (mother, brother in the Fleet Air Arm and sister) and was engaged for about five years, but broke it off.

The motive for her accepting the present task is, apparently, idealism. She felt that she had come to a dead end as a W.A.A.F., and was longing to do something more active in the prosecution of the war, something which would make more call on her capabilities and, perhaps, demand more sacrifice. This appears to be the only motive; the broken off engagement is old history, nor does she appear to have any romantic ideas of the Mata-Hari variety. In fact, she confesses that she would not like to have to do anything "two-faced", by which she means deliberately cultivating friendly relations with malice aforethought. The fact that she has already given some thought to preparing her mother for the inevitable separation and cessation of correspondence shows that she has faced some, at any rate, of the implications of the job. It is the emotional side of her character, coupled with a vivid imagination, which will most test her steadfastness of purpose in the later stages of her training.

OPPOSITE: *Student assessment of the suitability of '27 X 16' to operate in the field.*
RIGHT: *The report on Khan after she had completed training notes that she is 'not over-burdened with brains . . . unstable and temperamental' and that it is 'doubtful whether she is really suited to work in the field'. These phrases are angrily underscored by 'F', who comments, 'Makes me cross.'*

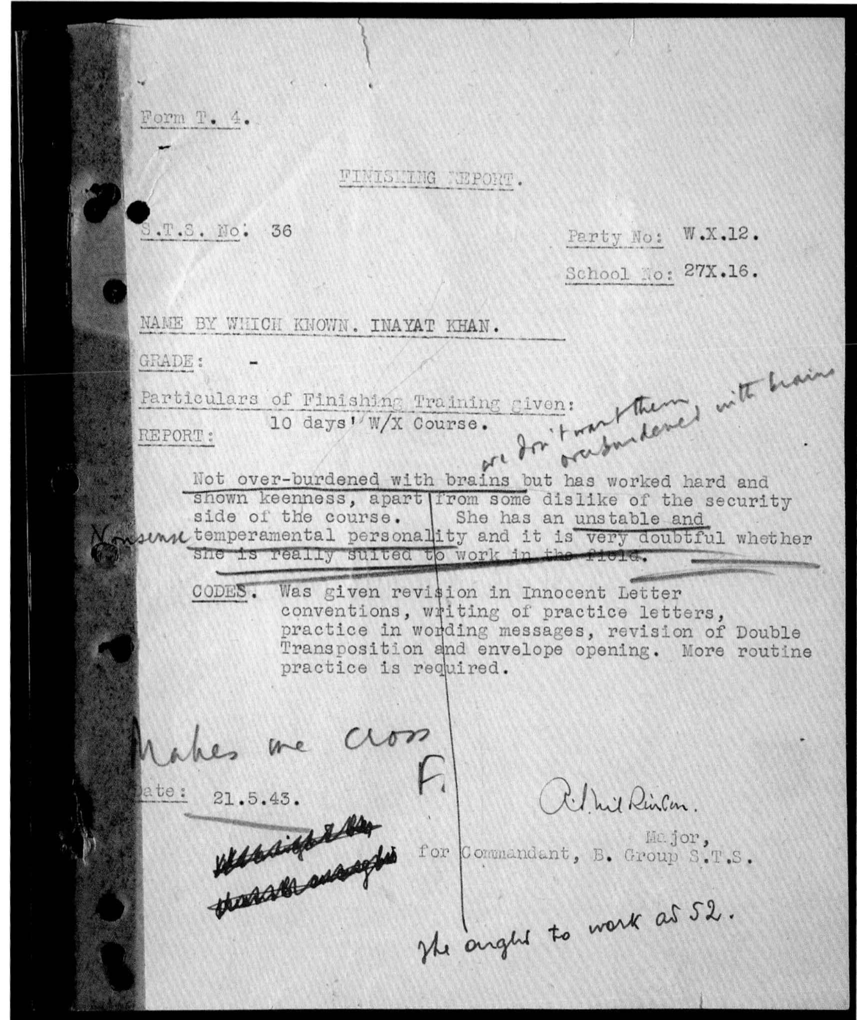

Form T. 4.

FINISHING REPORT.

S.T.S. No: 36 Party No: W.X.12.
School No: 27X.16.

NAME BY WHICH KNOWN. INAYAT KHAN.

GRADE: -

Particulars of Finishing Training given:
10 days' W/X Course.

REPORT:

Not over-burdened with brains but has worked hard and shown keenness, apart from some dislike of the security side of the course. She has an unstable and temperamental personality and it is very doubtful whether she is really suited to work in the field.

CODES. Was given revision in Innocent Letter conventions, writing of practice letters, practice in wording messages, revision of Double Transposition and envelope opening. More routine practice is required.

Date: 21.5.43.

for Commandant, B. Group S.T.S.

Major,



The second report was written when she had finished her SOE training, and shows opinion to be more divided: 'Not over-burdened with brains but has worked hard and shown keenness, apart from some dislike of the security side of the course. She has an unstable and temperamental personality and it is very doubtful whether she is really suited to work in the field.' Someone signing himself as 'F' (possibly Maurice Buckmaster, Head of SOE's 'F' for 'French' section) has taken exception to this, although it is a back-handed response: 'We don't want them over-burdened with brains . . . Makes me cross.'

F's reaction may have swung it. Less than three weeks later, Khan received a copy of the third document here, her mission instructions. She was to work in Paris under the assumed identity of a nurse, Jeanne Marie Renier. Her code name would be Madeleine. Her mission was to act as a wireless operator for a local resistance network.

Fifteen months after this document was typed, Khan was dead. The resistance network that Khan was joining had been uncovered by the SD, the intelligence agency of the SS. Shortly after she was smuggled into northern France, the SD arrested all of the other radio operators in the network. But, as Khan had said in her letter, she wanted to do something that was very brave and everyone admired, and she refused an offer to

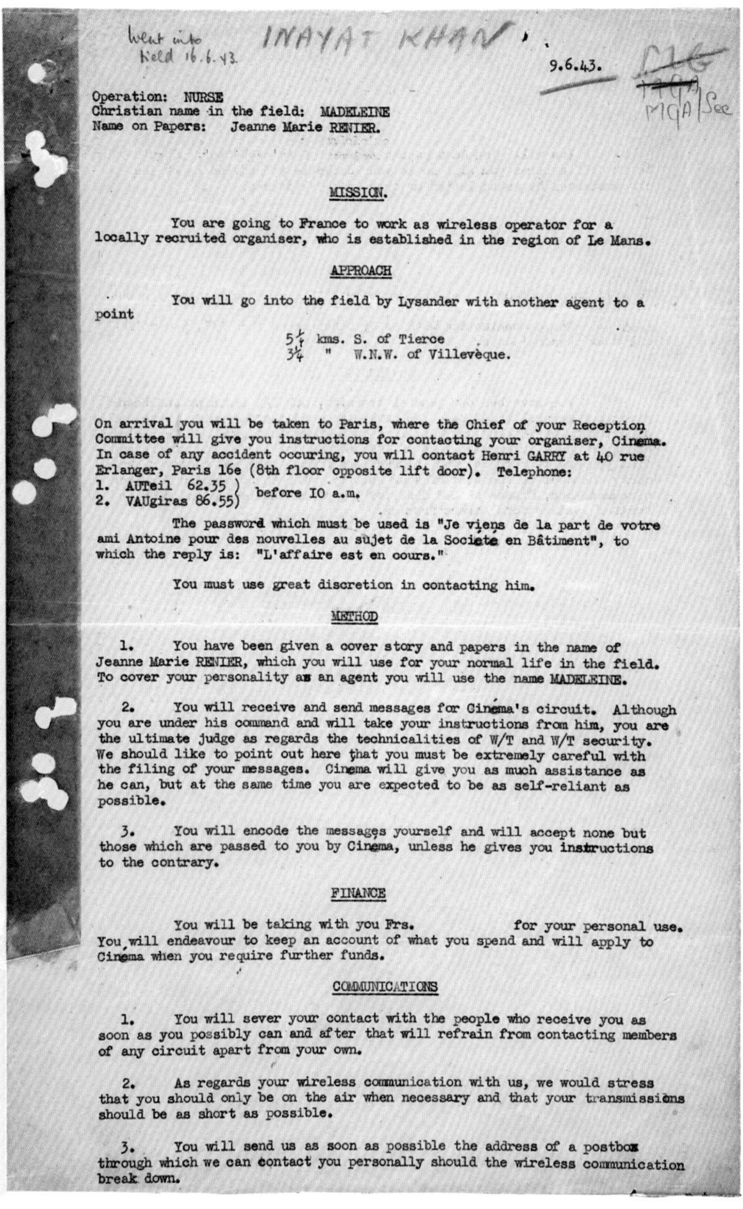

Went into field 16.6.43. INAYAT KHAN.

9.6.43.

MGA/Sec

Operation: NURSE
Christian name in the field: MADELEINE
Name on Papers: Jeanne Marie RENIER.

MISSION.

You are going to France to work as wireless operator for a locally recruited organiser, who is established in the region of Le Mans.

APPROACH

You will go into the field by Lysander with another agent to a point

5¼ kms. S. of Tierce
3¾ " W.N.W. of Villevèque.

On arrival you will be taken to Paris, where the Chief of your Reception Committee will give you instructions for contacting your organiser, Cinéma. In case of any accident occuring, you will contact Henri GARRY at 40 rue Erlanger, Paris 16e (8th floor opposite lift door). Telephone:
1. AUTeil 62.35 } before IO a.m.
2. VAUgiras 86.55}

The password which must be used is "Je viens de la part de votre ami Antoine pour des nouvelles au sújet de la Sociéte en Bâtiment", to which the reply is: "L'affaire est en cours."

You must use great discretion in contacting him.

METHOD

1. You have been given a cover story and papers in the name of Jeanne Marie RENIER, which you will use for your normal life in the field. To cover your personality as an agent you will use the name MADELEINE.

2. You will receive and send messages for Cinéma's circuit. Although you are under his command and will take your instructions from him, you are the ultimate judge as regards the technicalities of W/T and W/T security. We should like to point out here that you must be extremely careful with the filing of your messages. Cinema will give you as much assistance as he can, but at the same time you are expected to be as self-reliant as possible.

3. You will encode the messages yourself and will accept none but those which are passed to you by Cinéma, unless he gives you instructions to the contrary.

FINANCE

You will be taking with you Frs. for your personal use. You will endeavour to keep an account of what you spend and will apply to Cinéma when you require further funds.

COMMUNICATIONS

1. You will sever your contact with the people who receive you as soon as you possibly can and after that will refrain from contacting members of any circuit apart from your own.

2. As regards your wireless communication with us, we would stress that you should only be on the air when necessary and that your transmissions should be as short as possible.

3. You will send us as soon as possible the address of a postbox through which we can contact you personally should the wireless communication break down.

Left: *Khan's mission brief. She was to act as wireless operator for a group near Le Mans. Her agent name was to be Madeleine.*
Opposite: *Transcript of the interrogation of the senior Nazi intelligence officer who remembered Khan.*
Opposite, top far right: *Letter to Khan's mother, informing her that her daughter is missing.*
Opposite, bottom far right: *Later report on Khan's work in France, paying tribute to her accomplishment and bravery.*

escape back to England. For months she moved from place to place to make her broadcasts, maintaining the essential radio link between the resistance network and London.

Khan was finally betrayed. The National Archives holds a record of the later interrogation of Hans Kieffer, the Nazi's senior intelligence officer in Paris: 'I remember the English W/T operator Madeleine … we were pursuing her for months … after her capture [she] showed great courage and we got no information whatsoever out of her.' Khan had been so ferocious that Security Service officers were nervous of getting too close to her.

Kieffer continues with the story of an escape attempt. Khan had managed to get on to the roof of the building in which she was being held. She might well have got away successfully but, cruelly, a chance air-raid

Translation of the Voluntary Statement made by the Commandant of the Paris Gestapo, Hans Kieffer.

--------

Deposition, etc.

1. I remember the English W/T operator, Madeleine, and recognise her on the photograph shown to me. We were pursuing her for months and as we had a personal description of her we arranged for all stations to be watched. She had several addresses and worked very carefully. All addresses were constantly watched for her, and through Bommelburg (head of the German Secret Police in Paris) we had an address of relations of PHONO. We had drawn into this enquiry a great many secret agents and eventually she was caught by Vogt at this later address. The owner of the flat was a friend of Madeleine.

2. Madeleine, after her capture, showed great courage and we got no information whatsoever out of her. We had, however, found a good deal of material which helped in her interrogation. In particular she refused to give her security checks. Immediately after her arrest she made an attempt at escape, when she got on to the roof through a bathroom situzted on the 5th floor. She was re-arrested after the alarm had been given by Vogt. She remained about 2 months in the Avenue Foch and made a second attempt at escape in the company of Major Faille and Bob. After about 1 hour Bob and Madeleine were found on the second floor of a neighbouring house. Thereupon I arranged immediately for Madeleine and Faille to be transferred to Germany. Madeleine and Faille had again refused to give their word of honour not to attempt further escapes. Bob signed a paper saying that he would not make another attempt

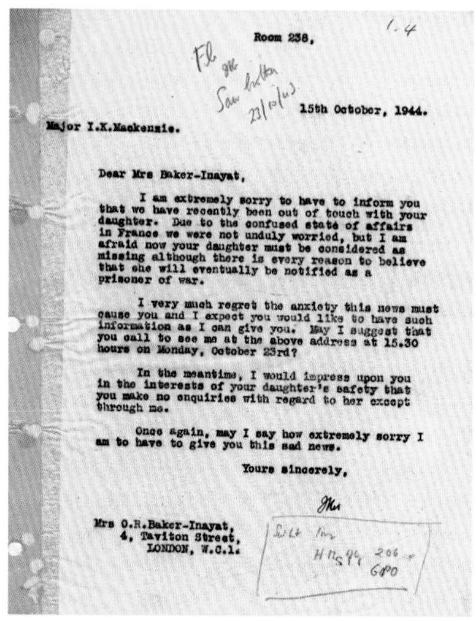

Room 238,

15th October, 1944.

Major I.K.Mackenzie.

Dear Mrs Baker-Inayat,

I am extremely sorry to have to inform you that we have recently been out of touch with your daughter. Due to the confused state of affairs in France we were not unduly worried, but I am afraid now your daughter must be considered as missing although there is every reason to believe that she will eventually be notified as a prisoner of war.

I very much regret the anxiety this news must cause you and I expect you would like to have such information as I can give you. May I suggest that you call to see me at the above address at 15.30 hours on Monday, October 23rd?

In the meantime, I would impress upon you in the interests of your daughter's safety that you make no enquiries with regard to her except through me.

Once again, may I say how extremely sorry I am to have to give you this sad news.

Yours sincerely,

Mrs O.R.Baker-Inayat,
4, Taviton Street,
LONDON, W.C.1.

A/S/O. INAYAT-KHAN, N. Joined W.A.A.F.: November, 1940.
Trade :

This officer, went to the Field on 16th June 1943, as a W/T operator to one of our most important organisers. Shortly after her arrival the Gestapo became extremely active in her area. Her group was penetrated and, on the arrest of the organiser and his chief Lieutenants, it finally collapsed.

The Gestapo's knowledge of her movements appeared to be such that her capture seemed almost a certainty - on one occasion she returned to her home to find them awaiting her; she was involved in a shooting match at GRIGNON but managed to escape. She was therefore instructed to return to England. She, however, pleaded to be allowed to remain and lie low for a month. At the end of this time she reported that she felt her security re-established as a result of arrangements she had made and subsequent events have fully justified her course of action.

This officer's devotion to duty enabled contact with this country to be maintained and as a result it was possible to re-inforce and re-construct the group. It is unique in the annals of this Organisation that a Circuit which was so completely disintegrated should be able to be rebuilt and this must be attributed to the conduct of this young woman, who, regardless of all personal danger, remained at her post - often alone - and always under the threat of arrest. She has also been instrumental in facilitating the escape of thirty Allied airmen shot down in France.

warning caused the area to be locked down and she was caught. Already classified as 'highly dangerous', the ferocious escapee had to be dealt with. Khan was sent to Dachau concentration camp. On arrival she was taken directly to the crematorium, where she was shot in the head.

Khan's brave death could not be acknowledged during the war. However, in 1949 she was posthumously awarded a British George Cross, the highest civil decoration of the United Kingdom, and the French Croix de Guerre with gold star. She is a woman for our times as much as for the 1940s: an Indian-American Muslim, who gave her life for Britain, in the fight against those who wanted to destroy the Jews. A monument to Khan has been erected in central London, close to her former home.

# *The* NAUGHTY DOCUMENT
## 'The Percentages Agreement'

ABOVE: *Churchill and Stalin.*

OPPOSITE: *Churchill's proposal for the division of power in Eastern Europe. The handwriting is Churchill's, the giant tick is Stalin's.*

# 1944

CHURCHILL WOULD LATER call this his 'Naughty Document'. Written in his own hand during a late-night meeting with Stalin, it is a quickly scribbled plan for carving up postwar Europe. The giant tick was made by Stalin, to indicate his approval of Churchill's proposal.

At this point in the Second World War, the Western Allies were pushing east from Normandy, while Stalin's forces were overrunning Poland, Hungary, Czechoslovakia, Romania and Yugoslavia. The Allies remained in close contact, but the pressing question now was not how victory might be achieved. Victory was in sight. No, the pressing question was, what would happen when the war was won?

In his memoirs, Churchill gives an account of how the document came into being in October 1944. Churchill and his Foreign Secretary, Anthony Eden, flew to Moscow for talks. The meeting became known as the Fourth Moscow Conference and its principal objectives were to negotiate Soviet entry into the war with Japan, and to reach agreement over the future of Poland. The men agreed that Russia would annex eastern Poland as part of the Soviet Union, and Poland would take German territory to the west. Late in the evening, with Poland carved up, talk turned to the future of the rest of Eastern Europe. Churchill and Stalin were sitting in the Kremlin, together with their translators but without the Americans. Churchill recalled:

*The moment was apt for business, so I said, 'Let us settle about our affairs in the Balkans. Your armies are in Romania and Bulgaria. We have interests, missions and agents there. Don't let us get at cross purposes in small ways. So far as Britain and Russia are concerned, how would it do for you to have 90 per cent predominance in Romania, for us to have 90 per cent of the same in Greece, and go 50/50 about Yugoslavia.' While this was being translated I wrote out a half sheet of paper:*

Note written by P.M. during [conv]ersation with Marshal Stalin at the Kremlin [9].10.44. Attached is Interpreter's translation. (Red ink added later).

169

Roumania

Russia 90%

The others 10%

Greece Great Britain 90%
(in accord w USA.)

~~The others~~ 10%
Russia

Yugoslavia 50/50%

Hungary 50/50%

Bulgaria Russia 75%

The others 25%

*No delicate diplomacy or careful discussion, just the fate of millions determined by the shrug of great men of power, scribbled on a scrap, sealed with a handshake. Churchill claimed to have got cold feet about how history might regard the casual exchange.*

ROMANIA *Russia 90% the others 10%*
GREECE *G. Britain 90% in accord with USA ~~the others~~ Russia 10%*
YUGOSLAVIA *50/50%*
HUNGARY *50/50%*
BULGARIA *Russia 75% the others 25%*

The half-sheet of paper was passed across. Stalin ticked it, and passed it back.

What did Churchill think he was doing? He wanted to do business in a way that Stalin would understand, and which flattered the dictator. No delicate diplomacy or careful discussion, just the fate of millions determined by the shrug of great men of power, scribbled on a scrap, sealed with a handshake. Churchill claimed to have got cold feet about how history might regard the casual exchange. In his memoirs, he says to Stalin: 'Might it not be thought rather cynical if it seemed we had disposed of these issues so fateful to millions of people, in such an offhand manner? Let us burn the paper.' Stalin replies: 'No, you keep it.'

But what, exactly, were all these percentages supposed to mean? That Yugoslavia would be physically split in two, 50/50, with each ally controlling one half? That they would share voting rights, with Russia getting a 75 per cent 'vote' on what went on in Bulgaria, and Britain and the US a 25 per cent vote? Was this talk of 'percentages' just diplomatic code? Did they really mean that Britain would control Greece (which hung over its routes to India), that Russia would control its near neighbours in Eastern Europe, and that everything else was up for grabs? Or did these percentages not really mean anything at all – which was why Stalin had no problem putting his mark to the paper?

It is hard to say what effect, if any, the document had. Britain and Russia took it seriously enough that their foreign ministers, Eden and Molotov, discussed it the following day, and finessed the percentages. But when Churchill sent a draft of the discussion to Stalin, the dictator struck out any reference to percentages and spheres of influence. And yet, if the Naughty Document had no impact, it was remarkably prescient. Romania, Bulgaria and Hungary were to become one-party communist states. Greece became a one-party junta under British influence. Fateful to millions, indeed.

# *The* QUEEN'S OATH

## Elizabeth II's Coronation Oath

## 1953

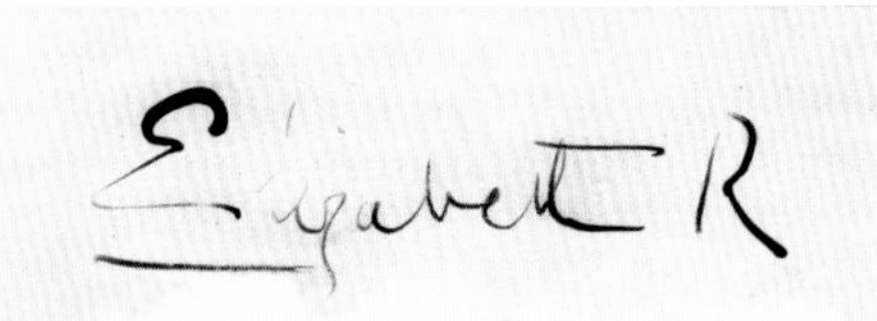

ABOVE: *The Queen at her coronation (from* Picture Post*).*
ABOVE LEFT: *The Queen's signature on her oath. A spurt of ink on the 'E' makes the rest of the signature faint.*

ON 2 JUNE 1953, Elizabeth II was anointed with holy oil in Westminster Abbey. She was presented with symbols of her rule: spurs, a sword, an orb, the royal sceptre. She was crowned Queen, and she was proclaimed to her people. But before all of that, Elizabeth had to sign an oath.

The Queen had entered Westminster Abbey in procession, knelt before the High Altar, and then settled in her 'chair of estate' (not the throne, not yet). She was then presented to the people by the Archbishop of Canterbury, turning in each direction of the compass to cries of 'God save Queen Elizabeth!' This done, the Archbishop read out the series of promises that make up the oath, and this document was laid before her. Elizabeth kissed the Bible, and picked up the pen.

Given the grandeur of the occasion, it is not surprising that Elizabeth's is not the most confident signature. You can almost see her mind working as she signs. A spurt of ink poured out at the top of the 'E', leaving the quill almost dry for the 'l'. The signature gathers confidence but dissolves the final 'th' into a 't'. She then dips the nib of her pen back into the ink before the final 'R' (for 'Regina', 'Queen', a title that Elizabeth had been using since her father died) is almost carved into the paper.

It is striking how little of the oath itself is concerned with good government. Elizabeth swore that she would govern various countries of the Commonwealth (some of which were to fall away from her rule in the coming decades), then simply swears that: 'I will to my power cause Law and Justice, in Mercy, to execute in all my judgements.'

No, the great bulk of the oath is concerned with religion. Elizabeth swore to 'maintain the Laws of God, and the true profession of the Gospel'; to maintain 'to the utmost of my power' the Protestant Reformed Religion; to 'preserve inviolately' the settlement of the Church of England; to preserve the Bishops and Clergy

Elizabeth R

I solemnly promise and swear to govern the Peoples of the United Kingdom of Great Britain and Northern Ireland, Canada, Australia, New Zealand and the Union of South Africa, Pakistan and Ceylon, and of my Possessions and the other Territories to any of them belonging or pertaining, according to their respective laws and customs.

I will to my power cause Law and Justice, in Mercy, to be executed in all my judgements.

I will to the utmost of my power maintain the Laws of God and the true profession of the Gospel. I will to the utmost of my power maintain in the United Kingdom the Protestant Reformed Religion established by law. And I will maintain and preserve inviolably the settlement of the Church of England, and the doctrine, worship, discipline, and government thereof, as by law established in England. And I will preserve unto the Bishops and Clergy of England, and to the Churches there committed to their charge, all such rights and privileges as by law do or shall appertain to them or any of them.

The things which I have here before promised, I will perform and keep.

So help me God.

OPPOSITE: *The coronation oath, which was first read out by the Archbishop of Canterbury. The Queen laid her right hand on the Bible and swore to uphold the oath, before signing the document.*

*For all that the oath is a throwback to seventeenth-century Protestantism, the promise to uphold 'Reformed Religion' does not mean that the monarch cannot uphold Catholicism as well. When a tradition belongs so obviously to another age, perhaps it is just a reminder of a very long history.*

of the Church, their churches, and 'all such rights and privileges as by law do or shall appertain to them or any other of them'. These were not very current preoccupations, even for 1953. Rather, they are a legacy of the events of 1688.

That was the year of Britain's 'Glorious Revolution'. England had been a Protestant country for around 150 years when in 1685 James II came to the throne. As we saw in the Declaration of Flora MacDonald on page 116, James II promoted Catholicism, which led to political insurgency and eventually to the King being forced to flee the country to be replaced by his Protestant daughter Mary and son-in-law William of Orange. At their coronation, kings and queens of England had long sworn an oath to maintain the laws and customs of the country, but the text was vague and ancient. The men who had persuaded William and Mary to take the crown needed to reassure the nation that their intentions were legitimate. Plus, this was a golden opportunity to make sure that no more Catholics could ascend the throne. Parliament therefore passed the Coronation Oath Act, which obliges all British monarchs to swear an oath in these terms. When Elizabeth swore to uphold 'the Protestant Reformed Religion', it was an oath against James II's Roman Catholicism; on the other hand, the promise to uphold 'the Bishops and Clergy', was a rejection of seventeeth-century Protestant Calvinism, which denied a hierarchy of bishops. Thus the Church of England's middle road was embedded in the State.

Every British monarch since William and Mary has sworn this oath in nearly identical terms – Queen Anne, the four Georges, William IV, Victoria, and on into the twentieth century. As things stand, the next British monarch will have to swear the oath, too. But should the Coronation Oath Act be repealed, or replaced? Should it be replaced by an oath that recognises a wider spread of faiths, or that does not refer to religion at all? Should it be expanded to embed other values or systems – truth, say, or equality and democracy? The Act, and the oath, are oddities from another age. But perhaps that is the very reason why they should stay. Orbs and sceptres are oddities, too. For all that the oath is a throwback to seventeenth-century Protestantism, the promise to uphold 'Reformed Religion' does not mean that the monarch cannot uphold Catholicism as well. When a tradition belongs so obviously to another age, perhaps it is just a reminder of a very long history.

# WINSTON'S COMICS

## Comics Bought for Winston Churchill

# 1955

Left: *'Vampire At The Window', a story from* Black Magic *comic.*

In 1955, waves of filth were sweeping across the Atlantic. British children were exposed to unprecedented levels of depravity – by comics (or, as they were called with a note of British disdain, 'American-style comics'). Those shown here were bought by civil servants for Prime Minister Winston Churchill, to help him assess the extent of the threat.

Comics from America had arrived in Britain as early as the 1890s, but they really gained traction in the 'Golden Age' of comic books, from the late 1930s to the end of the 1940s. Between 1938 and 1941, Superman, Batman, Wonder Woman, the Green Lantern, the Flash and Captain America all appeared for the first time. These superheroes were strong, fine and pure, and invariably triumphed over the forces of evil. They were even co-opted into the war effort. Superheroes fought the Axis powers and the Japanese, regularly clobbering the Führer himself.

Victory in the Second World War meant less need for black-and-white models of moral certainty. Popular English pre-war titles, such as *The Gem* and *The Magnet* (featuring Billy Bunter), were shouldered aside by fresher, cheekier comics, such as the *Dandy* and the *Beano*. In America, the nation turned to crime. By 1947 there were over forty crime titles in circulation, the biggest of which, *Crime Does Not Pay*, outsold both *Superman* and *Captain Marvel*. Their stories revelled in a murky world of gangsters, guns and misdeeds.

In the 1950s a strong push-and-pull developed between a thrill-seeking younger generation and a

Opposite: *The comics bought for Winston Churchill include three Westerns (*Rod Cameron, Casey Ruggles *and* Jesse James*), two Horrors (*Black Magic *and* Frankenstein*), a Crime (*Famous Yank Comics*) and a Superhero (*Captain Marvel*).*

Comics Bought for Winston Churchill

generation who had not fought a war to allow this kind of muck to go on sale. In 1954, there were 132 prosecutions under the Obscene Publications Act. Mickey Spillane's first Mike Hammer novel was banned; *Madame Bovary* was subject to three destruction orders; and in the same year, Dr Fredric Wertham published *Seduction of the Innocent,* which ascribed juvenile delinquency to comic books. Actually, juvenile delinquency wasn't the half of it. According to Dr Wertham, Batman was clearly gay and Robin was his lover. Wonder Woman was a bondage-loving lesbian. Superman was a fascist. The book was a bestseller.

ABOVE: *In* Captain Marvel, *on uttering the word 'Shazam!', young Billy Batson is struck by a lightning bolt and transformed into 'the world's mightiest mortal'.*

*A civil servant was sent out to buy comics for the Prime Minister, and came back with three Westerns, two Horrors, a Superhero and a Crime. One of the Horror titles,* Black Magic, *had been particularly targeted by anti-comics campaigners.*

In the UK, the campaign against comics included a deputation to the Government from the Archbishop of Canterbury and an anti-comics exhibition by the National Union of Teachers. When a private member's bill on comics was threatened, the Government felt that it had to act.

A civil servant was sent out to buy comics for the Prime Minister, and came back with three Westerns, two Horrors, a Superhero and a Crime. One of the Horror titles, *Black Magic,* had been particularly targeted by anti-comics campaigners. The edition shown on page 281 includes a cover story, 'The End of His Rope', about an Indian rope trick, where you age at the top of the rope. Inside, other stories include 'The Sniper', about a soldier helped by a ghost; 'Number 23', about a man obsessed with the number 23; and 'Jack the Ripper', in which the killer emerges from his grave to kill tourists.

The comics include two tales written by Mr Stan Lee, the man who would go on to create Spiderman, the Hulk, Iron Man and the Fantastic Four. Lee wrote 'Sweet Little Old Ladies', about a gangster who hides away in the home of some ladies who turn out to be witches and boil him in a pot, and 'Vampire at the Window', about a detective solving a vampire mystery, who turns out to be a vampire himself. The thought of Winston Churchill reading Stan Lee doesn't seem quite real.

The following year, Parliament passed the Children and Young Persons (Harmful Publications) Act 1955. The Act was aimed squarely at comics, condemning 'stories told in pictures' about the commission of crime, acts of violence or 'incidents of a repulsive or horrible nature' that were likely to fall into the hands of children and which might corrupt them. The offence was punishable by imprisonment for up to four months.

But there was a twist in the Act. To stop overexcited campaigners prosecuting every comic in sight, the Act provided that prosecution could be brought only with the agreement of the Attorney General. This is an old trick for dealing with a nation that is having a fit of the moral vapours, a way for Government to appear to 'Do Something', while curbing the enthusiasm of the crusaders. The Attorney General received numerous referrals, but it was fifteen years before anyone received permission to prosecute. Churchill cannot have been too shocked by what he saw.

# 'I INTENDED *to* FIND DAVID *and* SHOOT HIM'

## Ruth Ellis's Confession

# 1955

RIGHT: *David Blakely and Ruth Ellis, celebrating after a car race. Blakely was spending his inheritance on designing and building sports cars.*
OPPOSITE: *Ruth Ellis's confession.*

**CHAMPAGNE FROM PAPER CUPS**

David Blakely had been placed second in a race. Ruth Ellis ran to him, with a bottle of champagne. "He kissed me in front of everyone," she says. "The champagne foamed over the car. David shouted: 'What a christening, darling!' We drank out of paper cups."

**Chunk of bread started triangle**

CHUNK of bread Blakely, Ruth Ellis and it sailed across a Desmond Cussen.

RUTH ELLIS SIGNED this confession less than three hours after she had murdered her lover. Three months later she would be hanged for the crime. She was the last woman executed for murder in the United Kingdom, and her execution would lead to international protests and major changes in the law. The two sides to Ellis – on the one hand, a naïve and confused young woman, on the other, a determined and efficient killer – are laid bare in this vivid testimony.

Ellis's life had been a pattern of abuse. Her family moved around regularly in search of work for her father, and to stay one step ahead of questions about his treatment of Ellis and her sister. By the age of fifteen, she had escaped into wartime London, working in factories and taking waitressing jobs, and at seventeen she had her first child, Andy, by a French Canadian soldier who abandoned her before the birth. At twenty-four, she married an alcoholic dentist, by whom she had a second child. He too abandoned her before the child's birth. But Ellis was more than just a victim. Vivacious and fun, with the peroxide blonde curls of a Hollywood starlet, she was both a good-time girl and an ambitious and capable organiser. Maurice Conley, a London vice merchant, appointed her manageress of the Little Club on the Brompton Road, above which she lived in a rented flat. It was at another of Conley's clubs, in August 1953, that Ellis first met David Blakely.

Blakely was, in the words of one his associates, a 'good-looking, well-educated, supercilious shit'. Three years Ellis's junior, he was in the process of squandering a modest inheritance on a grand plan to design and build sports cars with his friend Anthony Findlater. Blakely moved in with Ellis within two weeks of their meeting. In her confession, the words 'I started to live with him' are crossed out and replaced with 'he started to live with me'. The order of events was important to Ellis. The flat was hers. Blakely was the sponger.

METROPOLITAN POLICE **STATEMENT OF WITNESS** No. 992

Hampstead Station. "S" Divn. 11th April, 1955.

Name Ruth Ellis (Mrs) Age 9.10.26

Address 44, Egerton Gardens, Kensington W.14.

Occupation Model.

Statement I have been cautioned that I am not obliged to say anything unless I wish to do so, and that anything I do say will be taken down in writing and may be given in evidence.

Ruth Ellis

I understand what has been said. "I am guilty". I am rather confused." About two years ago I met David Blakeley when I was manageress of The Little Club, Knightsbridge, my flat was above that. I had known him for about a fortnight when ~~I started~~ RE ~~to live with him and~~ he started to live with me and has done so continuously until last year when he went away to Le Mans for about three weeks motor racing. He came back to me and remained living with me until Good Friday morning. He left me about ten o'clock a.m. and promised to be back by eight p.m. to take me out. I waited until half past nine and

Signature Ruth Ellis, Signature witnessed by L. Gill Det Insp. "S"

Use both sides if necessary. (If this is done, *both* sides of the form must be signed and witnessed).

2.

he had not phoned although he always had done in the past. I was rather worried at that stage as he had had trouble with his racing car and had been drinking. I rang some friends of his named Findlater at Hampstead but they told me he was not there although David had told me he was visiting them. I was speaking to Mr Findlater and I asked if David was all right. He laughed and said, "Oh yes he's all right". I did not believe he was not there and I took a taxi to Hampstead where I saw David's car outside Findlaters flat at 28 Tanza Road. I then telephoned from nearby and when my voice was recognised they hung up on me. I went to the flat and continually rang the door bell but they would not answer. I became very furious and went to David's car which was still standing there and pushed in three of the side windows. The noise I made must have aroused the Findlaters as the Police came along and spoke to me. Mr Findlater came out of his flat and the Police also spoke to him. David did not come home on Saturday and at

Signature Ruth Ellis    Signature witnessed by P.G. Gill Det Inspr S

Use both sides if necessary. (If this is done, *both* sides of the form must be signed and witnessed).

M.P.-48635/200,000 Jan./1953 G25 (4)

Continuation of Statement of ......

nine o'clock ...
phoned Findl...
Findlater ans...
"I hope you a...
holiday" and ...
you have ru...
banged the ...
all day tod...
to phone but ...
About eight ...
I put my ...
I then took a ...
hidden and ...
This gun was ...
years ago in ...
name I do ...
security for mo...
a curiosity ...
was loaded ...
but I knew ...
looked at it. ...
in my bag ...
and shoot ...
to Tanza Roa...
David's car ...
address. ...
and walked ...
the nearest ...

Signature Ruth Ellis

Use both sides if necessary. (If this is ...

Above and opposite: *Ruth Ellis's confession (starting on page 285) was made in the early hours of Easter Sunday, 1955, less than three hours after the killing. The words 'I intended to find David and shoot him' (third page) meant that she would be tried for murder.*

Ellis and Blakely's troubled relationship was a creature of mid-1950s London. It was a time of racy living, hard drinking and jazz clubs, pulled by a criminal undertow. It was also a time of strong class barriers. Blakely told Ellis that he loved her, but there was never a chance that this middle-class boy would marry a brassy, working-class girl like Ellis. Once, when the couple were out near Blakely's family home in Buckinghamshire, Blakely kept Ellis in the car and brought her drinks from the pub, rather than risk their bumping into his mother. Blakely appealed to Ellis's aspirations to improve herself while viciously scratching at her insecurities.

The relationship was highly sexual and increasingly violent. Both carried bruises from drink-fuelled rows. Blakely would disappear for days and Ellis would stalk his old haunts, convinced he was seeing other women. In March 1955, Ellis discovered

No. 993

Ellis (Mrs)
orning (Sunday) I
again and Mr.
I said to him,
ving an enjoyable
about to say, "Because
mine" and he
down. I waited
Sunday) for David
id not do so.
this evening (Sunday)
Andria to bed.
which I had had
t in my handbag
me about three
flat by a man whose
member. It was
t I accepted it as
did not know it
t was given to me
morning when I
en I put the gun
tended to find David
I took a taxi
nd as I arrived
away from Findlaters
missed the taxi
down the road to
here I saw David's

Signature witnessed by P.G. Gill Det Insp "S"

s of the form must be signed and witnessed).

993

Continuation of Statement of Ruth Ellis (Mrs)

car outside. I waited outside until he came out with a friend I know as Clive. David went to his car door to open it. I was a little way away from him. He turned and saw me and then turned away from me and I took the gun from my bag and I shot him. He turned round and ran a few steps round the car. I thought I had missed him so I fired again. He was still running and I fired the third shot. I don't remember firing any more but I must have done. I remember then he was lying on the footway and I was standing beside him. He was bleeding badly and it seemed ages before an ambulance came. I remember a man came up and I said, "will you call the Police and an ambulance?" He said "I am a Policeman." I said "Please take this gun and arrest me." This statement has been read over to me and it is true. Ruth Ellis

Statement written down and read over by Det. Gill Detective Inspector "S" in the presence of Det. Supt Crawford and Det Chief Inspector Davies

Signature

Signature witnessed by

Use both sides if necessary. (If this is done, *both* sides of the form must be signed and witnessed).
M.P.-51917/30,000 Apr./1954 G28 (4)

she was pregnant. Blakely punched her in the belly, causing her to miscarry, and then left to go racing at Le Mans. He returned shortly before Easter. On Good Friday, Blakely left in the morning to visit the Findlaters in Hampstead, promising to be back in the evening. When he didn't show, Ellis was incensed. She went first to the Findlaters' home, then tracked David down to a local pub. Ellis's confession explains what happened next.

*When I put the gun in my bag I intended to find David and shoot him … I was a little way away from him. He turned and saw me and then turned away from me and I took the gun from my bag and I shot him. He turned around and ran a few steps around the car. I thought I had missed him so I fired again. He was still running and I fired the third shot. I don't remember firing any more but I must have done. I remember then he was lying on the footway and I was standing beside him. He was bleeding badly and it seemed ages before an ambulance came. I remember a man came up and I said, 'will you call the Police and an ambulance?' He said 'I am a Policeman'. I said 'Please take this gun and arrest me'. This statement has been read over to me and it is true.*

Tel. No.: WHItehall 8100

...xt.

...ommunication on the ...of this letter should be addressed to :—

THE UNDER SECRETARY OF STATE,
Home Office, London, S.W.1.

and the following number quoted :
CCS 600/1

Your Ref.

18E

201

HOME OFFICE,
WHITEHALL.

11th July, 1955

Sir,

I am directed by the Secretary of State to inform you that, having given careful consideration to the case of Ruth Ellis, now lying under sentence of death in Holloway Prison, he has failed to discover any sufficient ground to justify him in advising Her Majesty to interfere with the due course of law.

I am, Sir,

Your obedient Servant,

F. A. Newsam

The Commissioner of Police
of the Metropolis,
New Scotland Yard,
S.W.1.

16

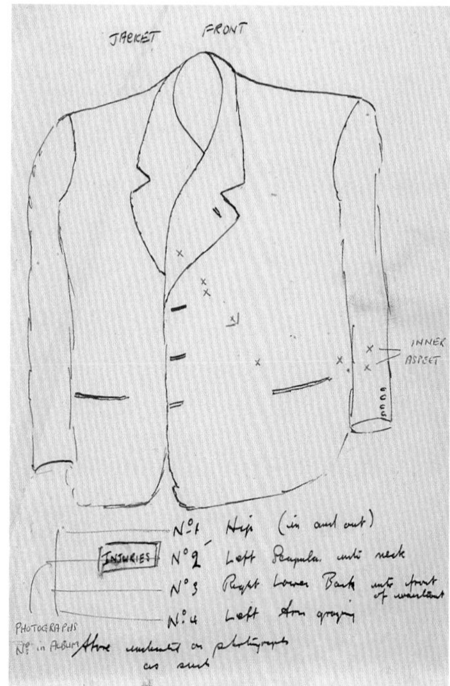


ABOVE: *Police drawing of Blakely's jacket, showing the entry points of the bullets.*

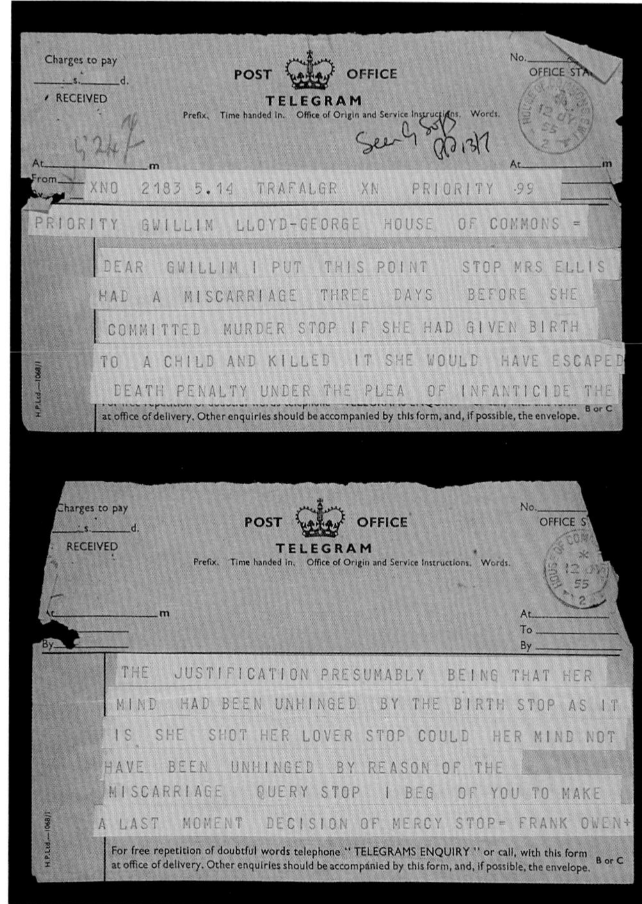

Charges to pay
s. d.
RECEIVED

POST OFFICE
TELEGRAM

Prefix. Time handed in. Office of Origin and Service Instructions. Words.

From XNO 2183 5.14 TRAFALGR XN PRIORITY 99

PRIORITY GWILLIM LLOYD-GEORGE HOUSE OF COMMONS =

DEAR GWILLIM I PUT THIS POINT STOP MRS ELLIS HAD A MISCARRIAGE THREE DAYS BEFORE SHE COMMITTED MURDER STOP IF SHE HAD GIVEN BIRTH TO A CHILD AND KILLED IT SHE WOULD HAVE ESCAPED DEATH PENALTY UNDER THE PLEA OF INFANTICIDE THE

at office of delivery. Other enquiries should be accompanied by this form, and, if possible, the envelope.

Charges to pay
s. d.
RECEIVED

POST OFFICE
TELEGRAM

Prefix. Time handed in. Office of Origin and Service Instructions. Words.

THE JUSTIFICATION PRESUMABLY BEING THAT HER MIND HAD BEEN UNHINGED BY THE BIRTH STOP AS IT IS SHE SHOT HER LOVER STOP COULD HER MIND NOT HAVE BEEN UNHINGED BY REASON OF THE MISCARRIAGE QUERY STOP I BEG OF YOU TO MAKE A LAST MOMENT DECISION OF MERCY STOP= FRANK OWEN+

For free repetition of doubtful words telephone "TELEGRAMS ENQUIRY" or call, with this form at office of delivery. Other enquiries should be accompanied by this form, and, if possible, the envelope.

ABOVE: *This telegram to the Home Secretary argues passionately that Ellis's recent miscarriage, caused by Blakely and not taken into account at her sentencing, should be grounds for mercy.*

OPPOSITE: *Letter written on behalf of the Home Secretary, refusing a reprieve. The Government had recently been re-elected on a manifesto that favoured the death penalty.*

The statement was given in the early hours of Easter morning at Hampstead Police Station, less than a mile from the killing. The damning admission from Ellis – that 'when I put the gun in my bag I intended to find David and shoot him' – meant that the killing was premeditated, not accidental or spur-of-the-moment. The moment she signed against those words, there was little chance that Ellis would escape a murder charge.

But there is a lie running through the statement. Donald Cussen was a middle-aged businessman who had met Ellis in the clubs, and had become infatuated with her. Cussen bankrolled Ellis, and became her shoulder to cry on. Cussen came to hate Blakely. And it was Cussen who had given Ellis the gun, Cussen who had shown her how to cock and fire it, and Cussen who drove Ellis to Hampstead on the night of the killing. But Ellis makes no mention of the man who set her up to do this. Ellis is being manipulated by men, even in her confession.

Under English law at the time, there were only four defences to murder: innocence, insanity, provocation and self-defence. The determined premeditation of the crime meant that none of these defences was available

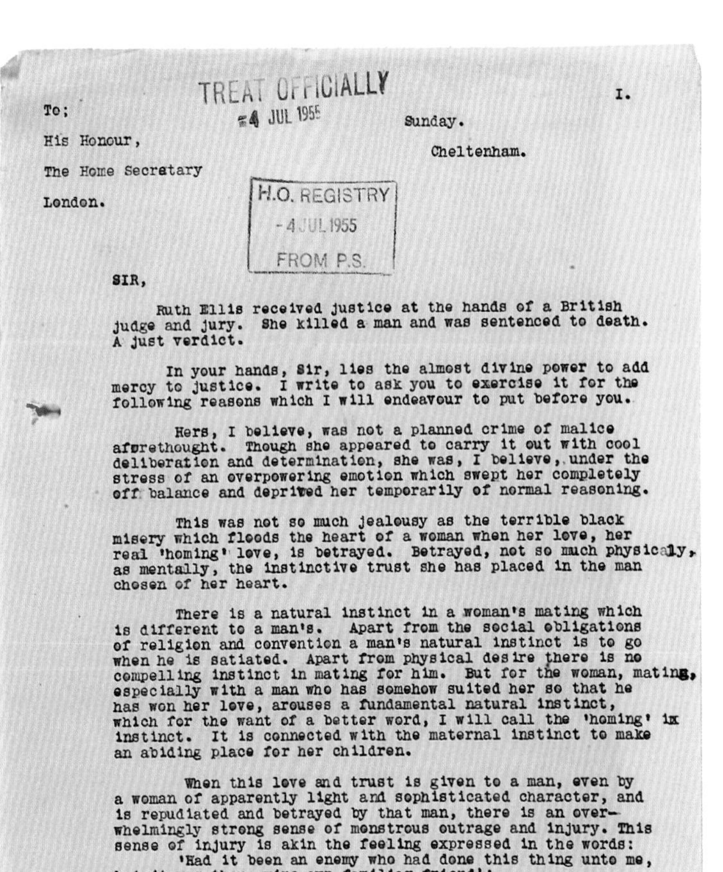

TREAT OFFICIALLY
4 JUL 1955

To;

His Honour,

The Home Secretary

London.

I.

Sunday.

Cheltenham.

H.O. REGISTRY
-4 JUL 1955
FROM P.S.

SIR,

Ruth Ellis received justice at the hands of a British judge and jury. She killed a man and was sentenced to death. A just verdict.

In your hands, Sir, lies the almost divine power to add mercy to justice. I write to ask you to exercise it for the following reasons which I will endeavour to put before you.

Hers, I believe, was not a planned crime of malice aforethought. Though she appeared to carry it out with cool deliberation and determination, she was, I believe, under the stress of an overpowering emotion which swept her completely off balance and deprived her temporarily of normal reasoning.

This was not so much jealousy as the terrible black misery which floods the heart of a woman when her love, her real 'homing' love, is betrayed. Betrayed, not so much physically, as mentally, the instinctive trust she has placed in the man chosen of her heart.

There is a natural instinct in a woman's mating which is different to a man's. Apart from the social obligations of religion and convention a man's natural instinct is to go when he is satiated. Apart from physical desire there is no compelling instinct in mating for him. But for the woman, mating, especially with a man who has somehow suited her so that he has won her love, arouses a fundamental natural instinct, which for the want of a better word, I will call the 'homing' ix instinct. It is connected with the maternal instinct to make an abiding place for her children.

When this love and trust is given to a man, even by a woman of apparently light and sophisticated character, and is repudiated and betrayed by that man, there is an overwhelmingly strong sense of monstrous outrage and injury. This sense of injury is akin the feeling expressed in the words:
'Had it been an enemy who had done this thing unto me, but it was thou, mine own familiar friend!'

I believe that it was this tremendous sense of out-

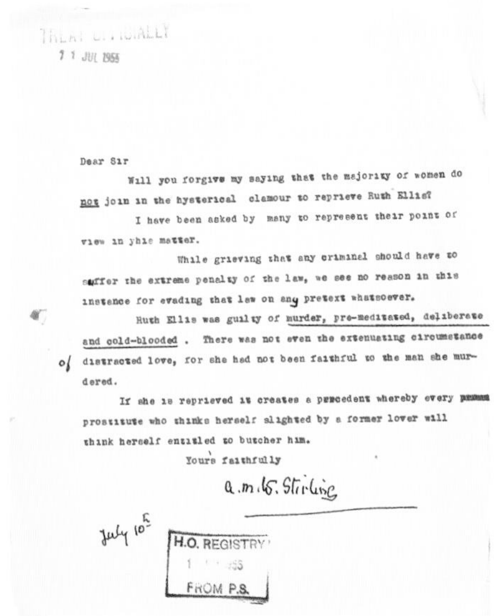

TREAT OFFICIALLY
11 JUL 1955

Dear Sir

Will you forgive my saying that the majority of women do not join in the hysterical clamour to reprieve Ruth Ellis?

I have been asked by many to represent their point of view in yhis matter.

While grieving that any criminal should have to suffer the extreme penalty of the law, we see no reason in this instance for evading that law on any pretext whatsoever.

Ruth Ellis was guilty of murder, pre-meditated, deliberate and cold-blooded . There was not even the extenuating circumstance of distracted love, for she had not been faithful to the man she murdered.

If she is reprieved it creates a precedent whereby every prostitute who thinks herself slighted by a former lover will think herself entitled to butcher him.

Yours faithfully

A. M. W. Stirling

July 10th

H.O. REGISTRY
1 [illegible] 1955
FROM P.S.

LEFT AND ABOVE: *The public was strongly divided about Ellis, and the Home Office was deluged with letters arguing both for and against a reprieve.*

to Ellis. Her trial lasted just a day and half, and none of the mitigating details – her miscarriage, Cussen's involvement – emerged. The 'blonde tart' (as someone shouted from the Public Gallery) was presented as a cold killer, who had finished off Blakely at point-blank range. The jury took less than half an hour to find her guilty. The judge drew a black cap on to his head, and sentenced her to be hanged.

The prospect of executing a mother of two for a *crime passionel* prompted a deluge of protest at home and abroad, and many letters urging clemency are preserved in the National Archives. It is striking that although polls in the UK have for decades shown a majority in favour of the death penalty, surveys at the time showed a majority against killing Ellis. But the Government had recently been re-elected on a pro-death-penalty platform, and was in no mood to grant a reprieve. Ellis was executed at 9 a.m. on 13 July. Her body was buried inside Holloway Prison.

Ellis's death had some important consequences. The following year, a new defence to murder was introduced, of 'diminished responsibility', an abnormal and temporary state of mind caused by a series of damaging events, which reduces a murder charge. Ten years later, the death penalty was suspended. Fifteen years later, it was abolished altogether.

# MADE *in* DAGENHAM

## Letter and Telegram to Harold Wilson

## 1965

RIGHT: *Caught in the cross-fire – Harold Wilson, British Prime Minister and Labour Party leader.*

POOR HAROLD WILSON. In June 1965, these two screaming documents hit his desk. One was from a group of furious women; the other was from a panicking man. It must have felt like sitting in a wind-tunnel. On 7 June 1968, 187 women workers at the Ford Motor Company's factory in Dagenham, Essex, went on strike. The women were sewing machinists, who produced seat covers for Ford Cortinas. Ford had proposed a new pay scale at the factory, under which the women would be paid just 85 per cent of the wages of men on the same grade. The women objected. Ford's management told them to do their worst. The women walked out.

The strike quickly hit the national news, and the Labour Government tried to intervene. It convened a Court of Inquiry to examine the strikers' demands, under the chairmanship of Sir Jack Scamp. The court recommended that Ford should undertake an internal review of their pay scales. But the internal review simply confirmed that the women's pay rates should stay where they were. The system was rigged.

The letter is sent by the 'Woman workers of Fords of Dagenham' and is not signed by any individual. These were friends, women from the same part of town, united in fury and defiance. Harold Wilson may have been Prime Minister, but that wasn't going to stop the women of Dagenham telling him how it was:

*Dear Mr Wilson,*

*You can call all the enquiries you wish, we women at Fords have the backing of a great number of MPs, we will not go back to work, we are fighting a great fight equal pay for women, we at Fords have started the ball rolling our Unions are backing us, funds are coming in we are all set for battle, Fords is the beginning, soon it will be every industry in Britain out because of us women of Fords, we will force you to give us all equal pay, or strike with our Union's blessings, we're sorry for Fords, sorry for the men out of work, but more sorry for ourselves its all for us now. Some women may be hard up we'll help them from our growing funds, make no mistake most of us have husbands still working, that's why we can fight you all, we are only our own money short, we will live. Give us what we want, not only us at Fords all Women everywhere, we refuse to go back, so what can you and the Government and Mrs Castle* [Barbara Castle, see below] *& Jack Scamp do. Nothing I mean nothing, we are sitting pretty, our Unions are backing us. Show this to Barbara, we don't care MPs are with us, soon everyone will be with us we will make Fords shut down completly, who cares, we don't.*

*Woman Workers at Fords of Dagenham*

*Give us what our Unions demand equal pay*

① N.A Women Workers of Fords.

② P 24/6 - Press Office June - 1968.

Dear Mr Wilson, urgently

You can call all the enquiries you wish, we woman at Fords have the backing of a great number of M.P'S, we will not go back to work, we are fighting a great fight equal pay for women, we at Fords have started the ball rolling our unions are backing us, funds are coming in were all set for battle, Fords is the begining, soon it will be every industry in Britain out because of us women of Fords, we will force you to give us all equal pay, or strike with our unions

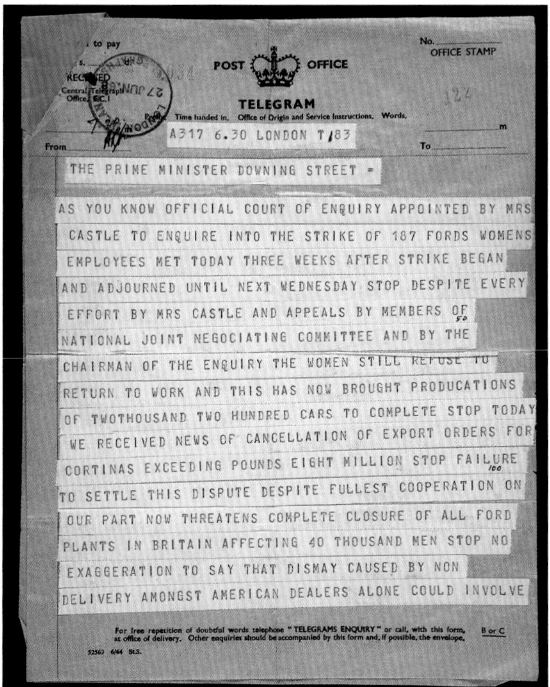

POST OFFICE TELEGRAM

A317 6.30 LONDON T/83

THE PRIME MINISTER DOWNING STREET =

AS YOU KNOW OFFICIAL COURT OF ENQUIRY APPOINTED BY MRS CASTLE TO ENQUIRE INTO THE STRIKE OF 187 FORDS WOMENS EMPLOYEES MET TODAY THREE WEEKS AFTER STRIKE BEGAN AND ADJOURNED UNTIL NEXT WEDNESDAY STOP DESPITE EVERY EFFORT BY MRS CASTLE AND APPEALS BY MEMBERS OF NATIONAL JOINT NEGOCIATING COMMITTEE AND BY THE CHAIRMAN OF THE ENQUIRY THE WOMEN STILL REFUSE TO RETURN TO WORK AND THIS HAS NOW BROUGHT PRODUCATIONS OF TWOTHOUSAND TWO HUNDRED CARS TO COMPLETE STOP TODAY WE RECEIVED NEWS OF CANCELLATION OF EXPORT ORDERS FOR CORTINAS EXCEEDING POUNDS EIGHT MILLION STOP FAILURE TO SETTLE THIS DISPUTE DESPITE FULLEST COOPERATION ON OUR PART NOW THREATENS COMPLETE CLOSURE OF ALL FORD PLANTS IN BRITAIN AFFECTING 40 THOUSAND MEN STOP NO EXAGGERATION TO SAY THAT DISMAY CAUSED BY NON DELIVERY AMONGST AMERICAN DEALERS ALONE COULD INVOLVE

For free repetition of doubtful words telephone "TELEGRAMS ENQUIRY" or call, with this form, at office of delivery. Other enquiries should be accompanied by this form and, if possible, the envelope.

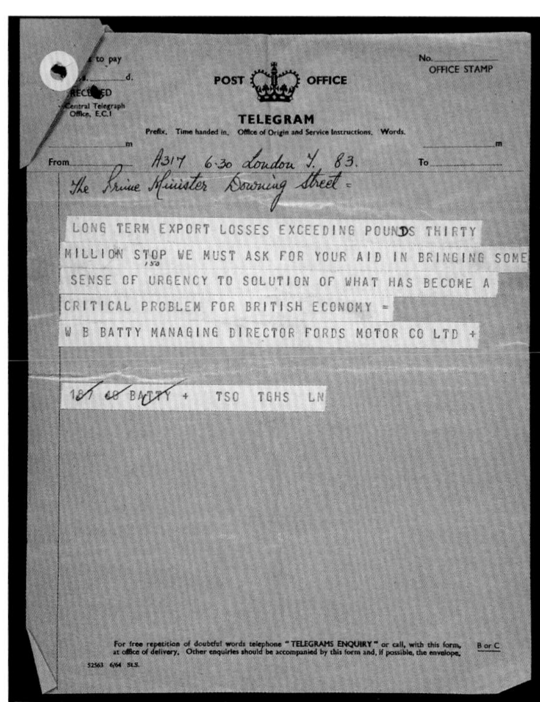

POST OFFICE TELEGRAM

A317 6.30 London T. 83.

The Prime Minister Downing Street =

LONG TERM EXPORT LOSSES EXCEEDING POUNDS THIRTY MILLION STOP WE MUST ASK FOR YOUR AID IN BRINGING SOME SENSE OF URGENCY TO SOLUTION OF WHAT HAS BECOME A CRITICAL PROBLEM FOR BRITISH ECONOMY =

W B BATTY MANAGING DIRECTOR FORDS MOTOR CO LTD +

187 60 BATTY + TSO TGHS LN

For free repetition of doubtful words telephone "TELEGRAMS ENQUIRY" or call, with this form, at office of delivery. Other enquiries should be accompanied by this form and, if possible, the envelope.

OPPOSITE: *First page of the letter to Harold Wilson from the women workers of Ford's.*

ABOVE AND ABOVE RIGHT: *Telegram to the Prime Minister from Ford UK's Managing Director, William Batty.*

Harold Wilson was getting it from both sides. The telegram shown was received on 27 June 1968 from the managing director of Ford UK:

AS YOU KNOW OFFICIAL COURT OF ENQUIRY APPOINTED BY MRS CASTLE TO ENQUIRE INTO THE STRIKE OF 187 FORD'S WOMENS EMPLOYEES MET TODAY THREE WEEKS AFTER STRIKE BEGAN AND ADJOURNED UNTIL NEXT WEDNESDAY STOP DESPITE EVERY EFFORT BY MRS CASTLE AND APPEALS BY MEMBERS OF NATIONAL JOINT NEGOCIATING COMMITTEE AND BY THE CHAIRMAN OF THE ENQUIRY THE WOMEN STILL REFUSE TO RETURN TO WORK AND THIS HAS NOW BROUGHT PRODUCATIONS OF TWO THOUSAND TWO HUNDRED CARS TO COMPLETE STOP TODAY WE RECEIVED NEWS OF CANCELLATION OF EXPORT ORDERS FOR CORTINAS EXCEEDING POUNDS EIGHT MILLION STOP FAILURE TO SETTLE THIS DISPUTE DESPITE FULLEST CO-OPERATION ON OUR PART NOW THREATENS COMPLETE CLOSURE OF ALL FORD PLANTS IN BRITAIN AFFECTING 40 THOUSAND MEN STOP NO EXAGGERATION TO SAY THAT DISMAY CAUSED BY NON-DELIVERY AMONGST AMERICAN DEALERS ALONE COULD INVOLVE LONG-TERM EXPORT LOSSES EXCEEDING POUNDS THIRTY MILLION STOP WE MUST ASK FOR YOUR AID IN BRINGING SOME SENSE OF URGENCY TO SOLUTION OF WHAT HAS BECOME A CRITICAL PROBLEM FOR BRITISH ECONOMY – W B BATTY MANAGING DIRECTOR FORDS MOTOR CO LTD

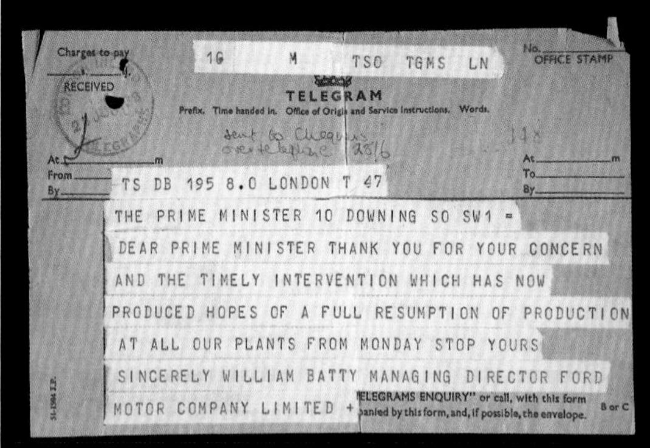

TELEGRAM

16 M TSO TGMS LN

TS DB 195 8.0 LONDON T 47

THE PRIME MINISTER 10 DOWNING SQ SW1 =
DEAR PRIME MINISTER THANK YOU FOR YOUR CONCERN
AND THE TIMELY INTERVENTION WHICH HAS NOW
PRODUCED HOPES OF A FULL RESUMPTION OF PRODUCTION
AT ALL OUR PLANTS FROM MONDAY STOP YOURS
SINCERELY WILLIAM BATTY MANAGING DIRECTOR FORD
MOTOR COMPANY LIMITED +

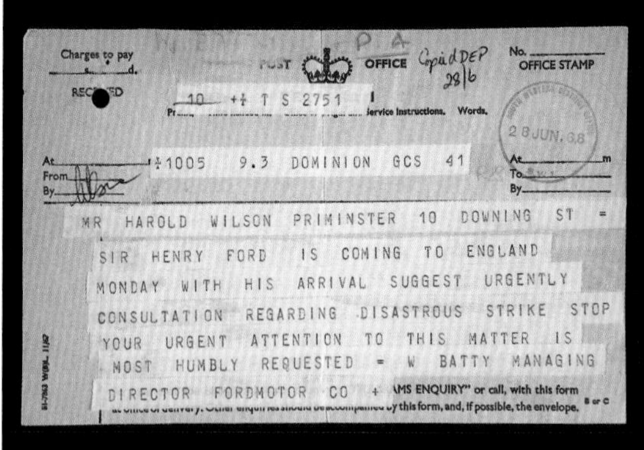

POST OFFICE

10 +½ T S 2751

÷1005 9.3 DOMINION GCS 41

MR HAROLD WILSON PRIMINSTER 10 DOWNING ST =
SIR HENRY FORD IS COMING TO ENGLAND
MONDAY WITH HIS ARRIVAL SUGGEST URGENTLY
CONSULTATION REGARDING DISASTROUS STRIKE STOP
YOUR URGENT ATTENTION TO THIS MATTER IS
MOST HUMBLY REQUESTED = W BATTY MANAGING
DIRECTOR FORDMOTOR CO +

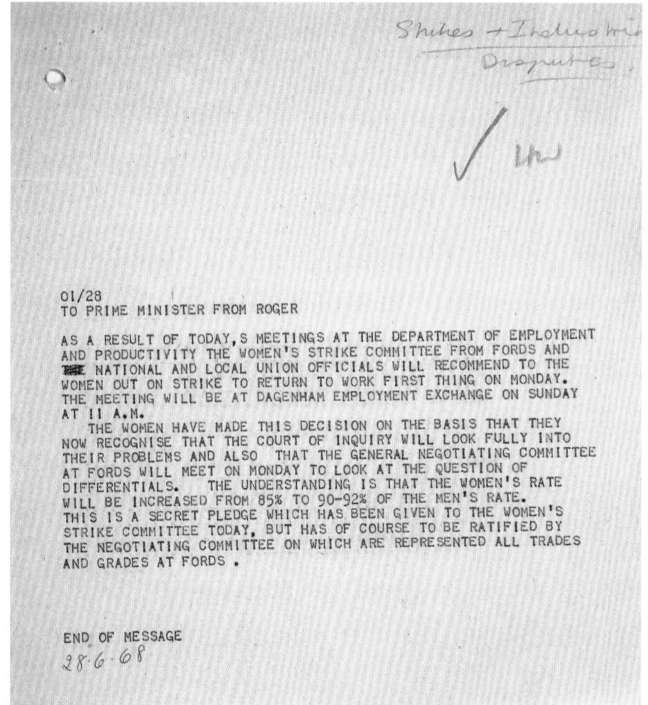

Strikes + Industrial Disputes

01/28
TO PRIME MINISTER FROM ROGER

AS A RESULT OF TODAY,S MEETINGS AT THE DEPARTMENT OF EMPLOYMENT AND PRODUCTIVITY THE WOMEN'S STRIKE COMMITTEE FROM FORDS AND THE NATIONAL AND LOCAL UNION OFFICIALS WILL RECOMMEND TO THE WOMEN OUT ON STRIKE TO RETURN TO WORK FIRST THING ON MONDAY. THE MEETING WILL BE AT DAGENHAM EMPLOYMENT EXCHANGE ON SUNDAY AT 11 A.M.

THE WOMEN HAVE MADE THIS DECISION ON THE BASIS THAT THEY NOW RECOGNISE THAT THE COURT OF INQUIRY WILL LOOK FULLY INTO THEIR PROBLEMS AND ALSO THAT THE GENERAL NEGOTIATING COMMITTEE AT FORDS WILL MEET ON MONDAY TO LOOK AT THE QUESTION OF DIFFERENTIALS. THE UNDERSTANDING IS THAT THE WOMEN'S RATE WILL BE INCREASED FROM 85% TO 90-92% OF THE MEN'S RATE. THIS IS A SECRET PLEDGE WHICH HAS BEEN GIVEN TO THE WOMEN'S STRIKE COMMITTEE TODAY, BUT HAS OF COURSE TO BE RATIFIED BY THE NEGOTIATING COMMITTEE ON WHICH ARE REPRESENTED ALL TRADES AND GRADES AT FORDS .

END OF MESSAGE
28.6.68

ABOVE RIGHT: *William Batty was particularly anxious because of an impending visit to England by Henry Ford, grandson of the company's founder.*
ABOVE LEFT AND LEFT: *Expressions of relief that the dispute had been resolved and the strike was over.*

It would take a woman to resolve the strike. Barbara Castle was Secretary of State for Employment and Productivity. The strikers saw her as one of them – in their letter, she is simply 'Barbara'. Castle invited the women to tea in her office. She dismissed the men present, and then opened the drinks cabinet. She also went to work on Ford's mulish management. A tiny compromise was reached, which allowed Mr Batty to save face: an immediate 8 per cent pay increase, and parity with the men the following year. The women went back to work, triumphant.

Although this was a local strike, you can see from this letter that the women had a wider mission, 'a great fight for equal pay for women'. The following year, a rally was held in central London to demand equal pay. The year after that, the Equal Pay Act 1970 was passed, sponsored by Castle. The Act prohibited inequality in pay and conditions between men and women. It was a good day for angry letters.

# *The* TRUTH *is in* HERE
## The British X-Files

# 1981

*What does all this stuff about flying saucers amount to? What can it mean? What is the Truth?*

WINSTON CHURCHILL, personal minute, July 1952

ABOVE: *Photograph taken by the US Air Force of the clearing in Rendlesham Forest where a UFO had been spotted. The UFO was reported to be triangular, two or three metres tall, with a red light pulsing on its top and blue lights underneath. At the site, branches had been torn off trees and higher-than-normal levels of radiation were found.*

LIGHTS IN THE SKY. Men in black. Crop circles. Alien visitors. All these phenomena and more are recorded in these reports, submitted to the Government, of unidentified flying objects and other strange happenings – the British 'X-Files'. They include a report of one of the most famous events in UFO history – the Rendlesham Forest Incident.

Tales of unidentified flying objects peak at times of national anxiety. The Government's files start shortly before the First World War, when the country was on the lookout for German Zeppelins. People were watching the skies again during the Second World War, when another spike in UFO sightings occurred, and again during the Cold War years, amid fears of Russian attack. The highest number of reported sightings came in the late 1970s and early 1980s. In 1978, Steven Spielberg's *Close Encounters Of The Third Kind* was released in the UK, with its eerie tale of alien contact. The number of UFO sightings reported in the UK increased to 750, almost double the previous year's figure.

The report on the famous incident was written by Lieutenant Colonel Charles Halt, a senior officer stationed at a US Air Force complex in Rendlesham Forest, near the Suffolk coast. In the early hours of 26 December 1980 (in his report, Halt was a day out), a security patrol saw strange lights outside the back gate of the complex and went to investigate. They found the forest illuminated by a metallic, triangular object, two or three metres high. A red light pulsed on its top, blue lights beneath. They thought that the object was either hovering, or standing on legs. As the patrol approached, it quickly escaped between the trees.

The next day, higher than expected levels of radiation were found at the spot where the UFO had been seen, together with torn branches and depressions in the ground. And that night, the lights were back.

Lieutenant Colonel Halt led a small team into the forest to investigate. He took with him a small tape recorder, and recorded a vivid blow-by-blow account of what they saw (you can hear it yourself by searching for 'Rendlesham Halt tape' on the internet). Having scouted the landing site, they saw the pulsing object

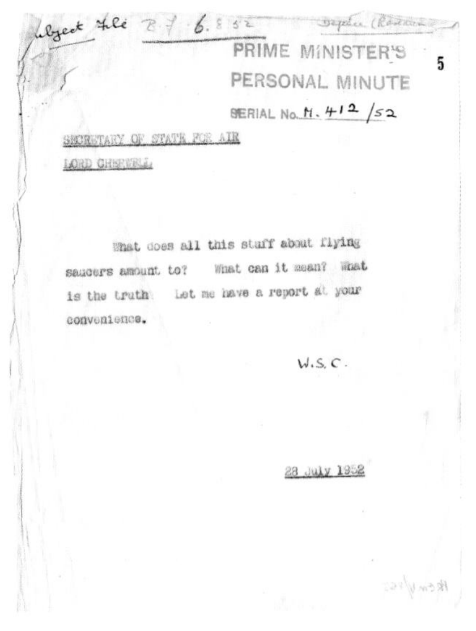

PRIME MINISTER'S PERSONAL MINUTE 5

SERIAL No. M. 412 /52

SECRETARY OF STATE FOR AIR

LORD CHERWELL

What does all this stuff about flying saucers amount to? What can it mean? What is the truth? Let me have a report at your convenience.

W.S.C.

28 July 1952

ABOVE: *A 1952 memorandum from Prime Minister Winston Churchill, baffled by the UFO reports.*

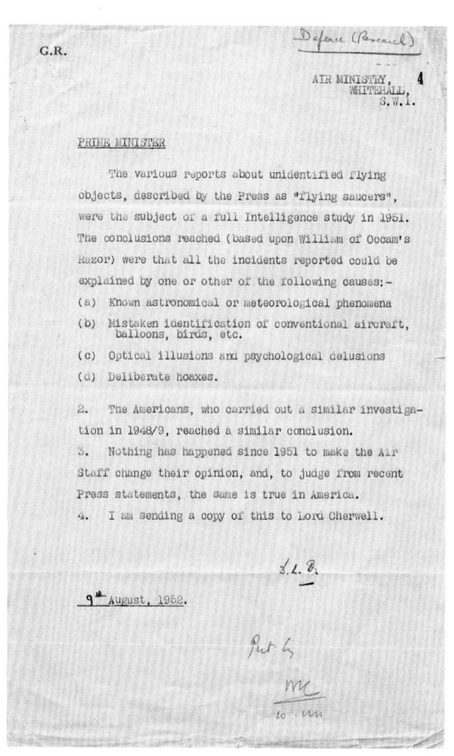

G.R.

Defence (Research)

AIR MINISTRY, 4
WHITEHALL,
S.W.1.

PRIME MINISTER

The various reports about unidentified flying objects, described by the Press as "flying saucers", were the subject of a full Intelligence study in 1951. The conclusions reached (based upon William of Occam's Razor) were that all the incidents reported could be explained by one or other of the following causes:-

(a) Known astronomical or meteorological phenomena
(b) Mistaken identification of conventional aircraft, balloons, birds, etc.
(c) Optical illusions and psychological delusions
(d) Deliberate hoaxes.

2. The Americans, who carried out a similar investigation in 1948/9, reached a similar conclusion.
3. Nothing has happened since 1951 to make the Air Staff change their opinion, and, to judge from recent Press statements, the same is true in America.
4. I am sending a copy of this to Lord Cherwell.

9th August, 1952.

LEFT: *The response to the Prime Minister's question. The tone is helpful, but weary.* OPPOSITE: *Report of the incident by Lt Col Charles Halt. Did he see a meteor shower? A lighthouse? Or did he see flying objects that cannot be identified?*

again through the trees. It seemed to move towards them, and then smaller lights rolled off it. Other lights joined them in the sky; half-moon lights became full moons; the horizon was scattered with red, green and blue lights; a beam of light appeared to be focused towards the ground.

The impression on the tape is of a man stumbling around the woods in the dark, who has gotten himself thoroughly spooked. The memo is altogether more sober. It was written two weeks later, on the advice of the base commander, who felt that the incident had to be reported to the UK Ministry of Defence (MoD). The National Archives' files show that MoD officials were curious but sceptical, attributing the lights to US military manoeuvres, beams from the nearby Orford Ness Lighthouse, lights used by poachers, or bright stars. Boringly, they may have been right: there was a meteor shower on 26 December, low, bright stars, and beams from the lighthouse were in the group's line of sight. Nevertheless, the airmen claim to this day that what they saw was genuine.

UFOs always cause huge excitement. Quite right too, since there is no doubt that they exist – in the sense that, when you put aside sightings that can be attributed to unusual cloud patterns, weather balloons and the like, there remain sightings, by reliable witnesses, of flying objects that have not been identified. The real question for each sighting is not whether the UFO exists – but what is it?

And the British X-Files, far from helping answer the question, have rather taken the wind out of it. For decades, the British Government refused to reveal these reports, so, of course, it was engaged in a cover-up. It held top-secret files that would reveal the truth, but when these files were made public in the mid-2000s, the event was an anticlimax. Hundreds, indeed thousands, of UFO sightings had been reported, but they were no different in character from other well-known sightings. The civil servants who dealt with UFO reports come across rather sweetly – less men-in-black, more mildly irritated at having to deal with this stuff.

DEPARTMENT OF THE AIR FORCE
HEADQUARTERS 81ST COMBAT SUPPORT GROUP (USAFE)
APO NEW YORK 09755

REPLY TO ATTN OF: CD

13 Jan 81

SUBJECT: Unexplained Lights

TO: RAF/CC

1. Early in the morning of 27 Dec 80 (approximately 0300L), two USAF security police patrolmen saw unusual lights outside the back gate at RAF Woodbridge. Thinking an aircraft might have crashed or been forced down, they called for permission to go outside the gate to investigate. The on-duty flight chief responded and allowed three patrolmen to proceed on foot. The individuals reported seeing a strange glowing object in the forest. The object was described as being metalic in appearance and triangular in shape, approximately two to three meters across the base and approximately two meters high. It illuminated the entire forest with a white light. The object itself had a pulsing red light on top and a bank(s) of blue lights underneath. The object was hovering or on legs. As the patrolmen approached the object, it maneuvered through the trees and disappeared. At this time the animals on a nearby farm went into a frenzy. The object was briefly sighted approximately an hour later near the back gate.

2. The next day, three depressions 1 1/2" deep and 7" in diameter were found where the object had been sighted on the ground. The following night (29 Dec 80) the area was checked for radiation. Beta/gamma readings of 0.1 milliroentgens were recorded with peak readings in the three depressions and near the center of the triangle formed by the depressions. A nearby tree had moderate (.05-.07) readings on the side of the tree toward the depressions.

3. Later in the night a red sun-like light was seen through the trees. It moved about and pulsed. At one point it appeared to throw off glowing particles and then broke into five separate white objects and then disappeared. Immediately thereafter, three star-like objects were noticed in the sky, two objects to the north and one to the south, all of which were about $10^{o}$ off the horizon. The objects moved rapidly in sharp angular movements and displayed red, green and blue lights. The objects to the north appeared to be elliptical through an 8-12 power lens. They then turned to full circles. The objects to the north remained in the sky for an hour or more. The object to the south was visible for two or three hours and beamed down a stream of light from time to time. Numerous individuals, including the undersigned, witnessed the activities in paragraphs 2 and 3.

CHARLES I. HALT, Lt Col, USAF
Deputy Base Commander

# INDEX

(page numbers in bold indicate primary entries)

# Picture list *from The National Archives*

| Page Number | Image and Date followed by Reference at The National Archives |
|---|---|
| 1 | A letter captured from a Dutch ship on its way to Amsterdam, 1780 HCA 30/341 |
| 2 | One of a series of letters received by King's Proctor asking him to intervene in the divorce, 1936-1937 TS 22/1/1 |
| 3 | A secret token used in the French Revolution, 1798 PC 1/42/140 |
| 5 (top) | An illustrated page from the Domesday Abbreviato, 1216-1272 E 36/284 |
| 5 (middle) | An illumination from the Valor Ecclesiasticus, 1509–1547 E 344/22 |
| 5 (bottom) | A page from the journal of Grenville Collins, 1676–1679 ADM 7/688 |
| 6 (top) | A secret token used in the French Revolution, 1798 PC 1/42/140 |
| 6 (middle) | One of a series of cartoons satirising the future George IV and Queen Caroline, 1818– 823 TS 11/115 |
| 6 (bottom) | A photo depicting the Rendlesham Forest incident, 1980 DEFE 24/2034) |
| 7 | A page from the account of Sir Thomas Hawley for soldiers' wages, 1415–1416 E 101/612/53 |
| 8 | An illuminated page from the the Domesday Abbreviato, 1216–1272 E 36/284 |
| 9 (top) | A letter from Richard III, 1483 C 81/1392 |
| 9 (middle top) | The covering note to the "Anonymous Letter", 1816 HO 42/150 |
| 9 (middle bottom) | Oath Recitation of John Balliol, 1292 E 39/21 |
| 9 (bottom) | A telegram from the Titanic, 1912 MT 9/920/C |
| 10 (top) | A page from the 1911 census as "defaced" by a suffragette, 1911 RG 14/227 |
| 10 (middle top) | The "Tide Letter" from Princess Elizabeth, 1554 EXT 11/25 |
| 10 (middle bottom) | A page from Captain Cook's journal, 1770 ADM 55/40 |
| 10 (bottom left) | A manorial roll illustrating the devastation wrought by the Black Death, 1346 DL 30/63/803 |
| 10 (bottom middle) | One of a series of cartoons satirising future George IV and Queen Caroline, 1818–1823 TS 11/115 |
| 10 (bottom right) | A letter sent from someone claiming to be Jack the Ripper, 1888-1891 MEPO 3/142 |
| 11 (top left) | A page from a notebook recording clandestine marriages, 1744 RG 7/511 |
| 11 (top middle) | A secret token used in the French Revolution, 1798 PC 1/42/140 |
| 11 (top right) | A note from the police investigation into George Orwell, 1936 MEPO 38/69 |
| 11 (middle top) | The "Percentages Agreement" between Churchill and Stalin, 1944 PREM 3/66/7 |
| 11 (middle bottom) | The United States Declaration of Independence, 1776 EXT 9/1 |
| 11 (bottom) | Caxton's printed indulgence, 1476 E 135/6/56 |
| 12 (top) | A page from Great Domesday, 1086–1087 E 31/2/1 |
| 12 (middle top) | A register of "non-conformist" baptisms, 1738 RG 4/2486 |
| 12 (middle bottom) | The final version of the Magna Carta, 1225 DL 10/71 |
| 12 (bottom) | A page from the Treaty of Versailles, 1919 FO 211/517 |
| 14–15 | An illustrated page from the Domesday Abbreviato, 1216–1272 E 36/284 |
| 16 | A page from Great Domesday, 1086–1087 E 31/2/1 |
| 17 | Tudor binding for the Domesday Book, date unknown E 31/3 |
| 18–19 | A spread from Great Domesday, 1086–1087 E 31/2/1 |
| 21 | The final version of the Magna Carta, 1225 DL 10/71 |
| 23 | An exchequer roll featuring caricatures, 1233 E 401/1565 |
| 24 | An exchequer roll featuring caricatures, 1233 E 401/1565 |
| 26 (left) | An illumination from the Domesday Abbreviato, 1216–1272 E 36/284 |
| 26 (right), 27 | Illustrations from the Domesday Abbreviato, 1216–1272 E 36/284 |
| 28 | An agreement by the competitors to the Scottish Throne to receive judgement as to their claims from Edward I, 1291 E 39/18 |
| 29 | Seal of John Balliol, 1292 E 39/21 |
| 30 | Oath Recitation of John Balliol, 1292 E 39/21 |
| 31, 32, 33 | A clerk's sheet music, 1325 E 149/7 |
| 34–35 | Edward III's request for prayers, 1347 SC 1/37 |
| 37 | A manorial roll illustrating the devastation wrought by the Black Death, 1346 DL 30/63/803 |
| 38, 39 | Manorial rolls illustrating the devastation wrought by the Black Death, 1348–1350 DL 30/64/806 |
| 40-41 | An illumination from the Valor Ecclesiasticus, 1509–1547 E 344/22 |
| 42, 43, 44–45 | Pages from the account of Sir Thomas Hawley for soldiers' wages, 1415–1416 E 101/612/53 |
| 47 | Caxton's printed indulgence, 1476 E 135/6/56 |
| 50–51 | A letter from Richard III, 1483 C 81/1392 |
| 52 | The seal of Elizabeth I, 1586–1603 SC 13/N3 |
| 53, 54 | The Wassington seal, 1401 DL 25/689 |
| 55 | An illumination from the Valor Ecclesiasticus, 1509–1547 E 344/22 |
| 56 | An illuminated page from the Valor Ecclesiasticus, 1509–1547 E 344/22 |
| 57 | Illuminations from the Valor Ecclesiasticus, 1509–1547 E 344/22 |
| 58 | The "Tide Letter" from Princess Elizabeth, 1554 EXT 11/25 |
| 61 | Reverse of the "Tide Letter" from Princess Elizabeth, 1554 EXT 11/25 |
| 62–63 | The coroner's report into Amy Robsart's death, 1561–1562 KB 9/1073 |
| 66 | The Roanoke map, 1585 MPG 1/584 |
| 68–69 | The Ealing census, 1599 E 163/24/35 |
| 70-71 | A page from the journal of Grenville Collins, 1676–1679 ADM 7/688 |
| 72 | A page from the accounts of Edmund Tylney, the Master of the Revels, 1604–1605 AO 3/388/13 |
| 73 | A portrait of William Shakespeare, date unknown PRO 30/25/205 |
| 74 | A page from the accounts of Edmund Tylney, the Master of the Revels, 1604–1605 AO 3/388/13 |
| 75 | Declarations of Guy Fawkes before and after torture, 1605 SP 14/216 |
| 76 | The Monteagle letter, 1605 SP 14/216 |
| 77 | Warrant from James I for the torture of Guy Fawkes, 1605 SP 14/216 |
| 79, 80 | The oath signed by the Walloons, 1574–1600 MFQ 1/565 |
| 81, 82, 83, 85 | Pages from the transcript of the trial of Charles I, 1649 SP 16/517 |
| 86, 87, 88, 89 | Pages from the journal of Grenville Collins, 1676–1679 ADM 7/688 |
| 91 | The will of Nell Gwyn, 1687 PROB 1/48 |
| 92, 93, 94 | Pages from the will of Catherine of Braganza, 1705 PROB 1/56 |
| 96–97 | A secret token used in the French Revolution, 1798 PC 1/42/140 |
| 98 | A page from William Brainie's diary documenting life at Fort Commenda, 1714 T 70/1464 |
| 100, 101 | Pages from William Brainie's diary documenting life at Fort Commenda, 1714 T 70/1464 |
| 103 | A page from Captain Gordon's letter describing the hunt for Blackbeard, 1718 ADM 1/1826 |
| 104 | A page from the log for HMS Pearl during the hunt for Blackbeard, 1718 ADM 51/672 |
| 108 | The indictment of Dick Turpin, 1739 ASSI 44/54 |
| 109, 110 | Pages from the register of "non-conformist" baptisms, 1940 RG 4/2486 |
| 111 | The "Woman's Almanack" upon which the baptisms were recorded, 1940 RG 4/2486 |
| 112 | A page from a register of clandestine marriages, 1744 RG 7/215 |
| 114–115 | A spread from a notebook recording clandestine marriages, 1744 RG 7/511 |
| 117, 118 | Pages from a copy of Flora MacDonald's declaration, 1746 SP 54/32/49E |
| 120, 121, 122 | Pages from Captain Cook's journal, 1770 ADM 55/40 |
| 125 | Case proceedings from the Longman & Lukey trial, 1773 C 12/71/22 |
| 127 | The United States Declaration of Independence, 1776 EXT 9/1 |
| 128–129 | Three Dunlap prints of US Declaration of Independence, 1776 EXT 9/1, EXT 9/76 & EXT 9/93 |
| 130 | Jan Teerlink's captured wallet, 1803 EXT 11/140 |
| 131 | A sample of the seed packets captured during the Anglo-Dutch Wars, 1803 EXT 11/140 |
| 132, 133 | Letters captured during the Anglo-Dutch Wars, 1780 onwards From top-left, anti-clockwise: HCA 30/321; HCA 30/750; HCA 32/1697; HCA 32/473; HCA 32/408; HCA 32/883; HCA 30/735; HCA 30/341 |

| Page | Picture |
|---|---|
| 134 | The spine of the Book of Negroes, 1783 PRO 30/55/100 |
| 135, 136–137 | Pages from the Book of Negroes, 1783 PRO 30/55/100 |
| 138 | Correspondence from Port Jackson, Australia, listing Mary Wade, 1789 CO 201/4 |
| 140–141 | A report requesting clemency be shown in the case of Mary Wade among others, 1789 HO 47/9 |
| 142 | Bligh's signature as featured in his HMS Bounty's logbook, 1789 ADM 55/151 |
| 143, 144, 145, 146, 147 | Pages from the logbook of HMS Bounty, 1789 ADM 55/151 |
| 149 | Tuki's map of New Zealand, 1793 MPG 1/532 |
| 150 | The front cover of the Treaty of Amity, 1794–1798 FO 94/2 |
| 152, 153 | Pages from the Treaty of Amity, 1794–1798 FO 94/2 |
| 154,155 | Secret tokens used in the French Revolution, 1798 PC 1/42/140 |
| 156–7 | One of a series of cartoons satirising the future George IV and Queen Caroline, 1818–1823 TS 11/115 |
| 158, 159, 160 | The "anonymous" letter, 1816 HO 42/150 |
| 162, 163, 164, 165, 166 | Cartoons satirising the future George IV and Queen Caroline, 1818–1823 TS 11/115 |
| 168, 169 | George Stephenson's patent, 1822 C 54/10096 |
| 170, 172–3 | Pages from the "Begging Grate" book, 1822–1829 PRIS 10/6 |
| 175 | "The New Poor Law" poster, c.1834 HO 44/27 |
| 177 | Cholera warning poster addressed to emigrants, 1853 CO 384/92 |
| 178 (left) | "Prevention of cholera" poster, 1848–1849 MH 13/245 |
| 178 (right) | Correspondence relating to a cholera outbreak and its potential causes, 1853 MH 13/245 |
| 179 | "A Few Blessings of the Public Health Act" poster, 1848–1871 MH 13/81 |
| 180 (left) | "Plain Directions for the People" pamphlet, 1855–1880 MH 98/25 |
| 180–1 | A patent for a "Sanitary Belt and Cholera Repellent", 1848–1849 BT 45/9 |
| 181 | "Instructions for District Visitors in the Time of Cholera", 1855–1880 MH 98/25 |
| 183 | A poster advertising a "great public meeting" in support of the Chartists' cause, 1839 HO 40/41 |
| 184 | A poster warning those who intend to attend a Chartists meeting, 1839 HO 40/41 |
| 186, 187 | Exhibitors' tickets for the Great Exhibition 1851 BT 342/2 |
| 188–9 | A map of the routes to the Great Exhibition as featured on a glove, 1851 BT 43/422 |
| 190 | A plan illustrating the Charge of the Light Brigade, 1854 MPN 1/23 |
| 192, 193, 194 | The differing reports of Ragland and Lucan relating to the Charge of the Light Brigade, 1854 WO 1/369 |
| 196, 197, 198, 199 | Papers relating to the case of Dr James Barry, c. 1865 WO 138/1 |
| 201 | The crew list for the Mimosa, 1865 BT 99/230 |
| 202 | A petition from the settlers requesting assistance, 1865 CO 78/52 |
| 204 | A portrait of David Livingstone, 1870 COPY 1/16 |
| 205 | A page from David Livingstone's letters, 1869–1874 FO 2/49B |
| 206 | David Livingstone's map of British discoveries in Malawi and Mozambique, 1859 MPK 1/422 |
| 208 | A page from David Livingstone's letters, 1869–1874 FO 2/49B |
| 209 (left) | 'The Claimant Running' caricature, 1873 COPY 1/22 |
| 209 (right) | A portrait of Mrs Arthur Orton, 1871 COPY 1/17 |
| 210 | A Daguerreotype of Roger Tichborne in France, 1868–1873 CN 28/1 |
| 211 | A portrait of Tom Castro, the claimant, 1873 COPY 1/23 |
| 212 | The trial report of the Tichborne case, 1873 TS 36/70 |
| 214, 215, 216 | Papers relating to Karl Marx's request for naturalisation, 1874 HO 45/9366/36228 |
| 217, 218, 219 | Photographs and records of prisoners at Wandsworth, 1872–3 PCOM 2/290 & PCOM 2/291 |
| 220 | A page from Lt. John Chard's despatch from Rorke's Drift, 1879 WO 32/7737 |
| 221 | A plan showing the defence of Rorke's Drift, 1879 WO 32/7737 |
| 222 | A page from Lt. John Chard's despatch from Rorke's Drift, 1879 WO 32/7737 |
| 224 (top) | A police notice seeking information on the Ripper murders, 1888 MEPO 3/140 |
| 224 (bottom), 226, 227 | A selection of the "Ripper" letters MEPO 3/142 |
| 228–9 | Exhibits "A" and "B" and the envelope for both, as featured in the trial relating to Oscar Wilde, 1895 CRIM 1/41/6 |
| 230 | Marquess of Queensberry's statement, 1895 CRIM 1/41/6 |
| 231 | Correspondence relating to Oscar Wilde's request to send his autobiographical manuscript out of prison, 1897 PCOM 8/434 |
| 232–3 | A photo depicting the Rendlesham Forest incident, 1980 DEFE 24/2034 |
| 234 (top) | The census return defaced by Louisa Burnham, 1911 RG 14/2277 |
| 234 (middle and bottom) | The Maud household's census return of 1911 featuring an apology from the husband of a suffragette, 1911 RG 14/227 |
| 236 (top) | A letter from the Paddington registrar seeking guidance over a Mrs Ayrton, who was refusing to complete the census form, 1911 RG 14/80 |
| 237 (bottom) | A letter from the Census Office replying to a registrar's concerns, 1911 RG 14/80 |
| 237 (left) | A photo showing survivors from RMS Titanic being picked up by the Carpathia, 1912 COPY 1/566 |
| 237 (right) | A portrait of Jack Phillips, Marconi operator on RMS Titanic, 1912 COPY 1/565 |
| 238 (both), 239 (top both) | The last telegrams from RMS Titanic, 1912 MT 9/920C |
| 239 (bottom) | A spread from the register of deceased passengers, 1912 BT 334/52 |
| 240 | A map of Somme as featured in the war diary of VIII Corps, 1916 WO 95/820 |
| 242, 243, 245 | Somme War Diary Entry, 1916 WO 95/820 |
| 246 | A map of Somme as featured in the war diary of VIII Corps, 1916 WO 95/820 |
| 247, 248, 249 | Documents relating to Sassoon's declaration and its consequences, 1917–1919 WO 339/51440 |
| 251, 252 | Pages from the Treaty of Versailles, 1919 FO 211/517 |
| 253, 254 | A collection of police files covering the abdication, 1935–1936 MEPO 10/35 |
| 255 | The signed "Instrument of Abdication", 1936 PC 11/1 |
| 256 | A collection of police files covering the abdication, 1935-1936 MEPO 10/35 |
| 257 | A letter from King George VI to the Prime Minister about his brother, 1938 PREM 1/467 |
| 258, 259, 260, 261 | A collection of the police files kept on Eric Blair, 1936 MEPO 38/69 |
| 263, 264 | The memorandum on a "super-bomb" by Frisch and Peierls, 1940 AB 1/210 |
| 266, 267, 268 | A "Report from the Front" of the capture of prisoners at St Nazaire Prisoners, 1942 DEFE 2/127 |
| 269, 270, 271, 272, 273 | A collection of documents found within Noor Inayat Khan's Special Operations Executive file, 1943–1944 HS 9/836/5 |
| 275 | The "Percentages Agreement" between Churchill and Stalin, 1944 PREM 3/66/7 |
| 277, 278 | Queen Elizabeth II's signature on the Coronation Oath, 1953 C 57/17 |
| 280, 281, 282-3 | The US comics assessed by Winston Churchill, 1954–55 EXT 5/19 |
| 284 | Newspaper cutting featuring Blakely and Ellis, 1955 HO 921/237 |
| 285, 286, 287 | The confession of Ruth Ellis in her own hand, 1955 MEPO 2/9888 |
| 288 | A letter in which Ruth Ellis's plea for clemency is rejected, 1955 HO 291/235 |
| 289 (left) | Drawing of jacket showing the injuries to Blakely, 1955 MEPO 2/9888 |
| 289 (right top and right botom) | Telegrams to the Home Secretary requesting leniency be shown, 1955 HO 291/238 |
| 290 (left) | A letter from the public to the Home Secretary regarding the Ruth Ellis murder and her sentence, 1955 HO 291/235 |
| 290 (right) | A letter from the public to the Home Secretary regarding the Ruth Ellis murder and her sentence, 1955 HO 291/236 |
| 292, 293, 294 | Correspondence relating to the industrial action of "Women Workers of Fords", 1968 PREM 13/2412 |
| 295 | A photo depicting the Rendlesham Forest incident, 1980 DEFE 24/2034 |
| 296 | Prime Minister's question about flying saucers and the response, 28 July 1952 PREM 11/855 |
| 297 | Halt's report of the Rendlesham Forest incident, 1980 DEFE 24/1948 |

# Other picture credits

*AKG*: 78, 90 (right); *Alamy*: (The Art Archive) 34, (GL Archive) 49, (North Wind Picture Archives) 65, (Lebrecht Music and Arts Photo Library) 102, 116, 124, 126, 167, 213; *Bridgeman Art Library*: 139; Corbis: (The Gallery Collection) 59; *Getty Images*: (Hulton Archive) 148, (Roger Viollet Collection) 228, (Museum of London/Heritage Images) 235, (Time Life Pictures) 262, (Hulton Archive) 277, (Ray Bellisario/Popperfoto) 291; *Imperial War Museum*: 241; *Mary Evans Picture Library*: 46, 62, 90 (left), 99, (Edwin Mullan Collection) 107, 113, 151, 171, 174, 186, 191, 221, 250, (Marx Memorial Library) 274;*The National Library of Wales*: 200; *The Trustees of the British Museum*: 20; *TopFoto*: (The Granger Collection) 36, 182, 265

1 3 5 7 9 10 8 6 4 2

Published in 2014 by Ebury Press, an imprint of Ebury Publishing

A Random House Group Company



The Random House Group Limited Reg. No. 954009

Addresses for companies within the Random House Group can be found at www.randomhouse.co.uk

A CIP catalogue record for this book is available from the British Library

The Random House Group Limited supports the Forest Stewardship Council® (FSC®), the leading international forest-certification organisation. Our books carrying the FSC label are printed on FSC®-certified paper. FSC is the only forest-certification scheme supported by the leading environmental organisations, including Greenpeace. Our paper procurement policy can be found at www.randomhouse.co.uk/environment

Edited by Sue Lascelles, Nicola Crossley and Marion Paull
Designed by David Fordham
Picture Research (excluding pictures from The National Archives) by Victoria Hall

Printed and bound in China by C&C Offset Co., Ltd

ISBN 978 0 0919 4335 6

his Maj:ties Pearle under my Command made to his
petition lately Layed before him in Counsell.
to this I shall very briefly lay before their Lordsps: a
that action with Thatch alias Blackbeard
they were so near, that the compliment past betwixt them o
ing each other quarters; Thatch observing all his men
ve them a broade Side; his guns being Sufficiently
wan Shot, partridge Shot, and others; with this broad
s and wounded (most by the Swan shot) one & twenty
, Mr. Maynder finding his men thus exposed, and
order his men down into the hold, giving himself
baft; ordering the midshipsman that was at the helm, o
utler his pilate to aquaint him with any thing that shou
. Thatch observing his decke clear of men, presently
el his own, and then Sheers on board Lieut: Maynard
enters himself the first man, with a rope in his hand
r make fast the two Sloops: Mr. Butler aquainting
ard with this, turned his men upon deck, and was himsel
tly among them: where in less then six minuets tyme
and five or Six of his men were killed; the rest of the
jumped in the water where they were demolished,
being dyscovered some dayes after in the reeds by the fouls
g over him: the Sloop in wch the Kings people were in, had
tune to have the three officers that commanded them killed
f his Sloop: & another Shot through the body in Thatchs Sl